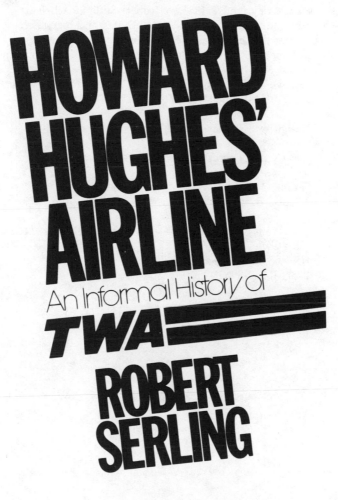

HOWARD HUGHES' AIRLINE

An Informal History of

TWA

ROBERT SERLING

St Martin's / Marek
New York

HOWARD HUGHES' AIRLINE: AN INFORMAL HISTORY OF
TWA. Copyright © 1983 by Robert Serling. All rights
reserved. Printed in the United States of America. No
part of this book may be used or reproduced in any
manner whatsoever without written permission except in
the case of brief quotations embodied in critical articles or
reviews. For information, address St. Martin's / Marek,
175 Fifth Avenue, New York, N.Y. 10010.

Design by Kingsley Parker

Library of Congress Cataloging in Publication Data

Serling, Robert J.
  Howard Hughes' airline.

  1. Trans World Airlines—History.   2. Hughes, Howard
1905-1976.   I. Title.
HE9803.T7S47 1983   387.7'065'73   83-9630
ISBN 0-312-39631-7

First Edition

10 9 8 7 6 5 4 3 2

To John Corris and Jerry Cosley
of TWA, without whose help and
support this could not have been
written

Contents

Prologue

They gather in clusters around the hotel lobby, each group a tiny island of old comradeships being refueled by the nostalgia of mutual remembrances.

On their heads are golf caps in red and white, the colors of the airline they once served. This is one of the gatherings of the TWA Seniors Club, some 5,000 retired employees organized into regional chapters; their accumulated airline experience adds up to at least 125,000 years, for TWA is one of the nation's oldest air carriers, and most of the members spent at least twenty-five years in its service.

There are senior captains forced to retire by federal edict at age 60 but who look young and fit enough to fly a Boeing 747 that same afternoon. There also are the veterans of the Ford trimotor and Fokker F-10 days, men who move slowly and laboriously but whose eyes sparkle when they spot a fellow airman from their own era. The years drop from stooped shoulders, the tired lines evaporate from leathery faces, as they recall and remember:

"*. . . and when the prop left that Alpha, it took the whole damn engine with it and old Harry was left with nothin' but a tail-heavy glider. . . .*"

"*. . . My God, could those DC-2s pick up ice. . . . I remember one trip outa Pittsburgh and we ran into precip—she was flying like an iron bathtub. . . .*"

Mechanics:

"*. . . the goddamn engine wouldn't start because it needed a new condenser which we didn't have. So I built one out of a sardine can. . . .*"

Hostesses:

"*. . . girdles and tight bras—Lord, all we needed were chastity belts. . . .*"

Reservations agents:

"*. . . he was courting this opera singer in New York and we booked him on a transcontinental flight once a week for twenty-six weeks. . . .*"

Characters:

"*. . . he was the only captain I ever knew who'd take off his uniform as soon as he boarded and fly across the Atlantic in his pajamas. . . .*"

Incidents:

". . . a belly landing on railroad tracks. Nobody got a scratch, but one woman became hysterical because a blanket fell over her head and she thought she had gone blind. . . ."

Nuggets mined out of memories, stories mostly pried from the common denominator of virtually all airline people, a sense of humor; the ability to laugh in the face of adversity, or at least to remember all the adversity with a kind of wry perspective that is roughly akin to that of battle survivors. This is natural, for airline humor is like military humor. It is based largely on reminiscences of mistakes, bumbling and inanities that somehow acted as life jackets in every sea of crisis.

Thus, the sound of laughter is an integral part of every Seniors' meeting— warm, infectious laughter from men and women whose airline lives have combined the routine and the raucous, the dull and the daring, the commonplace and the crises. This, of course, is true of the entire airline industry and its breed. Every air carrier history is similar almost to the point of repetition, just as the human cast of each airline has its identical counterparts on another. The plots, characters, events and tribulations are virtually interchangeable—companies started on shoestrings and then riding an economic roller coaster that soars to prosperity one minute and near-bankruptcy the next.

Yet there is something unique about TWA; it doesn't quite fit the mold. Its travails were not only more convulsive than most but seldom were the fault of the airline and its people. As much as any other airline in the world, TWA is a carrier built on a foundation of loyalty that has withstood the terrible buffeting of decisions, deeds and circumstances beyond the control of officers and employees alike.

This is reflected in the atmosphere of a Seniors' meeting, where one can sense the unity and pride that helped the airline survive. Admittedly, a large measure of this exists with every carrier, but at TWA it seems to have been applied with a branding iron. Another airline that equals it is Delta, but this is comparing oranges with apples; Delta's sense of unity and pride grew out of a special brand of management paternalism thriving naturally and easily in an atmosphere in which loyalty was projected downward as well as upward, whereas TWA's was a simple yet powerful weapon of survival amid constant management instability. There was more than one occasion when loyalty was the only glue that held TWA together. It was and still is the pivot around which the airline revolves.

Retiree business cards carry the title "Goodwill Ambassador" under each senior's name, cards they leave at travel agencies where they regularly drop off TWA schedules and brochures. They don special red blazers and on their own time, with no compensation, act as tour guides at major TWA bases. On October 3, 1982, the last day of the major league baseball season, a retired captain named Harold Neumann, whose retirement avocation is sky-writing, climbed into his airplane and flew over the Kansas City Royals' Stadium. Some 30,000 fans saw him write FLY TWA three times. The stunt cost him $300.

They never cease trying to sell their old airline, yet these are men and women with memories of times they couldn't get their paychecks cashed because of rumors that TWA was broke, of times when the airline was run by committee because it had no president, of times when they competed against modern jets with obsolete piston aircraft. They still have the blessed resilience, so typical of the airline breed, that saw them through those troubled periods. When they themselves travel, they uncomplainingly sweat out each boarding, cognizant that their relatively low priority passes leave them vulnerable to being bumped by a last-minute paying passenger or somebody with a higher priority pass. With the wiliness of coyotes, they have learned how to avoid most such hassles, carefully choosing certain flights on certain days or perhaps relying on the sympathy of their still-employed modern counterparts who look upon the retirees with a kind of "someday-I'll-be-in-their-shoes" awareness. Even so, the combination of operational knowledge and fraternal camaraderie doesn't always work; the most patient person in the world has to be an ex-airline employee with first-hand experience of what can go wrong on any given flight, from overbooking to bad weather to mechanical delays. They have learned to swallow disappointment, put up with inconvenience, and improvise their way out of being stranded.

Classic is the case of a TWA senior and his wife who were pass-riding from New York to Athens via London and Paris. They were bumped from the flight in Paris and all later Paris–Athens planes were booked solid for the next two days. Staying in Paris had no attraction; they had visited there many times.

"Athens is supposed to be the highlight of the trip," the husband observed. "Let's try another way to get there."

The "other way" was simple if circuitous. They flew back to New York and there caught a TWA nonstop to Athens that left only an hour after their Paris flight arrived in Kennedy.

This rather cosmopolitan solution is more than just another jet age story. TWA itself is an unusual hybrid of cosmopolitanism and Midwest provincialism. Its routes are global, but its roots are in America's heartlands; the core of the airline's technical operations is in Kansas City and has been for almost a half-century. This dual personality can be seen in the very makeup of the Seniors' Club; one member may recall the old airmail days while another talks about Spanish art or French cuisine, and a third remembers catering to the demands of prima donna movie stars. A fair-sized proportion of retirees have served in both domestic and international stations, a phenomenon virtually every TWA veteran traces to the influence of one man: Howard Hughes.

To TWA, he was Satan or Saviour, depending on one's perspective of this incredibly complex, undeniably brilliant and totally unpredictable maverick. It was a baby-faced visionary named Jack Frye who dreamed of transforming a financially ailing, purely domestic carrier with a long history of playing second fiddle to United and American into a globe-girdling giant. But it was Hughes who bankrolled the dream into reality, just as it was his ego and strange insecurity that almost wrecked this massive accomplishment. From the era of the DC-3 to the dawn of the jet age, Howard Hughes dominated TWA, shaping its destiny as one would mold a piece of clay.

The title of this book may smack of sophistry; as I write these words,

TWA is fifty-five-years old and Hughes controlled the airline for only twenty of those years. Yet to call TWA "Howard Hughes' airline" is not to stray far from historical truth. He sowed many seeds in two decades, some productive and others destructive, and the fruit they bore still exists in the inanimate yet intensely alive corporate body of a magnificent airline. He ruled with ruthlessness and often by whim, a man never seen by anyone but a tiny cadre of employees. His physical presence was about as solid as ectoplasm; he held no office, never attended a board of directors' meeting and wasn't even a board member, but his authority was that of an all-powerful dictator. During the twenty years of his absolute command, TWA had six presidents, and at least three of them never saw Hughes in person after taking office. At one time, TWA actually operated without a president for almost three years, floundering and leaderless.

This was the kind of atmosphere in which the troops, officers and rank-and-file alike, labored and fought their competitive battles. They worked under some of the most able chief executives in airline history, but these were men constantly hamstrung, interfered with and overruled by the awesome authority of an invisble man who not only owned TWA but, from all accounts, loved it more than any other of his possessions. One of the mysteries of TWA's turbulent history is that Hughes could be so cruelly blind to the effects of his egocentric, one-man rule over the entity that provided the major outlet for his most beloved interest: aviation.

But it is also an anomaly that the airline could survive the vicissitudes of leadership-by-whim. It suffered through occasional equipment inferiority, equipment delays and even equipment misappropriation—all due to a man who thought nothing of taking a TWA plane out of scheduled service for his personal use, who overrode the advice of his own technical experts in choosing new aircraft, and who let his fear of bankers almost ruin TWA's ability to compete in the technological revolution that came with the jets. That it did survive these difficulties is due to one inescapable fact: the loyalty of the men and women who were the heart of the corporate body.

It is only fair to acknowledge that sometimes TWA stayed alive because of Howard Hughes, not in spite of him. Hughes saved the airline from possible bankruptcy and helped forge its development into one of the world's greatest international carriers. Some of his influence and his instinct for showmanship still prevail. He had nothing to do with the much-admired and occasionally imitated gimmick of mounting spotlights on the tails of TWA aircraft, yet it is pure Hughes and he would have loved it. If there is a residue of resentment toward what Hughes did *to* the airline, there also are fond memories of what he did *for* it. It is surprisingly easy to find TWA veterans who still remember his eccentricities with a kind of grudging admiration for another part of the Hughes legend: his fierce independence and stubborn courage. It is as if the years have erased all the blacks and grays, leaving only the bright colors of this remarkable buccaneer whose idiosyncrasies are now viewed more with wry fondness than bitterness.

And this, too, is typical of the airline breed—a willingness to forgive and even forget the occasional faults of their leaders, the wrong decisions and ill-conceived policies that affected lives and careers as well as corporate balance sheets. TWA certainly has no monopoly on officialdom's errors, just as its people have no monopoly on keeping an airline flying despite those mistakes. Most carriers have endured bloody upper-echelon quarrels, recessions, cynical politics and bureaucratic procrastination and ineptness. Nor can TWA lay exclusive claim to marching under the banners of loyalty, of having pride in the past and faith in the future. Certainly it is not the only airline to recover gallantly from the traumatic stigma of a fatal crash—although it must be admitted that it has a history of getting involved in unusually significant accidents. Notre Dame's Knute Rockne was killed aboard a TWA plane in a crash that spelled the end of wooden transports. Two midair collisions, each involving a TWA aircraft, led in one instance to the creation of the Federal Aviation Agency and in the other to major air traffic control reforms. It was a TWA pilot who, for the first time in history, forced federal investigators to reverse a finding of pilot error—one that implied deliberate suicide.

It would be unfair to wrap the TWA story solely around the magic name of Howard Hughes. His was only a lengthy chapter. There were deeds of drama long before he arrived on the scene, and by the nature of his self-centered rule, there had to be continuing controversy after he left center stage. Nor was his the only figure of stature and color. The tragic Jack Frye, for example, was an unsung hero of commercial aviation. There were presidents like beloved Ralph Damon, perhaps the only TWA chief executive whom Hughes really respected; irascible Carter Burgess, a man of courtly southern grace with a tongue like barbed wire, who conducted station inspections with white gloves; Charlie "Two-Pants" Thomas, who looked like a mild-mannered haberdasher but who started the chain of events that ended the Hughes reign; brilliant Charles Tillinghast, who finished what Thomas started; and TWA's present chief, soft-spoken but steely-spined Ed Meyer, who steered TWA along its most precarious path—through the shoals of chaotic airline deregulation.

But in the end, the saga of Trans World Airlines still remains unique in the annals of aviation for one simple reason: no other airline ever had a Howard Hughes. He was a 22-year-old millionaire getting ready to shoot the first scenes of his aviation epic, *Hell's Angels,* the day TWA was born on the back of an envelope passed among four men in a small room at a private New York City club.

Part One
(1928-1939)

1

Shotgun Marriage

The quartet in the room at the Engineers Club consisted of an airline operations expert, a lawyer, a wealthy aviation entrepreneur, and the world's most famous flyer. It was the fall of 1928, and on the envelope they were examining intently was scrawled a crudely drawn map of the United States, done in pencil with the names of several cities dotting what looked like a child's impression of America's geographical outline. Significantly, the dots were stretched from the East Coast to the West Coast. This was the initial blueprint for the nation's first transcontinental airline.

The "artist" was Col. Paul Henderson, vice-president of National Air Transport, which operated an airmail route from Chicago to Dallas via Kansas City. Before joining NAT, the tall, stern-visaged, bespectacled Henderson had been assistant postmaster general, and in that capacity he had been instrumental in developing the transcontinental airmail service via a network of landing fields and lighted beacons so the mail could be flown at night.

Henderson was tense as he watched his three companions inspect his handiwork. One was Chester W. Cuthell, a prominent attorney invited to the meeting as a legal advisor. The second, youngest man in the tiny room, was a whipcord-slender ex-airmail pilot who, a little more than a year before, had written his name into history by flying the Atlantic both solo and nonstop from New York to Paris. Charles A. Lindbergh was present not so much to add his illustrious name to the budding venture, but to provide technical expertise.

The fourth man, Henderson's boss at NAT, was a Canadian-born financial genius who had once been a reporter on the *Wall Street Journal*. By 1928, Clement Melville Keys already had amassed both fortune and fame in the infant aviation industry. After leaving the *Journal,* Keys had organized an investment firm and wound up buying control of the Curtiss Aeroplane and Engine Company at the end of World War I. From the manufacturing of aircraft, he moved into the fledgling airline industry, bidding successfully for the Chicago–Dallas airmail route when the federal government decided to turn mail carrying over to private operators.

NAT was only part of the fast-growing empire that Keys had astutely organized under a holding company, North American Aviation. He also had his sights set on two established carriers—Pitcairn Aviation, operating the New York–Miami airmail route, and Maddux Airlines, an outfit organized by a Los Angeles car dealer named Jack Maddux, which served a San Diego–Los Angeles–San Francisco route against the formidable opposition of Harris "Pop" Hanshue's Western Air Express. Keys' intent was to form a lucrative link between his airframe/engine products and the airlines he ran under the North American Aviation flag.

Clement Keys, scholarly both in appearance and cranial capacity, was no romantic visionary; he probably would have thrown up at any rendition of Tennyson's ". . . saw the heavens fill with commerce, argosies of magic sails, pilots of the purple twilight, dropping down with costly bales." To the sentimentality of *Locksley Hall*, Keys would have wanted to add the phrase, "and making money hand over fist." He was a pragmatic businessman out to make as much profit as possible from any venture into which he poured his considerable resources. Unlike his rival at Western Air Express, Pop Hanshue, Keys actually discouraged passenger traffic. At NAT, he doubled air fares with just that purpose in mind. His reason was eminently practical, in keeping with his logical mind; NAT had won a New York–Chicago mail route that involved flying over the dangerous Allegheny Mountains, and Keys figured passenger traffic would be nil anyway after a couple of inevitable accidents. It was typical of Clement Keys that a remark he once made became axiomatic in the airline industry: "Ten percent of aviation is in the air, ninety percent on the ground."

It was pragmatism that led him to the meeting at the Engineers Club. Under his direction, Henderson had been sounding out various railroad officials, particularly Gen. W. W. Atterbury, who headed the mighty Pennsylvania Railroad, on the possibility of operating a combined airplane/train service coast to coast. Such a project appealed to Keys' inherent sense of caution; the planes would fly safely during the day with passengers transferring at night to the less risky mode of travel by rail.

Now, Henderson was awaiting the reaction to his scribblings on the envelope. "If you like the idea," he offered humbly, "it's just a job of work. If you don't, then there's no harm done."

There was silence as the three men continued to study the crude map. Henderson impatiently and rather unnecessarily added the explanation: "We're not ready to fly all night yet, but we can use the railroads at night and fly by day. I figure we can make the trip from here to California in two days."

Lindbergh, ever the technician, observed that it would take considerable time to establish the operation. "There isn't an airport on that route with the facilities for transport service," he warned.

"And how do you know you can interest the railroads in an airline?" Cuthell, the attorney, asked.

"I don't know for certain," Henderson replied, "but I do know that General Atterbury and the Pennsylvania Railroad have been in touch with aviation for some time. As I see it, we have two immediate jobs—sell the idea to the Pennsylvania and raise the money. I don't believe either one will be difficult."

Clement Keys raised his eyes from the envelope and smiled thinly. "No trouble at all about raising the money," he said quietly.

Before the four men left the room, they had agreed on the framework over which the first air/rail transcontinental passenger service would be built. They decided on the Pennsylvania and Santa Fe Railroads as the logical links between plane and train, with Columbus, Ohio, as the first transfer point. New York obviously was to be the eastern terminal with Los Angeles and San Francisco sharing equal status as West Coast terminals. The dots on Henderson's envelope laid out the tentative route—New York to Columbus via train; Columbus, Indianapolis, St. Louis, Kansas City, Wichita and Dodge City by air; Dodge City to Las Vegas, New Mexico, via train; Las Vegas to Los Angeles by air via Albuquerque, Winslow and Kingman, Arizona, with a connecting flight at Los Angeles for San Francisco.

Over the ensuing months, only three changes were made in Henderson's original route: Waynoka, Oklahoma, replaced Dodge City as the second transfer point; Clovis, New Mexico, was picked over Las Vegas as the third, and it was decided not to operate a San Francisco connecting flight at Los Angeles—primarily because the westbound trip arrived at Glendale too late in the day. The revisions were largely the work of Lindbergh, hired as chairman of the new airline's technical committee at the modest annual salary of $10,000 plus a gift of 25,000 shares of stock in the company. The stock, valued at $20 a share at the start, went up ten points as soon as Lindbergh's connection was made public.

Lindbergh earned every cent of his compensation; not the least of his contributions was his permission to use his name. Incorporated as Transcontinental Air Transport on May 16, 1928, TAT quickly became known as "The Lindbergh Line," and it was no empty sop to promotion and publicity. All decisions by the board of directors were subject to the approval of Lindy's committee if they involved technical or operational matters. Lindbergh's participation was aimed primarily at assuring safety, from selection of the aircraft to be used to the establishment of a weather-reporting network involving seventy-nine stations. Years later, aviation historian R.E.G. Davies was to observe: "In many ways the formation of TAT marked a definite step in the progress of civil aviation in the United States. In contrast to all the airlines which had been formed hitherto, TAT was formed to carry passengers."

TAT's capitalization was for $5 million—a large sum for those days but an amount to be exceeded three decades later by the price of a single jetliner. Keys, Henderson and the directors literally handed Lindbergh a blank check to develop the route. Between the date of incorporation and the inauguration of service lay more than a year of meticulous preparation at a cost of some $3 million, of which less than one-third was spent on the aircraft themselves.

The allocation of capital underlined Lindbergh's influence and authority. His committee investigated six multi-engine candidates: the Curtiss Condor, Keystone Patrician, Boeing 80-A, a Sikorsky biplane, the widely used Fokker F-10 and the all-metal Ford trimotor, affectionately known as the "Tin Goose." The new Condor, built by Keys' own company, seemed to be an obvious selection, but Lindbergh didn't want it. He agreed with Pop Hanshue, whose opinion of the Condor was bluntly expressed when someone asked him when Western would buy the luxurious airliner: "Not until they build a tunnel through the goddamned Rockies."

Like Hanshue, Lindbergh considered the Condor underpowered, nor did he want any transport built largely of wood and with a biplane design whose very struts and wires amounted to built-in headwinds. He preferred the sturdy if slow and noisy Ford trimotor. Keys, bowing to Lindbergh's consid-

5

erable influence, didn't object, although there was some sentiment for buying the faster wooden Fokker.

Some $1 million was allocated for the establishment of the weather stations, and another huge chunk went toward airport improvements. Lindbergh flew over the projected route for several months, inspecting the primitive facilities, and reported that east of Wichita, the cities to be served would provide airports meeting his strict specifications. West of Wichita, however, TAT had to supply its own fields, terminal buildings and hangars. Construction of these began early in 1929, including the "air passenger stations" as the terminals were then called. They were of Indian- or Spanish-type architecture, built of hollow tile and furnished with handsome replicas of old Spanish furniture.

TAT not only built these airports but even ran the lunch rooms and rented out various concessions. Through the years, the airline never stinted in trying to make them as attractive as possible. At Albuquerque, for example, valuable Western paintings were hung on the terminal walls and there was a system map made of hammered brass and studded with turquoise stones that marked each city served. (Many years later, when the airport was turned over to the city of Albuquerque, regional sales representative Fred Spuhler came in to help with the formalities and discovered that while the map was still hanging, the paintings were missing. Spuhler finally located them in the basement, and all but one are still on display at the Albuquerque airport. Spuhler, however, appropriated the map, which was given to senior vice-president E.O. "Oz" Cocke for his California ranch house.)

Paintings and maps were somewhat less important than runways. Each airport had a different soil structure and TAT had to hire experts to determine what soil treatment was best for every runway. At Waynoka, Clovis and Winslow, the runway surface consisted of a four-inch base saturated with oil. At Kingman, oil was spread on the natural soil, then was allowed to settle before being re-oiled several times.

The directors elected Keys president and Henderson vice-president and general manager. Lindbergh's all-important technical committee included William Mayo, chief engineer of the Ford Motor Company; C.S. "Casey" Jones, a veteran airman who had done everything from managing airports to acting as Will Rogers' personal pilot; and Maj. Thomas Lamphier, freshly retired from the Army Air Corps where he had commanded the First Pursuit Group, who was designated as Lindbergh's assistant. Lamphier's first job was to scout the country for experienced pilots, a task in which he was aided by two middle-echelon officers. One was Paul Collins, a World War I airman and former airmail pilot who had been named general superintendent of TAT in charge of pilot personnel. The other was tough, crusty John A. Collings, who would run TAT's Eastern division out of Columbus. Collings had been practically weaned on Ford trimotors; he had barnstormed in a Tin Goose and once served as Ford's chief test pilot when the trimotor was being developed.

The trio's recruiting efforts were aimed at other airlines—mostly those flying the mail—plus aircraft companies and the military. They hired from two categories: first pilots (captains), who were the most experienced, particularly on multi-engine aircraft, and second pilots (copilots), who were drawn largely from the Army and Navy. Of the initial thirty-eight men chosen, seventeen needed additional training to meet Lindbergh's exacting standards. They were mostly Army-taught fliers unused to airplanes as large as the Ford. The others really were experienced, far more than most airmen of that era, when pilots were prone to pad logbooks in order to land an airline job.

Lindbergh himself informed the directors that TAT had acquired the cream of the aerial crop. "The entire nation was included in a study of personnel," he wrote. "As a result, the average flying time of our first pilots is about 3,000 hours, including an average of 500 hours on trimotors alone."

Several of these early employees went on to become legendary figures in TWA's history—men like Cliff Abbott, Joe Bartles, Jack Zimmerman and Otis Bryan. Abbott and Bartles were Army-bred pilots stationed at Selfridge Field when John Collings landed a new trimotor there and spread the word that he was hiring flight crews for a new airline. The salary, he announced, would be $300 a month plus expenses. This happened to be $54 a month more than Abbott and Bartles were making as Air Corps birds, and they resigned their commissions, following Collings back to Columbus where they began training as second pilots. "There were nine of us in our class," Abbott recalled. "Nobody had more than six hundred hours."

At 21, Bryan was the youngest recruit, and like all his rookie brethren, he marveled at the size of the Fords. TAT had purchased ten trimotors at a cost of $813,000, a sum that included spare engines and parts. Although the Tin Goose was designed to carry twelve passengers, it was decided to install only ten seats to provide more room and comfort in keeping with a Ford trimotor advertisement of the day: "More stable than a yacht, swifter than the wind, a new exultation, the thrill of an indescribable experience, complete, luxurious relaxation." Naturally, the ad failed to mention the trimotor's less desirable qualities such as its noise level, which was roughly as loud as a boiler plate factory. The only way to converse with the person sitting across the aisle was to pass notes back and forth, and the cockpit was even noisier than the cabin. Otis Bryan remembers that the ten seats always rattled thus adding to the din, but he also recalls how reliable and well-built those Fords were. "Henry Ford once said," Bryan adds, "that if one of his trimotors ever had an accident attributed to faulty construction, he'd never build another airplane. He never had to make good on that promise."

Pilots training on the airplane discovered a few idiosyncracies, such as Ford's unexplainable decision to mount instruments for monitoring oil temperature, oil pressure and RPMs for the outboard engines outside the cockpit on a panel positioned on an inner strut. Ford claimed they were easily visible day or night—they were illuminated electrically—but it was no wonder that TAT's airmen were required to possess 20/20 vision. The aircraft had to be trimmed constantly via a hand-crank located on the cabin ceiling, thus giving rise to the legend that you could always tell a Tin Goose pilot because he had three arms. The glass in the cockpit windshield was installed vertically, which caused confusing reflections from lights on the ground. And the trimotor had to be wrestled as much as flown. The controls were stiff, slow to respond, and any kind of turbulence made pilots wish they had taken up weight-lifting as a hobby. Strong arms were a necessity for stopping the airplane, too; there were no brake pedals, and in a landing roll, copilots had to tug on an iron bar between the two cockpit seats to activate the brakes. The control yokes were a masterpiece of improvision—they came right off the Model-T Ford.

These flaws notwithstanding, the Tin Goose still was the safest airplane of its day. And TAT was determined to make safety the cornerstone of its operations, with passenger comfort and convenience a high priority. The latter goal extended beyond flight itself. In addition to buying eight tractors, eleven trucks and eleven gas refueling trucks for ground operations, TAT also ordered thirteen "Aerocars" designed by the same Bill Stout who created the Ford trimotor. These were car-drawn trailers seating fourteen passengers and built of wood and fabric, like most airplanes of that era. They were to be used to carry passengers between airports and downtown areas and were supplemented by another eleven automobiles. The gas refueling trucks were TAT-developed and could pump sixty gallons a minute out of two tanks. Nothing like them had ever been seen at an airport.

TAT's first airplane was a little Stearman biplane flown by the airline's construction engineer, Jack Herlihy, who used it in his survey work over the western region. In November of 1928, John Collings of the Eastern division flew to Detroit and accepted delivery of the first trimotor, christened *City of Columbus* in honor of the eastern terminus. From then on, delivery of the remaining nine Fords progressed on schedule.

Lindbergh insisted on equipping the aircraft with a new-fangled device: two-way radios. The transmitters were installed in the rear of the cabin and reception was erratic. Static interference was frequent, but the sets were the best available and TAT was the only airline to have them. The private wires of the two railroads became part of the TAT communications system, buttressed by seven airline stations located at Columbus, Indianapolis, Waynoka, Clovis, Albuquerque, Winslow and Kingman.

Lindbergh demonstrated his usual foresight by convincing the airline hierarchy that day-only flying was a temporary expedient. TAT not only equipped the company-owned airports with runway lighting but the city-owned airports as well. The money-starved Department of Commerce had recommended portions of the TAT airway for lighting, but it was the airline that footed the bill; even the area between Clovis and Waynoka, served by the Santa Fe, was lighted.

No fewer than seventy trained weather observers were hired—thirty-three by the Santa Fe, fourteen each by TAT and the Pennsylvania Railroad, and nine by the U.S. Weather Bureau. They were assigned to their stations in time for the "dress rehearsal" flights, which lasted seventeen days and covered 50,000 miles. Of equal importance to the airline was public interest; at least a thousand people applied for seats on the inaugural flights, impressed not only by the promised 48-hour coast-to-coast schedule but by such luxuries as in-flight meals served by uniformed "couriers." These early-day flight attendants were not a TAT first; Western Air Express had employed stewards on its Los Angeles–San Francisco route for more than a year before TAT launched its transcontinental service. Most of TAT's initial couriers were sons of Pennsylvania Railroad executives.

Nor, as it turned out, was TAT's the first air/rail transcontinental operation. Three weeks before TAT inaugurated service, Universal Aviation Corporation started a 67-hour service between New York and Los Angeles; the

New York Central carried passengers to Cleveland where they were transferred to a Universal Fokker F-10 trimotor that flew them to Garden City, Kansas, via Chicago, St. Louis and Kansas City. The Santa Fe took them from Garden City to Los Angeles.

Universal's coup, however, had little effect on TAT's far more ambitious and better-planned operation. For one thing, it was almost twenty hours slower and involved only one flight leg. Nor could Universal come close to matching TAT's justifiable flaunting of "The Lindbergh Line," and its beautifully orchestrated publicity. Lindbergh's wasn't the only prominent name connected with the airline. Amelia Earhart was appointed "assistant to the general traffic manager," although her job tenure was short-lived and her duties predictably vague. (In 1929, women airline executives were about as plentiful as surviving dinosaurs.) Her chief task seems to have been the christening of a Ford trimotor on static display at New York's Penn Station, although TAT publicity releases claimed she had been hired to develop interest in air travel among women.

The $5 million investment in Transcontinental Air Transport was put on the line July 7, 1929, at 6:05 P.M. Eastern Time when Lindbergh, sitting in the office of California governor C.C. Young, pressed a button. Three thousand miles away, at Penn Station, a light flashed—the signal to start the Pennsylvania's *Airway Limited* on its way. A band played "California Here I Come" as the train pulled out and headed west toward Port Columbus, the air/rail exchange station that had been built seven miles east of the Ohio capital. The train was on time but the inaugural wasn't; the start of service originally had been set for May 1, long before Universal's scene-stealing effort, but construction delays, political red tape and other factors had caused successive postponements to June 1, then June 15 and finally July 7—"the day we were properly ready," as Keys put it.

Two Fords, *City of Columbus* and *City of Wichita*, were poised at Port Columbus where some 5,000 spectators stood through a drizzle to watch nineteen passengers transfer from train to plane. They weren't all paying passengers. Three were TAT officials, including Miss Earhart and Henderson, who also brought along his son; two were officers of the Pennsylvania Railroad, and three represented the news media.

The train arrived at 7:55 A.M. July 8, and twenty minutes later the two trimotors were speeding west. Lunch consisting of cold meats, sandwiches and coffee was served in flight between St. Louis and Kansas City. The aircraft landed on schedule just before 6:30 P.M. at Waynoka. The four enroute stops were timed to consume not more than fifteen minutes each. At Waynoka, the passengers boarded a Santa Fe train for Clovis where two more Fords took over the final leg to Los Angeles.

The eastbound inaugural left Grand Central Air Terminal at Glendale with Lindbergh himself piloting the *City of Los Angeles*—a trimotor christened by movie stars Gloria Swanson and Mary Pickford just before its takeoff. Also present was Douglas Fairbanks, Miss Pickford's husband. It was the start of a long love affair between Hollywood celebrities and the airline that someday would be called TWA.

Lindbergh flew the trimotor only as far as Winslow and waited there for the arrival of the *City of Columbus*, which he flew to Los Angeles. Of more

9

significance than his flying two legs of both the east- and westbound trips was a telegram he sent to General Atterbury of the Pennsylvania. After congratulating Atterbury on "the opening of a new era of passenger transportation," Lindy added these visionary words:

I believe that the significance of this service lies not alone in the fact that we are bringing the Atlantic and Pacific coasts within 48 hours of each other, but rather it opens the way to what heretofore has been an impossible dream—the elimination of daytime travel. The present service requires two business days to cross the continent. Our night service, which is now in the process of organization, will require but one, and I am confident that the next decade will bring about overnight travel between New York and California over our lines. From a technical standpoint, the system is ready for operation. Every precaution which modern methods have developed has been taken for the safety of our passengers and I feel confident that we start operation today with a system which combines the elements of safety, comfort and rapidity of travel in their highest degree.

It was a curious yet highly prophetic way to congratulate the president of a railroad, one in which Lindbergh in effect predicted the eventual demise of the railroad as the primary carrier of long-haul traffic. Such a development would take another quarter of a century to come about, but it was TAT that had launched not just a gimmick but the forerunner of modern air travel.

In some respects, however, the Lone Eagle's vision was somewhat clouded. The system may have combined "the elements of safety, comfort and rapidity of travel in their highest degree," but Lindbergh should have added the phrase, "within the state of the present art." In virtually every respect, and despite all the careful planning, the air/rail service fell short of expectations, from revenue to the all-important aspect of safety.

On September 3, less than two months after the brave inaugural, a TAT Ford *(City of San Francisco)* left Albuquerque enroute to Los Angeles; Winslow was to be the next scheduled stop, but the flight never made it. All radio contact was lost after the plane departed Albuquerque, and a massive ground and air search was launched, covering 50,000 square miles of rugged terrain in western New Mexico and eastern Arizona.

Only after four days was the twisted wreckage of the trimotor discovered, on the south side of 10,000-foot Mt. Taylor in New Mexico, by a Western Air Express pilot flying an F-10 on a regular trip. The captain, George Rice, was later to become TWA's manager of flying for the Western region, but on this day, he was merely the bearer of sad news. After he radioed the wreckage's position, ground searchers reached the site and found all eight occupants dead. Ironically, less than two months later a Western F-10 crashed into the same mountain, killing all five aboard.

Traffic fell off sharply after the TAT accident and dwindled to the vanishing point after the second crash. TAT tried hard to mask the questionable safety of air travel under the facade of what then passed as luxurious comfort. It offered such amenities as free gold fountain pens and lunches served on gold plates with lavender tablecloths and napkins. The food itself, TAT boasted justifiably, was catered by the Fred Harvey Company, which operated the famed Santa Fe dining service. The airline even offered what was advertised as "the first aerial motion pictures in the history of aviation." On October 8, 1929, TAT passengers on the westbound flight from Columbus to Waynoka spent part of the 9-hour trip watching a newsreel and cartoons featuring Oswald the Cat. Someone in publicity hadn't done his homework, however; Britain's Imperial Airways had shown the first in-flight movie more than four years before TAT used the gimmick. In April of 1925, passengers on an Imperial flight to Europe were shown a full-length feature, Arthur Conan Doyle's *Lost World,* thus presenting the fascinating anomaly of viewing prehistoric monsters in the cabin of a 20th-century aircraft.

Meals and movies notwithstanding, TAT's traffic stayed depressed, and not even a drastic fare reduction helped. At the start of service, the New York–Los Angeles combined air/rail fare ranged between $337 and $403, depending on the class of train accommodations one chose. TAT's share was $290, amounting to about 16 cents a mile. TAT pegged a reduced fare at $267 and waited confidently for an avalanche of new business that failed to materialize. The memories of those black headlines, "GIANT AIRLINER CRASHES—ALL ABOARD PERISH," were too fresh.

More than safety was involved, of course. The average American viewed air travel as more of an exciting stunt than a mode of getting from one place to another. The air passenger of 1929 was not only scared but uncomfortable. Added to the almost intolerable noise level of the Ford trimotor was the statistical fact that one out of every two occupants got air sick. The couriers not only handed out cotton to plug in ears, and chewing gum to relieve eardrum pressure on takeoffs and landings, but also had to point ominously to the availability of the "burp bags," those wax-lined receptacles as essential as the seats. If the bags became full, which could and did happen, the only recourse was to praise the foresight of William Stout and Ford in providing windows that could open. Eventually, psychological research studies would establish a direct correlation between fear and nausea, yet even the bravest passenger was not immune to the effects of motion sickness. The Fords were more stable than the lighter Fokkers, but they still rolled and bucked in bad weather.

TAT's pilots normally cruised at 3,000 feet except on the Clovis–Los Angeles leg where the mountainous terrain required higher operating altitudes. This presented the additional problem of thin air. Some crews leaving or approaching Los Angeles flew through the passes of the mountains east of the city. Others preferred to put more space between their aircraft and the rugged ridges that invited disaster. This involved climbing to as high as 16,000 feet—the Tin Goose's official ceiling—but at that altitude some passengers simply blacked out until the plane had cleared the mountains and descended to more breathable air.

TAT pilot Cliff Abbott was flying one trip on which he had the devil's own time keeping level. One minute the Ford would be nose-heavy, and a few minutes later it would be tail-heavy. Abbott grew arm-weary winding the stabilizer trim above his head and finally decided to look back at the cabin to see if anything was amiss.

There was. A big man, weighing about 200 pounds, was walking up and down the aisle as if on a constitutional hike. Abbott turned the controls over to his copilot and went into the cabin.

"I'd like to ask what the hell you think you're doing?" he demanded.

"I'm counting the number of turns you're taking on that stabilizer," the man said affably.

"You mind telling me why?"

"Not at all. I'm Anthony Fokker and I wanted to see how this plane's stability compares to the one I build."

Abbott had to laugh. As a pilot, he knew that Fokker was thin-skinned about the Tin Goose. It was no secret that the Ford's airfoil, general dimensions and overall design had been copied from a Fokker trimotor that had parked overnight at Ford's Dearborn airport some years before. While its crew was being entertained by Ford officials, Ford engineers sneaked into the hangar and took copious notes and measurements. The only real difference between the two planes was the Ford's all-metal construction.

From Henderson, Lindbergh, Collins and Collings on down, the crews had safety drummed into their skulls and screwed into their navels. "Don't take chances" was TAT's unofficial but highly prevalent motto—which was admirable but also frequently resulted in canceled trips because of weather. Around the airline industry, the running gag was that TAT stood for "take a train." In the winter of 1929, schedule reliability became a shambles. Only too frequent were the occasions when the couriers had to take passengers off planes, put them on the first available train and accompany them to whatever city might have a flight that could take off; it was no wonder that included in the items carried by every courier was a supply of railroad tickets or vouchers.

A young TAT ticket agent named Oz Cocke met one train at Kansas City carrying deplaned passengers and broke the news that they'd have to continue their journey by rail. As he finished his apologetic speech, a man grabbed his arm.

"Could you take me out to the airport before the train leaves?" he asked imploringly. "I've been traveling all the way from Los Angeles and haven't seen an airplane yet. I just want to see what one looks like."

TAT, subordinates and officers alike, never stopped trying. The chief steward of the Pennsylvania Railroad was hired as a consultant to work up improved menus. He developed a meal service that recalled the typical cuisine of an ocean liner—bouillon in the morning, tea and toast in midafternoon and hot lunches consisting of broiled chicken kept warm in thermos jugs. Another innovation was radio service for passengers; they could send or receive personal messages via the plane's radios, and it is recorded that during the 1929 stock market crash, many TAT passengers communicated with brokers that way. It is not stretching the imagination too far to suppose that a millionaire boarding a TAT flight in Los Angeles might have found himself penniless when he reached New York forty-eight hours later.

The Great Depression had not yet taken its full stranglehold as 1929 ended, but already the Pennsylvania's General Atterbury was having his doubts about the air/rail venture that was steadily hemorrhaging red ink. Six or seven occupied seats on any leg was considered an excellent showing, for the usual load consisted of two or three intrepid souls. Desperately, in January of 1930, the airline cut fares again—down to less than $160. Traffic did pick up; in the first two months TAT carried nearly 6,800 passengers, which represented a 450 percent increase over the previous two months. But TAT could not have made money even if its Fords had flown to full capacity; the airline's share of the $160 fare was too small. Things were so bad that on several occasions, employees received IOUs instead of paychecks.

Clement Keys was not one to watch a $5 million investment go down the drain. The sagging fortunes of the air/rail service was only one of his setbacks, for he had lost control of NAT in a bitter and bloody fight with another aviation conglomerate, United Aircraft and Transport Corporation, under whose corporate flag flew the banners of Boeing Air Transport, the Boeing Airplane Company, the engine manufacturer Pratt & Whitney, Chance Vought (a successful builder of Navy planes), the Hamilton Propeller Company, Stearman Aircraft and Sikorsky Aviation. This formidable aviation colossus was capitalized to the tune of $146 million, dwarfing North American Aviation.

United Aircraft had seized NAT by secretly acquiring one-third of its stock. Keys counterpunched with a brilliant maneuver: he changed NAT's bylaws to reduce the quorum limitation and simultaneously issued 300,000 new shares to North American. This would have turned back United's invasion, but a court ruled the whole Keys strategy illegal, and United Aircraft took over NAT.

Minus NAT, Keys turned to merger as a means of bolstering North American's shredded holdings. On February 13, 1930, he finally reached an agreement with Jack Maddux to bring Maddux Airlines under the TAT roof. It was a deal carrying two major benefits for TAT: first, Maddux was the world's largest Ford trimotor operator, and the merger added fifteen trimotors to the TAT fleet; second, it gave TAT a Los Angeles–San Francisco route.

Almost simultaneously, Keys moved in another direction—toward the far-flung routes of Western Air Express. For by now, Keys knew that the air/rail concept was dead. The 48-hour transcontinental schedule wasn't fast enough to wean passengers away from all-train service, and TAT's air routes were too brief to be viable. In the first eighteen months of operation, his air/rail service lost $2.7 million. But in Pop Hanshue's well-run WAE, which operated as far east as Kansas City, Keys saw a chance to create an all-air transcontinental service.

Early in 1930, he wrote Hanshue and invited him to a meeting at his home in New York City. The letter freely admitted the purpose: to merge Transcontinental Air Transport with Western Air Express. The merged carrier, Keys emphasized, would start out with a combined train/plane combination but would eventually operate solely by air.

Hanshue, who openly dreamed of extending WAE all the way to the East Coast, discussed the Keys letter with his directors. From them he obtained permission not only to reject the merger proposal but also to decline meeting with Keys merely to discuss it. His answering letter, however, was not completely negative.

We believe the future problems of a transcontinental air and train, or all-air service, should await further development before attempting to join these forces into a one-company operation.

As an alternative, we suggest joining with you in a transcontinental service, each company providing equipment and operating independently in its particular territory to meet the necessities of a continuous through service.

We are substantially influenced by the fact that we are a western group of men for the primary purpose of serving a populous center of the western territory. We are experienced in and equipped for flying in the high western altitude and over western terrain. If we permit ourselves to become absorbed in a national system, we ultimately would lose our identity and control and our local interest. . . .

Keys handled the rebuff with surprising graciousness, tinged with just a wee bit of hypocrisy. He accepted the rejection "in the spirit in which you made it" but added the hope that one way or another, Western Air Express would be merged into the transcontinental picture "even though it seems very remote at this time." It wasn't that remote and Keys knew it; he was well aware (and may even have ordered it) that Col. Paul Henderson would quickly inform the Post Office Department of Western's refusal to merge. Henderson's report caused Warren Irving Glover, second assistant postmaster general in charge of airmail contracts, to write Hanshue that he was making a grave mistake. "Things are moving pretty fast in the passenger game," Glover informed Hanshue, "and I hope Western Air Express will not be squeezed out of the picture."

The somewhat politically naive Hanshue rejected this implied warning as quickly as he had rebuffed Keys. In a political sense, WAE's home base of Los Angeles was an isolated outpost; by contrast, Keys and Henderson knew in which direction the Washington political winds were blowing. And the source of the storm was none other than President Herbert Hoover's postmaster general, Walter Folger Brown.

Walter Brown was a Harvard-educated lawyer from Toledo, Ohio. Always impeccably dressed, he nevertheless was not the stuffed shirt his sartorial splendor, steel-rimmed glasses and stern countenance seemed to portray. He loved sailing, camping and cooking, for example, all hobbies that clashed with his stiff demeanor. He insisted on wearing a top hat while carrying out official duties that took him away from his office. Because of that habit, he required a limousine with a ceiling high enough for his Lincolnesque chapeau. Yet under the rather Victorian facade he had erected for public view was an intelligent, skilled public servant with a deep sense of responsibility toward a job traditionally held by political hacks.

Brown was no hack. He had received his political training from Mark Hanna of Ohio, one of the toughest political bosses in American history. From his first day in office when he opened the traditional leatherbound portfolio given to all new cabinet officers, he was intrigued with commercial aviation. The portfolio describing the duties of the postmaster general included a phrase that caught his eye—"to encourage commercial aviation." Brown at the time didn't know an aileron from a landing gear, but he was willing to learn, and he went, figuratively speaking, from kindergarten to college in two years.

In that period, he conducted an intensive study of the U.S. air transportation system, then composed of forty-four airlines whose economic health resembled that of the citizens of a Latin American country—either wealth or poverty. At one end of the spectrum were the well-financed giants like United, North American and Aviation Corporation (AVCO), the latter another conglomerate, launched early in 1929 by financiers including W. Averell Harriman and Robert Lehman, that controlled more than a half-dozen scattered carriers. At the other end of the spectrum were the small, undercapitalized operators clinging to their mail contracts, without which they would have folded overnight.

To Walter Folger Brown, this sprawling, hodgepodge system made no sense. And the plan gestating in his astute mind was designed to get rid of the marginal operators, consolidate the survivors into a more efficient and logical route system and, in doing so, to redraw the nation's air map. What he basically envisioned was a transcontinental network operated by three carriers—one flying a northern route, the second a central route and the third a southern route. United's acquisition of NAT, followed by its absorption of Varney Air Lines, already had provided the first real transcontinental airline over Brown's northern route—New York–San Francisco via Chicago. Now the postmaster general moved to achieve the rest of his plan. All he needed was legal authority, and he was handed that tool by passage of the Watres Act in April 1930.

The legislation had been introduced by Rep. Lawrence Watres of Pennsylvania and Sen. Charles McNary of Oregon, both Republicans. Its real purpose was to squeeze the smaller airlines out and foster the growth of passenger traffic. This would be achieved by its two main provisions: the first stated that any airmail operator with two years operating experience could exchange its current authorization for a ten-year route certificate and pioneer rights would be recognized—which sounded fair except that the Watres Act defined an airline with "pioneer rights" as the "lowest responsible bidder who has owned and operated an air transportation service on a fixed daily schedule over a distance of not less than 250 miles and for a period of not less than six months prior to the advertisement for bids." That definition automatically disqualified a number of small pioneer airlines flying minuscule routes, many less than 100 miles. Under the second provision, the practice of paying the airlines by the weight of mail carried was scrapped in favor of a new system based on payment by the space offered. The maximum mail subsidy rate would be $1.25 a mile, regardless of whether the space was filled. It seemed outwardly reasonable, but in reality it was a death blow to the smaller carriers with relatively little mail capacity. While it drastically reduced mail revenues for the larger airlines, it also forced them to increase their passenger-carrying operations to make up for the lower mail income, which is what Brown wanted all along. He was convinced that the future of America's air transportation lay not in carrying mail but in carrying people.

When the Watres Act was passed and signed into law, the postmaster general moved quickly to extend its effects beyond what the law intended. The job of advertising for new airmail bids was the responsibility of the Post Office Department, and Brown's notice included a new eligibility requirement: every operator had to have at least six months experience flying at night over routes of 250 miles or more. Technically, this eliminated TAT, which was still operating only in the daytime, but Lindbergh's foresight paid off; obviously TAT was capable of night flying and Brown was later to stretch a point in not holding the airline to his stiff requirement.

Finally, the Watres Act gave the postmaster general authority to extend or consolidate routes "when in his judgment the public interest will be promoted thereby." This rather vague statement was nothing but a blank check that Brown proceeded to fill out and cash.

Early in May, Brown summoned various airlines to Washington for a series of meetings. The guest list itself underlined Brown's ambitious plans; he invited only the heads of the large airlines. Later he was to explain, "There was no sense in taking the government's money and dishing it out to every little fellow that was flying around the map and was not going to do anything."

The meetings were not exactly secret, as critics were to charge, they just weren't very well publicized. Between May 19 and May 30, Brown discussed his blueprint for the nation's future air travel with top officers of the carriers he had summoned. Pop Hanshue, glowering and unhappy because he sensed trouble, represented Western Air Express. Present for TAT was a rather curious choice—D.M. Sheaffer, chief of passenger transportation for the Pennsylvania Railroad. Keys apparently selected him because Sheaffer was chairman of TAT's executive committee, but there wasn't much doubt that Clement Keys was calling the shots from behind the scenes. Also on hand were high-ranking officials from United Aircraft, AVCO, Eastern Air Transport and several other carriers. Among the uninvited, interestingly enough in light of future developments, was tiny Delta.

The twelve days of heated discussion and debate went down in history as the infamous "Spoils Conference," and the harsh sobriquet was not entirely unwarranted; to those participants who bought Brown's plan literally went the spoils. The postmaster general laid out the ground rules right from the start. He praised United's new New York–San Francisco service but added tersely that no single airline should have a monopoly on coast-to-coast operations. There had to be two more transcontinental competitors in addition to United's northern route; one would involve a central route via such cities as Pittsburgh and St. Louis, the other a southern route via Dallas and Oklahoma City.

He emphasized that he would not approve any transcontinental route to be served by an amalgam of airlines with connecting flights; each of the three routes would have to be operated by a single carrier even if it meant merging existing ones. Brown then suggested that the airline executives meet among themselves to work out various consolidations.

As Brown privately suspected, the jealous and mutually distrustful chieftains couldn't reach any agreement. They returned to his office and asked him to arbitrate their differences. This was simply another blank check. Brown's key decision was to choose TAT as the operator of the central route, giving the southern route to the AVCO conglomerate, which would operate as American Airways. The postmaster general acknowledged there was a slight loophole in the TAT award; it had never flown at night, which theoretically rendered it ineligible. But the solution was simple, Brown said:

all TAT had to do was merge with Western Air Express, which had considerable night-flying experience.

Hanshue was enraged. He was there under duress anyway, and early in the proceedings when someone asked him what he thought of the meetings, he had snapped, "I think you're all crazy as hell!" Now, with Brown's cards on the table, he furiously pointed out that WAE already was operating large segments of both the central and southern routes. Brown quietly repeated his TAT–WAE merger suggestion.

"But this will prevent us from bidding on the southern route," Hanshue protested. "We're flying as far east as Dallas now."

"Of course it will," the postmaster general agreed. "So I advise you to sell your Los Angeles–Dallas operation to Southwest Air Fast Express [an American Airways subsidiary]."

Hanshue, as lacking in diplomacy as in political finesse, told Brown he could go to hell. The meeting broke up with Hanshue refusing to budge. That same night, Sheaffer phoned him and asked if he could see him. Wearily, Hanshue agreed and listened to the railroad official representing TAT and Keys propose an even less palatable plan: TAT would take over Western Air Express through an exchange of stock.

Pop was too tired to explode again, and with rare civility, he told Sheaffer he doubted whether his directors and officers would want to lose control of their operations. Sheaffer insisted that he at least sound out some of WAE's major stockholders; Hanshue did and subsequently informed Sheaffer they were adamantly opposed. When the conference resumed, Brown could not budge the fiery little leader of Western Air Express from a position set in concrete. Hanshue finally left Washington, returned to Los Angeles, and in a somewhat calmer mood, wrote the postmaster general a carefully composed letter outlining his reasons for not wanting to merge with TAT or to sell the Los Angeles–Dallas route.

Brown's response was a phone call to Hanshue requesting a meeting between just the two of them. When Hanshue got to Washington, he found Brown in a pleasant, even conciliatory mood. By now, the postmaster general was aware of Sheaffer's proposal for a direct takeover, and Brown knew he couldn't ask Hanshue to swallow that bitter pill. Instead, Brown suggested that a new company be formed holding the assets of both TAT and WAE on a fifty-fifty basis. A third partner in the venture, Brown proposed, would be Pittsburgh Aviation Industries Corporation (PAIC), a company founded by several Pittsburgh industrialists. PAIC actually wasn't an airline; it had built an airport near Pittsburgh and ran a flying school there plus an air taxi service. But the latter was operated over what would be a small segment of the proposed central transcontinental route, and PAIC was insisting it held pioneer rights to that segment. In truth, PAIC didn't meet the requisites of the Watres Act; it had never flown a "fixed daily schedule," but among its backers was the Mellon family, with plenty of clout in the Republican party.

Brown already had convinced TAT it had to take in PAIC as a minority partner for the central route, holding ten percent of the stock. Hanshue objected but futilely. He argued in vain with Brown and finally departed with only the promise to "talk to my associates." This he did, only to dis-

17

cover that his directors—all Republicans—were now convinced that merger was the only course. In a last-ditch meeting in New York's Savoy Hotel, he pleaded with his board for more than an hour, offering to take the fight all the way to the White House. Pop Hanshue was the only man in the room, however, willing to take on the Hoover administration. By July 1, 1930, Hanshue had begun formal merger negotiations, which stumbled along until Mr. Brown put his well-polished shoes down on the bickering.

Hanshue had been objecting to giving PAIC five percent of Western's holdings in the new company; because the minority partner was on the eastern leg of the central route, he insisted, PAIC's ten percent share should come out of TAT's stock. Sheaffer was equally firm, arguing that TAT and WAE each should give up five percent to PAIC. When Hanshue and Sheaffer informed Brown they were stalemated, the postmaster general came up with a compromise: reduce PAIC's interest to only five percent, with Western and TAT each providing 2.5 percent. He presented the formula on a take-it-or-else basis. "If you don't agree this time," he warned, "I'll hold up awarding any mail contract until the issue is settled."

Faced with this ultimatum, Hanshue caved in. A tentative merger agreement was reached July 16 and was subsequently approved by the shareholders of both carriers with two new provisions. First, Western was to retain management control of the new airline for one year, with Hanshue serving as president, in exchange for giving TAT voting control. Second, Western would not have to contribute any cash to the new corporation. Pop wrung one final concession: Western Air Express would be allowed to survive as a separate carrier, operating its original Los Angeles–Salt Lake City route along with a San Diego–Los Angeles spur.

On October 1, 1930, Walter Folger Brown awarded the southern transcontinental route to American Airways and the central route to the child of a shotgun marriage. Officially known as Transcontinental and Western Air, Inc., it quickly became known by its initials: TWA.

Through the merger, the new airline had acquired virtually the entire Western Air Express fleet: twenty-one Fokker F-10s and two Fokker F-32s (a four-engine giant whose mechanical problems were commensurate with its size), plus some five hundred employees. The latter included an asset of far greater importance than $1.3 million worth of aircraft.

A full year before the Spoils Conference, Hanshue had bought into a struggling little air carrier named Standard Airlines that began by operating single-engine Fokkers between Los Angeles and Tucson via Phoenix, and later expanded its service to El Paso. Several months later, Hanshue bought out the airline entirely and merged it into Western's system, bringing with it the two ex-stunt pilots who had founded Standard. Their names were Paul Richter and Jack Frye.

2

"... The first thing we have to do is get a new president."

William John Frye was his full name, although in the years to come it would be virtually impossible to find anyone in TWA or the entire airline industry who knew it.

It was Jack Frye to all, from the most humble TWA employee to his own peers. Even the prestigious publication *Who's Who in Aviation* listed him only by his nickname. It is not exaggerating to say there was no man in aviation better liked or more respected than this big, curly-haired man who always seemed to have an ingratiating grin on his round, florid face. He was a true visionary, a pioneer airman from the helmet and goggle days weaned on flimsy wood-and-canvas biplanes, who never lost sight of the future even as he grappled with the present.

Frye was born in Sweetwater, Oklahoma, in 1904, the son of a cattle rancher, and left home at the age of 18 with his brother Don and two friends. They headed west to California in hope of landing some of those highly remunerative jobs supposedly in great abundance. But there was no pot of gold at the Los Angeles end of the rainbow, and Frye suffered through such menial occupations as newspaper boy, dishwasher and soda jerk. Discouraged, he was about to sail for Australia when a companion backed out at the last minute, and Frye returned to his job in a drug store soda fountain. On such a minuscule, prosaic turn of events was the future of an airline determined.

He was making $25 a week at the drug store when he became acquainted with Burdette Fuller, a veteran pilot who ran a little flying school and barnstorming operation in the Los Angeles area. Fuller gave Frye his first airplane ride for $5 and the youngster was hooked, even though the flight lasted only fifteen minutes. Fuller agreed to give him flying lessons at the going rate of $20 an hour; considering Jack's $25-a-week salary, it was no wonder it took him several months before he accumulated seven-and-a-half hours of instruction and was allowed to solo. A natural pilot, Frye gained enough experience to qualify as an instructor, and Fuller offered him a chance to buy into the business, including half-interest in one of the two Jennies he owned.

At the time, Jack was flat broke, but his brother Don loaned him enough to buy the partnership. Frye was only 20 when the papers were signed, but he had found his niche—along with a friendship that would last a lifetime. One of the instructors at Burdette Field was Paul Edmund Richter from

Colorado, and like Frye, the son of a rancher. Richter, too, had left home for California, but he had his sights on flying right from the start. Frye taught him to fly and he was good enough to be offered a job as a movie stunt pilot. He became a member of the "Thirteen Black Cats," which at the time constituted the most elite group of daredevils in Hollywood.

The Black Cats were run by Ronald "Ron" MacDougall, another partner in Fuller's Burdette Airport and School of Aviation. MacDougall's original goal was to corner the market for all film stunt work involving airplanes, cars, motorcycles and boats, and he advertised the outfit as "the world's greatest stuntmen—the only fliers who will do anything at a fixed price." The fees ranged from $80 for a simple parachute jump to $1,500 for blowing up a plane in midair and then jumping. Slightly under this top scale was a $1,200 price for crashing an aircraft into a house or tree or spinning it into the ground.

Frye joined the Cats, too, after acquiring a bit more experience, although his heart was never really in stunt flying. It was a subject he discussed with Richter as they got to know one another better and began to form a relationship that was almost fraternal. He also struck up a close friendship with another Burdette graduate, Walter Hamilton, who had won a pilot's license but had more of a bent for the mechanical end of airplanes than for flying them. Walt Hamilton was originally employed by the Duesenberg Auto Company, where he worked his way up to foreman and engineer. A true genius with engines, Hamilton loved to spend hours in the shed that housed Burdette's few tools and an old lathe, tinkering and repairing.

To both Richter and Hamilton, Frye confided his dream—to own his own company. The obvious target was Burdette itself and it was typical of Jack Frye that he spawned this grandiose idea after spending only two years working for Fuller. In 1925, the trio had saved up enough money to own three airplanes outright with a few thousand dollars left over, which they pooled to make Fuller an offer. Tired of his shoestring operation, Fuller sold out to the company Frye and his two compatriots had organized, Aero Corporation of California. The deal included the airport lease, two 8-year-old Jennies and Hamilton's beloved maintenance shed. In one year, Aero was making money. Frye and Richter wrangled regional distributorships for the Alexander Eaglerock and Fokker transports, and sales were brisk enough to establish branch offices in both California and Arizona.

Aero was a catchall operation, an aerial version of "have tux, will travel." Its flying school was considered one of the best in the nation and was one of the first to be certified by the Department of Commerce. Hamilton supervised another lucrative sideline, aircraft maintenance, expanding the old Burdette shed into modern hangars completely equipped with the best overhaul tools available. By the end of 1925, Aero was operating a fleet of seven Eaglerocks for charter flying, crop dusting, sky writing, aerial photography and towing advertising banners. When Frye and Richter added things up at the close of the year, they found they had carried more than 8,000 passengers on charter and scenic flights, so they did what came naturally; they started an airline.

It was formed as a subsidiary of Aero on February 3, 1926, but service didn't start until November 28, 1927. Under the name Standard Airlines, the new carrier operated single-engine, six-passenger Fokker F-7s between

Los Angeles and Tucson via Phoenix. The Fokkers lacked lavatory facilities, so Frye authorized an optional stop at Yuma, whose primitive airport at least had a ladies' rest room. Inasmuch as women passengers were not exactly numerous, Standard didn't have to make many landings there. At Tucson, passengers could board a Texas and Pacific Railways train and eventually reach the East Coast seventy hours after leaving Los Angeles. When Standard's route system was extended to El Paso later that year, Frye worked out a deal whereby the Texas and Pacific Railways would carry passengers from El Paso to Sweetwater, Texas, where they would board a Southwest Air Fast Express Ford trimotor (the company's initials were a natural, the letters forming the acronym SAFE) and be flown to St. Louis. From there they traveled the New York Central to New York, and the total elapsed coast-to-coast time was under sixty hours.

The *Official Aviation Guide,* first published in 1929 as the industry's schedule bible (later it became *Official Airline Guide),* listed Standard's top officers as "Lieut. Jack Frye, president; Lieut. Paul Richter, vice-president and treasurer, and Walter Hamilton, vice-president in charge of operations." The military titles were derived from brief Army stints Frye and Richter did in the early twenties. Both could have called themselves "Captain," because on more than one occasion, they flew scheduled trips, either subbing for a pilot or simply because they felt like getting back in a cockpit.

Frye was, from all accounts, a perfect boss—compassionate, informal and demanding only in the sense that he worked as hard or harder than anyone else. One of his secretaries, Florence Suddarth, once described him as "quiet, calm, like a seasoned sailor guiding his ship safely through a storm."

"He worked with us and for us," she wrote, "so that the distinction of 'employer' and 'employee' was never particularly stressed." She considered Richter and Hamilton cut out of the same cloth, commenting that the men and women of Standard didn't just like them, they worshipped them.

In truth, the trio formed a team, Frye and Richter in particular. Jack was the planner and the promoter. Paul was eight years Frye's senior, the more practical, his innate conservatism serving as light but firmly held reins on Frye's impulsive nature. Although Standard was small, its executives won a reputation in the industry for efficiency and for having excellent employees. Some of the latter included youngsters who couldn't afford flying lessons but were allowed to work for their instruction, a practice Frye had started when he first took over the Burdette operation. One such young hopeful was Lee Flanagin, who shelled out a dollar for a ride in one of Jack's Jennies and was bitten by the flying bug. He went to work for Aero as a mechanic in exchange for flying lessons and started flying Fokkers when Standard was launched. He was to become one of TWA's outstanding pilots and a favorite of Howard Hughes, as well as being very close to Frye and Richter.

"Jack was the go-getter, the dreamer," Flanagin remembers today. "Paul was the businessman who always had to keep Jack from going too fast and too far."

The cautious Richter, however, did not stand in Frye's way when Pop Hanshue approached Jack with an offer to buy into Aero, parent company of the airline. Frye, who was pouring every cent of profit back into Standard, welcomed the cash transfusion and put Hanshue and another large Western stockholder on Aero's board of directors. From that vantage point,

Hanshue got an even clearer view of the Frye/Richter combination; he openly coveted their services as much as he did Standard's routes, and just before the Spoils Conference, Western Air Express acquired Standard, taking in Frye, Richter and Hamilton as vice-presidents in charge of the Standard division. During the brief period Standard was part of WAE, it was operated as a separate airline. Under the terms of the TAT/Western merger agreement, Hanshue was forced to hand over Standard's routes to American, which to this day claims Standard as one of its predecessor carriers. (A plaque donated by American commemorating the November 28, 1927, inauguration of service by "a predecessor company" is displayed at Tucson International Airport, the nation's first municipally owned field.)

But the trio of Frye, Richter and Hamilton didn't go with American. They went to work for TWA, and when Postmaster General Brown wielded his menacing shotgun, he had no way of knowing he was handing the new airline a future president.

The reluctant father of the groom, Harris Hanshue, played virtually no further role as far as TWA was concerned. He was TWA's first president in name only, a disillusioned figurehead who had stepped on too many toes and made too many enemies, including Clement Keys, who never forgave Hanshue for his recalcitrant attitude toward the merger. Early in the spring of 1931, Hanshue became seriously ill with pneumonia, and during his unlamented absence, Richard W. Robbins, a top official at PAIC, took over as TWA's managing director. When Hanshue emerged from the hospital, he found Robbins running the airline and quickly read the signs. Four months before his one-year presidential tenure was over, Hanshue relinquished his TWA post and went back to Western Air Express. In his own words, he was "relieved" of the presidency and his appraisal was accurate. He was forced out, and the man who did most of the shoving was a member of TWA's board of directors, diminutive but dynamic Ernest R. Breech, a troubleshooter for General Motors who had been named a director at GM's request.

The giant auto firm had a large stake in TWA, and several other aviation ventures, including Fokker Aircraft's U.S. division, all operated under a subsidiary called General Aviation. GM had loaned Hanshue $800,000 to keep Western going after the merger and also, through General Aviation, had acquired 60,000 shares of stock in WAE, which gave it control of the airline. Most of those shares became TWA stock when the merger was consummated, and with that kind of leverage, General Motors began calling a few shots. First, it placed one of its vice-presidents, C.E. Wilson, on the TWA board. Then, because TWA's corporate headquarters were in New York and Wilson had too many duties in Detroit, GM chose Breech to succeed Wilson as a TWA director. Breech didn't like the way Hanshue was running—or not running—the airline. He so informed John Lee Pratt, second only to Alfred Sloan in the General Motors hierarchy. Breech told Pratt:

We're going to have to get hold of this thing or it's going to go broke. It has no top-management direction. Hanshue is really not operating as a president. Some of the directors are meddling in the affairs of the company. One of them, representing a stockholder, is negotiating in Washington for airmail contracts. Another one has the responsibility of negotiating oil and gasoline contracts, and a third is interested seemingly in the purchase of equipment for the airline, or at least in planning the purchase of equipment. The president seems to be responsible for little more than to show up at the office each day.

Pratt asked Breech what he thought should be done. Breech suggested a smaller board with an executive committee that had no conflicts of interest.

"The first thing we have to do is get a new president and send Hanshue back to California to run Western Air Express, which is what he wants to do," Breech added with his customary bluntness.

Pratt asked him if he had anyone in mind and Breech recommended Robbins, who already was on the TWA board and had gotten his feet wet filling in for Hanshue during the latter's illness. It was Breech who called a special directors' meeting at which Hanshue's resignation was accepted and Robbins was elected president; Ernie was to tell a writer many years later that he was especially proud Lindbergh attended that meeting and expressed his approval of the board streamlining plan.

When Dick Robbins assumed command, he was heading an airline losing $200,000 a month, with its new mail revenues insufficient to support the unprofitable passenger operations. From behind the scenes, Breech continued to wield his influence. He handpicked a new controller in the person of another GM executive, Frank G. Wilson, and kept a close eye on the airline's financial health. Yet the man he had picked to head TWA, Robbins, was something of a figurehead himself; the real boss of TWA was none other than Frye, who was named vice-president of operations. Richter, whose vice-presidential status ended temporarily with the merger, was superintendent of TWA's Western Division with headquarters in Kansas City. Hamilton was there, too, as division maintenance superintendent overseeing the care and feeding of TWA's hodgepodge fleet. It consisted of former TAT and Maddux Fords, a pair of Lockheed Vegas, formerly owned by Maddux, and most of Western's Fokkers plus WAE's two huge F-32s; the last were used briefly as backup planes and eventually retired. One of them wound up as a gas station in downtown Los Angeles.

The pilot corps also was of the hodgepodge variety. There were TAT veterans like Abbott, Bartles, Howard "Sonny Boy" Hall, Bryan and Jack Zimmerman. From Maddux came Daniel Webb Tomlinson IV, otherwise known as "Tommy." He was Navy-trained and had once commanded a crack Navy fighter squadron as well as leading a Navy aerial stunt team called "The Three Seahawks." At Maddux, he had risen to the position of operations manager and chief pilot, but when he joined TWA it was as a lowly copilot.

Tomlinson wasn't to stay a copilot very long. Like Lindbergh, he was as much a scientist as an airman, a man with insatiable curiosity, a plethora of new ideas and the willingness to try them out if given a chance. Frye, with a sharp eye for talent, spotted him early and promoted him first to captain and then to be his personal assistant and a member of Lindbergh's still-existing technical committee.

Other Maddux employees were to carve their own niches in the TWA story. One was a captain named Larry Fritz who, like John Collings, had been a Ford test pilot. Another was Johnny Guy, a feisty mechanic specializing in engine overhaul. Guy was working in a Los Angeles garage when Tomlinson brought in his car for repairs; he liked Johnny's style and offered him a job with Maddux at sixty cents an hour, less than what he was making at the garage. That he accepted Tommy's offer was not unusual; the early history of the airlines is replete with examples of men who left better-paying jobs for the challenge and excitement of commercial aviation. If the present was decidedly uncertain, the future seemed to hold promise.

Fear remained the youthful industry's biggest burden. Any accident would depress traffic for months, not only for the carrier directly involved but all airlines. It was bad enough if a mail plane went down, but when passengers were victims, public confidence took a dive—as it did on the blackest day in TWA's young history.

The date was March 31, 1931, five months after TWA had inaugurated a 36-hour coast-to-coast service entirely by air and three months before Breech shook up the high command.

On that rainy morning, Frye was in his office at 10 Richards Road, TWA's operations headquarters at the Kansas City airport. A stickler for maintaining schedule, he was fretting over delayed Flight 5, westbound to Los Angeles and still on the ground in Kansas City. Flight 5 was formerly a Western Fokker trimotor still bearing the red and silver colors of Pop Hanshue's airline; its captain, 32-year-old Bob Fry, was a former Western pilot. An hour behind schedule because of weather, the delay bothered Frye even more than usual; the passenger list included a very special VIP: Notre Dame football coach Knute Rockne, bound for Hollywood where he was to act as technical advisor on a projected football film.

Not that Rockne would have complained about the delay. With the exception of humorist Will Rogers, no prominent American was a firmer supporter of commercial aviation than the flat-nosed Norwegian. He flew frequently, often on TWA, and like Rogers, he was always extolling the virtues of air travel. But to Frye, a posted schedule was something to be followed like the dictates of the Bible itself, and it was with relief that he finally watched, from his office window, the six booked passengers come out of the terminal building and board the Fokker. Rockne was the last in line, behind five businessmen whose jobs ranged from insurance to designing department store fixtures.

Fry, acting on a captain's prerogatives, made the decision to leave; it was still drizzling, with heavy thunderclouds around the airport, but he had been advised of clearing weather ahead. Jack Frye did not question his judgment; Bob Fry was an above-average pilot who had once served with the Marines in China as a sergeant-pilot. The copilot, Jess Mathias, would be handling radio communications as well as the duties of cabin attendant. (TWA, in an economy move, had dispensed with the services of its couriers.)

Watching from his office window, Frye saw Flight 5 wheel away from the ramp area and taxi toward the runway. He didn't go back to work until the Fokker had taken off and headed west. He had no thought of impending disaster nor did he have any reason to; the Fokker F-10 had been in airline service longer than the Ford and had an excellent safety record. Some pilots

24

liked it better than the Tin Goose because it was easier to fly, more responsive and faster, with a higher ceiling and a slightly greater payload.

The chief reason for the Fokker's superior performance, of course, was its lighter construction. The F-10's fuselage was built of welded-steel tubing covered with fabric, but the wings were made entirely of wood. Even the skin was extremely thin plywood and the spars were carved out of spruce and birch. The Ford, weighing two and a half tons more than the Fokker, had a wing built on the same principle as a cantilever bridge. There were three main metal spars and five auxiliary spars that gave the entire wing massive strength. Both the wing and fuselage were made of a corrugated alloy called "Alclad," a combination of aluminum and duralumin; the whole airframe was riveted together. The Fokker's spars were attached with glue. And this was the source of the hidden malignancy eating away at the sinews of NC-999, the TWA Fokker carrying eight men to their ultimate fate.

Flight 5 was droning toward Wichita, only twenty-five minutes away from landing, when the TWA radio operator there tried to contact Mathias. The static was bad but the operator finally heard the copilot say, "I can't talk now. I'm too busy." He tried to add something but his words were garbled and Wichita asked, "What are you going to do?"

This time Mathias's voice came in loud and clear. "I don't know," he radioed.

Darkish gray, low-hanging clouds filled the sky over farmers working the rolling hills in the southern Kansas wheat and cattle country. Several looked up at the sound of airplane engines and saw the red and silver Fokker emerge from the overcast, banking as if the pilot was looking for a place to land. The viewers watched first with curiosity and then sudden horror as they heard a loud crack—one said later it was more of a bang—as the right wing severed. The Fokker nosed over and dove toward the ground, twisting slowly as it plunged the final 1,500 feet. Halfway in the dive, the onlookers saw five bodies fall out of the disintegrating fuselage, hitting the earth almost simultaneously with the plane. The airliner went in nose first with a sickening roar, followed by an eerie silence as the witnesses ran toward the shredded but unburned wreckage. Rockne's body was identified by a coroner who found a rosary clutched in the right hand.

Accident investigations in 1931 were under the jurisdiction of the Commerce Department's Aeronautics Branch. The initial supposition was pilot error; it was theorized that Fry, battling turbulence, pulled up so sharply that the wing failed. Then investigators found ice chunks around the wreckage site and an engine missing its propeller—evidence leading them to conclude that a piece of ice had been thrown from a prop hub, breaking off a blade and creating such severe vibration that the wing snapped. Five days after the crash, they had to discard this theory because the propeller was found intact.

The newspapers were pressing for a quick solution of a tragedy that had wiped out a national figure. Media pressure led the government to issue a public statement blaming the crash on icing. The third and apparently final conclusion contended that the Fokker had picked up ice which "rendered inoperative certain of its instruments." This, the statement continued, caused NC-999 to go into a steep glide and that "when coming out of this maneuver, the change of direction occurred at such unusual rapidity as to build up an enormous load on the wing, which in turn brought about the wing failure." The primary cause, the department said with mistaken smugness, was weather.

What the Commerce Department not only didn't say but completely ignored was the fact that the Aeronautics Branch already had evidence of the Fokker's vulnerability to spar deterioration, which could go undetected until it was too late. Branch officials were privately expressing their concern that there was no way to inspect the inner spars without tearing off the outer plywood skin—an expensive, time-consuming task. They also were worried about aileron rigging; the Fokker factory had recommended to all F-10 operators an adjustment that supposedly would alleviate a tendency toward tail heaviness, but one airline had advised the Aeronautics Branch that the "fix" caused control problems. With the new rigging, the airline reported, the ship went into a bank easily but required overcontrol to bring it out. The airline warned that some pilot could get into trouble in turbulence because the controls were too slow.

How many F-10s the Aeronautics Branch inspected before the Flight 5 accident was never disclosed, but Federal Aviation Administration historian Nick A. Komons says flatly, "By the eve of the Rockne crash, the Branch felt it had enough evidence to justify grounding the aircraft immediately."

But it wasn't grounded immediately. Not until May 4, five weeks after the tragedy, did the Department of Commerce announce that no Fokker F-10 built before 1930 could be flown with passengers aboard until the inner spars had been inspected. The planes, however, could still carry mail provided that the pilots wore parachutes. Curiously, the announcement skirted the real reason for the grounding. Examination of Flight 5's wreckage had revealed the real killer of NC-999. Moisture had seeped into the wing's interior, weakening the glue and causing structural failure under what should have been normal stress loads. Instead of disclosing the true grounding motive, however, the government merely said the Fokkers were to be taken out of passenger service for inspection and maintenance and that no structural problems were involved.

Jack Frye hit the ceiling. In its ruling, the government was implying that faulty maintenance had caused the Rockne crash. The F-10's designer, Dutch-born Anthony Fokker, already had angrily accused TWA of operating the flight in known bad weather. Furiously objecting to the grounding, Fokker declared that "the United States will not see Fokker airplanes blown from the sky merely by the error of maintenance of one operator."

Frye ignored both the government's implied and Fokker's direct accusations, except to publicly urge that such criticism await the official findings. Those findings eventually were to blame the fate of Flight 5 on wood rot, but long before this verdict was announced Frye already had permanently grounded TWA's Fokker fleet. A few planes were sold and the remaining were burned after their engines and seats had been removed. Other U.S. carriers operating the airplane gradually phased them out of service and ended forever the use of wooden transport aircraft in this country.

Lindbergh could have been forgiven for saying "I told you so," but once the Fokkers were banished from the fleet he devoted his energies to making the surviving Fords more efficient. He bumped into young Otis Bryan one day and asked him how he liked the Tin Goose.

"Fine, but it's too slow," Bryan complained. "It cruises at ninety."

Lindbergh nodded. "If we put cowlings on the engines," he mused, "we'd add about fifteen miles an hour."

This was done, but TWA's traffic department, headed at the time by a conservative vice-president named T.B. Clement, objected to advertising the Ford as a 105-mile-an-hour airliner on the grounds that people would be afraid to fly that fast. Clement ordered a compromise: it was advertised as a 100-mile-an-hour transport. Actually, it made little difference how the planes were described or how much stronger the Ford was than the disgraced Fokker. Not only did fear remain a major factor, but the Depression was in full sway and not many people could afford to fly. TWA, along with most airlines, stayed alive mostly from mail revenues. These were of sufficient volume to warrant the purchase of a fleet of planes designed solely as mail carriers.

The fleet was made up of Northrop Alphas, a sleek single-engine, low-wing monoplane designed by the brilliant Jack Northrop, who had worked for Lockheed before forming his own company. Northrop was a disciple of Germany's Dr. Adolf Rohrbach, inventor of the so-called "stressed skin" principle that even today is still the cornerstone of every transport structure. Rohrbach devised a means of making the outer skin carry a large proportion of an aircraft load by reinforcing it with box-shaped interior metal spars. Northrop had applied this design to the Alpha but improved on it; he not only reinforced the fuselage skin with duralumin hoops, but installed crisscrossing metal spars inside the wings that allowed the stressed skin on the wing itself to carry the entire load. Not even the doughty Ford was as strong as the Alpha. The Tin Goose's fuselage skin was not stressed and some old-timers remember the day Capt. Pat Gallup landed a Ford at Harrisburg, Pennsylvania, where the field was extremely rough. As he taxied up to the terminal, the cabin door fell off. Gallup discovered that the fuselage had buckled at the door opening.

But the Alpha had its troubles, too, as any veteran of the air mail days can testify. TWA originally bought twelve of them and eventually lost about half the fleet to various accidents. The airplane was not free from those mysterious gremlins known as "design bugs." The Alpha, for example, had a tail wheel with no covering and carbon monoxide fumes could go up the open wheel well and find their way to the cockpit. Pilot Ted Hereford landed one day, walked into operations and began disrobing. Everyone thought he was drunk and this theory persisted until a short time later when Harry Campbell fainted after a Northrop landing. Revived, he continued on to St. Louis where he collapsed again and had to be hospitalized. When his affliction was diagnosed as carbon monoxide poisoning, maintenance designed a leather sock for the tail wheel that ended all episodes of fainting pilots.

The pilots who flew the Alphas on mail runs constituted the cream of TWA's cockpit personnel. In the early days of the mail contract, the company assigned the mail runs to the most junior pilots, but it didn't work out. The Alpha was not an easy bird to fly. It had an extremely narrow landing gear that invited ground-looping. After a few nonfatal mishaps involving the less-experienced crews, Collings, Richter and Frye decided to man the Alphas with senior airmen like Abbott, Bartles, Bryan and Hereford. They also had Hamilton widen the gear, which eliminated ground-looping but didn't alleviate the considerable in-flight risks.

Seldom was a mail flight canceled. The boys flew in weather that would have grounded an eagle. Almost any kind of precipitation rendered the primitive radios inoperable because of static, and the pilots might as well have tried to communicate by yelling. President Robbins decided one day to find out what flying the mail was like and was bundled into one of the narrow passenger seats of an Alpha westbound out of Newark. The pilot was Walt Seyerly, strictly a seat-of-the-pants birdman who hated instrument flying. On this particular night, the weather was horrendous and Seyerly flew under the overcast so he could see ground lights. The overcast, however, was hugging the tree tops and Walt hedgehopped all the way to Columbus, making several stops at emergency fields when visibility got too bad. The white-faced Robbins staggered off the plane at Port Columbus and never boarded another mail flight.

One trick all the pilots utilized was to follow railroad tracks when radios were blocked out by static and light beacons became invisible in fog, rain or snow.

"You'd find a track," Cliff Abbott reminisces, "and turn on your landing lights. You'd fly as low as one hundred feet and even in heavy snow the tracks would shine just like ribbons of steel. We'd follow them for miles and miles."

Abbott had one particularly hazardous flight between St. Louis and Kansas City. His own laconic description tells the story:

Otis Bryan was heading east at two thousand feet and picking up ice. I was westbound at twenty-five hundred feet over Columbia, Missouri, and Otis managed to contact me on the radio, warning me I'd be icing up before I reached Kansas City. He was right. I got such a load of ice that the Alpha would hardly fly. It took off the antennas and aerials and the de-icers were working only on one wing. I just couldn't hold it and went into a spin. I put the nose down and by keeping it down and using full throttle I could just barely keep it from spinning again. I tried to climb to get away from the ice but this didn't work and at five hundred feet I was getting ready to bail out when I saw two red lights ahead. I knew they were the lights of the Booneville [Missouri] bridge so I let down a couple of hundred feet and when I did that I came out of the clouds.

I flew around at full throttle for about fifteen minutes trying to melt the ice and finally decided to land at Booneville. I put the nose down and retarded the throttle but when I did that, the plane stood on its nose. Even with full throttle I couldn't regain flying speed. It was so doggone heavy with ice, it just came down. I saw a road and headed for it, but all I could do was keep the tail down and we hit the ground hard. I thought the gear was going every which way but somehow it stayed together. I taxied to a gas station on the side of the road and put in some automobile gas. The next morning I took off, using aviation gas for the takeoff and the auto gas for cruising at reduced throttle.

TWA advertised the availability of seats in its mail planes—they could carry six persons—but never sold one nor even tried. There was a fatal exception to that rule, however. Otis Bryan landed in St. Louis one night and was accosted by a woman doctor who said she had to reach Philadelphia because of an emergency. Bryan demurred but she was insistent.

"Well, the weather's bad," he told her, "but I'll take you as far as Columbus."

They reached Columbus safely, and Bryan turned the plane over to Hal George, who told Bryan he wasn't taking anyone on his leg of the flight. "It's zero-zero in heavy snow all the way to Pittsburgh," he informed Bryan. "She just can't go."

Bryan advised the doctor of George's verdict but she refusd to take no for an answer. She insisted on talking to George and finally convinced him she was willing to accept the risks. Their first stop was Pittsburgh, but George couldn't find the airport—he was flying through a blizzard. He turned back to attempt an emergency landing at Steubenville, but at that point he began picking up ice. The Alpha went into an unrecoverable spin and crashed, killing both occupants.

Like most airmen of that era, TWA's were fatalists, living with danger as part of their modest-paying jobs; captains made $500 a month and copilots $300 (until 1934, they were still being called first pilots and second pilots respectively), with a small bonus for flying the night mail. There was no pilots' union then, and Bryan remembers that flying 100 hours a month was not uncommon; 100 hours a month may not seem like a long stint, but one hour in a noisy, vibrating Ford or an ice-vulnerable Alpha was the equivalent of eight hours in a modern jet.

Laughter, generated mostly by practical jokes, relieved tension. Crashes were so frequent that TWA started running out of mail planes. Two were lost in the same day on the Harrisburg–Pittsburgh leg when their pilots had to bail out because of ice. Abbott landed in Columbus one day and was met by a worried John Collings.

"Look, we can't afford to lose any more airplanes," he told Cliff. "If there's any ice—I don't care how thin it is—cancel the flight."

Abbott agreed and took off for Newark on the first leg of the mail flight. He was supposed to head right back on a westbound trip, but the forecast called for icing between Harrisburg and Pittsburgh and Abbott cancelled. The second leg, flown by Skip Taylor, landed at Newark and Abbott relayed Collings' warning.

"The hell with him," Taylor growled. "I'm going back to Columbus."

He got away with it, but Collings wasn't pleased. The short-tempered flight superintendent of the eastern division was hell on erring pilots, as Taylor was to find out. It was a practical joke that helped do him in. He had the habit of talking in his sleep, and some pilots caught him napping in the Columbus crew lounge. They went into "radio communications" with the sleeping pilot: "Pittsburgh to Flight Six . . . it's zero-zero down here . . . you can't land. . . ."

"Roger," mumbled the sleeping Taylor. "I'll go onto Philadelphia. . . ."

There were too many such incidents involving the somewhat flaky Taylor; they reached the radarlike ears of John Collings, who fired him "for psychological reasons."

Another casualty was Benny Howard. He was flying a Ford from Winoka to Wichita and was following the usual navigation aid over that leg—a gas pipeline that ran right by the Wichita airport. Unfortunately, he flew too low trying to keep the pipeline in sight; the landing gear brushed some trees and he almost crashed. The near mishap might have gone unnoticed except that virtually the entire TWA board of directors was on board and Benny was fired for careless flying.

The Achilles' heel of any really safe airline operation was weather forecasting. In the early thirties it was in its infancy, although the Guggenheim Foundation had brought to the United States Dr. Carl-Gustaf Rossby, a Swedish meteorologist trying to spread the new gospel of forecasting weather by means of tracking air masses. He lectured on the theory at the California Institute of Technology where one of his students was Irving Krick, who worked nights as a Western Air Express cargo clerk. Krick, who was to become dean of private weather forecasters, wrote a thesis on the subject of air mass prognostication and wangled an interview at TWA. He began by pulling his thick tome out of a battered briefcase, which was a mistake.

The interviewer, whose name has been lost to posterity, shook his head. "No thanks," he said hastily, being a man who considered weather forecasting a first cousin of betting on horses.

"But this thesis applies the air mass theory to airline operations," Krick argued. "Now these maps I've drawn . . ."

The interviewer got rid of him by suggesting that inasmuch as Krick already worked for Western, he might try his ideas out on that carrier. Krick did, much to the subsequent benefit of Western, which gradually adopted the new method. But for a long time, the rest of the industry relied on their old forecasting tools. Gordon "Parky" Parkinson, a young meteorologist hired by TAT in 1929 to establish weather stations between St. Louis and Amarillo, recalls how primitive those tools were.

"We were aware of the air mass concept but it hadn't really been proven and our stations relied mostly on interpreting cloud formations, along with balloon devices for measuring ceilings," he says. "If you could expect certain kinds of clouds, you could expect certain kinds of weather."

It often was hit-and-miss, however, and Parkinson readily admits the shortcomings. But one of his proudest memories concerns a weather forecast he made out of Columbus. He came upon it a few days later and saw that someone had written on it, "excellent forecast!" Under this praise was the name "Charles Lindbergh." Parky still has that yellowed sheet of paper.

The gesture was typical of Lindbergh, the consummate professional who appreciated professionalism in anyone else, even a youthful meteorologist. He was very close to Jack Frye in those days, and when they did get together to discuss airline problems, the chief subject of conversation was the need for a Ford trimotor replacement. Lindbergh insisted that any new airliner should have the capability of safely taking off from any field and climbing to a safe altitude with one engine shut down, a requirement that supposedly could be met only by a plane with three engines. He and Frye began jotting down potential specifications for such a transport, but while they were in the planning stage, word came that rival United had ordered sixty Boeing 247s, a revolutionary all-metal, low-wing airliner with two engines and a cruising speed of 155 miles per hour. Frye promptly approached Boeing on the possibility of buying 247s for TWA and was told, in effect, "Fine, but you'll have to wait until we finish the United order."

"How long will that take?" Frye asked a Boeing official.

"About two years."

It was a worried Frye who began polling his TWA colleagues on what kind of a transport could compete against the heralded Boeing that overnight would make TWA's Fords obsolete. Even though Frye had eliminated the all-air transcontinental overnight stop at Kansas City, thus cutting the coast-to-coast schedule to about twenty-seven hours, United was promising to fly the 247 from New York to the West Coast in twenty hours.

The consensus showed a decided preference for a trimotor, both from a technical and public relations point of view. Lindbergh wanted three engines to meet his engine-out takeoff requisite—the ability to climb out of a high-altitude airport like Winslow with one engine inoperative and still have enough power to clear the Continental Divide's mountains. The sales department felt the public still needed the reassurance of three engines; passengers were used to trimotors and might never accept a twin-engine transport.

In the summer of 1932, Frye mailed identical two-page letters to the heads of five aircraft manufacturing companies. The first four were Glenn L. Martin, Consolidated, Curtiss-Wright and GM's own General Aviation.

The fifth recipient was a small, struggling firm in Santa Monica whose only successful commercial airline sales venture had been a two-seater mail plane sold to Western Air Express. The largest aircraft it had ever built was an experimental two-engine flying boat of modest proportions. Nor did it have one iota of experience in designing a metal airplane—all of which meant nothing to its president, Donald Wills Douglas.

3

Black Was for the Good Guys

The letter was brief. Dated August 2, 1932, it was addressed to the Douglas Aircraft Corporation, Clever Field, Santa Monica, California, and marked ATTENTION: MR. DONALD DOUGLAS. It read:

Dear Mr. Douglas:

Transcontinental & Western Air is interested in purchasing ten or more trimotored transport planes. I am attaching our general performance specifications covering this equipment and would appreciate your advising whether your company is interested in this manufacturing job.

If so, approximately how long would it take to turn out the first plane for service tests?

Very truly yours,

Jack Frye
Vice-President
in charge of Operations

P.S. Please consider this information confidential and return specifications if you are not interested.

The attachment was a one-page list of requirements for the new airliner describing what TWA wanted in the way of power (three engines of at least 500 horsepower each); weight (maximum gross of 14,200 pounds or two tons more than the Ford); range (1,060 miles without refueling); capacity (at least 12 passengers); top and cruising speeds (185 mph and 146 mph respectively) and service ceiling (21,000 feet on three engines and 10,000 feet on any two).

The specifications ended with a key admonition, one that obviously reflected Lindbergh's input. "This plane fully loaded," it emphasized, "must make satisfactory take-offs under good control at any TWA airport on any combination of two engines." Whether monoplane or biplane—and Frye indicated he favored the former—it had to be of metal construction, particularly in the main internal structure. And it would have to land no faster than 65 mph, the same as the Tin Goose.

Of the five companies Frye approached, Douglas was the first to respond. Don Douglas received the TWA airmail letter Monday, August 5, and spent

Tuesday conferring with his young engineers, a collection of talent that read like a future aviation *Who's Who*. The chief engineer was James "Dutch" Kindelberger, and under Dutch were such someday-to-be-famous aircraft designers as Art Raymond, Ed Heinemann, Jerry Vultee, Fred Stineman, Frank Collbohm and Ken Ebel—Kindelberger and Vultee would go on to head their own companies. Douglas had a faculty for hiring the best young minds in the business—Jack Northrop had once worked for him and his stressed skin ideas were considered gospel around the Santa Monica plant.

Douglas quickly found out his "Young Turks" were unanimously opposed to the TWA demand for a new trimotor, with Kindelberger leading the way. "Why build anything that even looks like a Fokker or Ford?" he asked, and his associates nodded in agreement. Dutch argued that the Rockne crash simply had turned people off the trimotor concept, and to this psychological drawback he added a few technological points. Aerodynamically, a three-engine airplane like the Ford made no sense; the outboard engines did most of the work and the nose-mounted center engine "couldn't be used to swat flies," as a critic of trimotors once claimed. This was probably a gross exaggeration, but in truth, the center engine contributed little because of its location and the strut-clogged outboards, suspended underneath the wings, generated their own headwinds.

Don Douglas himself brought out the latest issue of *Popular Mechanics*, which contained a cutaway drawing of the Boeing 247.

"Take a look at this," he said, holding up the magazine. "It looks pretty good to me."

Several hours of discussion produced a unanimous verdict: it was possible to design a twin-engine transport that would not only exceed TWA's requirements but would be markedly superior to the 247. The Douglas team didn't know it at the time, but the vaunted Boeing entry was already being scaled down in size and power. The drawing Douglas had shown his engineers was that of a 16,000-pound airliner capable of carrying twelve passengers. The 247 United eventually would put into service would gross only 12,000 pounds while carrying ten passengers. The original design called for new Pratt & Whitney Hornet engines with sufficient muscle to power a 16,000-pound airplane, but United's pilots objected on the grounds that an 8-ton bird couldn't be landed safely, and they also preferred their reliable but less powerful Wasps to the unproven Hornets. Boeing didn't agree with this conservative reasoning, but with a sixty-plane order on the books and no other competitor in sight, neither United nor Boeing were worrying.

They should have been and would have been if they had been privy to the events transpiring in Donald Douglas's small office. So, for that matter, would have General Aviation, which on receipt of the Frye invitation, had told its designers to start work on a new trimotor that would meet TWA's specifications. The GM subsidiary had every reason to feel confident. It, in effect, controlled the airline through its parent company, but it was unaware of either Jack Frye's streak of independence or the unexpected speed with which Douglas reacted.

After his Tuesday meeting with his engineers, Douglas dictated on that same night a reply to the Frye letter:

We are interested in submitting a proposal in answer to your bid invitation for the design of a new transport plane. When will it be convenient for some of our engineers to get together with your technical people and present our views?

In the next five days, the Douglas team had forged a proposal for a new twin-engine airliner carrying twelve passengers, faster and with a longer range than the 247. On the sixth day, Art Raymond, Kindelberger's top assistant, boarded a train for a meeting with TWA officials in New York. He was accompanied by Harry Wetzel, Douglas vice-president and general manager, who was the company's production and financial expert. They took a train to give Raymond a chance to compose a passable presentation out of the mass of notes, drawings, technical data and rough blueprints that had emerged from the engineering sessions. By the time they arrived at New York's Penn Station, Raymond had filled five large notebook pads, cramming them with facts and figures on nearly a thousand individual items from the width of the cabin aisle (sixteen inches) to the location of two hand fire extinguishers.

Significantly, the two Douglas envoys met first with Frye and his closest associates—Richter, Hamilton and Tommy Tomlinson. Kindelberger, who knew Frye well, had told Raymond that Jack was the man to sell, not TWA president Dick Robbins. By now, Robbins was head of the airline in name only and Clement Keys was entirely out of the picture. Late in 1931, while Keys was vacationing in Europe, some of his most trusted friends had misappropriated millions from Keys' investment firm. Keys spent his entire personal fortune to repay these obligations but was still $1 million short. To get the million, he sold out his interest in North American, which wound up as part of the General Motors empire that controlled not only TWA but Eastern.

Raymond and Wetzel had talked to the four TWA men for more than an hour when three more airline officials joined the meeting. Robbins came in bringing with him Lindbergh and Harold E. Talbott, Jr., North American's chairman. Wetzel's eyebrows lifted in pleasant surprise because Talbott happened to be a good friend of Donald Douglas. As things turned out, however, that friendship wasn't needed; Raymond's lucid, unemotional presentation painted for the TWA delegation a picture of a superb new transport that would leave the 247 eating its exhaust trail.

For three more weeks, Raymond and Wetzel thrashed out the technical and financial details that had to be settled prior to the signing of a formal contract. Lindbergh threw in an unexpected curve when he enlarged one crucial specification—the item calling for the ability to take off from any TWA airport on "any combination of two engines." That requirement, Lindbergh pointed out, was irrelevant inasmuch as the proposed Douglas plane would have only two engines. What Lindbergh wanted was "a guarantee that the plane will be able to take off with a full load from any field along TWA's routes on one engine and then be able on one engine to climb and maintain level flight over the highest mountains on the way."

Raymond phoned this new requirement to Douglas who asked if it could be met.

"I'm ninety percent certain it can," Raymond sighed, "but it's the other ten percent keeping me awake at night.'

Douglas consulted with Kindelberger who snorted, "There's only one way to find out—build the damned thing and try it!"

On September 20, 1932, TWA president Robbins signed a contract for the delivery of one airplane at a price of $125,000 to be paid in gold bullion. If development costs exceeded that figure, Douglas would foot the bill. The agreement further stated that if the $125,000 prototype performed to TWA's satisfaction, the airline could purchase up to sixty additional planes at $58,000 per aircraft, also in gold bullion. The engines would be extra.

The prototype was officially designated "Douglas Commercial Model One"; it was more familiarly known by its initials: DC-1.

The day Douglas received the famous Frye letter, his company's stock was selling at $7.12 a share. When the DC-1 contract was signed, the price went up to $16—for various reasons there was a feeling of optimism about the unborn airplane before the first metal was cut. It was still just a paper airplane, but even on paper it looked like a thoroughbred with sleek yet sturdy lines that hinted at speed and strength.

Frye and Lindbergh were especially impressed with certain pivotal design features, some innovative and some modifications of existing hardware. The DC-1, for example, would achieve TWA's required 65-mph landing speed by means of retractable wing flaps—nothing really new except that they had never been tried before on an airplane that big. The wings themselves would be a fresh version of Jack Northrop's cellular web construction internally, and built in three sections: a center stub that was an integral part of the fuselage and bolted to two outer wing panels, the latter swept back slightly to improve the airfoil. The center wing section, enormously strong, eliminated the need for a long main wing spar, which was the rival 247's biggest drawback; the Boeing's main spar ran smack through the center of the cabin, necessitating the installation of small steps so passengers could walk over the spar hump.

The TWA brass liked the DC-1's dimensions, too. The cabin ceiling would be high enough so that a six-footer could walk upright; the 247's interior was far more cramped even with two fewer seats. Art Raymond added a few more key items when he flew back to California from the three-week marathon negotiating sessions aboard a TWA Ford trimotor. He informed Douglas that the flight demonstrated exactly what the DC-1 had to provide in passenger comfort—better seats, for instance. The Ford had leather-covered wicker seats that Raymond described as "about as comfortable as lawn furniture." When the trimotor climbed to get over a mountain range, the cabin became so cold that Raymond's feet almost froze. The lavatory in the rear was tiny. And the noise! Raymond told Douglas and his fellow engineers that the new airliner had to have plenty of soundproofing even if it added weight. The plush if lumbering Curtiss Condor had been the first U.S. airliner to employ the new-fangled gimmick of soundproofing material, a whopping 70 pounds of it; three decades later a TWA jet would carry two tons.

Such improvements as superior seats, cabin temperature control and soundproofing meant, of course, that TWA's $125,000 contribution was going to fall far short of meeting full development costs. It also became apparent that the $58,000 price tag on each production model was far too low, but Douglas plowed ahead with its ambitious engineering exercises. Douglas was spurred on by knowledge of competition—not so much from Boeing, which had painted itself into a corner with the $4 million United order, but from GM's powerful General Aviation and its projected trimotor. Actually, this airplane was never really in the running but Douglas didn't know that. There is reason to believe Lindbergh was keeping Douglas from getting too complacent by hinting broadly that TWA was very much interested in the General Aviation trimotor.

In truth, the GM transport never got off the ground, thanks to none other than the ubiquitous Ernest Breech; he never liked the plane, and Lindbergh's fears about the DC-1's single engine performance evaporated with the news that the Hamilton Standard Propeller Company had developed an adjustable pitch prop; the blades could be set at one angle for takeoff and at another during cruise when the bigger "bite" of air wasn't needed. That was all Douglas needed to make the DC-1 the only contender, and it was all Ernie Breech needed, too. In May of 1933, General Motors named him president of North American Aviation, Inc., the subsidiary governing the three airlines GM controlled—TWA, Eastern and Western Air Express—along with General Aviation. One of his first acts as president was to cancel the trimotor project, for even before the DC-1's maiden flight it was apparent Douglas had a winner.

The DC-1 took to the air for the first time on July 1, 1933—a test flight that came close to wiping out the $307,000 Douglas estimated had been spent on design and construction. Both Wright Cyclone engines, chosen by Douglas over Pratt & Whitney Hornets, kept cutting off and on, quitting in a modest climb and surging back to life in the subsequent dive. Chief test pilot Carl Cover said the airplane handled well but he couldn't explain the engine tantrums. Neither could anybody else; the Cyclones ran perfectly on the test blocks. But five days after the initial flight, Douglas engineers discovered that the carburetors had been installed backward. Once this was corrected, the mysterious engine gremlins disappeared and the test flights resumed. Frye assigned Tommy Tomlinson to ride herd on the program, and Tomlinson kept sending back glowing reports. The DC-1 was meeting or surpassing all TWA specifications.

One requirement was that the airplane must climb to 21,000 feet with a full load. With Tomlinson acting as copilot, the new transport reached 22,000 feet carrying 18,000 pounds of sandbags and lead ingots that simulated the allowable maximum weight of passengers, crew, fuel, mail and cargo. What's more, the DC-1 took off with that load using less than a thousand feet of runway.

The plane's strength exceeded all expectations. They ran a steamroller over the wing and the skin didn't even wrinkle. On one test flight, the DC-1 was landed inadvertently with the wheels still retracted; the only damage was the pilot's red face and two bent propellers. The plane was faster than anyone hoped, too. During one flight it achieved 227 mph, and by the time Tomlinson got through playing with the airplane he had set fourteen different point-to-point speed records.

Tommy was in the cockpit, along with balding, mustachioed Douglas test pilot Eddie Allen, the day the DC-1 undertook the most critical test of all: a one-engine takeoff at Winslow Airport with a full load. The plan was to start the roll normally on two engines; at the instant the aircraft became airborne, Tomlinson was to cut the power on the starboard engine by one-half, at which point Allen would raise the gear. This would be a "dry run" followed by a second takeoff on which Tomlinson was supposed to cut all starboard power by flipping the ignition switch.

Tommy proceeded to throw Allen a surprise curve. They started the dry run takeoff and Tomlinson, instead of reducing power partially, hit the cut-off switch just as the wheels broke ground. Allen immediately shoved the port engine to full power. The DC-1 trembled and staggered like a badly hurt boxer but kept climbing, all the way to 8,000 feet and well above the surrounding mountains.

"What the hell did you do that for?" Allen demanded when his blood pressure was back to normal.

Tommy grinned. "You work for the manufacturer, but I work for the customer—I just wanted to see if the old girl's as good as you guys claim she is."

She was even better. They flew all the way to Albuquerque at 8,000 feet on one engine and never lost a foot of altitude. When they landed, Tomlinson wired President Robbins in New York: "This is it!"

The test program also demonstrated that the DC-1 was 20 percent more economical than even Douglas was promising, a bonus achieved by a then unique method of determining precise engine power at any given moment of flight. It enabled Wright and Douglas to devise cruise power tables that provided pilots with the most efficient power settings according to altitude. Aviation historians justifiably give Douglas the lion's share of credit for this revolutionary transport, but the role of Curtiss-Wright in its success has been sadly underplayed.

Wright gave TWA an unusual guarantee on its Cyclones—for the first time, an engine manufacturer promised that certain components would run a specific number of hours, and if the part didn't last that long, the airline could get a replacement at a price reflecting full credit for any unused hours. It was much like the warranty on an automobile tire, and Bob Johnson, a Curtiss-Wright field engineer who worked on the DC-1 program, says the unprecedented guarantee literally forced Wright to build a better product.

"For example, we guaranteed a Cyclone cylinder for three thousand hours, and at the time most cylinders were lucky to last five hundred," he adds. "This put great pressure on Wright to perfect its cylinders because if anything went wrong before the three thousand hours were up, we had to pay for it."

TWA took delivery of the DC-1 in December 1933, only thirteen months after the original contract was signed. Tommy Tomlinson, representing the airline, handed Donald Douglas a check for $125,000 instead of the specified gold bullion; Franklin D. Roosevelt had taken the country off the gold standard by then, and Douglas settled for a check. But the manufacturer knew he had set too low a price on the production airplanes and stood to lose the company's collective shirt if TWA held him to that $58,000 figure. Douglas flew to New York aboard the DC-1 for the first time—Tomlinson was at the controls—and went into a huddle with Robbins and Frye. His chief argument was that inasmuch as gold was no longer legal tender, the contract was null and void.

There wasn't much haggling; Frye was too enamored to be seriously recalcitrant. TWA agreed to sign for twenty-five airplanes at $65,000 each, and the $7,000 increase actually was a bargain. The revised contract called for a fourteen-passenger transport instead of a twelve-seater, an increase made possible by a decision to lengthen the fuselage by two feet with an additional window on each side. This vital revision was another nail in the 247's coffin; the DC-2 series would not only be faster but far more viable with those two extra seats. And even though the first twenty-five DC-2s would fall $266,000 short of meeting Douglas's break-even point, orders from other airlines—notably American and Eastern—took the program out of the red. Anthony Fokker had a demonstration ride on the DC-1 and promptly wangled European sales and distribution rights. It was Fokker who sold the DC-2 to its first foreign customer, Holland's KLM.

"This airplane," Don Douglas proudly related at a chamber of commerce dinner some years later, "was to lead the company and American commercial aviation into new horizons."

True, but before the DC-2 reached those horizons, the U.S. airline industry flew into a storm that threatened its very existence.

The seeds of potential disaster had been planted in Walter Brown's Spoils Conference, and they sprouted under a figurative watering can held in the hand of an Alabama senator named Hugo Black.

Black was chairman of a special Senate committee investigating ocean mail contracts, the principal means by which the federal government subsidized the nation's merchant marine. He was an aggressive, smalltown lawyer with a built-in prejudice against big business, a bias that he shared with the new president of the United States. In years to come, Hugo Black would become a distinguished Supreme Court justice of great influence and integrity, but in the early days of the New Deal he was an ambitious, headline-hunting lawmaker who chafed under dull ocean mail hearings that produced little copy and little attention.

He found his *cause célèbre* thanks to the inquisitive nose of Fulton Lewis, Jr., a young reporter for the Hearst newspapers in Washington. Lewis happened to be having a drink one summer day in 1932 with William Briggs of the Ludington Line, a small air carrier operating an all-passenger service between New York and Washington via Philadelphia. It had been founded by the Ludington brothers of Philadelphia, who knew little about the airline business but were smart enough to hire two men who did—Paul Collins and Eugene Vidal, both refugees from old TAT. Collins and Vidal (father of writer Gore Vidal) had left TAT after quarreling with Clement Keys, and under their guidance, Ludington became the first airline to make money carrying just passengers. Its small fleet operated hourly schedules between the three cities, much like today's Eastern shuttle, but when it tried for a mail contract over that route, Postmaster General Brown rejected the bid and gave the contract to Eastern.

It was shortly after the award that Briggs, a relatively minor Ludington official, met with his friend Lewis and casually mentioned he couldn't understand Brown's decision. Lewis idly asked why and Briggs said Ludington's bid was only twenty-five cents a mile; it had to be below Eastern's bid, he added, although he didn't know the exact figure.

Lewis didn't think much about the matter until a few days later when he read a Post Office Department announcement that Eastern had been awarded a Washington–Philadelphia–New York mail contract for eighty-nine cents a mile. The reporter remembered what Briggs had told him and he smelled a distinct odor. In subsequent years, Lewis was to become a prominent radio commentator with conservative political views, but in this era, just before the dawn of the New Deal, he was an idealistic crusader. For weeks he searched Post Office Department records before he hit a rich lode—accounts of Brown's behind-the-scenes activities at the Spoils Conference.

Lewis finished his research and in January of 1933 sent a full report to William Randolph Hearst at San Simeon. The publisher, who had given Lewis permission to dig into the history of airmail contract awards, knew that the outgoing postmaster general was a close friend of one of his own top aides. He refused to clear the reporter's material for publication and Lewis was left holding a bag of apparent scandal with no place to air the contents.

The bag remained closed for about a year until Lewis, with Hearst's permission, told Black what he had unearthed about Walter Folger Brown. Quietly, the senator began his own investigation, drawing largely on the smaller airline operators only too eager, at long last, to voice their accusations of skullduggery and under-the-table dealings. The picture they drew for Black fit neatly into his own preconceived image of giant corporate sharks feeding on tiny, helpless competitors. The portrait was more a caricature than a realistic painting, but there was enough truth in it to warrant legitimate concern. Of the twenty-seven contracts awarded in the wake of the Spoils Conference, twenty-four had gone to airlines controlled by the giant holding companies like North American, AVCO and United. And in the crusading, anti-business atmosphere of the New Deal, to an administration brought into power by a disillusioned public, it made little difference that Brown's motives had been sincere and actually helpful to the growth of commercial aviation. His only real crime was that he had been faithful to a now-discredited philosophy that held that large corporate size meant more efficiency.

It was a Pandora's box that Lewis had opened. The subsequent Black hearings actually failed to prove that Brown had done anything in the slightest way illegal. He had been dictatorial and ruthless but with full legal authority for his actions and, in his own way, he had tried to be fair. He insisted, for example, that smaller airlines forced to relinquish their routes to the conglomerates be given adequate compensation. He logically explained Eastern's award over Ludington—the larger Eastern bid involved airmail service that was part of a major north-south network embracing almost the entire Eastern seaboard, whereas Ludington proposed to fly the mail only on the lucrative Washington–New York segment. And Brown made the award contingent on Eastern's buying out Ludington at a generous price. At the hearings, Brown held up well under Black's relentless questioning. The real victims of all the testimony were the holding companies controlling the nation's air transportation system, and Black went after them even before his committee began taking testimony early in March of 1934.

Late in January, Black had gone to the White House for a private meeting with FDR. They had lunch and during that session, Black poured into Roosevelt's willing ears his tale of chicanery and back-alley intrigue. With no real evidence to go on, except for the Lewis report, which was more implication than direct accusation, Black urged the president to cancel all existing airmail contracts on the grounds that they had been obtained by fraud and conspiracy.

Roosevelt actually knew little about the situation, but he was impressed by Black's evangelistic fervor—plus the fact that the consummate politician in FDR quickly recognized a chance to further embarrass the already humiliated Hoover administration. He made no commitment to Black except to think it over for a few days, but the senator considered this promise such sufficient encouragement that he turned all his files over to U.S. Solicitor General Carl Crowley. Crowley condensed the data, allegations and still-incomplete evidence into a 100-page report, which he handed to Postmaster General James S. Farley. In typical fashion, Big Jim thumbed through the verbose copy and growled, "I can't wade through all that—just tell me about it."

Crowley's oral condensation boiled down to a recommendation that all airmail contracts be cancelled. Farley was shaken by the implications and promptly set up a meeting for the next afternoon. Present would be himself, Crowley, Black and the president of the United States. Neither Farley nor FDR read Black's file of raw material or Crowley's lengthy summary. Roosevelt accepted both men's verbal briefings as factual, and so did Farley—with one important exception. The postmaster general expressed his doubts that the Army could fly the mail. He urged the president not to cancel the contracts and suggested that the Post Office Department merely issue new bids for all airmail routes.

Farley's opposition impressed Roosevelt to the extent of sending an emissary to Brig. Gen. Benjamin Foulois, chief of the Army Air Service. The emissary, Second Assistant Postmaster Harlee Branch, asked Foulois point-blank: "If the President should cancel all contracts, do you think the Army could carry the mail?"

There are two theories about the general's reply. One holds that Foulois, whose service had been starved for funds, saw in that blunt question a glittering opportunity to win praise and, not incidentally, fresh appropriations. The second theory is that Foulois was influenced by recent attacks from Col. William "Billy" Mitchell, whose widely publicized criticism of the Army implied that its air arm couldn't lick a South American banana republic. Whatever his motives, Foulois could not bring himself to admit he really did not know the answer. Instead, with brave but tragic confidence, he told Branch, "Yes, sir. If you want us to carry the mail, we'll do it."

His assurance was relayed to FDR. At 4 P.M., February 9, 1934, Franklin D. Roosevelt cancelled all airmail contracts effective in ten days, citing postal laws that gave the postmaster general punitive authority if conspiracy to obtain such contracts was apparent. At midnight February 19, FDR ordered, the Army would start flying the mail. It was to prove one of Roosevelt's worst decisions, not only because it convicted the airline industry without a trial, but because it would send twelve pilots to their deaths.

For the airlines, TWA included, the White House order was catastrophic; they were still deriving approximately 60 percent of their income from mail operations. TWA's relatively small Alphas alone generated almost as much revenue as what the airline took in from passengers. It was small consolation that the forthcoming DC-2 would be a moneymaker. TWA wasn't scheduled to take delivery of its first plane for several months, and by that time the damage from loss of mail pay could well be fatal.

While the public generally accepted the mail contract cancellation with equanimity (most Americans were still infatuated with their dynamic and colorful president and thought he could do no wrong), there were plenty of prominent citizens who raised strong objections. Will Rogers, certainly no Roosevelt-hater, commented that "it's like finding a crooked railroad president and then stopping all trains." A large proportion of the nation's press attacked FDR's decision editorially and gave front-page space to any well-known citizen willing to voice his opposition. There was no shortage of prominent opposing voices.

Lindbergh spoke for the majority of the industry when he wired Roosevelt.

> Your present action does not discriminate between innocence and guilt, and places no premium on honest business. Your order . . . condemns the largest portion of our commercial aviation without just trial.

From crusty Eddie Rickenbacker came a prophecy. He was then an official at North American, working directly under Ernie Breech, and reporters interviewed him in GM's New York headquarters the day after the cancellation announcement. The weather outside was foggy and rain-sodden, something the captain noted as he spoke.

"The thing that bothers me is what's going to happen to these young Army pilots on a day like this," he said grimly. He went on to point out that military pilots were not trained for mail-carrying operations, nor were their planes equipped for bad-weather flying. It was a deadly combination, he warned, that could "pile up ships all across the continent."

Rickenbacker knew the score. Even as he voiced that warning, there were only three pilots in the entire Air Service who had logged as many as 5,000 hours. A parsimonious Congress had slashed military spending so ruthlessly that the Army could afford to let its airmen fly only 175 hours a year—almost every minute of it in good daytime weather. By contrast, the average airline pilot flew that much in three months in all kinds of weather and often at night.

Furthermore, General Foulois could muster a force of only 200 officers and less than 400 enlisted men to do a job that had kept some 7,000 airline pilots and technicians busy. By the military standards of the day, the Army's fleet was adequate but to fly 27,000 miles of airmail routes. It was in way over its head.

It was Jack Frye, ever the promoter and schemer, who came up with an idea for one dramatic, final act of defiance by the airlines, and it was typical of him that he did not try to make it an all-TWA show. On February 10, the day after Farley read FDR's thunderclap announcement to a stunned press, Frye phoned Rickenbacker and invited him to participate. He chose Captain Eddie for two reasons: his prominence as America's greatest World War I ace, and the fact that Eastern, TWA's sister airline in the General Motors family, also had chosen the DC-2. Frye's plan was to try for a transcontinental speed record, using the DC-1 as a means of demonstrating that the airlines were better qualified to fly the mail than the Army. (There had been press reports quoting some Army officials saying that the industry's pilots, planes and operational procedures weren't any better than those the Army was going to provide.) "Let's show the bastards they don't know what they're talking about," Frye told Rickenbacker.

The captain agreed to the defiant gesture immediately and promised to come out to the West Coast in time to meet Frye's deadline—Jack wanted to leave Burbank with the last load of privately carried mail so they could arrive in Newark before midnight of February 19. He also suggested that Rickenbacker bring with him as many sympathetic newspapermen as he could muster. "We'll need every inch of publicity space we can get," Frye said.

Enlisting reporters he could trust was an easy task for Captain Eddie. He arrived in Los Angeles accompanied by a journalistic contingent primed to exploit the stunt. On February 17, the day before the scheduled departure, Frye and Rickenbacker held a joint press conference at which Frye announced that takeoff would be at 9 P.M. the following night.

"Our meteorologists are predicting that a blizzard will move into the Newark area about twenty minutes after we arrive," Frye explained.

"Hadn't you better leave Burbank earlier, then?" a newsman asked.

Rickenbacker fielded this one. "The purpose of this flight is to demonstrate the efficiency of a privately run air transportation system," the captain replied. "I want the American people to know that air transport has progressed to the point at which we can call our own shots." He paused, milking drama out of every word. "We'll leave on schedule."

There was a press breakfast the morning of the 18th. It had just begun when someone handed Rickenbacker a copy of the *Los Angeles Times;* the black headlines reported that three Army pilots had been killed flying to their assigned airmail stations. Two had died when their plane hit a Wyoming mountain and the third had crashed trying to land in a heavy fog in Idaho.

Rickenbacker handed the paper to Frye, his hawklike face flushed with anger. "That's legalized murder!" he said loudly, and a reporter asked quickly, "Jesus, Eddie, can we quote you?"

"You're damned right you can quote me," the captain snapped.

The "legalized murder" crack preceded the DC-1 across the country, the wire service teletypes and radio wires carrying it faster than the plane could fly, but not much faster. Frye and Rickenbacker didn't leave Burbank until 10 P.M., delayed by an unexpectedly heavy load of mail—stamp enthusiasts had jammed the sacks with envelopes they hoped would become collectors' items. A huge crowd witnessed the takeoff, with Frye in the left seat and Rickenbacker acting as copilot. Jack waved as he closed the cockpit window and began taxiing toward the runway.

Frye later credited Rickenbacker with doing his fair share of flying duties, but in truth he was being generous to a man who had little experience at the controls of a heavy transport plane. When they weren't on autopilot, Frye did the flying, and TWA had few pilots who were much more competent. They sped nonstop to Kansas City, the first refueling stop, landing in a light snow. When Frye checked the weather ahead, he was warned that a blizzard was moving down fast from the Great Lakes—it would roar into Columbus, their next refueling stop, before they landed.

"The hell with it!" Frye decreed. "Let's go."

The DC-1 arrived in Columbus just ahead of the storm. Aided by stiff tailwinds, Frye had "bent the throttles" to achieve a cruising speed of nearly 230 mph. TWA mechanics swarmed over the plane and hurried the refueling process, for the blizzard swept in while the DC-1 was on the ground. When they took off, the ceiling was down to virtually zero, and Frye, flying on instruments, climbed to 19,000 feet where they broke out of the overcast, sucking on oxygen tubes to stay conscious. The DC-1 roared over the "hell stretch" of the Alleghenies, the Cyclones growling defiance at the menacing mountains that had killed so many pilots. They flashed into Newark ahead of the predicted storm, some three hours ahead of schedule. When the wheels touched down at Newark, the DC-1 carrying the red letters "TWA" on its fuselage had set a new transcontinental speed record of thirteen hours and four minutes. It had been more than a gallant gesture; it was a symbolic one, for the new airliner had conquered weather that was a forerunner of what the Army would face with its inadequately trained pilots and inadequately equipped planes.

The day after Frye and Rickenbacker proved their point, the Army began flying the mail into the teeth of the worst winter weather in the annals of the United States Weather Bureau. Its brave efforts were doomed from the start, as the subsequent deaths would demonstrate so grimly. In truth, the Army's record was not as bad as some historians have claimed; only four pilots were killed actually flying the mail—the others died on training or ferry flights. Rickenbacker's "legalized murder" crack was an impulsive bit of hyperbole, understandable under the emotional circumstances but not entirely justified. The passage of time has created a kind of opaqueness, exaggerating memory of the past into a bloody image of planes "dropping out of the sky like acorns," as one writer so colorfully but inaccurately put it.

A fairer perspective is to examine how efficiently the Army did its job under terrible handicaps, and this is where the politicians who shoved the military into a meat grinder must be faulted. The undermanned military force trying to do a civilian job could operate only 16,000 miles of airmail routes compared to the 27,000 miles the airlines had served. It cost the government $2.21 to fly every pound of mail the airlines had carried for fifty-four cents. The Army airmen had been given no time to survey their routes, and they were using largely pursuit and observation planes that were not only inefficient but ill-equipped for instrument flying.

At TWA, Dick Robbins ordered the following notice posted on all company bulletin boards the day before the Army began its ill-fated operations:

TO ALL T & W A PERSONNEL:

Effective February 28th, 1934, the entire personnel of T. &. W.A. is furloughed. Between now and that date, the Management will work out

43

plans which will involve the least possible hardship to the personnel and make arrangements for the continuance of its curtailed schedules.

Faithfully yours,

Richard W. Robbins
President

The "arrangements for the continuance of its curtailed schedules" consisted of keeping enough people on the payroll to run two daily Ford trimotor transcontinental flights, one in each direction. Only those with the highest seniority were retained, but the compassionate Frye wasn't satisfied. Mechanic Johnny Guy was in his office a few days after the furloughs went into effect and personally watched Frye put in a telephone call to Donald Douglas.

"We're absolutely convinced the Army can't do the job and we'll get those contracts back," Frye told Douglas. "I'm going to go ahead with our DC-2 contract, Don, but if we go through with it, I want you to hire all the furloughed TWA maintenance people willing to go out to Santa Monica and keep them there until we go back to flying the mail. Do I have your word?"

Douglas pledged to take on as many TWA people as he could. Frye then put in a call to Curtiss-Wright and made a similar pitch. After extracting the same promise from Wright, Frye notified TWA maintenance personnel they could find jobs either in Santa Monica or Paterson, New Jersey, and that TWA would fly them and their families to either city at no cost—plus free transportation back to their old jobs if and when the airline's mail contracts were restored.

"It was a hell of an offer," Guy still marvels. "Remember, this was the last stage of the depression and there weren't any jobs to be had. I'll tell you one thing—Jack Frye never really got the credit he deserved. TWA never had a finer president."

The handful who remained on the airline's payroll took pay cuts, including officers like Frye, Richter and Hamilton. One of the fortunate few was Tommy Tomlinson; Frye kept him flying the DC-1 on various test hops. The aircraft was more of an airborne laboratory than a commercial transport, although TWA had used it briefly on the night mail run between Kansas City and Los Angeles, and also as a pilot training aircraft. Paul Richter's private scrapbook contains notes, correspondence and clippings indicating that Tomlinson conducted tests on rubber de-icing boots which threw off ice when they flexed, experimental navigation aids and night flying equipment along with different engines. Pratt & Whitney Hornets were tried out for a short time before TWA decided to go back to the Wright Cyclones.

Johnny Guy was among the TWA contingent sent out to Santa Monica. He was assigned to the DC-2 program as an inspector and test flight observer working under Ralph Ellinger, who was the airline's factory representative at Douglas. Typical of the mechanics who took advantage of Frye's offer was Al Jordan; he was to rise to a vice-presidency, but in 1934 he was just a furloughed apprentice eagerly grabbing a chance to work at the Douglas plant.

"I thought I was on vacation," Jordan chuckles today. "I was making fifty cents an hour which was fifteen cents more than TWA paid me, and I was living with three other bachelors in a rented beach bungalow."

Jordan is one of the few still-living TWA veterans who remembers Dick Robbins. "He was from south Kansas originally, and he had a turkey farm. The first Christmas I worked for TWA, back in 1932, he was sending dressed turkeys to friends all over the country. He'd bring them to the hangar in Kansas City, crated and kept on ice until we found some flight with space to ship 'em out."

There were times when Robbins must have felt resigned to returning to his turkey farm. While the Army was struggling with its impossible task, TWA was losing $250,000 a month, even with its truncated payroll, and the DC-2 assembly line was pumping out planes that the airline couldn't operate or afford to buy. Things didn't look much better as the Army gained experience and began to operate with reasonable efficiency. Certainly it was operating more safely; its last fatal crash was March 31, and for the next two months, the military safety record was spotless.

But it was the first month, not the next two, that changed the course of events. Roosevelt reportedly would have been content to let the Army carry the mail permanently—he had been infected by Black's venom toward the industry. But long before the Army's performance began improving, FDR had been stung by the spate of devastating headlines about the early accidents. Combined with unceasingly angry editorials, those first fatalities convinced the president he had erred. He was furious at Foulois, giving him a face-to-face tongue lashing. Nor were the Black hearings generating the kind of evidence that would have justified his impulsive cancellation of private contracts.

Jim Farley was taking most of the editorial heat, but faithful to his creed of political loyalty, he told no one publicly that he had warned FDR not to pull the trigger. While most of the press blamed Farley, it was the postmaster general who finally took Roosevelt off the hook. FDR announced he would seek legislation permitting new airmail contracts, and Black promptly introduced the Air Mail Act of 1934—a punitive measure designed to spank the industry even as the airlines got back their routes. It was a far-reaching law, requiring the separation of airlines from all aircraft manufacturing companies. It also banned all executives who had attended the Spoils Conference from holding office in their respective companies, and it reopened all airmail routes to competitive bidding.

The Air Mail Act broke up the vast General Motors aviation empire, including the three airlines that had operated under the GM banner. But this wasn't enough for some of the smaller carriers, hungry for the prime routes and fearful that they'd never be able to outbid the big boys. To placate them, Farley pulled what was perhaps a devious end run, but one that kept the industry from complete chaos. He talked Black into inserting a provision in the Air Mail Act forbidding any airline that had taken part in the Spoils Conference to bid on a new route.

Farley knew perfectly well that if the provision were enforced, it would mean demolition of the airways. The small airlines were incapable of taking over the whole air transportation system. They would be a collective Jonah trying to swallow a whale. So, privately, Farley informed the airline chiefs that the provision was strictly a face-saving device. All an affected carrier had to do, he advised, was change its corporate name.

American Airways thus became American Airlines. Eastern Air Transport was changed to Eastern Airlines. United Aircraft & Transport switched its name to United Air Lines. Western Air Express organized a temporary dummy operating company, General Airlines, in which Western held all the stock.

TWA's rewrite job carried the imprint of Ernie Breech. Under the Air Mail Act, GM's subsidiary, North American Aviation, was forced to dispose of its TWA and Western stock. But Breech had spotted a loophole: there was nothing in the new law that prevented a company manufacturing aircraft, engines or instruments from holding an airmail contract itself. North American, which owned 100 percent of Eastern Air Transport, simply merged the airline into the parent company and operated both firms under the name Eastern Airlines. Breech couldn't mastermind this deal with TWA or Western. North American didn't own them outright, but he figured out a way to legally circumvent the act.

He simply organized two brand-new airlines, incorporating them under the respective names of TWA, Inc., and WAE, Inc. He took over the presidency of both companies until he could find the right talent for each. Under its new corporate name, TWA bid successfully for its old transcontinental mail route from New York to the West Coast. They used Ford trimotors sold to TWA, Inc. by the still existing Transcontinental and Western Air, Inc. to carry the mail. The latter stayed in business, operating its new DC-2s but carrying only passengers. Robbins remained as its president.

The wily Breech knew the Post Office Department would eventually object to the inefficient Fords carrying the mail. And as he expected, the Department suggested that maybe the "old" TWA, the airline flying modern DC-2s, could merge with the "new" TWA holding the mail contract. This was what Breech had intended right from the start. The only catch was that Robbins had to be a casualty. Under the Air Mail Act, as an officer of a company banned from holding an airmail contract, he'd have to resign along with several directors.

Breech, who liked and admired Robbins, had to tell him the Post Office Department's merger proposal would require his resignation. Robbins took it graciously. "In the interests of the stockholders," Robbins said, "you have no choice but to accept."

On December 27, 1934, Breech dispatched a young lawyer named George Spater to Dover, Delaware, for the purpose of filing new papers incorporating the new airline under its old name once more—Transcontinental & Western Air, Inc. At the same time, he announced that Jack Frye would be TWA's new president.

4

The Frye Era Begins

Frye didn't want the job and he so informed Breech, who had summoned him from Kansas City to New York for a meeting on the subject of high command.

"The Board of Directors has selected you unanimously," Breech said. "What's your problem?"

"I'd rather be a good vice-president of operations than a rotten president who'll lose his job," Frye explained.

But Breech wasn't about to accept this reasoning. He had been a long-time admirer of Frye; he liked Jack's style of leadership. Frye was as good a pilot as any of his underlings and better than most. When TWA had won its new mail contract, it had been Frye who flew the first trip, and it was not the first time Jack had flown a mail run. Shortly after the airline had acquired its Northrop Alphas, the crews began complaining that Frye's established mail schedules were too tight. He didn't respond verbally or in writing; he simply showed up at the Newark airport one night, took a pilot off his assigned westbound night mail trip, and climbed into the Alpha cockpit himself. He made the regular stops at Pittsburgh, Columbus, Indianapolis and St. Louis on schedule and landed in Kansas City on time. There were no further complaints.

It was a demonstration that gladdened the heart of Ernest Robert Breech, who all his life considered most airline pilots overpaid prima donnas doing more griping than flying. He thought of them as whiners and troublemakers. So in December of 1934, Jack Frye took over TWA, at the age of 29, the youngest air carrier president in the country. He drew a salary of $13,500 a year. Brash, energetic and fiercely competitive, he was the quintessential airline leader at a crossroads in aviation history. Frye grasped the import of the 247/DC-2 revolution; he saw them as major technological advances, yet also recognized them as mere streaks of light in the dawn of a new air age. They may have taken the youthful industry out of rompers and into knickers, but not into long pants—not yet. They represented the first tentative, uncertain steps toward making air transportation respectable, toward giving the passenger priority over the mail sack.

The airline industry of 1934 was light years away from what it had been only two years before. The average seating capacity of the commercial transport fleet in 1932 was less than six, and of the 450 airliners flying, 80 percent had only one engine. A total of twenty-four airlines carried fewer than 500,000 passengers that year; they offered 700 daily flights (in another three decades they would be operating some 13,000 flights a day) and traffic was so thin that the industry ran its own air traffic control system—and would until 1936.

The element of fear was not only still present but all-pervasive, and deservedly so. In 1932, a relatively safe 12-month period, there were 108 accidents, sixteen of them fatal. The industry's fatality rate was nearly fifteen deaths for every 100 million passenger-miles flown, and this meant the commercial airplane was 1,200 times more hazardous than trains and 400 times more dangerous than busses. The chances of a 1932 airline pilot getting killed on his job were roughly 300 times greater than they are today, a situation partially attributable to the fact that a pilot in 1932 didn't have to be qualified to fly on instruments. Most of TWA's pilots were, thanks to the considerable night flying the airline did, but they were among the few exceptions to the rule. It was no wonder that in 1932 air travel insurance was nonexistent. In fact, most regular life insurance policies contained a provision cancelling all protection while the policy holder was on an airplane.

This was the world in which Jack Frye had been raised—an existence of such precarious economics that more than a half-dozen airlines in 1932 had agreed to carry card advertisements on the interior walls of their planes, much like the ad placards seen on streetcars and busses. The practice would last only a year. Too many industry leaders (Frye included) thought they were undignified, but the placards were indicative of the airlines' desire to scrounge as much revenue as possible.

This also was a world that by 1935 had changed drastically. Hugo Black's anti-industry crusade was not without its blessings; in demolishing the interlocking structures of airlines and their manufacturing conglomerates, he had returned industry leadership back to the pioneering breed that was its original core. For while the Air Mail Act had wiped out individuals, it failed to touch men like Frye, American's C.R. Smith, Eastern's Rickenbacker and United's Pat Patterson—the industry's younger echelon with fresh views, attitudes and gamblers' instincts.

It was an unhappy time for the airline executives forced to leave office, the most tragic victim being Pop Hanshue, whose only crime had been to attend a meeting where he was mugged and whose consequences he had tried to block. Hanshue was to live only two more years; he died in 1937 of a cerebral hemorrhage that might well have been diagnosed as a broken heart.

Frye's first move at TWA was to name his top assistant. Paul Richter became vice-president of operations. The executive offices were moved from New York to Kansas City, and the centralized headquarters was a far more efficient location for overseeing the new DC-2 transcontinental fleet. As the nation's first DC-2 operator, TWA's advertising was built around the new airliner offering 15-hour (actually, it was 15 hours and 23 minutes eastbound and nearly 17 hours westbound) coast-to-coast service. Safety, speed and comfort were emphasized. The ads cited "the atmosphere of the living room with its deeply upholstered, fully reclining and reversible chairs and the spacious cabin with its *unobstructed* aisle [a large needle aimed at United's 247 spar steps]." For the fearful, the ads offered soothing technical verbiage.

. . . The first plane represents an investment of approximately $300,000. . . . The unusually exhaustive tests through which it has passed prove that the Douglas Luxury Airliner is the fastest multi-motor passenger plane in the world, can fly fully-loaded on only one of its 710 horsepower Wright Cyclone engines, has a lower landing speed than any transport plane of its size due to the air brakes with which it is equipped. . . .

The advertising puffs happily refrained from mentioning the DC-2's idiosyncracies, which could be both exasperating and dangerous. Some of TWA's best pilots cut their airmen's teeth on the airplane—among them Frank Busch, Bob Buck and Hal Blackburn, to mention a few.

"When we met up with a United 247," Blackburn recalls fondly, "we could go by them on one engine."

Speed was the DC-2's outstanding virtue in the air; but on the ground the plane was something else. It had an extremely stiff gear and for that reason, it invited hard landings. "When you logged a landing," Buck laughs, "you just logged the last bounce."

Raising or lowering the gear demanded the muscles of Tarzan and the suppleness of a circus acrobat. The very sound of a captain ordering "gear up!" was enough to fill any copilot with dreaded anticipation of what was to come: manual labor that would make a galley slave turn pale.

"There were seventy-two parts to the landing gear pump," retired TWA Captain Russ Black remembers, "and in cold weather they all seemed to freeze simultaneously. We had one pilot, Ken Fairchild, who was tugging at the gear handle so hard it came off in his hand."

Pilot/author Ernest Gann, who flew the DC-2 for American before his bestseller days, offers a classic description of another DC-2 foible: its taxiing difficulties. Gann wrote in his book *Flying Circus:*

When taxiing, the braking system in a DC-2 was activated by heaving on a horn-shaped handle protruding from the left side of the instrument panel. By simultaneous use of the rudder and handle, the desired left or right brake could be applied. Since there was inevitably a lag between motion and effect, the DC-2 was stubbornly determined to chase its own tail on the ground and in crosswinds, sometimes switching ends to the embarrassment of all aboard. Taxiing a DC-2 was an art rather than a skill, and even chaste-mouthed pilots were occasionally given to blasphemy.

This somewhat challenging characteristic is confirmed by Blackburn. "The brakes were horrible," Blackie says. "They weren't bad after you learned, but until then you had to be a contortionist." Another problem was the tail wheel, which had to be locked securely while landing or the plane would ground loop without warning. Then there was the tendency of the cockpit windshield to leak in rain, often with such force that many DC-2 pilots started wearing raincoats while flying through precipitation.

The DC-2's heating system, while preferable to no heating system at all, still left something to be desired. It was nothing but an airborne version of a steam radiator; one of the copilot's preflight duties was to reassure passengers that the assorted banging, gurgling, gasping and choking sounds emanating from the heater didn't mean the plane was coming apart. The wintertime complaint that the old Fords were too hot or too cold could also be applied to the DC-2. The de-icing boots, a rather primitive system, fell considerably short of winning pilot confidence. Its inadequacies, however, were partially compensated for by the fact that the DC-2 could carry an awesome amount of ice before it quit flying.

To this day, there are former TWA pilots who swear the DC-2 was a better airplane than its more famous successor, the DC-3. Hal Blackburn thought so and Bob Buck agreed. For one thing, it was faster than the DC-3 because it was lighter, with almost the same amount of power. Conversely, some TWA pilots were highly critical of the DC-2. The earlier models had propeller and tailfin icing problems. It was nose-heavy, had relatively poor directional stability, and aileron and rudder forces were rather heavy. One contemporary critic called the DC-2 "a good example of a flying barn door."

Yet it also was rugged and dependable, and the younger pilots worried far more about their captains than their airplanes. This was a period of transition for the veterans who had learned their trade in the fly-by-the-seat-of-the-pants days but now found themselves in the far more disciplined environment of instrument flight. Not until 1933 did the federal government require airline pilots to be instrument-qualified, an edict some of the old-timers considered unfair, uncivilized and unnecessary. Perhaps sensing that the younger men represented a new breed of professionalism, many veterans resented them enough to make their lives miserable.

The airline captain of 1935 often was an autocratic martinet who ate young copilots alive. The distance between the left seat of a captain and the right seat of a copilot was only a few inches, but in a practical sense they were divided by a vast chasm of rank, experience, authority and even attitude. Fortunate, indeed, was the copilot assigned to a captain who'd let him make a takeoff or even a landing now and then. Being allowed to fly one leg of a trip was considered an event in a copilot's life. The rookies mostly were expected to watch, learn, genuflect and keep their mouths shut except for laughing at the captain's jokes. Buck remembers that the unpredictability of some captains was the largest cross a young pilot had to bear.

"One captain would chew your ass out for touching anything," Buck relates. "The next captain would chew your ass out if you didn't touch anything. It could get very confusing."

Buck's first captain was a relatively friendly soul named Dutch Halloway. They flew together for six months and Halloway kept promising, "Bob, I'm gonna let you make a landing today." Shortly before reaching the site of the promised landing, Dutch would renege—"Little too much crosswind, Bob, so I'd better take it. But you can land at Albuquerque."

Coming into Albuquerque, Buck would be all primed only to have Halloway shake his head sadly. "It's dusk," he'd say in a tone of abject regret. "Dusk is absolutely the worst time to land. I'd better handle it."

This went on for the whole six months. On the last trip of their assigned schedules, Halloway had to land at an emergency field in Saugus, California, because the Burbank Airport was closed by fog. They put the DC-2's passengers on a bus and slept in the airplane. The next morning, Halloway phoned Burbank and found that the fog had lifted.

"Tell you what," he said to Buck magnanimously, "I'll let you make the takeoff out of here."

This, Buck reasoned, was even better than a landing. If he made the takeoff, the captain would have to raise the gear. They thundered down the Saugus runway, Buck grasping the yoke and hauling back as they accelerated to takeoff speed. Just as they broke ground, Halloway yelled, "Okay, I've got it! Gear up!"

Actually, TWA's captains were somewhat justified in their attitude toward a copilot's flying ability. The training requirements hadn't changed much from the Ford trimotor days; Buck had one week of ground school before he started flying the line. TWA was hiring only military pilots and in those days simply assumed they could learn the airline way of life with on-the-job training. Frank Busch, who joined TWA in 1935 fresh out of the Army Air Corps, remembers that his TWA schooling consisted of learning how to fill the water tank for the cabin heater, pass out lunch boxes, serve coffee, punch tickets "and pump up that goddamned gear."

"There was a brief ground school," Busch adds, "but no flying. They'd put you in with some captain and away you'd go. You have to realize, though, that if you had Army flight training, TWA felt you could hack it as an airline copilot. Army schooling was so tough that in my class we started out with a hundred and ninety-two pilots and graduated only eighty-seven."

Military reputations didn't impress the senior captains, however. They regarded themselves as having their own elite corps, and in the airline's earlier days, they even had their own insignia of sorts; their uniform sleeves carried a small star for every thousand hours logged. Hal Blackburn notes that at one time senior captains invariably flew out of Los Angeles while the younger crews had to fly the tougher routes in the east.

"The veterans wouldn't venture east of Kansas City," Blackie says. "Then passengers got to noticing the absence of those stars on crews boarding the eastbound flights at Kansas City, and TWA finally forced some of the older guys to move to eastern bases."

It was Frye who released TWA's copilots from a chore they dreaded more than foul-tempered captains: cabin service. In mid-1935, Frye authorized the hiring of TWA's first female cabin attendants, an area in which he hadn't exactly demonstrated a pioneering spirit. United had introduced stewardesses in 1930, and American followed suit three years later. Frye's reluctance apparently was based on surveys that showed that nearly 80 percent of the TWA passengers polled preferred to be served by copilots—or said they did. The evidence was to the contrary, for Frye discovered that the same passengers claiming they were happy with occasional copilot visits were going over to United and American because they had attractive girls. The passenger-oriented Frye bowed to the inevitable, as he had done previously when superstitious passengers complained about being assigned to seat number 13 in the DC-2. Frye just changed the seat number to 15.

Jack, however, refused to call the first cabin attendants "stewardesses"; he hated the expression. TWA's flight attendants, he decreed, would be designated as "hostesses." "They're serving our guests," he explained, and it was *hostess* from then until the 1970s when all airlines began using "flight attendant" for both male and female cabin personnel.

TWA adopted the industry rule that all cabin crew members had to be registered nurses, a precedent United had set five years earlier on the grounds that passengers would feel more secure with a medically trained attendant on hand. The prevalent medical problem, of course, was air sickness, which didn't require the ministrations of a registered nurse any more than those of a brain surgeon. But once United established the R.N. rule, everyone went along and would until World War II when nurses were in short supply.

A young nurse named Ida Staggers, who joined TWA in the DC-2 days and was to fly until she was 60, was typical of the early hostesses. She was an R.N. in a Kansas City hospital and was hired over the objections of Walt Avery, in charge of in-flight service; Avery interviewed her and thought her voice was too loud. He may have been right, because Ida came from a farm family with six sisters and one brother and had learned a long time ago how not to get pushed around. She sensed Avery's negativism, but she had made up her mind to be a hostess. She knew Paul Richter's secretary, so she wangled an interview with Richter and John Walker, vice-president of traffic. They hired her, unwittingly launching a career that one day was to make Ida Staggers the oldest airline hostess in the world.

Her training was on the skimpy side. "Being a nurse, we didn't have to learn very much," she concedes. "They showed us the airplane and where to find things. We had to learn ticketing and all the names of the top people in the company. We had a chart that listed Jack Frye on top and all the vice-presidents and other officers under his name along with their pictures. There weren't many names to memorize. We had to know connections, our routes and what towns we were flying over. And we had to know how to make out railroad tickets. If we came into a city and had to cancel, the hostess had to take her passengers to the train station, buy their tickets, get on the train with them no matter how long she had been on duty, and ride with them to the next city where they could board a flight again.

"I missed the first three days of training because somebody forgot to tell me when the class started. Even then, I was able to graduate and take my familiarization flight from Kansas City to Los Angeles—more than twelve hours. On my first regular trip, I had fourteen passengers on a DC-2 and nearly panicked. I thought I'd never get breakfast served. Imagine, fourteen people to serve in only two hours and ten minutes!"

Like their counterparts on other carriers, TWA's hostesses were vulnerable to pilot jokes. The girls were intelligent, personable and above average in maturity, but they still were aviation neophytes and fair game for the cockpit crews. The pilots would ring the hostess call button, put the plane on autopilot and hastily hide in the baggage rack just behind the cockpit. When she entered, all that would be visible was an empty glove on the throttle and an open cockpit window. Another heart stopper was the Frankenstein monster mask. This was a rubberized affair painted green and of great realism. The procedure was to don the mask on a night flight, turn down the cockpit lights until the only illumination came from the red glow of the instrument lights and press the call button. Enter the unsuspecting hostess. The captain would turn around, a flashlight held under his chin so the light played ominously over the green monster mask.

"Good evening, my dear," he'd rumble, and wait for the inevitable shriek.

Hostesses weren't the only victims. TWA had one captain who would open the cockpit door and roll nuts and bolts down the aisle until his passengers were positive the airplane was falling apart. He was the same character who obtained a white cane, donned a pair of dark glasses, and in full uniform, followed his passengers into his airplane, walking toward the cockpit while tapping the cane ahead of him. The final touch was real genius; under his arm was a book with a jacket he had had specially printed. It read: *How To Fly In 10 Easy Lessons.*

It would be in the interests of historical accuracy to reveal his name, but the truth is that those stunts have been credited to several pilots, the most frequently mentioned nominees being John Montgomery and Elmer "Bud" Gorman. Bud loved to wear various disguises. On one crew layover in Winslow, he noticed there was a hot poker game going on in the hotel lobby. He went to his room, donned the somber apparel of a minister (he actually *was* an ordained minister) and returned to the lobby where he marched with righteous indignation to the poker table.

"Sinners!" he bellowed, and dumped over the table, scattering chips, money and cards. In the confusion he managed to disappear, and by the time police arrived, Gorman had changed back into uniform and was helping everyone search for the mysterious minister.

At one time or another, Gorman was blamed (or praised) for every joke pulled on the TWA system. One of his accomplishments was bird mimicry, an entertaining but disconcerting hobby because of the way he employed his skill. Anyone trying to contact his flight usually was greeted with unidentified chirps, squawks and trills.

Gorman was not, however, guilty of the cruel chicanery perpetrated by Captain Richard Beck. A brand-new hostess boarded Beck's flight and, after takeoff, was summoned forward where Beck proceeded with stage one of his plot. Knowing that the girls were invariably curious about the mysterious dials, levers and switches adorning a cockpit, he moved the gear handle out of neutral into the "up" position, which activated a red light. The hostess spotted it immediately.

"Is anything wrong?" she asked nervously.

"Well, the tail wheel failed to retract," Beck explained, failing to mention that there was no such thing as a retractable tail wheel on a Douglas airplane.

"Is that dangerous?"

"Could be. You'd better come back to the blue room [lavatory] with me and I'll show you how to retract it manually."

The hostess complied and watched carefully as Beck pulled a strap over the commode. (It actually de-iced the radio antenna but she didn't know this.) "Do me a favor," the captain requested. "Our next stop's Amarillo and after we take off, come back here and pull that strap, just like I showed you. I'll ring the call button twice and that'll be the retraction signal."

The hostess pulled the strap out of Amarillo. She also pulled the strap out of Topeka, coming to the cockpit each time to report compliance. "The last time was pretty tough," she added. "There was a lot of turbulence so I had to sit on the john and brace myself against the bulkhead so I could get a good grip on the strap."

"I'm proud of you, honey," Beck said gravely. "God knows what would happen with a stuck tail wheel."

When they deplaned at Kansas City, there was a crew change and Beck made a point of listening to his hostess brief her replacement. "There's something wrong with the tail wheel. Maintenance is supposed to fix it but if they don't, here's what you have to do . . ."

"Are you kidding me?" the other hostess asked suspiciously.

"Why should I kid you? It's the only way to save the airplane!"

Practical jokes notwithstanding, the pilots began to arrive at a grudging respect for the girls—particularly after an incident involving a hostess named Nellie Granger. When her DC-2 crashed on a Pennsylvania mountain ridge, she was thrown clear. Bruised and battered, she climbed down the mountainside and summoned help. It was suspected that Frye decided to employ hostesses as much for safety as competitive reasons, and if true, Granger confirmed his judgment. Jack had been badly shaken by an accident that occurred before the first hostess was hired. On May 5, 1935, a TWA DC-2 left Albuquerque for Kansas City, operating as the second section of transcontinental Flight 6. The first section had trouble landing at Kansas City because of low visibility and ceiling, but finally made it down at 2:24 A.M. Meanwhile, the second section, commanded by Capt. Harvey Bolton, was in trouble.

His radio transmitter was faulty; a TWA mechanic at Albuquerque had checked it out and reported it would work on the company's daytime frequency but not at the frequency used at night. Bolton, a 29-year-old pilot whom Frye held in high regard, decided to proceed east anyway because the Weather Bureau was predicting clear skies ahead.

But enroute, the weather worsened, and Bolton, who found himself able to receive messages but incapable of sending, was told to try to land at Kansas City—the first section had made it. Running about a half-hour behind the first plane, Bolton arrived in the Kansas City area after the ceiling had dropped below minimums. He had less than 45 minutes of fuel left after circling the airport several times, and TWA meteorologist "Parky" Parkinson phoned an oil refinery adjacent to the field, requesting that they ignite excess gas so Bolton might spot the flames.

TWA dispatcher Ted Haueter finally checked an emergency field at Kirksville, Missouri, 120 miles northeast of Kansas City. Kirksville was below minimums, too. At 3 A.M., Haueter radioed Flight 6 to proceed on the northeast leg of the Kansas City radio beam and toward Burlington, Iowa, the next available airport. But Burlington was 250 miles away, and the dispatcher advised Bolton to land at the first available field.

Flight 6 headed northeast, but Bolton's luck was running out along with his fuel. He followed the beam toward Kirksville, and with his fuel gauges reading almost empty, he let down through the overcast, attempting to establish visual contact with the ground. The last weather report given Flight 6 was a 300-foot ceiling at Kirksville—400-feet below minimums but still providing Bolton with some margin of safety. The report was wrong; it was almost zero-zero at Kirksville and Bolton had more of a handicap than he realized. The beam presumably leading him toward the emergency field was faulty, and he was 16 miles off course. When he broke out of the fog, he was only a few feet from the ground and the DC-2 struck a 60-foot embankment, flipping over as it hit.

The copilot was killed instantly, along with four passsengers. Bolton, bleeding internally, crawled through the wreckage trying to help the six passengers who survived the impact. When rescuers finally arrived, Bolton refused to leave until all passengers were put into ambulances. He was finally taken from the scene on the back of a flatbed truck and died from loss of blood before reaching a hospital.

It was the first fatal crash of a DC-2 and TWA's first fatal accident since the Rockne tragedy. It received more than the usual press attention because one of the dead passengers was Senator Bronson Cutting of New Mexico. He had boarded Flight 6 in Albuquerque. His death led to a Senate investigation that subsequently resulted in major air safety reforms, not the least of which would be the establishment of an independent accident investigation board. The Department of Commerce, in looking into the Cutting crash, was literally investigating itself and proceeded to lay most of the blame on everybody but itself. TWA was criticized for such alleged sins as failing to carry an adequate supply of reserve fuel, undertaking an instrument flight with an inoperative radio and not dispatching the flight to a safe alternate field before it was too late. Bolton was accused of carelessness because he chose to continue his flight while knowing he could not communicate with the ground. The only criticism levied against the government was the Weather Bureau's inaccurate forecast and its failure to advise Flight 6 that Kansas City minimums had dropped below legal limits. Having thus swept its own, not inconsiderable part in the accident under a rug, the Department concluded by fining the captain of Flight 6's first section $200 for landing below minimums.

The Senate committee put most of the blame where it belonged—on the Department of Commerce. There would have been no accident, the committee held, if the northeast radio beam had been working properly. Rather than castigate the dead Bolton, the senators said he had been betrayed by "an inherent deficiency in the radio range and criminal negligence in weather reporting." The Senate report concluded:

> Bolton . . . displayed such nerve and coolness in the few minutes that followed [the accident] that no one could possibly allege carelessness, lack of loyalty toward duty, selfishness or a character that would shirk.

Another three years elapsed before Congress passed the Civil Aeronautics Act of 1938, establishing an independent Civil Aeronautics Authority and also an independent Air Safety Board. Both were the direct results of the Cutting crash. But Jack Frye was not the type to wait for the slow-moving wheels of legislative reform. There is no recorded evidence that he hired hostesses because of a belief that the presence of one on Bolton's plane might have saved more lives, including that of Bolton himself. Yet it would not have been unlike him; he was a caring, compassionate man, tough yet sensitive, with a gift for introspection. He never said it publicly, but he admitted to Richter and others that TWA had to bear some share of the blame for the fate of Flight 6.

Frye didn't punish anybody, not even Haueter, the dispatcher who had let the first section land illegally and also had allowed Bolton to circle Kansas City, wasting precious fuel. Haueter actually was a captain who set up TWA's widely copied dispatch system while Ted was flying the line, and

Frye subsequently made him a flight superintendent under Larry Fritz and John Collings. Frye went looking for answers to the future, not questions of the past. And in this respect, he turned to Tommy Tomlinson, a pilot who could have flown a bathtub if it were equipped with wings and an engine.

Just before the airmail contracts were cancelled, Frye had ordered two Northrop Gammas, a much faster version of the Alpha, ostensibly as mail planes. They were delivered while the airlines were in FDR's doghouse, and Frye converted one of them into a high-altitude experimental plane. He had always been fascinated by the potential of above-the-weather flying, from the standpoint of both safety and comfort, and had used the DC-1 as an aeronautical laboratory, equipping its Cyclones with two-speed blowers and electrically controlled props so the plane could reach 27,000 feet. Tommy Tomlinson had flown these DC-1 forays into the upper skies, and it was Tomlinson to whom Frye entrusted the Gamma flights.

Tommy's "toy" was a collection of borrowed parts, such as a special engine from Wright that included an experimental carburetor. The Army loaned TWA a turbo-supercharger to which TWA's maintenance specialists fitted improvised pumps for increasing fuel pressure. Starting in July of 1936 and continuing for the next six months, Tomlinson logged more than forty hours at altitudes above 30,000 feet, hours that included moments of terror. Once, groggy from lack of oxygen on a high-altitude flight from Kansas City to New York, he picked up the Newark beam but flew it in the wrong direction and found himself over the Atlantic 150 miles from land. He ran out of fuel near Princeton, New Jersey, trying to get back to Newark, and crash-landed on the side of a hill. On another test flight, the engine's turbo-wheel flew off and hit the wing, sending the Gamma into a dive from which Tomlinson was barely able to recover.

But the risks were acceptable, considering the knowledge acquired—data that would affect the future of commercial aviation. For what Tomlinson discovered in his high-altitude flights was the existence of what is now known as the jetstream—powerful stratospheric winds blowing from the west/northwest above 30,000 feet. TWA meteorologists like Gordon Parkinson didn't believe Tomlinson when he reported encountering winds of nearly 150 miles an hour. To Frye, Tomlinson gave an equally vital message: if an airline could operate all flights above 20,000 feet, it could avoid 80 percent of bad weather. Frye did believe him and began looking around for an airplane capable of doing the job.

Frye was planning a revolution while TWA itself was in the process of evolution—from the DC-2 to the DC-3.

If the DC-2 had been TWA's baby, the DC-3's parents were American Airlines and the tough-minded Texan who headed it—Cyrus Rowlett Smith, otherwise known as C.R. He had never been enamored of the DC-2, although he had bought it to keep pace with TWA and ahead of United. C.R. thought its fourteen-passenger payload was inadequate, and he noted with displeasure that going westbound, the DC-2 couldn't make the New York–Chicago run nonstop. Smith also experienced an unpleasant ride on a DC-2 between Buffalo and Chicago. He was accompanied by American's chief technical engineer, Bill Littlewood, and the plane was yawing sharply in turbulence and ice.

"I don't think much of this," C.R. growled. "Do you?"

Littlewood allowed that he wasn't happy, either. It was enough to start both men discussing ways to improve on the DC-2. In the fall of 1934, Smith placed a telephone call to Donald Douglas and for two hours expounded on his ideas for a better DC-2. Smith wanted more range, twenty-one daytime seats instead of fourteen, and sleeper facilities for fourteen passengers on an aircraft that could cross the nation with only four stops.

Douglas was hard to sell, primarily because he had a fair-sized backlog of DC-2 orders and saw little reason to improve on a classic. Nor did he like C.R.'s insistence on sleeping accommodations.

"Who the hell is going to buy a sleeper plane?" he complained later to Art Raymond. "Night flying is about as popular as silent movies."

But it was hard to argue with a man who was willing to buy twenty planes sight unseen—ten of them 21-passenger daytime transports and the rest sleeper planes. Douglas agreed to study American's specifications, and within six months his engineers, working closely with Littlewood, had come up with an acceptable DST, standing for Douglas Sleeper Transport; its more widely known name was DC-3. It would have a cabin twenty-six inches wider and three inches higher than the DC-2. It also would have automobile brakes operated by foot instead of the DC-2's cumbersome handle-activated brake arrangement. A major improvement was the installation of a dorsal fin just ahead of the tail to improve stability. The new fin was installed on later DC-3s; the first DST didn't have it and this was the airplane that Frye sent Tomlinson to test-fly.

Tommy's verdict was that American had bought a turkey, not an eagle. "A clunk," he informed Frye after flying the DST early in January of 1936. Tomlinson reported that the aircraft had failed one of its key tests; it didn't have the ability to get off the ground in less than 1,000 feet while carrying its full takeoff weight of 24,000 pounds. Considering the short runway lengths of most airports in the 1930s, this was a major deficiency and Tommy's recommendation to Frye was simple: forget about the DST or DC-3 and buy more DC-2s.

It turned out to be the wrong piece of advice, one that cost TWA crucial DC-3 delivery positions, but it's hard to fault Tomlinson. Among those sharing his original view toward the DST was Donald Douglas himself. Almost everything about the airplane bothered him. It had the same inherent stability problems as the DC-2; it was overweight and underpowered and Douglas never liked the idea of turning it into a sleeper plane. His prejudice was reinforced, albeit illogically, when the DST went on public display for the first time at the National Pacific Aircraft and Boat Show, carrying American's markings.

Douglas entered the huge Los Angeles Auditorium and marched over to the glistening new plane. There was a sign in front of it and his face turned crimson: "14 BIRTHS, 21 SEATS," it read.

More than that errant sign was changed. The adding of a dorsal fin cured the stability problems and beefed-up engines gave the DC-3 the necessary muscle. Overall, it *was* markedly superior to the DC-2, eliminating most of the latter's faults while retaining such virtues as ruggedness and reliability. Greater payload was its chief advantage over the older plane, and soon Frye knew he had to follow American's lead. Even United ordered the DC-3 in an abject admission that its 247 gamble had failed. It was the first airliner whose interior color scheme was designed to reduce airsickness. Research had shown that subdued shades like light blue and light gray worked better than bright reds and greens. Darker shades were used on the carpets and lower walls, implying strength and security, while lighter pastels went into the upper walls and ceiling to reduce the feeling of confinement. TWA's DC-3 interiors were roughly like American's and so, generally speaking, were everyone else's—with one glaring exception. Eastern's Rickenbacker insisted on a combination of a cream white and a somewhat bilious green for the interior, the latter virtually inviting nausea. But that was Captain Eddie; he loved to buck any industry trend on the theory that if it was good enough for him, it was good enough for his passengers.

By contrast, Jack Frye was very much passenger-oriented and promotion-minded. He revived the old in-flight movie stunt that had been tried in the Ford trimotor days, installing projectors in some of the DC-2s. And he had one of the most colorful airline public relations men in the history of the industry, the legendary Clancy Dayhoff, who would try anything short of murder to get TWA mentioned in the newspapers. Clancy was in charge of public relations for the western region, an ideal location with its proximity to Hollywood. TWA and American competed fiercely for the movie traffic between Los Angeles and New York, business that blossomed with the introduction of transcontinental sleeper service. United wasn't much of a factor in that market at the time; it didn't have New York–Los Angeles authority and served L.A. with connecting flights at Salt Lake City or San Francisco.

Frye ordered ten DSTs and eight regular DC-3s to start with. Prior to their delivery, the TWA timetables advertised "Douglas Skyliners on All Flights," a rather sly inference that TWA was operating the latest in Douglas equipment—which it wasn't. American put the DST/DC-3 into service in 1936 while TWA was still operating an all-DC-2 passenger fleet of twenty-seven aircraft, plus a few Ford trimotors converted to freighters. Frye had swung his own DC-3 deal by getting Douglas to switch the DC-2s TWA still had on order over to other carriers, particularly in Europe.

TWA's sleeper service was inaugurated June 1, 1937; the airline trumpeted it had spent an extra $10,000 per aircraft "to guarantee a more beautiful and more comfortable Skysleeper." This was true; in trying to go American and United one better, Frye had ordered special $500 seats. The interior colors and decor had come from the fertile mind of industrial designer Raymond Loewy. The major selling point, however, was speed. TWA's coast-to-coast schedule, described as "the shortest and fastest," actually was more direct than American's southern route and slightly quicker with the same number of stops, three.

The two prime westbound trips were Flight 7, which left Newark at 5:15 P.M. and arrived in Los Angeles at 7:25 A.M. the next day after stops in Chicago, Kansas City and Albuquerque, and Flight 5, departing Newark at 5 P.M., reaching Los Angeles at 7:04 A.M. with a stop at Columbus instead of Chicago. The only eastbound Skysleeper was Flight 6; it left Los Angeles at 4:30 P.M., stopped in Albuquerque, Kansas City and Chicago, and landed in Newark at 10:40 A.M. Newark, then the nation's busiest airport, would remain TWA's major east coast terminus until 1939, when LaGuardia opened.

The one-way transcontinental fare was $149.48 on a DC-2; there was a surcharge for flying the DST or DC-3—$4 extra for that $500 seat and $8 for berth accommodations between New York and Los Angeles. The cost wasn't unreasonable, but these were the immediate post-depression days, and both American and TWA went after the well-heeled movie and stage crowd. Robbie Robinson, who started working for TWA as a clerk in 1933, was in Los Angeles sales during the DST era and remembers how hard he had to scrounge for customers.

"The cream of our long-haul business was theatrical. We had to personally call on every sonofabitch in Hollywood who might have a reason to fly. If the guy had a wife who objected to his flying, we'd take the wife out to a fancy restaurant for lunch and soften her up with statistics on how safe air travel was. Some of us used to meet the ocean liners docking in New York, Los Angeles and San Francisco, and if there were celebrities on board heading for the opposite coast, we'd buttonhole them and try to talk 'em into flying TWA across the country."

Because the airline catered to the entertainment world, people like Robbie inevitably encountered their share of prima donnas. Robinson remembers Sonja Henie as being especially difficult. "Everytime she showed up for a flight, she'd have hundreds of pounds of excess baggage and then would go into a rage when we'd try to collect the extra charges."

Robbie ran into one such tantrum when her luggage checked in some 200 pounds over the allowable limit. She began screaming about the injustice of it all, but Robbie calmed her down with a compromise. "Your bags are four hundred pounds over," he lied, "but because you're such a good customer, Miss Henie, I'll charge you for only two hundred pounds and let you take the other two hundred pounds free."

This mollified her, but the Norwegian skating star, in Robinson's memory, never flew TWA without raising hell about something. "She was impossible. If you did her a favor, she'd expect the same favor from then on. But at least she traveled with us. The other side of the coin was Mary Pickford. She'd book space on a flight and then cancel. She'd book again and cancel again. Sometimes she'd cancel at the very last minute and other times she just didn't show up for the flight."

Finally Lou Marechal, Robinson's boss, sent him out to interview Miss Pickford on the theory that maybe she was booking on TWA and flying on American. Robbie posed this possibility to her.

"Oh, it's nothing like that, Mr. Robinson," she assured him. "The reason I decide to cancel is that I find the stars aren't right for me on the day I'm supposed to fly."

Of all the celebrities Robbie booked, Clark Gable and Carole Lombard were his favorites. They never complained, never demanded special treatment and were always understanding if a flight was delayed. Another frequent TWA customer was Harry Cohn, the tough, profane president of Columbia Pictures, who always insisted on occupying a lower berth aboard the sleeper flight to New York. Columbia's traffic manager, Max Seligman, would phone Robinson about a week before departure and make sure the lower was available. One day Seligman called with his usual request. "Robbie, the King's going to New York Friday and wants his usual space on Flight Six."

"No problem," Robinson said confidently. But when he checked reservations, only an upper was available and Robbie called Seligman back.

"I'll protect him in an upper," he promised. "He'll have priority on the first lower cancellation. . . . I'm sure something will open up by Friday."

Nothing did, however, and Robinson had to tell Seligman all week long that Harry Cohn was still stuck with the upper. Finally Cohn himself called.

"I can get the goddamned lower berth myself!" he yelled. "Who's your reservations manager?"

Mike Corley, Robinson told him, and Cohn phoned Corley who listened patiently while the movie mogul ranted about the unavailability of a lower berth. When Harry ran out of invectives, threats and pleas, Corley said softly, "Mr. Cohn, that airplane flies every day to New York at eight thousand feet."

"What the hell does that have to do with my lower berth?" Cohn stormed.

"Well, at eight thousand feet what difference does three feet make?"

There was silence. Then Cohn started to laugh. "I'll take the upper this time," he said grudgingly, "but don't let it happen again."

Such reasonableness on the part of the man Hollywood called "White Fang" was somewhat unique. Seligman once asked Robbie to put two pounds of kosher ham on a westbound TWA flight out of New York. "The boss says you can get it from Lindy's Restaurant," Max added desperately.

"There's no such thing as kosher ham," Robinson pointed out.

Seligman sighed. "You know that and I know that, but Harry Cohn apparently doesn't."

Robinson dutifully asked someone in New York to pick up two pounds of ham from Lindy's and left it up to Cohn to check out its dietary authenticity. Anyway, kosher ham was no less challenging than another Cohn request: he wanted TWA to take up a new radio he had just bought "and fly it around for a couple of hours."

"What for?" Robbie asked Seligman.

"He wants to know if it'll work at high altitudes," Max explained.

While this plea was refused, TWA's ability to cope with the demanding Mr. Cohn was typical of its public relations. Starting with the days of TWA's air/train service, the airline enjoyed a close relationship with the movie industry, recognizing the publicity value of having prominent personalities as regular customers. Occasionally, a celebrity returned the favor; Betty Seay Hawes, a hostess in the DC-3 era, remembers the time a TWA flight was grounded in Albuquerque because of weather. Eddie Duchin was a passenger, and he played a piano at the airport for two hours while sixteen other passengers and the crew listened in awe. But she also recalls that the vaunted sleeper planes weren't really all that comfortable.

"A lot of famous entertainers were afraid to fly," she reminisces. "Most of them preferred to take trains like the Super Chief; *that* was the way to travel across the country. The planes were faster, but they couldn't fly over the weather and nobody ever got an honest all-night sleep. We had to wake up passengers before every landing, to protect their eardrums, and Flight

Five eastbound would come into Los Angeles around seven A.M., which meant I had to start waking up people at six. It wasn't exactly the most gracious way to travel."

". . . they couldn't fly over the weather . . ."

More than anything else, this aeronautical deficiency stuck in Jack Frye's craw. But he also had plenty of other items to worry about. He wasn't getting along too well with TWA's board of directors, which was dominated by the airline's majority stockholder, former Yellow Cab magnate John D. Hertz.

Breech was the man who had brought Hertz into the TWA picture around the time the "old" and the "new" airlines merged at the suggestion of the Post Office Department. Ernie worked for Hertz at one stage and had been instrumental in getting Hertz to merge Yellow Cab into the General Motors family. Hertz subsequently became a partner in the prestigious New York investment banking firm of Lehman Brothers and served on North American Aviation's board. When the "new" TWA won a transcontinental mail contract late in 1934, Brecch convined Hertz to buy into the airline—to the tune of about 11 percent of the outstanding shares.

The nominal head of the board was Henry B. duPont, who was named chairman of the merged Transcontinental & Western Air, Inc. on December 28, 1934—the day after George Spater filed the incorporation papers. But duPont was chairman in name only; Breech continued to dominate. When Breech temporarily left the airline business and returned to fulltime duties as a General Motors vice-president, Hertz' influence increased because of the close relationship he enjoyed with Breech. Henry duPont resigned as board chairman in January of 1936, and for the next two years the TWA directors operated without a chairman. Presumably, one wasn't necessary with John D. Hertz running a board heavily populated with his handpicked choices. Frye served as a director and so did Richter. Another director, one of the few totally sympathetic to Frye, was young attorney George Spater whose law firm of Chadburne, Park, Whiteside & Wolff represented TWA and still does today. But for the most part, the TWA directors between 1936 and 1938 were subservient to John Hertz, and it was not a healthy situation for that crucial period. Frye had committed the airline to another technological expansion, and in doing so, he had set a collision course with Hertz.

For months Frye had carried in his pocket a clipping that he showed to anyone interested in the subject of aviation's future. It was a story quoting other airline presidents to the effect that nobody needed four-engine planes and that flying as high as 20,000 feet was crazy. Jack would display it as his example of the industry's backward thinking.

Frye's own beliefs were demonstrated before 1936 ended. He signed a contract with Boeing for six four-engine transports at a cost of nearly $2 million. They would be the world's first pressurized airliners, and they were destined to lead Jack Frye and TWA into the hands of Howard Robard Hughes.

5

". . . Well, why don't we buy TWA?"

The TWA that Jack Frye took into the pivotal year of 1937 was a carrier fairly representative of the quickly maturing airline industry.

It was solidly if not overwhelmingly secure financially, having wound up 1936 with a modest but encouraging profit of slightly over $200,000; the 1935 net had been only $19,000. It would carry in calendar year 1937 approximately 90,000 passengers, or about 10 percent of the total traffic flown by all domestic scheduled airlines of that year.

TWA was part of the so-called "Big Three," ranking behind American and United respectively in terms of miles flown, passengers carried, cities served and revenues. Later the Big Three would become the "Big Four," with Eastern joining the trio as the nation's largest domestic carriers. The sobriquet "Big Three" was well deserved; American, United and TWA shared 60 percent of the industry's total 1937 revenues, the other 40 percent being divided among the remaining eighteen airlines.

Of the twenty-one scheduled U.S. airlines, only one flew internationally, Pan American. The others included such familiar names as Delta, Braniff, Western and National, plus long-forgotten carriers like Boston-Maine Airways, Canadian Colonial, Hanford, Chicago and Southern, Miami-Key West Airways, Wilmington-Catalina Airline, Wyoming Air Service, Central Vermont Airways and a tiny company called Varney, which flew between Pueblo, Colorado, and El Paso. Varney was headed by a pilot who had been Beech Aircraft's West Coast distributor. Before taking over Varney, the airman had become friendly with TWA's Clancy Dayhoff.

Dayhoff wanted to shoot some promotional films of aerial scenes and had chartered a Beech from the young pilot, who decided to fly the photographic mission himself. Clancy liked him and invited him to the Biltmore bar when the flight was over. They talked at length, the pilot confiding his growing boredom with selling airplanes. What he really wanted was to get into the airline business.

Dayhoff had an idea. He explained that TWA was trying to get a New York–San Francisco transcontinental route but did not have much hope for success. Suppose the pilot started an airline that would operate between San Francisco and Winslow. TWA would provide financial backing and, because TWA already served Winslow, its flights could connect with the spur airline at the Arizona town and thus offer direct service between the East Coast and the northern California metropolis. The pilot was intrigued, and after several more drinks, they even thought up a name for their embryonic airline: Trans-Western.

Dayhoff left the bar long enough to phone Jack Frye, who told him to put the pilot on a TWA flight the next day. The two of them met in Kansas City where they agreed on the general details, subject to approval by TWA's directors. The pilot went back to the West Coast dreaming of becoming an airline president overnight. But when Frye informed John Hertz of the plan, Hertz refused to sanction it without an okay from his own lawyers. Their opinion was that the arrangement, while legal, was somewhat unethical, and Hertz ordered Frye to forget the whole thing.

It was the first real clash between Frye and Hertz, one that sowed seeds of future dissension. Hertz considered Frye too impulsive, and Frye thought Hertz was too cautious. The other party to the abortive scheme went on to become one of the most colorful giants in commercial aviation history; the pilot's name was Robert F. Six and shortly after he came close to becoming part of TWA, he bought into Varney and changed its name to Continental.

The incident, however, marked the start of a lifelong friendship between Frye and Bob Six. They were very much alike in several respects. Both were rugged, independent westerners with a willingness to gamble and a feeling for passengers that sometimes bordered on the flamboyant, though more often than not, their notions emerged as sound marketing instinct. The aborted plan to create the San Francisco–Winslow spur was not the only time Frye and Six would cross paths.

Frye's eagerness to crack the San Francisco–East Coast market, even if it was via the back door devised by Clancy Dayhoff, was typical of Frye's competitiveness. It was a trait absorbed by most of the people who worked for him. TWA's attempts to bump heads with United in the latter's San Francisco stronghold were to bear fruit in 1938, when TWA won San Francisco–Chicago authority, albeit via a circuitous routing. R. Dixon Speas, today one of commercial aviation's leading consultants, was a young TWA employee during the 1937–1938 period, working as a ticket agent in the Bay Area. Speas remembers that the airline's inaugural flight to Chicago went first to an unscheduled stop at Oakland before heading east.

"On the very first flight," Speas recounts, "we had only two or three legitimate passengers, so the local manager, Ole May, dredged up a plane-load of employee friends who brought empty suitcases to the airport. The whole purpose was to scare the United representative that May knew would be counting our passengers. They were checked in with much fanfare, after which the airplane took off, flew to Oakland, and off-loaded all but the two or three lonely souls who went on east."

One TWA salesman, Jimmy Scott, was assigned to meet incoming ocean liners from the Orient. He'd go out on the pilot boat and proceed immediately to the ship's purser for a list of all passengers heading east. To anyone already booked on United, Scott would offer free limousine service from the dock to a complimentary room at a hotel, another free limousine from the hotel to the airport, and a promise of no charge for excess luggage. United quickly learned of Mr. Scott's sales forays and counterattacked. UAL agents would ride the same limousines to the airport and while enroute would seek to persuade TWA-booked passengers to take United's more direct flights. It was easy persuasion for a long time; TWA's service out of the Bay Area went from San Francisco south to Fresno, west to Las

Vegas, and south again to Winslow where connections could be made with the eastbound transcontinental flights.

One of Speas' tasks was to phone new arrivals at the St. Francis and Sir Francis Drake hotels, following a prepared spiel that went like this:

"Good evening, sir [or madame], welcome to San Francisco. We understand you have just arrived from the east and so has TWA. Could we help you with your return reservations?"

Speas also called on other hotels and large firms trying to persuade their telephone operators to paste a little airplane cutout with TWA's reservations number on their switchboards. "Those were the days of strong and direct sales efforts," Speas adds.

The efforts had to be strong and direct for one simple reason: the success of the DC-3 resulted in most major airlines operating the same equipment. By 1938, the new Douglas airliner would be carrying more than 80 percent of all U.S. air traffic; its only competition was Lockheed's L-14 Super Electra, 45 mph faster than the DC-3 and just as advanced technically. The L-14 was the first transport to have full-feathering, constant-speed propellers, cargo compartments under the cabin floor instead of in the rear fuselage, integral fuel tanks, two-speed superchargers and Fowler flaps, the last even more efficient than the DC-2/DC-3 wing "brakes." But the fat-bellied Lockheed had two drawbacks: it carried only fourteen passengers and it went into service (on Northwest) with an unsuspected fatal flaw. A Northwest L-14 only three months off the assembly line lost its tail and crashed. When the accident was traced to tail flutter so severe as to cause structural failure, the L-14 became the first U.S.-built airliner to be grounded until the weakness was corrected.

So the ubiquitous DC-3 ruled the skies, and the airlines were hard pressed to convince the public each carrier was operating better DC-3s than the other guy's. TWA, possibly reflecting Frye's love affair with technology, emphasized those $500 special seats but dwelt even more heavily on the claim that "TWA's new Skysleepers carry a greater reserve of horsepower than any other land transport in America with 2,100-mile cruising range." American advertised: "a clean, cool overnight journey between New York and California with only three stops and the complimentary meals are delicious." But American also stressed security; one of its earlier DC-3 ads had passengers mouthing such quotes as: "Say, these new Flagships look like the *Hindenberg* with wings . . . I have never flown before, yet this new Flagship plane looks so big and steady, I have perfect peace of mind."

United's transcontinental sleepers featured a "Sky Room" described as "a courtesy lounge for all passengers and especially convenient for those wishing to retire late or arise early."

"It is *always* available," the advertisement added proudly and then went on to cite "two separate dressing rooms in addition to separate lavatories for men and women . . . hot and cold running water . . . Packard electric razors . . . courtesy toilet kits . . . electric kitchens for hot à la carte meals aloft."

All carriers benefited from the plane's reputation as the safest transport yet built. The newly formed industry trade organization, the Air Transport Association of America, announced that trip insurance would be available to air passengers for the first time—a $5,000 policy for twenty-five cents.

Significantly, this was the same premium charged rail and bus travelers, and *Time* magazine commented:

> That insurance companies can now bet $5,000 to two bits against a passenger being killed on a flight of some 800 miles is one of the best pieces of publicity the U.S. airlines ever had.

Such reassurance to the public couldn't have come at a better time. In the two-month period between late December of 1936 and the end of January 1937, the airlines suffered five major accidents and passengers were canceling reservations by the thousands. Some carriers, TWA included, saw their flights often running empty, carrying only mail and freight. Aviation needed a DC-3, although it was a long way from achieving aerodynamic perfection. Its considerable recent achievements, enhanced by the nostalgia for an era that is four-and-a-half decades in the past, have perhaps imbued the old gal with more virtues than she actually possessed.

"I've never been maudlin about airplanes," ex-TWA Captain Bob Buck admits. "I thought the DC-3 was a lousy airplane and I still do. I never shed a tear when we retired the last one. It was good only because it had two great engines in it. It flew like a damned brick outhouse on one engine and it had terrible stall characteristics."

Buck's criticism notwithstanding, the DC-3 *did* have its virtues, including great stability. Buck himself remembers one TWA captain, Ted Hereford, who could and did fly the DC-3 just by manipulating the trim tab. Once on a ferry flight between Columbus and Dayton, Hereford invited a hostess, deadheading to Dayton, to fly the airplane. She was at the controls for the whole 71-mile trip, and Hereford kept her there almost down to the ground. She never caught on that she wasn't actually flying anything but her imagination; Ted was using the trim tab with his knee, surreptitiously correcting every maneuver she made. When they were on final approach, Hereford began screaming at her: "Pull up! PULL UP! Are you trying to kill us?"

The stricken hostess finally deplaned, hair messed and face blotched with terror-generated sweat. Hereford thought it was funny but he was to get his comeuppance. He drew a copilot named Bronson White without knowing that White had been tipped off to the trim tab procedure. Hereford bet him he could fly all the way to the next stop without touching the yoke. They started their takeoff roll, Hereford planning to roll back the trim tab as soon as the tail wheel was off the ground. What he failed to notice was Bronson's own knee; the copilot had pressed it against a chain next to the yoke and connected with the trim stabilizer. When Hereford tried to move the stabilizer back, it refused to budge. He kept cranking and cranking but nothing happened. With the stabilizer all the way back, White suddenly took his knee away from the chain and the DC-3 practically stood on its nose.

Hereford just managed to avert a stall—not an easy task because he was simultaneously yelling at White, "You goddamned son of a bitch! . . ."

A captain with legendary skills was Jack Zimmerman, one of TAT's original pilots. Sociable, personable and unflappable, Zimmerman always wore his uniform cap cocked at a jaunty angle and flew airplanes the same way. Hal Blackburn, who served with him as a copilot, testifies as to Zimmerman's ability: "He'd put a DC-2 into a stall, come straight down and recover just before landing. I told him once, 'You bastard—some day you're gonna kill us both,' but he just laughed. He was a great guy and a magnificent pilot."

Blackburn was still a copilot when he and Zimmerman were among the TWA pilots assigned to a secret charter contract Frye had arranged with J. Edgar Hoover and the FBI. United originally had the contract but unfortunately for UAL, some of its employees had bragged about the hush-hush operation, and Hoover abruptly cancelled the arrangement. TWA flew the FBI charters for two years, and Blackie remembers his first assignment. He was based in Newark at the time and got a call to come to the airport.

"Should I bring maps?" Blackburn wondered.

"Yes."

"How many and to where?"

"Bring all of them," he was told.

Zimmerman was assigned as the captain, but he had been partying and confessed to Blackie he was in no shape to fly. "I'm stoned," he said frankly. "You take it the first leg and by then I'll be fine." They waited by their DC-2 in a hangar until Hoover and his aides drove up in a black sedan and boarded. It was the first of several charters that Blackburn and Zimmerman flew but to this day, Blackie doesn't know the exact nature of the trips except to recall that one involved a kidnapping case. What was more important was the fact that the FBI and its rock-hard chief were willing to rely on air transportation.

The industry and TWA were growing up. Gone were the Ford trimotors—the last ones had been phased out of the TWA fleet in 1934 after brief duty as freighters. The Alphas had departed the scene in 1935. Only the experimental Gamma remained, with Tomlinson continuing to fly his high-altitude missions, gathering data that was funneled directly to Frye's desk. More than any other contemporary, the TWA president was looking ahead—at a time when most of the bigger airlines were perfectly happy with the vaunted DC-3. The smaller carriers tried valiantly to convince the public that they, too, were part of the new era of modern equipment and modern methods. They boasted that "all our planes carry two pilots and two-way radios." Any transport with more than one engine was described with pathetic pride as "multi-motored." Those operating the by-then obsolete 247 resorted to the adjective "fast."

There was plenty of room to grow. In 1937, there still were scores of cities with populations of more than 200,000 that had no direct airmail service. The number of communities with municipal airports totaled 742, but only 27 percent of them were served by scheduled air carriers. The average airline passenger was no longer an adventuresome soul who flew for the thrill, bragging "I just flew to New York" in the same boastful tone he'd use if he were saying "I just went ten rounds with Jack Dempsey." Now he usually was a businessman going some place in a hurry. Whereas he once chalked up delays and cancellations as just bad luck, he now was blaming such misfortunes on the airlines themselves and was demanding good service and reasonable reliability. Leaders like Frye grasped what some of their colleagues did not or could not: the time was fast approaching when an airplane like the DC-3, because of its speed, altitude and range limitations, would become an anachronism. Frye, in particular, realized that the DC-3's limitations actually were a restriction on airline growth itself. It was, indeed, the most reliable, confidence-generating and viable transport plane built to date, but it still wasn't good enough to achieve what Frye, along with a handful of fellow airline officials, envisioned as a future target: the development of the airplane into a mode of mass transportation, dominating long-haul travel.

Even the well-deserved popularity of the DC-3 didn't change the fact that in 1937, only 1 percent of the nation's adult population had ever set foot on a scheduled airliner. The 1936 rate of traffic growth had been a dramatic 39 percent, thanks in large part to planes like the DC-2 and DC-3. But the 1937 increase in domestic passenger miles flown was less than 5 percent, disappointing when measured against the DC-3's dominance of the airways and the technical advances it represented. The meagerness of the gain merely buttressed what Frye was insisting—that the DC-3 wasn't capable of spurring air travel much more than it already had.

He was well aware that events in the making were destined to propel the industry toward new areas of both responsibility and opportunity. In the works as 1937 drew to a close, was legislation designed to end the quarrelsome, clumsy system of dividing government regulatory authority over the airlines among three federal agencies: the Post Office Department (mail contracts and routes), the Interstate Commerce Commission (mail rates and passenger/freight tariffs) and the Commerce Department's Bureau of Air Commerce (safety, airways and pilot/aircraft licensing).

Known as the Civil Aeronautics Act of 1938, it was commercial aviation's version of the Magna Carta in that it brought stability and reasonable regulation to an industry that had been walking a precarious tightrope between czarlike controls and competitive anarchy. The act created an independent, five-member Civil Aeronautics Authority that had jurisdiction over all civil aviation activities except accident investigation—that was entrusted to a three-man Safety Board, which operated independently even though it was part of the CAA. At the head of the agency was an administrator in charge of executive and managerial duties.

Thus the act established a quasi-independent agency of three separate but equal parts. Its greatest accomplishment was to eliminate specified duration of mail contracts, which in effect made all route awards temporary. Under the new law, route certifications became permanent but not exclusive; the CAA was given authority to provide competition in markets where the traffic justified the services of two or more carriers.

Nobody welcomed passage of the act with more eagerness than Frye. He had long chafed under TWA's stagnating route system, which in 1937 stood basically unchanged from the days of the TAT/Western merger. Its heart was the old transcontinental mail route stretching from New York to Los Angeles; sandwiched into that 3,000-mile airway were twelve intermediate cities—Philadelphia, Harrisburg, Pittsburgh, Columbus, Dayton, Indianapolis, St. Louis, Kansas City, Wichita, Amarillo, Albuquerque and tiny Winslow. A non-mail segment ran from Albuquerque to Los Angeles via the Grand Canyon, but it was operated only seasonally; a second non-mail route carried passengers between Chicago and Kansas City.

In 1937, TWA was granted two new airmail routes. The first was Chicago–New York via Ft. Wayne and Dayton; the second was the previously mentioned route between San Francisco and Winslow via Fresno and Las Vegas. Both were disappointing in terms of developing viable passenger traffic because of the required intermediate stops, but they still represented a foot in the door leading to a pair of major markets. As such, they were enough to encourage Frye's dreams of expansion. He was looking ahead to the projected 1939 New York World's Fair and San Francisco Exposition, and in the new Civil Aeronautics Act he visualized the eventual end of restrictions on TWA in both the Chicago and San Francisco markets.

He could look back on his first three years as TWA's president with pride. As 1938 began, the airline had slightly over 1,100 employees, with more than 600 based in Kansas City. To most of them, Frye and Richter came close to being father figures, each exuding a brand of leadership that blended paternalism with toughness. They earned affection through respect, and they continued to complement each other. Frye, the more visible and extroverted of the two, drew most of the attention, but he never forgot what Richter was contributing to the company. In an industry run by chieftains whose large egos were part of the territory, Jack Frye remained a modest, even self-effacing individual. Richter, in fact, though the quieter of the two, had a fearsome temper, whereas Frye was rather easygoing. In person, they were a Mutt-and-Jeff combination—Frye tall and husky, with a shock of hair resembling a floor mop; Richter comparatively small with the feistiness that seems to go with many men of short stature.

Richter was apparently self-conscious of his height. He had established a new personnel department "to insure better selection of new employees," according to its stated aims, but he exercised veto power over the department's decisions. One day a personnel interviewer rejected an applicant for a ticket agent's job because he was too short. Somehow Richter heard about it and asked the interviewer to justify his action.

"Mr. Richter, the guy was so short that it would have been hard for him to see over the counter and talk to passengers," the personnel man explained.

"Let him stand on a stool," Richter snapped. Then his eyes twinkled. "If size had anything to do with ability," he added, "I wouldn't be where I am today. I suggest you hire the applicant and forget about his height."

Richter had one little idiosyncrasy that George Spater remembers; he always slept with his head buried under a blanket but with his feet sticking out at the other end. Spater, who traveled with him a lot, swears he never broke this habit. "He'd climb into that hotel bed, pull the blanket over his head while kicking it off his feet, and that was the only way he could go to sleep. He was devoted to his wife, Daisy. When he was on a trip he'd call her every day. He and Frye were like brothers. Frye would think up some idea and Paul would put it into effect. And Jack was never short of ideas. He was a great believer in standards of service. He'd go over TWA's advertising copy word by word. He insisted that the airplanes looked clean."

"Dynamic" is the word most people who knew Frye use in describing him. When a savage hurricane flattened most of New England in the fall of 1938, Frye virtually shut down the airline and dispatched planes to Boston as part of the industry's emergency airlift. Air was the only way in and out of the city and TWA flew there with no operating experience in the area.

Bob Buck flew some of the mercy missions and witnessed pilots, assigned to a Boston flight, ask crews on other carriers, "How the hell do I get there?" "Just follow me," was the usual answer.

Frye was fair game for the Clancy Dayhoff types, being reasonably accessible for interviews and extremely tolerant of Clancy's eager-beaver, occasionally unconventional approach to public relations. When a Broadway producer began planning a new musical that would be part of the 1939 World's Fair, Dayhoff talked him into letting TWA pick up girls across the country and fly them into New York for auditions. Then he convinced Frye the publicity would be worth taking a plane out of service and assigning it to the cross-country casting flight for three days.

But it wasn't enough for Clancy to rely on legitimate applicants. He hired a comely young lady in Albuquerque, dyed her face and body with walnut juice, put a black wig on her head and passed her off as an Indian princess determined to represent her tribe at the fair. There was some suspicion, however, that Frye might have put him up to this; Jack was fascinated by Indian lore and for a long time wanted TWA to have a Western Indian motif. He even sent Clancy into a reservation with instructions to study the resident tribe and get some ideas for applying its style to such areas as advertising, aircraft insignia and interior decorating.

Dayhoff wore glasses and was professorial in appearance, if not in demeanor. He was an alumnus of Western Air Express, where he had won fame of sorts by composing the most misleading slogan in the history of commercial aviation. He happened to get into a conversation with weather expert Irving Krick, who was expounding on his ideas for predicting tailwinds. Dayhoff was fascinated and, armed with this suddenly acquired scientific knowledge, he began touting Western as "the airline with perpetual tailwinds." The slogan didn't last very long for two practical reasons: there weren't always tailwinds present, and not even Irving Krick could make one reverse course so it would benefit a flight heading in the opposite direction.

In spite of Dayhoff's occasionally misguided efforts, Frye liked him and put up with most of his wilder stunts—such as the time he staged a carrier pigeon race, for some obscure reason, between New York and Chicago. Dayhoff had joined the airline as a by-product of the TAT/Western merger and wasn't to leave the airline until 1948, when he quit to start a small newspaper. Later, Dayhoff spent several years as director of public relations for the Port of Los Angeles.

Dayhoff died in Ireland in 1974; his ashes were flown back to the U.S. where he received a PR man's version of a Viking funeral. Clancy's expressed wish was to have his remains dropped from a plane over his native Montana, but his wife Nan—the last of his several wives—decided to consult others on the practicality of such arrangements. So she turned to friends like Robbie Robinson, who called an informal meeting of the unofficial pallbearers. One of Dayhoff's oldest cronies and drinking buddies was an ex-TWA district sales manager named George Cousins who died about the same time as Clancy. The mourners decided it would be fitting to scatter the ashes of both departed souls over the Pacific, somewhere between Long Beach and Catalina—a kind of united-in-life, united-in-death symbolic gesture.

A boat was borrowed from Bob Prescott, president of the Flying Tiger

Line, for the solemn occasion; the ashes were dumped overboard, followed immediately by a full bottle of bourbon.

"It was very appropriate," Robbie sighs nostalgically. "We knew those two wonderful bastards would fight over that bourbon all the way to the bottom."

When Clancy worked for Frye, the height of media exposure in those pre-television days was to get on network radio. One such program was the popular *Voice of Experience,* on which Dayhoff arranged a personal appearance by Frye, TWA hostess Betty Seay and a TWA captain. It wasn't enough that they merely be interviewed, however; Dayhoff took the whole *Voice of Experience* entourage up in a DC-3, the announcer proclaiming dramatically, "Today's broadcast is coming to you from one of TWA's beautiful Skysleepers, thousands of feet above Hollywood and Los Angeles, first by radio shortwave from station KABD to station KABB, thence to KHJ in Hollywood and from there to the network."

The interviews followed a script written by Dayhoff, which, in light of what we know today about commercial aviation's drawbacks in the late 1930s, must be admired for the audacity of its sugar-coated reassurances. The narrator, known to the audience as the "Voice," began by thanking TWA Capt. Felix Preeg for flying the special trip and then addressed Frye:

> Mr. Frye, I think the best purpose we can serve in today's interview is for you to give authentic information to my listening audience on safety in air travel. A logical first question, then, in introducing Mr. Frye, is this: Would you say, sir, that hazard has been eliminated from air travel?

Frye, dutifully following Dayhoff's script, neatly circumnavigated the planted question.

> Voice of Experience, let me answer you this way. Has hazard been eliminated from earthbound modes of travel? The answer, I am sure, must of necessity be no. Now if you had asked me, "Have the hazards of the air been reduced to the minimum of the railway and the steamship?" I should reply by citing the greatest experts on life and death in the world—the actuaries in the large insurance companies who determine the mortality rates in every line of endeavor, in every mode of travel. Ten years ago, insurance companies did not encourage air travel, but today every air traveler in the United States can buy five thousand dollar trip policies for twenty-five cents. This is just as cheap a premium as offered to railway or steamship travelers.

The "Voice" replied:

> Well, Mr. Frye, since the insurance companies are hard-fisted businessmen, this action says plainly that in their opinion airplane travel is a very reliable means of travel. Tell me, Mr. Frye, what in your opinion has made the greatest contribution towards safety in the air?

Frye's reply:

> Two things, Voice of Experience—radio and development of de-

pendable instruments. Without them, we could not give America dependable air transportation. With radio, our planes are constantly in touch with ground stations, receiving weather information, and our pilots follow a skyway which, though invisible, is as well marked as a modern highway. In the cabin, your transport pilot is provided with mechanical eyes so that even though the ground is overcast, your pilot constantly knows his height above the earth and the plane's progress along the airway.

All of which was true—up to a point. In terms of 1938 technology, the TWA president was reciting the latest state-of-the-art developments in navigation aids. In terms of today's technology, such aids were primitive. Radar, distance measuring equipment, computerized flight directors, instrument landing systems, radio altimeters, all-weather landing systems, vastly improved weather reporting, grooved runways, high intensity approach lights, runway visibility measuring equipment and markedly superior pilot training are just some of the tools available in the jet age that were unheard of in Frye's day. Given the advantage of historical hindsight, his claims for air travel's safety sound pitifully naïve and perhaps a bit misleading.

Yet Frye was anything but naïve and he was not trying to mislead; he was striving for badly needed reassurance to the public while simultaneously conceding to himself that in safety matters, commercial aviation was still in its crib. Unlike some of his contemporaries, he refused merely to pay lip service to this vital area; others mouthed platitudes about safety, but Frye—while he was guilty of the same platitudes—actually tried to do something about making them come true. The pilot in him recognized aviation's drawbacks even as the dreamer in him yearned to correct those drawbacks, and he did his best with the tools he had.

Almost from the day he became president, he had laid down one inviolate rule: Safety had a higher priority than schedule performance, and this philosophy permeated down through the ranks. If a project was aimed at making flying safer, Frye backed it without hesitation. There was no revenue in Tomlinson's high-altitude experiments, but Frye considered them absolutely essential. He insisted that the radio and navigation equipment aboard all TWA aircraft exceed the government's requirements. He was especially supportive of Walt Hamilton and his maintenance crews; no one was prouder than Frye when big Walt received *Aviation* magazine's award for outstanding contributions to aircraft maintenance in 1936. He required all TWA pilots to attend meteorology classes and he poured company funds into a research project started by J.C. "Jack" Franklin, the airline's superintendent of communications.

One of the industry's major operational problems concerned the static that afflicted radio signal reception in rain or snow. Franklin, at first on his own and then with Frye's whole-hearted blessing, developed a rotating loop antenna electrostatically shielded from the effects of precipitation. It enabled a pilot to determine his exact position by using the antenna to take bearings on two transmitting stations. Simple triangulation established the aircraft position, and because the device was static-free, it also could be used to supplement the conventional voice radio antenna whenever needed. TWA made the new antenna available to all airlines simply because Frye felt increased safety benefited the entire industry. Innovations like the static-free antenna could never be used as a competitive weapon.

He was not so altruistic in his quest for other superior equipment, but in this area he ran afoul of Hertz and the Hertz-dominated board of directors. Even while the whole airline was gearing up for the new four-engine Boeings, Hertz began having second thoughts about the $1.6 million commitment. Those six B-307s, dubbed Stratoliners, promised to be as quantum a jump from the DC-3 as the latter was from the Ford trimotor. Scheduled for delivery sometime in the summer of 1938, they would carry thirty-three passengers in a daytime configuration with sleeping accommodations for sixteen plus chaise-lounge chairs for nine additional persons at night. The Stratoliner actually was an offshoot of the B-17 bomber, using much of the latter's engine, landing gear, wing and tail components but with a radically different fuselage. The 307's cabin would be dirigible-shaped and pressurized for comfortable flight above 20,000 feet; the cylindrical shape was dictated by its ability to allow the air to expand equally in all directions, thus reducing the possibility of excessive stress in any one area. Pressurization—the technique of compressing the thin air of the upper atmosphere into heavier, breathable air—was not new. Lockheed had flown a small pressurized transport in experiments for the Army Air Corps, and Tomlinson's Gamma flights had contributed considerable data on the high-altitude environment, but never before had pressurization been tried on an aircraft as large as the 307.

Frye's plans for the big new bird were grandiose. He signed Raymond Loewy to design the interior, with indirect lighting, large lavatories and separate dressing rooms. A contract was executed with Marshall Field for such furnishings as the chaise lounges. The TWA annual reports for the years of 1936 and 1937 mentioned the huge Boeings in glowing terms, pointing out that they would be flying TWA's routes long before any other airline could obtain aircraft in any way comparable. Frye began phasing out the DC-2 fleet in eager anticipation of realizing his dream: over-the-weather flying.

But the 1938 annual report contained just one brief, cryptic mention of the Stratoliner, and that was a reference to a "controversy" between TWA and Boeing over the B-307 contract. Only the traditional verbal sanitizing of a corporate annual report could have described the volcanic situation so obliquely. The controversy involved far more than the contract; it stemmed from the festering Frye–Hertz feud, which threatened to erupt into a full-scale battle for control of the airline's destiny. It was a war in which Frye found himself sadly outmanned. He and Richter were the heart and soul of TWA, but the financial blood was pumped by John Hertz, holding nearly 12 percent of the stock along with Lehman Brothers and dominating the largely subservient directors. And Frye's position had been weakened in that pivotal year of 1937; for all his service innovations and commitment to technical excellence, the airline had finished the year with a loss of more than $770,000. It was ink more of a pale shade than bright crimson, and actually quite a respectable showing considering the capital outlay for the DC-3 fleet, but it was red enough to convince Hertz that the Stratoliners were an unwanted luxury.

Hertz was no ogre; he simply had no real aviation background, neither knew nor understood the airline business and seemed to consider Frye a wild-eyed reformer. Aggressive and staccato-voiced, Hertz was a stocky, dark-complexioned man with a deep and abiding interest in horse racing— he owned thoroughbreds himself.

Hertz initiated the contractual dispute by ordering Frye not to make the required progress payments as the Stratoliners moved through the assembly process. In June of 1938, Boeing cancelled the contract after pressing TWA in vain for some money.

Johnny Guy was in Seattle at the time, working under Ralph Ellinger as TWA's factory inspector. His job was to file periodic reports on each Stratoliner—state of construction, any assembly line problems and so forth. One day Guy came to work and discovered that the TWA insignia had been stripped from two of the four planes then on the assembly line. He asked for an explanation and was told that the contract had been terminated because TWA had failed to make a scheduled progress payment. Guy called Kansas City and was abruptly ordered to Santa Monica to oversee repairs on a damaged DC-3; the Stratoliner project apparently was almost dead.

Frye was distraught. He regarded the 307 as a golden opportunity to beat all other airlines in acquiring four-engine equipment, and there was little doubt the industry was heading for bigger aircraft. As far back as 1935, TWA had joined four other airlines (Eastern, Pan Am, United and American) in forming a $300,000 pool to help Douglas develop a four-engine transport. This unprecedented arrangement was forged by United's Pat Patterson who had warned his colleagues that if any single airline tried to finance such a project, "we'd go broke, one by one."

Out of the pool deal came the DC-4E (for "experimental")—a triple-tailed giant three times the size of the DC-3 and about a third heavier and larger than the Stratoliner. The DC-4E actually flew six months before the 307 made its first flight, but the Douglas entry proved to be overweight. Designed to carry forty-two passengers by day and thirty in a sleeper configuration, its test flights were disappointing. The plane was too slow and uneconomical. Eventually the design would be scaled down to the highly successful DC-4, but in mid-1938—when the Boeing/TWA contract hassle erupted—Frye had a lukewarm attitude toward the new Douglas airliner. It was not only too heavy, it was unpressurized; not one of its five sponsors was happy about its performance, and they all refused to sign firm contracts until major design improvements were made. At this stage, the 307 looked like a better airplane, but now Frye saw his chance for getting a jump on the rest of the industry going out the window.

Glumly, he and Richter watched helplessly as Hertz and his lawyers sank into a legal morass with their counterparts at Boeing. TWA's official position was that the airline still owned its Stratoliners, and Ellinger, in fact, ordered Johnny Guy back to Seattle.

"You go there and inspect those airplanes as if we owned them," he told Johnny. It was a gesture obviously dictated by Hertz, whose refusal to make progress payments had precipitated the whole mess. The quarrel could have been settled at any time if Hertz had allowed the airline to honor that payment provision; Boeing had only two 307 customers—TWA and Pan Am (which had ordered four)—and stood to lose enormously on the Stratoliner project with only ten orders on the books. When the TWA contract was canceled, the only other 307 prospect was KLM, which showed only mild interest at best, and Boeing was faced with losses on six unsold airplanes.

But Hertz was adamant, and on December 15, 1938, TWA itself formally terminated the Stratoliner contract and filed a lawsuit charging Boeing with failure to deliver its airplanes on schedule—a curious claim by a man who didn't want the 307 to begin with. Boeing promptly countersued and, in calm retrospect, probably could have won the legal battle. The first contractual violation had been TWA's failure to make the required progress payments.

It was a discouraged, disillusioned Jack Frye who greeted 1939 with the strong suspicion that he had lost control of his airline—a well-founded suspicion. The key blowup, however, came not because of Frye, but Richter. Early that year, Frye and Richter attended a directors' meeting at Hertz's home in Chicago. By then, Paul was executive vice-president (Larry Fritz had replaced him as vice-president of operations) and remained one of the few supporters Frye had on the board. Another was the young lawyer, George Spater, who also was at the meeting and remembers how the volcano erupted.

On the agenda was Richter's request to install full-feathering propellers on all TWA aircraft. When he brought up the matter, Hertz asked rather tartly, "Is it necessary?"

The short-tempered Richter took immediate offense and accused Hertz of impugning his technical expertise. A brief argument ensued, ending when Hertz adjourned the meeting so they all could go out to the race track and see a couple of his horses run.

"It was probably a rather innocuous incident," Spater adds. "I honestly don't believe Hertz meant to raise a fuss. He actually knew nothing about ropellers and probably was more interested in getting the meeting over quickly so they could go to the races. But it was the proverbial straw that broke the camel's back. Richter and Frye were furious and Frye decided to do something about the situation."

What he did was to shape TWA's destiny for the next two decades. He flew to Los Angeles and saw Howard Hughes.

Frye and Hughes had known each other for years. They were not close friends, but aviation was a common bond and the two men shared a mutual respect. Jack was aware of Hughes' almost insatiable curiosity about every phase of flying. The eccentric millionaire once, briefly in 1932, had even worked incognito as a copilot for American Airlines under the name "Charles Howard." In 1936, Hughes made his first direct contact with TWA when he bought the airline's historic DC-1, intending to fly it around the world after installing additional gas tanks and more powerful engines.

Hughes took delivery on the plane in Kansas City and flew it to New York for the modification work; TWA chief pilot Harlan Hull served as his copilot. Later, Hughes was to change his mind about using the DC-1 on a world flight, switching to a Lockheed L-14 because it was faster. He parked the DC-1 at the Burbank Airport where it sat forlornly until an airport official called Hughes and asked how long the plane was going to remain there.

"Oh, that's where I left it," Hughes chirped in his high-pitched voice. "I forgot where it was."

(He finally sold the DC-1 to an English viscount; the Britisher used it as his personal plane for several months before selling it to a French company. In 1939 "Old 300" showed up in Spain as a personnel transport for the Republican government and after the Spanish Civil War served *Sociedad Anónima de Transportes,* forerunner of today's Iberia Air Lines. In December of 1940, the world's first and only DC-1 crashed while landing at Malaga, Spain. No one was injured but the aircraft was wrecked beyond repair.)

Purchasing the DC-1 was not the only contact Hughes had with TWA in the mid-thirties. At Frye's invitation, he flew one of the airline's DC-2s, and it was apparent that he was beginning to like Frye's way of doing business— a combination of incorrigible optimism and heady planning. Actually, Howard knew Richter better than Frye; Paul had been one of the stunt pilots Hughes hired during the filming of *Hell's Angels* and they remained friends—close enough for Hughes to call Richter whenever he came to Kansas City.

He called on one special occasion, which Daisy Richter, Paul's widow, still recalls. It was the day before Thanksgiving, 1936, and Richter invited Howard to dinner. Richter mentioned that several TWA people from California were coming to dinner the next day, including Capt. Lee Flanagin, whom Hughes also knew.

"We'd like to have you, too," Richter said.

"That's very nice of you," Hughes replied politely. "I'd like to come."

He showed up late—Daisy remembers her guests had just finished antipasto—and seemed ill at ease. Mrs. Richter adds: "He kept staring at our two-year-old daughter as if she were an alien from another planet. He obviously wasn't very comfortable around children, and there were a lot of them there. Lee Flanagin had brought one of his kids, and so did several others. All Howard did was play with a sugar bowl throughout the entire dinner. He didn't talk much—mostly to Paul and Lee. He was, well, just different. But a few months later, when Paul and I were in Los Angeles, he insisted on taking us to dinner at the Tropicana, and he was absolutely charming."

In later years, Frye told trusted associates about his meeting with Hughes; unfortunately he seems to have given varying accounts. Otis Bryan, for example, says both Frye and Richter flew to Los Angeles and met Hughes at his home on a Sunday morning either late in December of 1938, or early in January of 1939; the specific date is unknown. George Spater is not sure whether Richter was present, and his account differs in some respects from Bryan's.

As reconstructed by Bryan, the scenario went like this:

"We simply can't get along with John Hertz," Frye told Hughes. "It may be our fault, but we think it's his and we can't stay. We got the idea you might be interested in buying an airline. Pacific Air Transport (which operated between Los Angeles and Seattle) is for sale—if you'd buy it, we'd run it for you."

They discussed this and other possibilities until around 3 P.M., when they broke for a late lunch. When they resumed, Hughes asked Frye, "Does Hertz own TWA?"

"He's the largest stockholder, along with Lehman Brothers in which he's a partner," Frye replied.

"Well, then," Hughes said calmly, "why don't we buy TWA?"

Frye and Richter were stunned. "We never thought of that," Frye finally said. "TWA would cost a lot of money."

"I've got the money," Hughes drawled.

He instructed Frye to compile a stockholders list, which was to be mailed to him as soon as possible.

Spater's version, based on what Frye told him, differs in that it was Frye who kept insisting Hughes buy TWA. After confiding that it was impossible to work with Hertz, Frye rejected Hughes' first offer—to buy some manufacturing company that Jack would run for him.

"I like the airline business," Frye demurred.

"I could buy United," Hughes offered.

"I like TWA," Frye said firmly—at which point the two accounts merge into agreement that Hughes then ordered Frye to send him a list of stockholders. The TWA president returned to Kansas City where he obtained the stockholders list from the corporation secretary. Behind the locked doors of his office at 10 Richards Road, Frye copied names and addresses in longhand of all persons holding three hundred or more shares. The job was so tedious and time-consuming that he asked his secretary, after swearing her to secrecy, to finish the list and mail the names to Hughes' post office box in Los Angeles.

By the end of January, Hughes had acquired about the same amount of TWA stock as Hertz and Lehman Brothers held—approximately 12 percent. He notified Frye, who promptly confronted Hertz with the *fait accompli*.

"We're ready for a proxy fight," Frye declared. "Do you want one or are you willing to sell?"

Hertz, who had no real love for TWA or the airline business, caved in almost immediately and Lehman went along. Hughes wound up with approximately 25 percent of the stock and told Frye to go ahead with the Stratoliner deal.

Reportedly, Hughes purchased some 200,000 shares at $8 a share—that is the most widely accepted figure. Therefore, he bought into TWA initially for only $1.6 million and then began acquiring additional shares until he eventually held around 78 percent of the stock. As early as 1940, however, his shares amounted to a controlling interest.

For better or for worse, and there were to be large portions of both, Howard Robard Hughes had become part of the TWA saga—bringing with him the blessing of apparently unlimited financial resources and the curse of unlimited power.

Part Two
(1939-1960)

6

A Lady Named Connie

More than a readily available checkbook arrived at TWA with Howard Hughes—as Jack Frye found out right from the start.

The most immediate cross Frye had to bear was not Hughes' penchant for dominating anything he touched but his closest associate and most trusted advisor—a small-framed, dapper-mustachioed accountant named Noah Dietrich. Since 1925, when Hughes hired him as a kind of financial guru, Dietrich had performed invaluable services for a man strangely haphazard in money matters.

In some ways, Dietrich's relationship with Hughes was like that of Richter's to Frye; Noah and Paul had more in common than their short stature. They both had financial acumen, they were intensely loyal to their respective bosses, and each served as a calming buffer zone that the volatile Hughes and Frye had to cross enroute to acting on their more farfetched schemes. Dietrich, who looked enough like Ernie Breech to be his brother, may have lacked Richter's sense of compassion, but he was just as smart, tough-minded and realistic.

Hughes' entrance into the airline business came as a complete surprise and even a shock to Noah. By his own admission, he knew nothing about the TWA stock acquisition until it was well underway. What made the deal as unpalatable to Dietrich was that buying into an airline, an ailing one at that, was probably the last thing he would have advised Hughes to do. Dietrich viewed the still struggling, immature airline industry in the same way a banker would look on a wild-eyed gold prospector. It was not the type of investment that appealed to an accountant's neat, orderly mind through which the pros and cons passed in review. There is not the slightest doubt that Dietrich, privy to so many Hughes ventures, deeply resented not being consulted on this one—perhaps the riskiest, craziest of all—which may be, of course, precisely the reason Hughes didn't consult him. Hughes wanted to get involved with an airline, and he probably felt that Dietrich could talk him out of it. Noah may have been an antidote for Howard's greatest failing—an inability to make up his mind—but in this case, Hughes *did* make up his own mind. Included in Dietrich's resentful feelings about the deal was the man he felt had unduly influenced Hughes—namely, Frye.

"The rivalry between Frye and Dietrich started early," George Spater says. Dietrich himself never made any attempt to hide his dislike for and even contempt for the TWA president. Dietrich always felt Frye was after his scalp, and he had no respect whatsoever for Frye's business abilities. In his biography, *Howard,* Dietrich couldn't resist sniping at his adversary.

"The slogan of TWA at that time [of Hughes' stock acquisition] was 'An Airline Run by Fliers,'" Dietrich wrote. "It should have been run by businessmen. TWA suffered from chronic deficits, and I believed the blame belonged to Frye and his inept management."

That was hitting in a vicinity south of the belt; Dietrich had no grounds for serious criticism of TWA's operations in the immediate prewar years. True, the airline wasn't exactly in the best of health; Bob Buck remembers flying a lot of trips "when there was nobody on the airplane but the crew."

"There was a time in late 1938," he adds, "when we used to run out and cash our paychecks as soon as we got 'em because we were afraid they'd bounce."

But if the airline was having troubles, it still had the potential for growth, and that is what Howard Hughes saved when he rescued Frye from the confining clutches of John Hertz. Noah's recollections of that period are decidedly suspect. For example, in the biography he claimed that Hughes insisted Dietrich go on TWA's board of directors immediately after the stock purchase, but that two years later he resigned at Frye's demand. This is either poor memory or pure fiction; there is no record of Dietrich serving as a TWA director in this time period; he was not named to the board until 1946, and Frye himself was gone before Noah resigned. For that matter, Hughes never served as director. As his influence on the airline grew, he began putting his own men on the board, but before the war he showed little inclination to interfere.

At this point, Frye was at quarterback, which fed Dietrich's displeasure and distrust.

"In this period," George Spater says, "Frye dominated Hughes, not the other way around. I remember once that they were planning to go to a party together. Jack told Howard if he didn't get a haircut first, he wouldn't go with him. Damned if Hughes didn't send for a barber."

Otis Bryan, too, believes Dietrich kept pressing Hughes without success to let him run TWA. Noah's insistence finally reached the point where Hughes actually asked Frye if he'd mind Dietrich taking a more active role in the airline's business.

"No!" Frye snapped. "If you want to put Dietrich between us, I'm getting out."

"Okay," Hughes sighed. "You'll report directly to me."

But the Frye-Dietrich feud went on unabated. "All through the years," Bryan says, "Dietrich sat on the sidelines, sniping at Jack, always trying to get himself into a position of power within the airline. He never really did succeed, but eventually he was to be the main force in unseating Frye."

But Frye's unseating was a long way off. In 1939, a year in which TWA showed a loss of only $188,000 (the 1938 deficit was more than $770,000), Jack Frye and Howard Hughes became a working team, which Frye, not Hughes, captained. The two men were united at first by a piece of machinery with four engines and wings—the Boeing Stratoliner. Frye's crusade to put the revolutionary airplane into TWA's service had brought them together, and the 307 was to remain not only a common bond but a significant force in the airline's future development, even though, it must be added, the plane got off to a shaky start.

On a bright Saturday afternoon in March of 1939, the second Stratoliner off the production line left Seattle on what was supposed to be a routine test flight. Aboard were a Boeing test pilot, two engineers from the Dutch airline KLM, several Boeing technicians and TWA chief pilot Harlan Hull. Somewhere in the vicinity of Mount Ranier, the plane was seen disintegrating at an altitude of between 3,000 and 5,000 feet. There were no survivors, and investigators subsequently learned that the aircraft had been undergoing stability tests with two engines shut down. The 307 apparently stalled, began a spinning dive and structural failure resulted from the attempted pullout at high speed. Boeing added a vertical fin to the rear fuselage, increased the size of the rudder and installed a slotted leading edge on the wings—all aimed at improving stability.

The destroyed Stratoliner was one of the four ordered by Pan Am, which decided it would accept only the remaining three. TWA, too, pulled back on its original order of six; it revised the contract to five 307s after Hughes agreed to buy the sixth aircraft for his personal use, putting in a plush interior including divans, armchairs and a kitchen. What Hughes wanted with an airplane that big is a mystery, but Johnny Guy believes he was considering another world flight. One of the first thing he did was install bigger engines. Years later he was to sell his 307 to Houston millionaire Glenn McCarthy who eventually sold it back to Hughes. Howard offered it to TWA as a training plane and Ed Huff, then head of line maintenance, asked Guy to look it over. Johnny did and told Huff to forget it.

"It's out of date and would cost a fortune to renovate," Guy reported. But while he was examining old N-19904, he couldn't help but notice that the cockpit looked brand-new—"like it had just come out of the factory." To Hughes it had been just another toy to be enjoyed briefly and then discarded in favor of something newer. He sold N-19904 to a Florida real estate man who removed the wings and engines and turned it into a plush, powered houseboat.

The Stratoliner was no toy to Jack Frye; he spent a fortune preparing for its introduction into TWA's system and chafed under the enforced delivery delays. TWA had planned to open transcontinental Stratoliner service by mid-1939, but the Hertz-generated contract dispute pushed this schedule back to mid-1940. One casualty of the year-long postponement was Frye's intention of having a Stratoliner flight officially open New York's LaGuardia Airport late in 1939—the nation's newest and finest airliner symbolically becoming the first transport to serve the nation's newest and finest airport. But thanks to luck and the perseverance of Captain Jack Zimmerman, TWA still won the honor of being the first airline to land a transport at the airport.

Zimmerman was commanding Flight 18, a DC-3, which originated in Burbank and flew to Newark before proceeding to LaGuardia, the final destination. The new airport was on the verge of closing down because the ceiling and visibility were dropping below the respective minimums of 500 feet and one mile. But Zimmerman sneaked in ahead of the worst weather, landing at 12:03 A.M. as LaGuardia's first commercial flight.

It was one of the few victories TWA could score over larger American and United. Although the central transcontinental route had its advantages—it was shorter than American's southern route and enjoyed better weather than United's northern one—it was not as viable as either. TWA operated under two distinct handicaps: the area it served west of Wichita was sparsely populated; and, unlike TWA, both American and United served many more eastern cities, which fed traffic into their transcontinental routes. Boston offered a good example: Boston passengers wanting to fly to the West Coast simply took American to New York where they connected with a westbound American flight. TWA could not match the convenience of this single-airline service; most of the points it served were already on the transcontinental routes.

Frye and Richter tried hard to overcome such basic deficiencies. Their route applications in 1939 aimed at putting TWA into such markets as Boston, along with San Francisco–Los Angeles authority, but another major effort was directed at the purchase of a feeder line—tiny Marquette Airlines. Marquette operated ancient Stinson trimotors, but equipment was not what Frye sought; Marquette served a route between Detroit and St. Louis via Toledo, Dayton and Cincinnati. The purchase agreement was signed in October of 1939, but it would take almost two more years before it won final government approval. This procrastination was due in large measure to President Roosevelt's second major reorganization of the civil aviation regulatory establishment. While the Civil Aeronautics Authority was still considering the TWA-Marquette deal, FDR abolished the CAA and created a new Civil Aeronautics Board whose five members had virtual control over all airline economic and safety matters from route awards and fares to revocation of pilots' licenses. At the same time, FDR established a Civil Aeronautics Administration within the Commerce Department and headed by an administrator; this new CAA had jurisdiction over air traffic control and limited safety regulations. It issued airmen's certificates, for example, but had no revocation nor suspension powers. FDR's third reform was to wipe out the independent Safety Board and assign its accident investigation responsibilities to a new Bureau of Safety within the CAB.

This was the regulatory framework in which the industry was to operate until the jet age. It was neither the best nor worst of worlds and eventually would prove tragically inadequate in the vital area of safety, but Frye and his fellow airline chiefs at the time believed the reorganization was in their best interests. They were grateful for what the original act had accomplished. Before it was passed, half the private capital invested in the U.S. air transport industry had been "irretrievably lost," according to the old CAA's 1939 report to Congress. But they also recognized the act's basic weakness: a federal agency composed of three separate but equal components was theoretically good, but a practical mess. There was much confusion among the three groups, with lines of specific authority too vaguely drawn. Congress, having created the child, didn't like the way it was growing up. By the end of 1939, the CAA had more than 5,000 employees, and critics claimed they outnumbered those of the major airlines they were regulating.

In the turmoil of reorganization, many route cases such as TWA's acquisition of Marquette were put on hold, and Frye concentrated on his own reorganization plans—namely, fleet modernization. He was trying to get rid of as many DC-2s as possible (all would be sold by 1941), and in addition to the Stratoliners, he bought three more DC-3s. He was finally able to get some semblance of an Indian motif into the five 307s by assigning tribal names to each; they were christened *Apache, Cherokee, Comanche, Navajo* and *Zuni*. And they were the first TWA airplanes to drop those three proud words that had been painted on every fuselage since the early DC-2 days: "The Lindbergh Line." The Lone Eagle had ended his official connection with TWA; it was an amicable severance. The airline had outgrown its need for his technical advice as it acquired skilled personnel of its own, and Lindbergh himself had become deeply involved with Pan Am, another airline for which he had been performing valuable technical work and one that was destined to become TWA's bitter rival in the postwar years.

In place of "The Lindbergh Line," the TWA fleet carried above their cabin windows the words "The Transcontinental Line," and they looked especially good on the bulbous fuselage of the mighty Stratoliner. No one else had a transport to match it, for the DC-4 was still years away from airline service. It will always be a mystery why American and United did not seriously consider the Boeing 307, knowing its considerable lead time over the four-engine Douglas. It may have been distrust of its bomber heritage and probably concern that it seemed to be plagued by design bugs. The Mount Ranier crash undoubtedly cost Boeing dearly in terms of turned-off prospects. The fast corrective action did little to dissuade many airlines that the 307 was suspect, for TWA itself came close to losing a Stratoliner on a proving flight from Kansas City to Albuquerque.

Otis Bryan, who had just been named system chief pilot, was the captain, and there were thirteen other TWA people aboard including Ida Staggers and two other hostesses. The women were practicing making up berths when the big plane, flying at 20,000 feet over southeastern Colorado, plunged into a vicious thunderstorm with precipitation in the form of snow, sleet and hail. Ice formed in the carburetors, choking off the air supply to the engines, and all four quit almost simultaneously. Bryan found himself fighting some 40,000 pounds of deadweight that followed the inexorable laws of gravity—straight down.

The Stratoliner came out of the overcast at 500 feet and Bryan headed for the only level terrain in sight—a small plateau with a gaping canyon at one end. The aircraft hit the ground with wheels down; the impact drove them back into their wells but also jarred loose the belly baggage compartment doors—a freak development that prevented a catastrophe. The doors acted as plows that dug into the ground, slowing down the plane, which came to a stop only 200 feet short of the canyon.

All fourteen occupants climbed out unhurt into a pouring rain, grateful to Bryan.

"I had been in rougher landings," Ida Staggers chuckles. "Otis really put that airplane down in a pasture. We were so far from any town that no reporters or photographers showed up. A couple of days later I saw a head-line in a Colorado paper: 'Huge Airliner Makes Precautionary Landing.'"

The dearth of general publicity didn't keep the industry from hearing about the incident, however; the airlines' rumor/gossip network is just as efficient as a prison grapevine. Bryan actually flew the crippled airliner off the plateau a few days after the accident after it was propped up with pieces of angle iron so the wheels could be lowered. Boeing developed a better means of preventing ice buildup in the carburetors, but on top of the test flight crash, the forced landing did the 307's reputation no good whatsoever. Detractors snidely pointed out that even at 20,000 feet, weather could still be a problem and W. E. "Swede" Golien, a colorful TWA captain of that era, commented ruefully that the Colorado mishap simply proved "that with the Stratoliner we could get high enough to get into the middle of the roughest part of a storm."

It must be added, however, that TWA's pilots admired their new big bird immensely, and the veterans still remember it with respect. Enormously strong—a Boeing trademark—it was the first land transport so large and complex that it required a three-man cockpit crew, the third member being a flight engineer who monitored engine instruments and served as a "Mr. Fixit" whenever necessary.

"It was a nice airplane to fly," Bob Buck says. "A little squirrely on the ground and the cockpit visibility was bad. From the outside, the cockpit looked like a greenhouse with its wrap-around windows, but this was misleading. The pilot seats were so far back that the windshield seemed to be at the end of a tunnel."

TWA inaugurated Stratoliner service July 8, 1940, with Otis Bryan flying the westbound inaugural out of LaGuardia with movie stars Tyrone Power and Paulette Goddard among the passengers. He landed at Burbank fourteen hours and nine minutes later after intermediate stops in Chicago, Kansas City and Albuquerque—almost four hours faster than the average DC-3 westbound schedule. Jack Zimmerman commanded the first eastbound trip, landing at LaGuardia twelve hours and thirteen minutes after taking off from Burbank; this bettered the average DC-3 eastbound transcontinental time by some three hours. Overall, the Stratoliner's transcontinental flights were about two hours faster than the DC-3's and the difference would have been even greater if TWA had operated them at higher altitudes. Most 307 trips were flown at 14,000 feet; TWA was playing it conservatively. Even so, the Stratoliner won instant popularity because 14,000 feet was sufficient to clear most of the weather.

Five airplanes, however, were not a big enough fleet to be profitable. Training costs, the addition of a third crew member and heavier-than-normal advertising and promotional expenses all combined had an adverse effect on the 307's economic viability. Designed to carry thirty-three passengers by day and sixteen in the overnight berths, and considering the small number of Stratoliners in service, the 307 actually was too small. Frye knew this and so did the man who had saved the Stratoliner program. Howard Hughes already was dreaming of building the greatest airliner in aviation history.

The most unfavorable portrait of Howard Hughes depicts him as the ultimate parasite—a man who would have disappeared into obscurity if he hadn't inherited his father's wealth and parlayed it into an even greater fortune by living ungratefully off the brains, skills and blind loyalty of others far more intelligent than himself.

Noah Dietrich tried hard to foster that image, insisting (and probably believing) that Hughes was an abysmal businessman who would have squandered away his entire fortune if men like Dietrich hadn't been around to save him from his follies and lack of real talent. To Dietrich, Hughes was a classic case of "jack-of-all-trades, master of none," a dabbler with shallow knowledge of whatever fields he dabbled in.

There is some truth in this portrayal, but even more falseness. Hughes was undeniably brilliant and enormously skilled in areas in which he had no formal training. If he had ever really tried to master totally any given subject, he would have had to have been classed as a genuine expert. He had the instincts of genius, but none of the self-discipline required for genius to bear fruit. Impulsive and impatient, demanding yet curiously indecisive, inherently suspicious but at times incongruously trustful—these all were personality traits that covered the real Howard Hughes like the facade of one of his movie sets.

It is fashionable, for example, to recall his several failures in the motion picture industry (including *The Outlaw,* which admittedly epitomized a lack of both talent and taste). Yet two other films, *Scarface* (produced by Hughes and directed by Howard Hawks) and *Hell's Angels* (which Hughes produced and directed) became all-time classics. They demonstrated a feeling for the movie medium even more remarkable when it is realized that Hughes was in his twenties and totally inexperienced when they were made. They were not the products of a leech sucking on the talents of others; they were flawed yet brilliant examples of film-making by an amateur.

He showed brilliance in his aviation ventures, too. Hughes had no background in aeronautical engineering; he had never taken a single course even in the most basic rudiments of aircraft design, yet men considered experts in this highly technical profession marveled at what he accomplished seemingly on sheer instinct for what was right and wrong. Jack Real, now president of Hughes Helicopters and a former Lockheed test pilot and engineer, knew Hughes as intimately as anyone, including Dietrich. "Howard had all the attributes of a successful aeronautical engineer," Real says. "He had a continuing inquisitiveness that he never lost. He loved everything about airplanes and engines."

"Inquisitive" indeed described Hughes. It led him to investigate new concepts, and if he couldn't always execute them, he at least conceived ideas that were fresh and often inspired. He shared with Frye a visionary mind uncluttered by fears of the new and unconventional. In that spirit, as early as 1938 and long before the first Stratoliner was delivered, they had laid before Lockheed their general criteria for a new four-engine pressurized transport that would be bigger, faster and longer-ranged than anything then flying or on any drawing board.

Inquiries also were made to Consolidated and possibly to Douglas, although whether the latter was ever approached is something of a mystery. Several historians have written that Hughes never considered contacting Douglas because Howard was supposed to be *persona non grata* with Donald Douglas. This reportedly stemmed from an incident that had occurred some years earlier when Douglas was rebuilding a racing plane for Hughes. Howard not only kept interfering with the work, so the story goes, but made impossible demands and in the end, accused Douglas of overcharging him. Douglas, in turn, supposedly swore he would never again do business with Howard Hughes.

That Hughes had been extremely difficult is most believable, but a permanent moratorium on the part of Douglas is hard to swallow. A more logical supposition is that Hughes and/or Frye did contact Douglas but were cooled off quickly by the latter's lack of interest. First, they were looking for a pressurized aircraft and Douglas at the time was lukewarm toward this concept, and secondly, Douglas was committed to the DC-4 and didn't want to take on another large-scale project. At any rate, it was Lockheed that had the inside track. Its president, Bob Gross, had been very close to Hughes for a long time, and Howard had great respect for Lockheed's two top designers, chief engineer Hall Hibbard and Clarence "Kelly" Johnson, Hibbard's imaginative young assistant. Not many years later, Johnson would achieve recognition as one of the greatest aircraft designers in the history of aviation. It was a Hibbard/Johnson-designed Lockheed Model 14 that Hughes had flown around the world in 1938 and he admired the company's design philosophy. Gross, Hibbard and Johnson brought the preliminary drawings and data on the proposed airliner to Hughes and Frye at 7000 Romaine, the stubby stucco building that housed the Hughes empire headquarters in Los Angeles. The date was June 22, 1939; the rest of the TWA delegation—Richter, Tomlinson and Jack Franklin, TWA's corporation secretary—waited at the Biltmore Hotel.

At the time, Lockheed was designing a four-engine transport for Pan American, the Excalibur, far enough advanced to have reached the wooden mockup stage. It was slightly bigger than the DC-4 and had an extremely thick wing—this due to the insistence of Andre Priester, Pan Am's chief engineer, that the plane have an internal wing catwalk so a mechanic could have access to the engines in flight. Lockheed had no plans to pressurize the Excaliber, however, and Hughes wasn't interested, although his original specifications—hammered out in hours of discussions with Frye—were for a plane of this approximate size. Kelly Johnson thought Hughes was setting his sights too low in those specs—a 40-passenger airplane with sleeping accommodations for twenty, a 3,500-mile range, a cruising speed of between 250 and 300 mph, and a payload of 6,000 pounds.

Lockheed was recommending that the plane be powered by the untried but promising Wright 3350, the largest and most powerful aircraft engine in the world, still in the testing stage. Johnson pointed out at this first meeting that such an engine would make the Hughes specifications too conservative; with the 3350, the payload could be at least doubled or even tripled and this would mean a daytime passenger capacity of up to sixty.

Hughes, who as usual showed up late for this momentous appointment, seemed impressed but went into his habitual nit-picking and had numerous suggestions for changes. Frye later was to confide to aviation writer Doug Ingells that he could never forget the way Hughes looked, sitting on the floor as if he were at an Indian peace pow-wow, finally directing a key question at Bob Gross: How much would the plane Lockheed was proposing cost?

"I'd say four hundred and fifty thousand apiece," Gross quoted.

Hughes was silent for a moment. "TWA can't pay for them," he drawled. "The damned airline's broke. We can't take it to the banks. They'd think we were nuts talking about a three hundred-mile-an-hour airplane. Hell, I guess I'll have to pay for them myself." He smiled tightly at Gross. "Go ahead and build 'em, Bob. Send the bills to the Hughes Tool Company."

Later, Frye told Ingells, they were alone and discussing what had transpired. Hughes remarked, "When we get through with 'em, Jack, we'll have one hell of an airplane!"

There were several more days of conferences before Hughes, Frye and Gross agreed on final contract details. On TWA's side, the most vital requisite was secrecy. Frye, in particular, was adamant that American and United must be kept in the dark. Both were known to be talking to Douglas about the DC-4. Let them buy that airplane, Frye reasoned, and they'd be stuck with a transport hopelessly outclassed by the new Lockheed. What Hughes had demanded and Lockheed agreed to build was an airliner capable of crossing the United States in less than ten hours. The DC-4, Frye felt, was nothing but an overgrown DC-3, and the Excalibur posed no threat in the hands of an airline with no domestic routes.

Hughes agreed to buy forty airplanes, and Lockheed, in turn, agreed to give TWA exclusive rights to the first forty planes off the assembly line. It was an $18-million contract, up to then the largest in commercial aviation history. For that sum Hughes was buying for TWA a lead time of up to two years. So great was the desire for secrecy, that Hughes refused to have the contract typed by any Lockheed employee. The typist chosen was none other than Tommy Tomlinson's wife, a court stenographer by profession; she had come to Los Angeles with Tommy and was summoned from their Biltmore room to prepare the formal papers, which specified that Hughes Tool, not TWA, was buying the planes.

Secrecy was Hughes' middle name anyway, and he even imposed code names for the handful of TWA officials aware of the project. Hughes, for example, would be known as "God," and Frye was "Jesus Christ." Also secret was the name of the airplane. Designated in the project as the 0-49, it would be called the "Constellation."

It was a mystified Johnny Guy who was called into the office of Paul Richter in the spring of 1940, shortly after the fifth Stratoliner had been delivered. Guy, his inspector's job at Boeing finished, thought he had been summoned back to Kansas City to work under Vice-President of Engineering Tomlinson. He had no inkling of any other assignment until Richter greeted him warmly and asked him to shut the door.

"Johnny," he asked without preamble, "do you have any idea of quitting TWA?"

"No, sir, Mr. Richter," the surprised Guy replied.

"Well, before I tell you what I'm going to tell you, I want you to promise that you will not leave TWA without our permission. Will you give me your word?"

"Yes, sir, I will."

Richter proceeded to tell him that Howard Hughes had signed an agreement with Lockheed to develop a large four-engine transport with great range and speed, that the contract was between Toolco and Lockheed, and that only five people in the entire Lockheed organization knew the airline that would operate it. Those five, Richter added, were Gross, Hibbard, Johnson and two engineers assigned to the secret project—Don Palmer and Paul Deprane.

"There are only four of our own people in on this," Richter continued. "Frye, Tomlinson, myself and Franklin. You're the fifth. This is why I needed your promise."

Richter went on to explain that Hughes had "shopped around" to determine what manufacturers would be willing to undertake a new transport project under such conditions of total secrecy. He mentioned that Consolidated, designer of the four-engine B-24 bomber, had shown tentative interest but was unwilling to make the commitment Lockheed had. Guy, he said, would act as a coordinator between Hughes and Frye on one hand, and Lockheed on the other.

"Basically you'll be dealing with Mr. Hughes," Richter explained, "but you'll have to keep Jack Frye informed of all developments. Go out to Burbank and rent a house there. It has to have a large room you can use as an office. You must make sure there's nobody living on either side of you or across the street who works for Lockheed."

Guy's eyebrows shot up to full staff. "Mr. Richter," he protested, "that's a hell of an order. Almost everybody in Burbank works for Lockheed."

"Well, that's what they want," Richter said. "And that's not all, Johnny. To offset any possibility that someone might suspect what you're doing, the word Lockheed will be stricken from your vocabulary. You are not to mention that name in any correspondence. If you send a technical report to Hughes and Frye, and Lockheed's name appears anywhere in that report, take a razor or sharp scissors and remove it before you send in the report."

"If anyone asks what I'm doing in Burbank, what the hell am I supposed to tell 'em?"

"We've got more DC-3s on order. Officially, you're going out to Douglas as our factory representative. And you'll really be working at that job. At night and on weekends, you'll do your liaison work for Hughes and Frye."

"I had a hell of a time finding a house," Guy relates. "I finally rented one with nobody from Lockheed on either side or across the street, but I learned later that the guy in back of me worked for Lockheed. It was like being with the CIA. Richter warned me I couldn't even tell my wife and family what I was really doing in Burbank."

The house he rented was at 938 Cyprus Street. Lockheed would send Guy all data, drawings and engineering reports to that address in care of the Hughes Tool Company. He dutifully used a razor blade to excise any mention of Lockheed. This was to prevent anyone who broke into the files from knowing what they were all about. In his correspondence with Frye and Hughes, Guy used only initials, not names; it was "Dear H." or "Dear F." and Johnny signed his letters "G."

His contacts at Lockheed were Palmer and Deprane, the two Constellation project engineers. "Sometimes I'd have to meet them at night, so we'd go down to Griffith Park and find some secluded spot, or they'd come to my house. If it was necessary to see them in the daytime, I'd have to make up some excuse to leave the Douglas plant on an imaginary errand."

Such alibis didn't sit well with TWA people who knew nothing of Guy's moonlighting mission. Bill Hughes, the airline's superintendent of maintenance at the Burbank airport, would call Johnny at Douglas asking help in expediting of a spare DC-3 part. Invariably he was told that Guy was at such-and-such a company on business, but when Bill called that company, Guy was never there. They met at the TWA hangar one day and Bill announced that he was fed up.

"You little bastard," he snarled, "you're always fucking off some place!"

Guy's contacts with Hughes were in person as well as via the telephone and mail; they never became close friends but did achieve mutual admiration, and to this day Johnny Guy bristles when he hears a disparaging remark about Hughes.

"It was Hughes who footed the payroll more than once," Guy says with a touch of anger. "And if it hadn't been for those Boeings he saved, it's possible we never would have been an international carrier. Because when the war came along, we and Pan Am were the only airlines with airplanes capable of flying the Atlantic, and that's where we got our experience."

Yet Guy was not blind to his hero's faults. "Howard was nuttier than a fruitcake in many ways," he admits. "Eccentric and demanding as hell. The funny thing was, though, that he treated small fry like me just fine. The bigger a guy was the more disdain he showed and the worse he got."

They got to know each other well enough for Hughes to insist that Guy call him by his first name. Their common bond was Hughes' insistence on total secrecy and Guy's ability to follow all keep-your-mouth-shut orders.

"If you ever hear anything indicating that somebody knows about the project, let me know immediately," he once told Guy, who privately considered the elaborate precautions somewhat farcical. His censorship duties—eliminating any mention of Lockheed from every piece of correspondence—could get tiresome. If he had to send a parts list to Hughes, a component might be labeled "LAC Standard"—meaning it was a regular Lockheed Aircraft Corporation part. The letters "LAC" had to be removed from the document and Johnny says, "Some of the drawings looked like a piece of Swiss cheese when I sent 'em in."

Like everyone with whom Hughes did business, Guy was exposed to his habit of making phone calls at hours when most normal people were in bed. "He'd call at two A.M., wanting to talk to me about some design detail or data I had sent him. His main areas of interest were the cockpit layout and the cabin decor—colors and so forth."

Eventually, the project reached mockup stage. Lockheed built a full-size cabin with a complete cockpit, locating it in a large and secluded shed surrounded by a wire fence. The first showing was scheduled at Hughes' request for a Sunday at 5:00 A.M. Bob Gross, Frye, Tomlinson and Guy were present, as well as Lockheed's interior design specialist. Hughes showed up two hours late, unshaven and wearing sneakers. He entered the mockup without saying a word, and looked up and down the ersatz cabin. Only then did he speak.

"Hey, Jack," he yelled to Frye. "I don't like this. I don't like this interior at all. Get Raymond Loewy out here right away and tell him to style this damned thing."

End of mockup meeting. Hughes left without saying another word. Loewy was summoned and spent more than two weeks working with Lockheed on new interior color schemes and decor. Guy, who knew him from the DC-3 interior decorating days, called him periodically so he could relay progress reports to Hughes. One Saturday night Johnny reached Loewy in his room at the Beverly Hills Hotel and was told the decorating job was finished.

"I'm going back to New York tomorrow on your nine A.M. flight," Loewy said. "I'll return here in a couple of weeks and see the mockup results."

At 3:00 A.M. Sunday, Guy's phone rang; it was Hughes.

"Johnny, how's Ray Loewy doing?"

"Well, he's all through. He's turned his sketches over to Lockheed and he'll go back east this morning."

"Tell you what I want you to do. Bring him over to my house Monday afternoon at five."

Guy couldn't believe what he had heard. "Howard, he's leaving this morning and I don't think he can hang around."

"I want to see him. I have something I must show him."

"Look, he told me he has a meeting with the Studebaker car people Monday."

"I still want you to bring him over. Tell him I said so."

"I'll do my best," Guy said.

Loewy was packed and ready to leave the hotel when Guy called him at 7:00 A.M. to break the news. A calm and gracious man, Loewy wasn't happy but hid his justified indignation. "I don't know, Johnny," he protested mildly, "that Studebaker meeting is very important to me."

"So is a meeting with Hughes," Guy pointed out with some desperation.

"What does he want?"

"I wouldn't know. All he said was that he had something to show you."

Loewy agreed to make some phone calls in an effort to reschedule the Studebaker session. He contacted Guy about an hour later and reported that he had made the necessary arrangements. Monday afternoon, Guy picked Loewy up at the Beverly Hills and drove him to Hughes' home. A butler admitted them and asked that they sit in the living room. They did—for two hours. Hughes marched in at seven o'clock, shirt tails out and the inevitable sneakers on his feet.

"Johnny, you bring Ray back at nine," he ordered, and left.

Loewy and Guy went to the Brown Derby for supper and returned to the house promptly at nine. They waited two more hours for Hughes to appear and when he finally did, he was carrying a huge picture; he had drawn a rendition of some airliner seats.

"This is what I want for the Constellation," he said.

Patiently, Loewy tried to explain what he had done with the Constellation's interior and why these seats didn't fit the decor. Hughes merely nodded and left the room without further comment.

The whole episode provided a classic example of Howard's *modus operandi*. He was unreasonable but not deliberately mean; he simply had tunnel vision when he got involved with anything—a single-minded fixation on whatever he wanted at any given time, to the total exclusion of everything else including awareness that other people might be greatly inconvenienced by what was too often a whim.

The Loewy incident, however, was just an aberration when viewed in the context of Hughes' overall role in the Constellation program. It is not true that he designed the airplane, as so many chroniclers of the Hughes legend have written, but the overall concept was his. Hughes himself liked to take credit for the basic design and used to argue the point with Kelly Johnson, who really did design it. The tapering, graceful shark-shaped fuselage, the triple tail—these two instant-identification features of the plane everyone came to call the "Connie" emerged from Johnson's fertile brain. Some writers have credited Hughes with designing the wing but this, too, is untrue. The Connie's wing was an enlarged version of the one used on Lockheed's twin-engine fighter, the P-38, and Kelly also was the father of that famed warplane.

But it is equally true that the Connie might never have been, or at least would not have been built as soon as it was, if not for Hughes. That accolade never satisfied Howard. He was complaining to Jack Real once that he had more to do with the Constellation design than Johnson. Real laughed.

"Howard," he said, "you conceived it and Kelly designed it."

"I don't understand the difference," Hughes grumbled.

"Believe me, there's a big difference. What if I can get Kelly to admit that you conceived it and he designed it?"

"I'd have to know what the difference is," Hughes insisted—and Real was never able to explain it to him.

He should well have been satisfied with the conception credit, for he really worked at that job. It was not a case of pulling a few performance figures out of a hat and demanding, "Build me a plane that'll achieve those figures." For months before the crucial June 22 meeting in Los Angeles, he conferred constantly with Frye, Richter and Tomlinson over the specifications, making sure they matched TWA's needs, route structure and marketing potential. On one occasion he kept Frye on the telephone for eight hours dictating or discussing ideas he had for the plane; some were on the wild side (such as a lavatory in the first airplane for his exclusive use), but Frye admitted that some "also made a lot of sense."

Aviation reporter Doug Ingells once asked Bob Gross how much of Howard Hughes went into the Connie. Gross conceded that Hughes contributed a lot to the cockpit configuration, the control boost system (the 0-49 was the first transport to have fully hydraulically boosted controls like power steering on an automobile) and a number of interior details. One of the interior details involved the curtains for the sleeping berths; Lockheed was going to install them with zippers until Hughes objected and demanded that they use large buttons.

"Who the hell wants to get it caught in a zipper?" was his explanation.

Gross told Ingells:

"We had our ups and downs. But as the project moved along, we began to respect some of his ideas and he ours. Howard had more in-born engineering ability and know-how about systems and instruments than anyone gave him credit for, and he had a human-engineering touch that gave the plane a lot of personality. He gave a lot more to the effort than the dollar sign."

While TWA's future took the shape of a triple-tailed aluminum beauty, its present was not that rosy. Before 1940 was over, the airline would suffer another loss—more than $232,000—which was a far worse showing than in 1939. The reported loss of $186,000 for 1939 had been turned into a profit of some $107,000 due to adjusted mail revenues. But Frye remained optimistic. He attributed the red ink to many factors—the expenses involved in the Stratoliner's introduction, the cost of leasing Marquette's St. Louis–Detroit route while awaiting CAB approval of outright purchase, and heavy advertising and operational outlays involved in the hotly competitive New York–Chicago market. TWA now had nonstop authority but for years had operated under restrictions that enabled American and United to establish firm dominance; there was a lot of lost time to make up.

Not all the statistics were gloomy. In 1940, TWA carried slightly over 256,000 passengers—a whopping 57 percent increase from 1939. For all of its financial troubles, TWA was achieving a reputation for technical excellence, good service and unrelenting commitment to safety—all of which attracted passengers but also cost money. One little statistic is significant: in 1939, TWA operated almost 97 percent of its scheduled miles but less than 94 percent the following year. The explanation for that drop lay partially in the establishment of more conservative operating standards for 1940; Frye insisted on higher ceilings, greater visibility and better enroute weather before allowing a flight to be dispatched.

And he kept modernizing the fleet. The fifteen new DC-3s he ordered in the spring of 1940 were to carry twenty-four instead of twenty-one passengers, and they were to be equipped with more powerful engines, which also would be retrofitted on all current DC-3s. Such plans, however, ran afoul of gathering war clouds. Shortly after the contract with Douglas was signed, the government's new Priorities Board ordered restrictions on the delivery of commercial transports to the airlines. By the end of 1940, only four of the fifteen DC-3s on order had been released to TWA. Furthermore, the burgeoning defense effort threatened the whole structure of secrecy so carefully erected around the Constellation.

Lockheed officials were informed that a military task force was touring all aircraft factories to assess production capabilities and determine what commercial contracts they were obligated to fulfill. Hall Hibbard broke the news to Johnny Guy.

"We've got a problem," he warned. "They'll be in Southern California in ten days to two weeks. We can't keep this thing buttoned up much longer. We'll have to show them what we've got, so you'd better get hold of Howard."

Guy reached Hughes by the usual indirect route, phoning the Romaine office and leaving word for Hughes to call him back. Howard, as Johnny remembers it, took the setback calmly, but calmness was not his only reaction. Knowing that he couldn't expect the military to keep the Constellation under wraps for the benefit of TWA's competitive position, he made an unusual deal with Bob Gross.

The Lockheed president, a man of unimpeachable integrity, always had misgivings about designing the Excalibur for Pan Am while simultaneously and covertly working on a vastly superior transport for TWA. It did not seem ethical, and he discussed this frankly with Hughes who—not dreaming that TWA would someday be challenging Pan Am internationally—agreed to let Juan Trippe's airline into the Constellation project. In return, he exacted a promise from Gross not to sell the Connie to any U.S. airline with east-west domestic routes that competed with TWA. Thus, Lockheed would be allowed to offer the new plane to Eastern and Braniff, both north-south operators, but not American or United. It was an arrangement that greatly inhibited Lockheed's future sales, but also one rendered moot by Pearl Harbor; nobody but the Army was going to fly a Constellation until the war was over.

That "day of infamy" was six months away when Frye literally enlisted

TWA in the Air Corps. One day in May 1941, he called in Otis Bryan and confided he had just met with General Hap Arnold, chief of the Army Air Corps.

"Arnold's told me too many ferry pilots flying bombers to England are going down in the ocean," Frye said. "It's lack of experience, so Arnold wants us to start a training school. Teach 'em crew coordination and turn out some better-trained pilots and navigators. Otis, you go out and find us a training site."

Bryan took Frye's own plane, a Lockheed L-14, and toured the country before finally settling on Albuquerque; New Orleans was his second choice. Within weeks the school, dubbed "Eagle Nest," was in operation. Bryan took several TWA pilots off the line for instructors (they included Hal Blackburn, assigned to Eagle Nest as superintendent of instrument flight training, and Swede Golien, who headed four-engine transition training) and immediately ran into a problem: they could fly, but they had trouble communicating with their green students.

"Like most pilots in those days," Bryan says, "all they knew was how to fly an airplane, and that was true of ninety-nine out of a hundred. They didn't have the slightest idea how to teach—to relate to and communicate with students. I had taken a three-year course in public speaking and after a week of watching our guys talking to classes, I knew we were in for a disaster. So I contacted my old speech professor and got him out to Albuquerque to give a crash course for our instructors."

Blackburn, an articulate man, didn't need to be taught, but most of his brethren were reluctant orators. The professor insisted that each pilot be able to stand up in front of the class and talk extemporaneously for five minutes—a chore that ranked slightly below structural failure on their list of unpleasant experiences. Frank Busch, informed that he had to take the speech course, complained to Blackie:

"Well, we sailed across the Atlantic, we've flown across the Atlantic, and now we're gonna talk our way across."

But the professor managed to impart enough elocutionary skills for the boys to get their messages across. This in itself was no easy task because most of their pupils were raw youngsters. One of Eagle Nest's major assignments was to provide pilot and flight engineer instruction in four-engine equipment to greenhorns who had logged as little as seventy-five hours in twins. Blackie was in charge of a B-24 training flight one night and asked the baby-faced flight engineer trainee, "How's it going?"

"I don't know, sir."

"Well, does everything look okay?"

"I think so, sir."

"You *think* so?" Blackie demanded. "Don't you know?"

"Sir," the trainee confessed, "this is my first airplane ride."

No airline was better prepared for the aftermath of December 7 than TWA, but this was due not only to Frye's foresight, but that of Edgar Gorrell, president of the Air Transport Association. Shortly after Pearl Harbor, Franklin Roosevelt signed an executive order nationalizing the entire airline industry for the duration of the war. Fortunately for the carriers, FDR informed Gorrell of the document before putting it into effect, and the ATA chief raced to the White House.

Gorrell, a tough ex-Army colonel himself, bluntly told Roosevelt he didn't need to take over the airlines if all he wanted was an efficient military air transportation system. As far back as 1936, Gorrell had warned the industry it might be nationalized if war ever came and that it needed to set up an alternative. In essence, his plan was to create a civil air reserve that could be turned over to the military virtually overnight, furnishing not only transport aircraft, but ground and flight crews as well. Gorrell kept updating the plan almost to the eve of Pearl Harbor, and it was a ready-made blueprint for voluntary airline mobilization that he handed the president. Roosevelt listened carefully and then, with that ingratiating grin of his, tore up the executive order before Gorrell's eyes.

Even without nationalization, the airlines knew it was not going to be business-as-usual. Of the industry's fleet of 378 planes, more than 200 were taken over by the military—all in accordance with Gorrell's plan. TWA alone lost about half its fleet, incuding the five Stratoliners that Frye, in a burst of patriotism mixed with far-seeing acumen, already had agreed to turn over to the military's Air Transport Command before they were commandeered. By this action he incurred the gratitude of the War Department, which said TWA could keep more DC-3s than the airline normally would have been allowed under Gorrell's mobilization schedule. The Army conceded that by giving up five Stratoliners, TWA was providing the equivalent of ten twin-engine planes.

Hap Arnold wanted those five 307s desperately. As America entered World War II, the airlines possessed only fourteen commercial-type aircraft capable of flying the ocean and the military none. Six were Pan Am's huge but lumbering Boeing 314 flying boats, and the other eight were TWA's and Pan Am's Stratoliners. TWA, in other words, had the greatest number of transatlantic land planes and the crews to operate them.

On December 24, 1941, Jack Frye signed one of the most important documents in the airline's history—DAW 535 ac-1062, which directed TWA "to hire and train all personnel, procure necessary facilities, materials and supplies, and to secure necessary certificates of convenience and necessity, licenses and permits essential to providing air service on a worldwide basis for the United States Army."

The contract was the direct result of meetings Frye had held as early as December of 1940, when he saw both General Arnold and Robert Lovett, assistant secretary of war for air. In that first meeting he had told them that if war came, TWA's Stratoliners would be available to the government. When war did come, TWA still was the only domestic airline operating four-engine equipment; it was obvious what had to be done next.

On the same day the War Department contract was signed, Frye established the Intercontinental Division (ICD) of TWA to operate the services required under DAW 535 ac-1062. Thus, under wartime pressures and the uncertainties of a global conflict yet to be fought and won, he laid the foundations for his airline's future as an international carrier.

7

TWA Goes to War

Off they marched, men and machines. Within a year after Pearl Harbor, more than eight hundred TWA employees had gone into military service, and these included key management personnel. Paul Richter joined the Navy as a commander in the Naval Air Transport Service. Tommy Tomlinson went back into the Navy as a captain in the Training Command. Larry Fritz became a colonel in the Air Transport Command. Chairman of the Board T.B. Wilson departed to serve as General MacArthur's chief of transportation, and Walt Hamilton left for the Navy.

The fleet was decimated. Early in 1942, the government reneged on its agreement to let TWA have additional DC-3s as replacements for the Stratoliners; it received exactly zero and lost most of the ones it had ordered originally, thus reducing the fleet to approximately half its former size. But there were no complaints; TWA was in no worse shape than any other airline.

The five Stratoliners were gutted. Even the pressurization systems were removed to save weight as the 307s were converted into combined cargo and personnel-carrying aircraft with four auxiliary fuel tanks installed between the cockpit and cabin. Off came the proud red tail stripes and fuselage lettering, replaced by the Army's olive drab. The surviving DC-3s got a facelift, too; in place of "The Transcontinental Line" appeared the lettering "Victory Is in the Air—Buy Bonds."

The new ICD Division went to war in a hurry. It was set up hastily in makeshift quarters at Washington's new National Airport, which had opened only six months before Pearl Harbor. Otis Bryan had been named to run ICD—out of a room on the second floor of National's terminal building. The assignment came as a surprise to Otis. He had been at Eagle Nest overseeing the training program and decided to go home to Kansas City for Christmas.

He landed in Kansas City at about 6:00 A.M. and was greeted by a secretary from Frye's office.

"Mr. Frye wants to see you," she informed him.

"I'm tired and pretty grubby," Bryan said. "Let me get cleaned up first."

"No, he wants to see you right now, Captain Bryan."

Bryan sighed resignedly and went to Frye's office. There the president broke the news that he had signed over the Stratoliners to the Air Corps. "They want someone to set up a group to operate them between Washington and Cairo," Frye continued. "We don't have much time. Rommel's kicking the hell out of the British in Egypt and Montgomery's running short of proximity fuses for his artillery shells. That'll be our first load, and we're already stripping the 307s and installing extra fuel tanks."

"Okay with me," Bryan said. "Who's going to run this outfit?"

"You are. By the way, what the hell are you doing in Kansas City?"

"I thought I'd go quail hunting down in the Ozarks for a week," Bryan confessed.

Frye chuckled. "You can take my plane down there and go quail hunting for one day. Then get your ass back here and start the Cairo operation. You'll be based in Washington."

In two months Bryan had ICD organized and ready to move. Frye, who had decided to maintain an office in the capital for the duration, had invited all five members of the Civil Aeronautics Board to witness the dun-colored Stratoliner *Navajo,* loaded with proximity fuses, depart February 26, 1942, on the first flight. Typically, Bryan had assigned himself to command the first ICD mission, which had required the issuance of a temporary certificate from the CAB; even in wartime, TWA needed to comply with the bureaucratic red tape that granted official authority to fly to Egypt.

Someone asked Bryan if this would be the first time he had ever been out of the United States.

"Second time," Bryan said blandly. "I spent a week in Mexicali once."

Seventeen days later, Bryan was back at his ICD desk, the historic trip having earned a "well done" from Hap Arnold. The crew deserves mention: Milo Campbell, an ex-cowboy, was the first officer; Don Terry and Bill Noftsinger, second officers; Pete Redpath, chief navigator; W.R. Shook, radio operator and R.L. Proctor, flight engineer. The flight had taken them from Washington to Cairo via West Palm Beach; Puerto Rico; Belem and Natal in Brazil; Monrovia, Liberia; Accra and Kano in Nigeria and Khartoum. Bryan insisted on operating a survey as well as cargo mission, which is why the roundtrip took seventeen days. All along the route, Bryan conferred with Army personnel, gaining information on operational problems so he could establish future procedures and standards. He had no way of knowing how incredible that future would be. The *Navajo*'s flight was the first of nearly 10,000 wartime Atlantic crossings by TWA alone, compiling more than 15.6 million logged miles. Before the war ended, forty-three crew members were to lose their lives in nine crashes—none of them, incidentally, involving the Stratoliners. ICD's personnel was to reach a maximum of slightly over 1,700 persons at the height of its operations in 1944—more than TWA's total employment in 1939.

One of Bryan's first tasks was to hire radio operators and navigators. Most of the earlier navigators had come off ships. The flight engineers largely were drawn from the ranks of the mechanics. One of them, Ray Dunn, was to miss narrowly becoming president of TWA one day. Dunn, an aeronautical engineer who couldn't find work after leaving school, was hired by TWA as a mechanic in 1935. When the Stratoliner joined the fleet, Dunn was in the first flight engineers' class—one of five who survived the course from the thirty who began it. After flying the line for several months, he was named chief flight engineer and was assigned to Eagle Nest as an FE instructor. He was there on December 7, 1941, and remembers seeing a 30-caliber machine gun mounted on the roof of the hangar housing the training school when word of the Japanese attack reached Albuquerque.

Dunn flew a couple of 307 trips before taking over a new industrial engineering section at ICD, but he was only one of several on TWA's wartime payroll destined for future fame. The copilot on the first North Atlantic flight was Floyd Hall, Eastern's future president. Bob Rummell, who would be closely linked to Howard Hughes, joined TWA in 1943 as a young engineer under Jack Franklin.

The war also brought TWA's first male flight attendants since the TAT trimotor days. They were hired as pursers for the ICD trips that carried passengers, solely because the War Department adamantly refused to let hostesses work these flights. "We've got guys in places like Africa and Greenland who haven't seen a woman in two years," an Army official told Frye, who thereupon ordered Cliff Mutchler, in charge of cabin crews, to go find some men.

Mutchler's most available source was Eastern, the only major domestic airline that had refused to hire women. Captain Rickenbacker gave TWA grudging approval to hire men only because he knew Eastern had stewards about to be drafted and who would have to leave anyway. So ICD's first pursers were a half-dozen Eastern stewards extremely happy to be recruited; ICD was an honorable way out of the draft and its pay scale was considerably higher than that of the rather parsimonious Captain Eddie. One of the first EAL men hired, Russ Robbins, had first-hand knowledge of Rickenbacker's tight-fisted operation.

Russ had been a bellhop in Miami, making as much money in one day as his father made in a month. But the work was boring, and he quit to join Eastern at $80 a month. When TWA offered him an ICD job, Russ consulted with Don Avery, then EAL's director of customer service.

"How much do you think I should ask for?" he inquired.

"I'll tell you the same thing I'm telling everyone else," Avery advised. "Don't sign on for less than three hundred a month."

TWA proposed a starting figure of $150 and then agreed to $200, a sum that was not only satisfactory but downright seductive. At the time, Eastern was paying its stewards only $85 and the meal allowance was a dollar a day. A later recruit from EAL, Buddy Ledger, still marvels at how they existed on that allowance:

"All the stewards in Miami used to go to this little chili joint, where you got all the chili you could eat and all the Cokes you could drink for twenty-five cents. I used to go over there at ten in the morning with the other guys. We'd bring newspapers and magazines to read and we'd sit there all day eating chili and drinking Cokes. Along about noon the owner would come up and tell us we had to get out because the lunch crowd was coming. We'd say that's okay because we'll have chili for lunch, too. We'd read, play cards and shoot the breeze until five when we'd all have chili for supper. When TWA offered me a job, it was like finding a million bucks—almost three times the salary and a chance to fly overseas."

Ledger was hired after TWA had exhausted its supply of Eastern's draft-eligible men and was casting about for fresh bodies. His recruiter was Ernie Belshaw, whose own association with TWA had been quite fortuitous. Buddy was flying for Eastern, based in New York, and happened to live across the street from Belshaw. He saw Ernie sitting on his front steps one day, reading an EAL manual, and walked over.

"I'm with Eastern," he announced, "a steward. I couldn't help noticing your manual."

"I was just hired," Belshaw confided. "Matter of fact, I'm taking my first flight out today, down to Miami. The only trouble is, I haven't gotten my uniform yet."

"How can you work a flight out of uniform?" Buddy asked.

"Oh, I think the chief steward here is gonna lend me his."

Belshaw departed for Miami wearing his chief's uniform, which had enough hash marks on it to satisfy a South American general. It so happened that one of his passengers was TWA's Mutchler, who inquired about the stripes, which looked like a lined football field.

"Years of faithful service," Ernie assured him.

They landed in Miami where the chief steward at that base immediately spotted Belshaw in his borrowed uniform, and refused to believe it was acquired on loan. "You're fired," was his verdict and Belshaw headed back to New York the next day in disgrace. On the same plane was Mutchler, unaware of Ernie's severely demoted status. They got talking and Cliff asked, "How would you like to work for TWA?"

Negotiations were quickly concluded and Belshaw immediately went over to Ledger's house.

"Two things just happened to me," he said. "I got fired by Eastern and hired by TWA. I'm going to Washington tomorrow and fly overseas."

Buddy offered to intercede for him at Eastern, but Ernie declined. "The hell with them, this TWA job sounds great."

A few days later, Belshaw phoned Ledger. "How would you like to come over to TWA?"

"You're nuts," Buddy said.

"Nope. Mr. Mutchler says they need pursers for their overseas flights. You'll get two hundred and fifty bucks a month. I've already talked to him and he says to hire you."

Ledger departed forthwith for Washington where Belshaw greeted him with more warmth than the occasion demanded. Why was quickly ascertained.

"We have to write a manual for pursers," Ernie declaimed. "Nobody's ever gotten around to doing one, and this Mutchler thinks I know everything there is to know about the airlines. Hell, you know more than I do."

Actually, Belshaw was being a bit modest. He had once worked as a steward for a steamship line and was no stranger to travel service needs. But he knew little about the airlines and turned the manual writing job over to Ledger who then knew little about TWA.

"We sat down with an Eastern manual and copied it just about word for word," Buddy admits. "All we did was substitute 'TWA' for 'Eastern' whenever necessary and nobody ever caught on."

The need for more pursers increased as TWA's overseas operations expanded. One month after the inaugural Cairo flight, Arnold asked TWA to start flying the North Atlantic, and Bryan assigned three of the Stratoliners to this route—from the East Coast to England and beyond via Gander and Prestwick, Scotland. By fall, TWA was flying new C-54s, the military version of the DC-4, which would have been in airline service by now except for the war. It was a grim reminder to Frye of how close they had come to wiping out the competition with the Connie, which also could have been in service by 1942. But if the DC-4 was inferior to Lockheed's new giant, it was superior in many respects to the gallant Stratoliner.

The Douglas plane was about 50 mph faster, roomier and quieter; it had a tricycle landing gear, the first U.S. airliner to have this feature, whereas the 307 had a conventional single gear like the DC-3. The latter created problems on the heavily loaded ICD contract flights, for the Stratoliner was nose-heavy anyway and the problem was even worse in the military configuration, primarily due to the four extra gas tanks in the forward fuselage. On many 307 flights, nobody in the cabin could sit down during takeoff. All passengers and nonflying crew members would stand as close to the cockpit as possible; it was the only way to get the tail off the ground during the takeoff roll.

"Approximately an hour after takeoff," Russ Robbins recounts, "they'd start returning to their seats in order of rank. If there was a general on board, he'd be the first to sit down. After about two hours, everybody finally got a seat. But if you had to go to the john, which was in the rear section, somebody else had to go forward to balance the trim. That Stratoliner was really something. You never took off like in a normal airplane. You just bounced and bounced until it bounced high enough to raise the gear."

On Robbins' first crossing, he had fourteen crew members (including relief pilots and pilot trainees) and eight passengers aboard a Stratoliner. They were scheduled to leave National Airport at 8:00 A.M., and Robbins reported at 6:30 for a familiarization briefing. He had never seen a Stratoliner before. Fran Mann, a TWA commissary manager, walked him through the airplane once, emphasizing the galley with its cooking utensils, pots and pans and three hot plates.

"Where's the food?" Russ asked.

"There isn't any on board," Mann said. "You're the guy responsible for buying it."

There wasn't time to go grocery shopping, but Robbins talked a soft-hearted Army mess sergeant out of some meat and bread so he could make sandwiches enroute to Gander, a flight of nearly nine hours. At Gander he scrounged additional supplies to last until Prestwick, Scotland, fifteen and a half hours away; the heavily loaded Stratoliner averaged only 130 mph. Robins continues:

"After that, we pursers would spend most of our layovers buying food for our next flight. Some of it was hard to get; you needed ration coupons for sugar, for example, and TWA didn't have any coupons to give us. We'd go from store to store bargaining and begging, picking up whatever we could. Inevitably we had to rely on the black market. One thing in plentiful supply was canned fruit cocktails, which you could buy in large cans. Occasionally we'd acquire a black market turkey, chicken or ham. I'd take it home and my landlady would let me cook the night before a flight. I used a file cabinet to pack the food, and I'd take the cabinet out to the airport the next day."

The pursers' expense accounts went to Walt Menke. An accountant by training, he had joined TWA in 1940 as an assistant to a district sales manager and when war came, was assigned to ICD's finance section. The pursers liked the tall, easygoing Menke, who never questioned a single expense account even though the cost of black market food was astronomical. Years later, Robbins asked Walt why he had been so tolerant.

"Hell," Menke replied, "I knew you didn't have ration çoupons and had to buy that stuff illegally. Besides, the ICD contract was on a cost plus ten percent basis; if you spent five dollars, the company made fifty cents."

Ledger's first ICD assignment was on a C-54 flying personnel to Prestwick. They stopped at Nova Scotia to pick up a number of survivors from a ship torpedoed off Newfoundland—all construction engineers heading for a project in Greenland. Being torpedoed didn't scare them nearly as much as the prospect of flying over the ocean to Greenland.

"It wasn't a case of transporting them," Ledger says, "it was a case of dragging 'em on that airplane. We even needed MPs to help us, they were so scared."

Another purser who joined TWA at the time was Carlyle Smith. He had been a steward with Hanford Airlines and when war came, he went to work for North American in Kansas City building B-25 bombers and also serving as night bell captain in the Continental Hotel. TWA maintained a suite at the hotel, which Howard Hughes used whenever he came to see Frye.

"He wasn't as eccentric in those days as he was later," Smith says, "but he still never carried any money and wore those tennis shoes. If he had to go any place special, he didn't have a clean shirt so I'd go down to a little store, buy a shirt for a couple of bucks and charge Hughes ten.

"After I heard he had bought into TWA, I went to his room one night, knocked on the door and started talking to him. I told him I had been a steward with Hanford but lost my job when the Army took most of our planes and that I'd like to go with TWA. Hughes said he didn't know what he could do but would try. A few weeks later I got a letter with a two hundred dollar check and a ticket to Washington. I never saw Howard Hughes again."

The third plane TWA acquired for the ICD operations was the C-87, actually a B-24 Liberator bomber converted into a transport. It was big, ugly and lumbering and the pilots hated it. The C-87 had a reputation for catching fire with unnerving ease; it had a fuel transfer system on the rear wing spar visible from the cabin, with a little gutter that was supposed to carry any spilled fuel overboard. But on top of that wing section was all the radio equipment and a single spark could ignite the fuel.

Hal Blackburn flew C-87s occasionally and says, "If you lit a cigarette it could blow up." Otis Bryan agrees. "Throw a rock at one and you could set it on fire," Bryan swears. He wasn't kidding; the fuel gauges on the cockpit instrument panel were simply tiny windows through which the pilots could see the gas level. If something broke the glass—and it could be as accidental as hitting it with a foot—fuel would spray all over the flight deck. TWA lost a C-87 on a flight between Natal and Ascension Island and the wreckage was never found. Hal Blackburn to this day believes the aircraft simply exploded.

Long before the U.S. surgeon general issued the now routine warning message about cigarettes, the ICD crews found out that smoking could be hazardous to one's health. Carlyle Smith was working a C-54 flight commanded by Virg Elliott who, as was the custom, seldom objected if any high-ranking brass or civilian VIPs visited the cockpit. On this flight a passenger was up front with the crew and took out a cigar to light. Someone suggested it would be better to drop into the nose wheel well and smoke it down there so the fumes wouldn't bother anybody.

The passenger complied, but a few minutes later called up to Smith, who had entered the cockpit.

"Hey, Smitty, is it raining?"

"Raining?" the mystified pursur asked.

"I'm getting all wet," the VIP replied.

Smith looked down and almost had a coronary. They were in the middle of a fuel tank transfer and one of the fuel lines was leaking gas all over the cigar smoker. They got him out of the well in a hurry and no cigar has ever been extinguished so fast.

In the pioneering phases of ICD, TWA was required to operate aircraft without radio navigational aids. Only celestial navigation was allowed, and radio silence had to be observed except in approaching a land base, when an ICD flight could use radio for finding directions, reporting locations and answering recognition challenges. The reason was simple: the Germans monitored the airways constantly. For a time, TWA substituted for radio a device called the Aldis lamp, a kind of oversized flashlight that looked like a gun and was fired by a trigger. Its brilliant Morse code flashes could be mistaken for machine gun blasts and more than one ICD plane drew anti-aircraft fire as a result. One C-54, flown by Capt. C.S. Garber, apparently flashed a recognition signal with the Aldis lamp while flying over a convoy. It was promptly jumped by a British fighter and shot down, all aboard perishing. Another C-54, flying between Iceland and Newfoundland with a load of wounded, disappeared with no word that it was in trouble; investigators later deduced it was flying low when it was fired on by a German submarine. More fortunate was Capt. Stan Stanton, whose Stratoliner absorbed a direct hit from a sub that put a hole through the 307's tail, and still survived.

The firing incidents involving the Aldis lamp became so numerous that ICD was allowed to resume the use of radio. Actually, enemy fire wasn't nearly as dangerous as the weather and the unpredictable, insidiously subtle menace of fatigue. TWA pilots used to flying only eighty-five hours a month found themselves flying as many as two hundred hours over the same period; one captain made seven ocean crossings in eleven days. There were unsolved, unexplainable accidents in which fatigue was suspected as a primary cause but never proved—like a C-54 that flew into a cloud while approaching Stephensville, Newfoundland. Hidden in the cloud cover was a mountain. Eventually, the Air Transport Command decreed that no ATC flight crew member could fly an average of over one hundred hours a month for any three consecutive months.

Despite the dangers, ICD did prove something that would be of unestimable value after the war—namely, that flying the Atlantic in the wintertime was not inherently more dangerous than crossing it in the summer. At first the ICD crews flew the Great Circle route as being the most direct across the North Atlantic. But Bryan, and later his successor Hal Blackburn, soon had the pilots trying a new method of long-distance flying—so-called "pressure pattern" operations in which shorter mileage was less important than following the rotation of weather pressure areas. By this means they were able to pick up tailwinds that sharply reduced flying time even over longer distances.

Cliff Mutchler briefly replaced Bryan as head of ICD in late 1942, when Otis was made vice-president of war operations—a post created especially for him as Frye shuffled his command staff around. Blackburn, in turn, replaced Mutchler. John Collings took over as vice-president of operations when Larry Fritz went into the service, and Lee Talman was assigned temporarily to Paul Richter's job as executive vice-president.

Frye spent more time in Washington than Kansas City; Collings really ran the airline's domestic operations. Jack had developed a close friendship with Elliot Roosevelt, the president's second oldest son, and had TWA crews picking up cases of Scotch at Prestwick that were delivered to young Roosevelt later. There was nothing really immoral or illegal about this favor, and it is mentioned only to demonstrate that Frye was fast acquiring valuable political contacts. Gregarious and likable, Frye developed a circle of Washington cronies that began to resemble a list of who's-who-in-Washington; Harry Truman was one along with the five members of the Civil Aeronautics Board and a number of influential lawmakers who came to welcome the poker parties Jack loved to throw. Slowly but surely, he was laying the groundwork for what he had come to regard as TWA's postwar manifest destiny: international routes that would tie into the airline's domestic system. There was nothing he wouldn't do for ICD and this was natural; he knew the division was gaining experience to which he could point with pride when he applied for overseas routes.

The domestic side was riding the crest of wartime prosperity. Seldom were there any empty seats on a domestic flight. With the outbreak of war had come the government-dictated priority system:

Priority One: Those traveling on direct orders of the White House or personnel from the War or Navy Departments.
Priority Two: Military pilots enroute to aircraft ferry bases or military stations.
Priority Three: Military or civilian passengers traveling on essential war business.
Priority Four: Military cargo.

If a passenger didn't have one of the first three priorities, he had to take his chances of being bumped, either at the last minute before departure or somewhere at an intermediate stop. By and large, the airlines scrupulously observed the rules; Eddie Rickenbacker was bumped off one of his own Eastern planes by an enlisted man holding a Priority Three. A Los Angeles newspaper sent a reporter to New York to cover an important story and the eastbound trip took forty-four hours, not bad considering the number of times he had to give up his seat to a priority passenger. When the assignment was finished and he flew back to Los Angeles, he was enroute for nine days.

Gas rationing limited long-distance car travel, of course, and the trains were just as crowded as airplanes. In retrospect, the airlines performed something of a miracle. In 1943, for example, they carried 1.5 million more domestic passengers than in prewar 1939, using less than half the number of planes. Utilization was one reason; TWA's DC-3 Fleet was kept flying almost twenty-four hours a day. Even flights leaving at such ungodly hours as 3:00 A.M. were usually packed; inconvenient departures were about the only chance a nonpriority civilian had of getting on a plane.

One such passenger was a popular movie actress, Carole Lombard, who boarded TWA Flight 3 in Indianapolis at 4:00 A.M., January 16, 1942.

She had been in Indianapolis winding up a cross-country war bond tour. The Treasury Department had told her it would be happy if she sold $500,000 worth in the Indiana city, the last stop; she promoted sales of more than $2.1 million.

No more popular and genuinely liked film star ever lived. Bawdy, with the vocabulary of a stevedore, one of the most renowned practical jokers in Hollywood and a woman of great natural beauty, she was worshipped by everyone from lowly grips to studio executives. And among her admirers was her husband, as famous as she—Clark Gable.

Gable was the reason she insisted on flying back to California. She missed him and refused to consider taking the only alternative: a three-day train trip. Even leaving at 4:00 A.M., she expected to arrive in Los Angeles that same evening, accompanied by her mother and MGM press agent Otto Winkler. Neither of the latter two were happy. They disliked flying and the mother, Mrs. Bessie Peters, had an additional reason for preferring the train. She was a great believer in numerology and astrology and fearfully pointed out they would be leaving on the 16th day of the month; the number 16, according to numerologists, was a warning of an impending accident or death. The number 3 bothered her, too. There were too many 3s. The flight number. The DC-3 on which they'd be flying. They were a party of three. And Carole Lombard was thirty-three years old. The astrological portents were unfavorable, too, for Mrs. Peters' astrologist had warned her to stay off airplanes in 1942. It all added up to disaster, she told her disbelieving daughter, who merely laughed. Carole already had agreed to a compromise—to let a coin toss decide their mode of travel—train if it came up heads, plane if it was tails. Winkler flipped a nickel and it came down tails. The press agent went to work trying to arrange space but the only available seats were on Flight 3.

The trip originated in New York, and there was a crew change at St. Louis, where the captain who took over was 41-year-old Wayne Williams, a veteran from the airmail days and considered one of TWA's best instrument pilots. He had been hired in 1931, in fact, to teach instrument flying in the Ford trimotors. At the time he boarded Flight 3, he had accumulated an impressive 12,000 hours of logged flying time. His copilot, M.A. Gillette, was twenty-five and his logbook showed slightly over 1300 hours.

There was a brief hassle at the Albuquerque Airport before the DC-3 took off. Because of a heavy mail and priority cargo load, only nineteen passengers could be accommodated, and there were a number of Army pilots, all graduates of Eagle Nest, who had been ordered to report to their ferrying command base in Los Angeles. TWA boarded fifteen of them plus another serviceman and asked the Lombard party to give up their seats. Carole normally would have agreed; she was no prima donna, as TWA personnel who knew her would have testified. But tired, anxious to see Gable and not wanting to be stranded overnight, she insisted she was on a government mission and held as much priority as the Army pilots. She really didn't, not officially, but being Carole Lombard she won the debate without much objection from the three airmen who would have taken the seats.

Ordinarily Flight 3 would have flown nonstop from Albuquerque to Burbank, but Williams was informed of strong headwinds enroute and with his heavy load, he decided to make refueling stops at both Winslow and Las Vegas. He took off, approximately three hours late, at 4:40 P.M. with only 350 gallons of fuel. Only a few minutes out of Albuquerque, Williams asked for and received permission to bypass Winslow and proceed to Las Vegas. Flight 3 landed there shortly after 6:30, refueled and took off again a half-hour later—thus setting the stage for a tragedy that to this day intrigues TWA pilots who knew Wayne Williams.

Westbound flights out of Las Vegas followed an airway whose compass heading was 205 degrees, taking them safely to the south of Potosi Mountain, an 8,500-foot peak northwest of the Las Vegas Airport. Witnesses who saw Flight 3 take off told investigators it headed in a northwesterly direction. It was a clear night with good visibility.

The flight plan Williams had filed designated 8,000 feet as the cruising altitude—500 feet below the summit of Potosi Mountain. It further specified a Las Vegas departure heading of 218 degrees, almost directly toward that mountain. Also puzzling was the fact that the flight plan violated TWA's operating procedures, which required plans to be made out by the first officer and personally signed by the captain. Flight 3's carried only Gillette's name in printed letters; Williams never signed it, a mysterious omission suggesting that he probably never saw it.

Most of the airway beacons in the Las Vegas area had been blacked out because of the war emergency, but there was one still operative on January 16—Beacon 24, also known as the Arden Beacon, located about two and a half miles to the right of the center line of the Las Vegas radio range leg marking the airway. Flights heading southwest out of Las Vegas passed to the left of Beacon 24. But the Civil Aeronautics Board found that the last time Williams had flown the Vegas-Burbank leg, three weeks earlier, Beacon 24 was inoperative. A logical supposition is that Williams, seeing the lighted beacon, mistook it for one situated directly on course and, assuming he was on course, flew to the right of it never realizing that he was looking at Beacon 24.

While the CAB conceded this might have happened, it added these damning words:

In addition to this lighted beacon, however, the lights of the town of Arden and of automobiles on U.S. Highway No. 91, and farther on, the lights of the town of Goodsprings, afforded reliable reference points. Moreover, under contact conditions such as existed on the night of the accident, if the cockpit lights are kept dimmed, it is possible to see the outline of the mountains especially when the peaks are snow-covered as they were on January 16.

Furthermore, it appears . . . that the available radio range facilities were operating properly at the time of the accident. Had the captain and first officer been listening to the Las Vegas radio range, a moderate "A" signal would have been heard, which would have definitely indicated the plane was off course. . . . It seems obvious that the pilots were not using the radio range for navigational purposes.

Flight 3 impacted Potosi Mountain at a point 730 feet below the crest and exploded. All twenty-two aboard were killed instantly, and the CAB's subsequent verdict was pilot error—"failure of the captain after departure from Las Vegas to follow the proper course by making use of the navigational facilities available to him."

Some TWA pilots who knew Wayne Williams well never bought that finding. Says Frank Busch:

"On the Lombard plane were pilots Wayne and I had trained at Eagle Nest. We think what happened was that Wayne went back to the cabin to bull with them about me and some of the guys we all knew. He left the copilot flying the plane and the kid flew right into the mountain. The way we found Wayne's body, it didn't look as if he had been in the cockpit when they hit. He was the kind of guy who gave his copilots a lot of responsibility. They put me in with him and everytime we'd approach a thunderstorm, he'd leave the cockpit and I'd have to wrestle through the damned stuff. I finally got up the nerve to ask him why and he says, 'because those things scare me to death.'"

Gordon Parkinson, who spent forty years in various TWA operations posts, also knew Williams and what his fellow airmen thought of him. "The scuttlebutt from some pilots was that he was in the cabin talking to Carole Lombard. They couldn't prove this but it was widely believed because that's exactly what he might have done."

Otis Bryan, who knew Williams well, agrees. "He was a good friend of mine but he was a show-off. I don't mean that in a derogatory sense . . . he was a hell of a good pilot . . . but I can just see what happened. He had a copilot who was strange to him and that plane was no sooner off the ground than Wayne was back there talking to Lombard."

Lee Flanagin remembers Williams as "something of a daredevil . . . he'd try landings in zero-zero conditions."

To Ida Staggers, he was "a very dignified man; he was the captain on my very first trip and Frank Busch was the copilot."

Ida was chief hostess in Kansas City when Flight 3 crashed. It was her duty to notify the family of the hostess on the Lombard plane, Alice Frances Getz.

"She came from a farm in northern Illinois and there was no telephone. Personnel finally got me a number to call, that of a neighbor who had to drive a wagon over to the Getz farm, wake up Alice's father and drive him back to the phone. By this time it was about two or three in the morning and I still don't know why I didn't wait until later that morning. I don't even remember how he took the news, I was so stunned myself."

So was everyone else, Frye and Hughes included. Hughes reportedly sent Gable a personal condolence note and the actor apparently bore no grudge against the airline he and Carole had flown so often. There is no record of his filing a negligence lawsuit and one of his biographers, Warren H. Harris, says Gable actually talked Otto Winkler's widow out of suing with the promise that he would build her a house and provide her with a $100,000 annuity.

The Lombard accident drew more publicity than all the ICD crashes combined, but it also was quickly forgotten amid the black headlines of war. While Collings ran the domestic side, Hal Blackburn took over Bryan's job as ICD chief and soon won the respect of all pilots, including those who privately considered him a company-minded martinet. Like Bryan, Blackie never asked an airman to do anything he wouldn't do himself. He had flown and continued to fly many ICD missions himself. On one he was trying to duck German radar and flew so low that the ocean waves slapped against the aircraft's belly and salt spray covered the cockpit windshield.

At one point it came to Frye's attention that Blackburn had authorized TWA planes to fly over the German V-bomb experimental center at Peenemunde in France. He called in Blackie and demanded an explanation.

"We've been taking pictures of the facility," Blackburn confessed.

"Jesus, Blackie, it would be very serious if we had a TWA pilot shot down or captured."

"We won't do it anymore," Blackburn promised.

"See that you don't. By the way, did you get any pictures?"

"Yes, sir," Blackie said proudly.

"Keep it to yourself." Frye grinned.

On another occasion, Blackburn was told that TWA had to ferry a C-87 to Miami for delivery to Pan Am. He couldn't find a crew so he flew it himself, solo.

"If Bryan had found out, he would have fired me retroactively," Blackie smiles. "But hell, you do those crazy things in wartime."

He could be tough. Captain Al Sherwood was flying a C-54 and lost all four engines over the Atlantic when the carburetors iced up. When they came down to a lower altitude, Sherwood got the engines restarted and the passengers not only applauded but made sure Blackburn was advised that Sherwood's skill had saved them from death. Blackie called him in.

"You dumb sonofabitch!" he scolded. "If you had shot alcohol into those carburetors you wouldn't have had any trouble. Now you're a goddamned hero!"

According to Johnny Guy, Blackburn's assumption of command at ICD wasn't welcomed by non-flying personnel, and Guy was one of those in maintenance and engineering who had serious misgivings about Blackie's executive ability.

"We were wrong," Guy says. "I don't think in all my years at TWA that I ever saw an organization function as a group any better than ICD with Blackburn running it. He had a good understanding of human relations. After he took over, he got all department heads together and announced, 'Anybody here can call anybody else a son of a bitch providing the guy you're talking about is present. I don't want anyone coming to me with stories about somebody else.'

"He used to tell us, 'There's only one real problem in the world and if you can solve it, you've got it made. There are no technical problems nor political problems—just human relations problems.'"

Guy was ICD's chief engineer and had communications under his jurisdiction. "We had hired a new girl as a telephone operator and through some slipup she hadn't been paid for more than a month after coming to TWA. Everyone was loaning her money and her supervisor finally asked for a salary advance. I made out the papers and took them to Blackie to sign. He not only signed them but went down and personally apologized to the girl. That's what he meant by human relations."

Blackie tried not to play favorites, but he had a few—such as captains Larry Chippiano and Milo Campbell, two totally different men. Chippiano's ICD crews could have passed a Saturday morning inspection at West Point. He insisted on a spic-and-span operation, from shined shoes to spotless aircraft interiors. Yet Blackie remembers that for all Larry's spit-and-polish demands, the crews would tell Blackburn, "That Captain Chippiano's real tough but can I fly with him again?"

Campbell was just the opposite; an ex-cowboy, he dressed like and walked like one, with a pronounced western waddle. Milo's crews looked like a collection of unmade beds, but they worshipped him and invariably would ask Blackburn, "Can I fly with him again?"

Chippiano died during the war. He had taken Orville Wright for a ride in the first Constellation to come off the assembly line and that same night suffered a fatal heart attack. It was his fortieth birthday, and a sorrowful Blackburn couldn't believe what had happened. There was an autopsy and Blackie asked the doctor what he had found.

"All I can tell you," the doctor said, "was that if I had given him a physical that day I would have cleared him to fly. We do know he had a family history of unexpected coronaries at an early age. In other words, Captain, beware of your ancestors."

The ICD crews lost count of the VIPs they flew across the Atlantic. On Blackburn's first trip, his passengers included Generals George Marshall and Hoyt Vandenberg and Admiral Ernest King. On subsequent trips he carried Omar Bradley and Anthony McAuliffe of Bastogne fame—the general who said "Nuts!" to the German surrender demand. By the time the war ended, TWA pilots had carried not only the top military figures but a princess, two kings, a queen, two presidents and two premiers. Eisenhower, de Gaulle, Patton, Doolittle, Hopkins, Rickenbacker, Stimson, Arnold, Roosevelt, Stilwell, Chiang Kai-Shek—these were just a few of the names that appeared on ICD passenger manifests. And one TWA pilot became a favorite of the famous: Otis Bryan.

Bryan, early in the war, was sworn into the Air Corps as a major, even though he retained his vice-presidential status at TWA. As a major, he was subject to special orders and one of them was a lulu: he was picked to fly President Roosevelt on a trip to Casablanca in January of 1943. Roosevelt took a Pan Am Boeing flying boat on the first stage of the journey, landing in Africa at Bathurst, Gambia, where two TWA C-54s were waiting for him. Bryan commanded the first plane and Captain Don Terry, a colorful TWA veteran who always wore a white scarf and played a violin in the cockpit, was in charge of the escorting backup plane. Neither man, nor any of their respective crews, knew the identity of their number one passenger until he boarded; all they had been told was that they were to fly some high-ranking officials from Bathurst to Casablanca, fifteen hundred miles away.

It was, Bryan admits, the most memorable experience of his long career.

He recalls Roosevelt as being an excellent passenger—"very much interested in the territory over which we flew and always asking questions.

"But he didn't ask for special privileges. We had removed several seats so he'd have a bed, but I can't remember his using it much if at all. He said he'd rather sit up and stay awake because the others in the plane didn't have the same privilege. Another thing that impressed me was how chipper and good-natured he was when he boarded. It was about seven A.M. and he had been flying steadily for almost three days since leaving the United States, but you never would have known it.

"I admired him greatly. He had a strong personality and the ability to put you at ease right away. I was awed at first but we had some wonderful conversations."

Bryan narrowly missed not flying another presidential trip. The Air Corps took a dim view of the president of the United States traveling on what amounted to a chartered commercial airliner and decided to provide the White House with a presidential aircraft. The plane chosen was a modified C-87, its bomber interior converted into deluxe passenger accommodations; it even was given a name: *Guess Where II.*

This very special C-87 was the ancestor of today's *Air Force One,* but although it carried many dignitaries during the war—including Eleanor Roosevelt—FDR himself never set foot on it. The reason was simple: the Secret Service thought the C-87 had too many bugs. The men in charge of the president's security knew about the plane's vulnerability to fire and there also had been reports of other difficulties. When Roosevelt decided to hold a "Big Three" conference in Tehran with a stopoff at Cairo enroute, the Secret Service insisted that he use one of TWA's C-54s. The unhappiest man at this news was Major Henry "Hank" Myers, the man the Air Corps had picked as the president's personal pilot. It was Myers who had picked the name *Guess Where II* for the special C-87, an airplane he really loved.

Myers, a senior American Airlines captain before the war, suspected that TWA had pulled a fast one but this wasn't true. They couldn't have, not even with Jack Frye's connections. It was a Secret Service decision and thus did Otis Bryan get to fly the second presidential mission to North Africa, Cairo and Tehran in the fall of 1943. It proved to be not quite as uneventful as the Casablanca mission.

As usual, the crippled FDR had to be emplaned via a ramp, so his wheelchair could be pushed into the cabin. It was a sight that always jolted Bryan because it brought home starkly the extent of Roosevelt's incapacitation. "I knew we had been ordered to build ramps, but I only thought of them as a convenience. I was aware of FDR's polio but until I actually saw him being wheeled into the airplane, I didn't dream it had left him like that."

He was to be reminded again of Roosevelt's physical helplessness on the return flight, when the president wanted to visit Malta and Sicily enroute. Those stops, incidentally, were the result of a somewhat devious plot in which Bryan was a co-conspirator. FDR called him in before they left Cairo and confided that he wanted to go to Malta and Sicily.

"The Secret Service will tell me no," the president said, "but I'm also going to tell them that I not only want to stop at those two places, but also visit troops in Naples, a real combat area. They'll be so worried about my flying into Naples, they won't say a thing about Malta and Sicily. Is that okay with you, Otis?"

Bryan agreed not to make waves although he was later to wonder if he shouldn't have objected. Coming into Malta, Bryan discovered that a hydraulic pump had failed, making it impossible to lower the wing flaps. He sent his navigator back to inform the president they would have to land much faster than normal and there was an element of danger.

"Well, just do the best you can," Roosevelt said calmly. Then he chuckled. "Sounds like we'll have a good time."

Agents grabbed every pillow in sight and placed them around the president as cushioning protection. But they weren't needed. Bryan landed fast, at more than 100 mph, yet so gently that the tire blowouts he feared didn't occur. Later, someone asked Otis how it felt to make such a landing, knowing that one mistake might have killed the Free World's outstanding leader.

"That didn't cross my mind," Bryan insisted. "What really worried me was getting caught by German fighters just as we landed."

Actually, he did have reason to fear such unexpected attacks on an ICD plane carrying the chief executive. He strongly suspected the Malta flight was no secret to the enemy. While in Cairo, FDR had asked him to fly to Ankara, pick up the Turkish president and bring him back to Cairo. Otis landed at Ankara and was having coffee with the base commander when German propagandist Lord Haw-Haw's voice came over the radio.

"Major Bryan, Roosevelt's pilot, has just landed in Turkey," he announced much to Bryan's dismay.

"How the hell did he know that?" he demanded.

The base commander sighed. "They've probably got spies right in the Ankara control tower that the Turks operate. One of them evidently called Berlin the minute you landed."

The Air Corps had wanted Bryan to have a fighter escort into Turkey, but Otis refused. He figured just the presence of fighters invited trouble, and he wasn't too sure of the capabilities of the U.S. escorting planes. "To handle groups of those P-38 fighters was a problem in itself; those pilots weren't too experienced and they could get into trouble. I always tried to stay away from escorts because they couldn't help much at the moment you were the most vulnerable to getting jumped—on takeoffs or landings."

The last time Bryan flew FDR was in 1944, to the Yalta conference with Churchill and Stalin. Otis was shocked when he saw the president; in two years Roosevelt had aged fifteen. After the meeting, when the C-54 was droning toward the point where FDR would board a warship for the final leg home, he summoned Bryan to his stateroom. The president apparently was just bored, lonesome or depressed. "I guess he just wanted someone to talk to," Otis muses.

"He talked about Stalin and his mistrust of Churchill and vice versa. He said too much of his time had been taken up dealing with that situation."

Bryan was commanding that trip, incidentally, only because of Roosevelt. Hank Myers was supposed to be in charge with Otis as copilot, but FDR heard about it and insisted that Bryan be ranking officer. The president had nothing against Myers, whom he genuinely liked, but there seems to have been an unusual rapport with the TWA pilot. Bryan denies there was any friction between himself and Myers over the command choice, but if there was it is hard to blame Myers.

The Yalta trip marked the first time the *Sacred Cow* was used as a flying White House. This was the specially built C-54 that the Air Corps had ordered after the C-87 was rejected as a presidential aircraft. The *Cow,* so named by irreverent White House reporters, had started life as an ordinary C-54. But in October of 1943, a classified Air Corps telegram was sent to Douglas. Fuselage No. 78, identical to the seventy-seven transports that had preceded it down the assembly line, was hauled to a heavily guarded area where it was transformed into the most unique C-54 in the world. Its outstanding feature was a battery-operated elevator in the rear fuselage; the tell-tale ramps that FDR was required to use would never be needed again.

The overwhelming majority of ICD trips, of course, did not involve glamorous passengers and exotic ports of call. The fleet, numbering fewer than thirty aircraft even at its peak, hauled machine guns, aircraft engines, spare parts, mail, medical supplies, assorted military equipment and the most precious cargo of all—the wounded. In 1944 alone, ICD carried 60,000 passengers and 11.5 million pounds of high-priority cargo and mail. To keep the volume of wartime traffic moving on schedule, ingenuity became a way of life particularly at the more remote stations, where spare parts were either in short supply or nonexistent.

A mechanic named Red McKenney, who had spent thirty-seven days on a ship enroute to an ICD station in Africa, was once confronted with a balky engine that wouldn't start. The culprit was a failed condensor, and the next ICD plane wasn't due for another week. So Red built a condensor out of a sardine can, an even better job of improvisation than the one performed by a TWA flight engineer whose Stratoliner had been rendered *hors de combat* by an inoperative starter. The crew faced temporary maroonment at some out-of-the-way military base until the flight engineer spotted a captured Nazi bomber on the premises. An hour later the Stratoliner was on its way, thanks to a starter salvaged from the enemy aircraft and hastily retooled to fit the 307.

Cannibalizing for spare parts was a frequent recourse at stations where no excuses were accepted for delayed deliveries of vital materiel and personnel. Natal, Brazil, was such a station. It was the last stop before the long overwater flights toward the European and Middle Eastern war theaters, and a grounded airplane was an unacceptable sight.

John Cooper, now a TWA vice-president of maintenance, arrived at Natal enroute to Africa but was pulled off the C-87 on which he was riding with two other mechanics also heading for Africa. Mel House, the base supervisor, had been advised that Cooper was a skilled welder.

"We need you here," he informed Cooper. "Get your stuff off the plane."

Cooper had heard rumors that Natal wasn't exactly a paradise. "Not on your life," he protested. "I'd rather go to Africa."

House wouldn't listen and Cooper watched sorrowfully as the C-87 took off to the East. He was the luckiest welder in ICD; that C-87 was the one that disappeared with no trace of its fate. Eventually, he came to realize there were worse places than this most eastern point of Brazil, the biggest of

TWA's enroute stations. He was there eight months and sums up his stint with wry nostalgia.

It was tolerable, if you could get used to eating not much more than Spam. Natal itself was gorgeous, with a great beach. The flights would leave about nine P.M., heading for Ascension Island. We had about a dozen mechanics there plus a few passenger agents and clerks. The first thing we learned was how to steal stuff off airplanes, and we learned how to improvise. For example, a C-54 came through one day and it needed exhaust ball joints for an engine. I don't think there was a ball joint replacement within a radius of two thousand miles, so another mechanic, Jack Brown, and I worked all night scrounging through the spare parts. We finally found some old joints which we pruned down to fit an R-2000 engine.

There were always some wrecked airplanes around. If a plane came in with some faulty part you usually could cannibalize one out of a wreck. But even cannibalizing had its limits, so we'd resort to stealing stuff from aircraft parked there overnight by military transients. A pilot would leave his airplane and go off to get some sleep. He'd come back the next morning and find it had a wheel missing. The stealing got so bad that crews had to leave a guard by their airplane all night long.

The TWA mechanics worked from ten to twelve hours a day. The shifts varied; Cooper says some days he was on duty for only four or five hours, but there also were stretches of twenty-four hours without relief. For entertainment, there was a makeshift movie theater on the base, and the town of Natal wasn't too far away. Its main attractions were the Staff House, the hotel where the crews stayed, and the Wonder Bar, which all TWA Natal alumni remember with mixed feelings. It was a combined watering hole and occasional brothel, periodically raided by the local police or U.S. Marine MPs who constituted the security force. A bar and dance floor were downstairs, and upstairs were a few bedrooms reached by "the longest staircase in South America," to quote from one Natal veteran. The back of the building was equipped with a second-floor balcony from which the Pan Am flying boats taking off or landing could be seen on a nearby river.

One of Cooper's buddies at Natal was Slim Morgan, at this writing maintenance director at Los Angeles International. He was then a tall, gangling apprentice mechanic, one of the first assigned to Natal. Another was Lou Gordon, who had been Amelia Earhart's mechanic when she flew the Atlantic. In the early days of the war, Stratoliners were the only TWA planes to land at Natal, and Morgan recalls that they furnished some temporary headaches.

"They were a lot of fun," Morgan explains, "but they were always blowing cylinders. Jack Robinson was one of the TWA supervisors there, and we were having so much trouble with those cylinders that Jack went up to Washington to oversee a complete engine overhaul on a 307. He wanted to make sure everything was being done just right, and he stayed with that one plane and its four engines all the way through overhaul, including a test hop that was perfect. So they loaded it up for a trip to Natal, took off, and got as far as Richmond, Virginia, a hundred miles from Washington, when a cylinder blew and they had to land."

It is likely that Jack Frye's interest in Stratoliner performance diminished in proportion to progress on the Constellation project. It mattered little that TWA wouldn't be getting the new plane until the war was won. When that happy event occurred, Frye was determined that the airline would be ready for the expected postwar air transportation boom.

The airline had turned over its purchase rights for the Connie to the government; all TWA retained was an option to buy the forty it originally had signed for. A year before the war ended, Frye had Otis Bryan working on an estimate of how much it would cost to reinstate the old contract after the shooting stopped; the $450,000 per aircraft figure Bob Gross had quoted in 1939 obviously wasn't going to hold up. (In the end it would cost almost $1 million per plane.)

Once the secrecy pact was broken, Johnny Guy was able to stay at the Lockheed factory during the first stages of construction on the initial 0-49. At the time of Pearl Harbor, the fuselage was virtually completed and the wings and tail section about half-finished. When the Air Corps ordered it for use as a military transport, it was designated a C-69, and flight tests began early in 1943. On the first flight, the test pilot in charge was Boeing's Eddie Allen, borrowed because he had more experience flying four-engine equipment than anyone else in the world.

It remained for Frye and Hughes to give the world its first glimpse of the airplane on which they had bet TWA's future. At 3:56 A.M. Pacific time, April 17, 1944, they left Burbank in the Constellation prototype and landed in Washington six hours and fifty-eight minutes later—a record transcontinental flight and one that the *New York Times* hailed as an "outline of the shape of things to come in air transportation."

Hughes flew the first half of the trip and Frye the second. Hal Blackburn assigned a navigator, flight engineer and radio operator from ICD to help the two pilots, who reportedly had an argument before takeoff over which one was to fly the first leg. Also aboard were twelve TWA and Lockheed officials. Not until it was too late did the Air Corps, ready to accept delivery of the plane after the flight, find out that Hughes had ordered the Connie painted in TWA's colors—the double red stripes on the tail, the letters "TWA" in red on the rear fuselage, and the red-lettered "The Transcontinental Line" over the windows. Air Corps officials were furious when they saw the Connie land at National Airport that afternoon—a flying advertisement for an airline that didn't even own the plane. True, the paint used was not the kind used normally, but easily washable water colors. But the Army was peeved anyway; in the middle of a war, one did not upstage the United States Army Air Corps.

There is reason to believe Hughes did it not only to boost TWA but figuratively to tweak the nose of Hap Arnold; Hughes disliked him, considering him more of a politician than a general, and the feeling was mutual. The pair had more than one shouting match during these occasions when their paths crossed. Hughes' incorrigibility even went beyond the paint episode; he was supposed to turn the Connie over to the military almost as soon as he landed, but somehow he arranged to keep it for a few days so he could take various government and military officials on demonstration rides.

Up to this point, few TWA employees had much direct contact with Hughes and his idiosyncrasies. But almost from the moment he stepped off the plane—he was wearing a dark sports jacket and tie while Frye had a light-colored jacket over his inevitable pullover sweater—it was clear that Jack Frye was no longer running TWA by himself. Even the arrival time of 1:45 P.M. was later than scheduled due to Hughes; the Burbank takeoff had been delayed because Howard had been trying unsuccessfully to talk Ava Gardner into going on the flight.

Frye, in anticipation of the demonstration flights and for photographic publicity purposes, had Ida Staggers and eight other hostesses at National to greet the plane. The first demonstration hop was scheduled for the next day and Ida was in the cabin, discussing snack service with a TWA agent when Hughes boarded. He tossed an apple and small carton of milk wrapped in a yellow paper napkin into a seat and glared at Ida.

"She's not taking this flight," he said to the agent.

Ida, her face red, muttered, "That's fine with me," and stomped off the plane. The agent courageously confronted Howard.

"Mr. Hughes, we need the hostesses to serve lunch," he insisted.

"Let a couple of agents do it," Hughes snapped.

His reluctance to have any female on the plane was never explained, unless one buys the theory that he was still fuming over Ava Gardner's refusal to come on the trip. So Fran Schulte, chief passenger agent at National at the time, assigned subordinates to serve sandwiches and milk while the nine hostesses never got closer to the Connie than the bottom of the boarding ramp. Each day, Ida would greet Hughes as he boarded with a pleasant "Good morning, Mr. Hughes," and each day all she received in reply was a cold stare. On the last day, when Howard encountered her at the foot of the steps, she deliberately said nothing. Hughes looked surprised.

"Good morning, miss," he said pleasantly.

On one demonstration flight, Hughes insisted on showing off the Connie's ability to fly on reduced power. He cut one engine first and then a second, without realizing that his passengers—including the entire Civil Aeronautics Board and other high government officials—thought there was something wrong with the plane. Jack Nichols, a TWA vice-president, rushed to the cockpit and told Hughes he had a cabin full of frightened people.

"Hell," Hughes laughed, "I'm gonna cut a third engine; thatll show 'em what this plane can do."

Nichols, fearing a stall if Hughes did what he intended, pleaded that it was too risky.

"If we crashed it would mean the end of TWA," he pointed out.

Hughes hesitated, then restarted the two engines. When Frye heard about it, he just shook his head. He was tremendously conscious of TWA's safety image—and that of all airlines. George Spater flew to New York with Jack once on an Eastern DC-3 and on takeoff, the EAL pilot put the nose up more sharply than Frye thought was warranted. He summoned the steward and sent a note up to the cockpit. Spater says the handwritten message evidently questioned the pilot's sanity and the marital status of his parents, for a few minutes later the captain sent a return note to Frye telling him, in effect, to mind his own business.

"For the rest of the trip," Spater sighs, "they argued back and forth via notes."

But that was Jack Frye. He had lost too many colleagues, friends and trusting passengers to tolerate rule deviations. Before the war ended, he was to mourn the deaths of Jack Nichols, Milo Campbell and another TWA employee in a bomber crash. In his planning for the postwar aviation world, there was no room for carelessness and defiance of operations procedures. In the Connie, he figured, he would have a virtually foolproof airplane that would bring TWA unprecedented prosperity and a secure future for himself. He would be proven wrong.

Advisor Col. Charles Lindbergh prepares for a 1933 flight in Northrop Alpha ship No. 12, the same plane that TWA volunteers restored to flying condition for the Smithsonian in 1976.

Above: A rare photograph of Paul Richter (left) and Jack Frye before they started Standard.

Jack Frye—more at home in a cockpit than behind a desk. He could outfly most of TWA's skilled crews.

Captain Otis Bryan and friend. The picture was taken in a C-54 enroute to Casablanca.

The uniforms changed but not the spirit. *Top:* the first jet age outfits; *Below:* one of TWA's first graduating hostess classes.

Hostess with the Mostest—Ida
Staggers

TWA's most famous—or infamous—hostess uniforms. Left to right: the English pub, French cocktail dress, Roman toga and Manhattan lounging pajamas. The latter was the most popular.

TWA's most significant aircraft

The original Constellation

The Boeing 767

A Ford trimotor leaves Los Angeles on the eastbound transcontinental inaugural, July 1929. The contraption on the right is the TAT "Aerocar," forerunner of airport limousines.

The DC-1. Tommy Tomlinson commanded the record-breaking flight proclaimed on the fuselage. "Old 300" ended its career in Spain.

Tommy Tomlinson, shown with TWA's flying laboratory—the Northrop Gamma

One of TWA's most beloved leaders—
Ralph Damon

Left, Carter Burgess on one of his feared inspection tours. With him is Gordon Gilmore, who molded one of the country's finest public relations departments.

The Boeing 307 Stratoliner, world's first pressurized airliner

Left to right: Oz Cocke, Warren Lee Pierson and Charlie Thomas. The controversial 880 is the top aircraft.

Three of TWA's leaders in the post-Hughes years. Left to right: Charles Tillinghast, Ernest Breech and Bud Wiser. The building is the Breech Training Academy.

8

Peace—It Wasn't so Wonderful

War's end found TWA with a somewhat bloated payroll exceeding 11,000 men and women, more planes than it had before Pearl Harbor and bright prospects. All the massive responsibilities and commitments of global conflict hadn't deterred Jack Frye from following his dreams. If he had managed to keep the airline's feet planted firmly in the realities of the present, he also had pointed them toward a rainbow-hued future. The new route applications TWA filed in 1943 alone called for:

- Adding ninety-nine communities to the thirty-four TWA was serving domestically.
- Authority to fly between Los Angeles/San Diego and Honolulu.
- International service to London, Paris and Cairo.

To the last, in 1944, the airline added an application for a round-the-world route involving more than twenty countries. All this added up to the biggest postwar expansion plan of any carrier, but in the 1944 annual report, Frye refused to buy the argument that TWA might be overextending itself.

> To some, this program (international) may appear excessively ambitious. Such is not the case. While initial operations over this international route involve flying approximately 68,000 miles per day, this is less than the present scheduled daily mileage of TWA's domestic routes. The capital outlay to establish this round-the-world route is estimated at $16.5 million, which would consist principally of expenditures for aircraft. The Company's ability to finance is well in excess of such a sum.

Frye's optimism stemmed not only from his own unquenchable enthusiasm but from the support of Howard Hughes, whose interest in global flight had already been demonstrated tangibly. Hughes, as much as Frye, wanted TWA's routes to circumnavigate the globe. There is reason to believe, in fact, that it was Hughes who sometime during the war suggested to Frye that the airline change its name while retaining its initials. And in 1945, TWA registered the name Hughes reportedly proposed: Trans World Airlines. Not for another five years would it be official; Frye was too busy to worry about corporate name changes.

He decided to move ICD's postwar operations from Washington to Wilmington, Delaware. The latter had the advantage of being about halfway between New York, which would be TWA's main international gateway, and the capital, where he had established his own headquarters. He had a home in suburban Arlington, Virginia, a place large enough for the voluminous entertaining and the poker games he loved. The house had an adjoining swimming pool where Frye tested various models of life rafts for the Constellation, inflating them and throwing them into the pool.

Paul Richter came back from the Navy to resume his post as executive vice-president, while Lee Talman was named a senior vice-president with responsibilities largely in finance. John Collings continued as vice-president of transportation—actually operations—because Larry Fritz decided not to return to TWA. Oz Cocke, who had been one of the airline's first ticket agents, by then had climbed the corporate ladder to vice-president of traffic.

These were the stars of Frye's executive team, but at this critical period he seems to have also populated the airline with a number of persons whose contributions and qualifications were questionable. George Spater, who worked closely with Frye throughout the war as his chief legal counsel, remarks that "one of Jack's greatest weaknesses was inability at picking people. He was impressed by Ph.D.'s and various university degrees or high military rank, and he kept hiring what I'd have to term as a whole series of nuts."

Spater charitably refrains from identifying them individually, but the top echelon of management definitely appeared over-endowed with officers lacking airline experience. There were three men on the 1945 roster who were vice-presidents of precisely nothing—their duties and lines of authority were as vague as their titles. And Frye's board of directors at that time, while it was largely Frye-selected, was not really pro-Frye. Spater comments:

"One of the important things to remember, in light of what was to happen, is that none of the TWA directors were really Jack's friends. He didn't do what so many presidents do—appoint cronies. A lot of the directors represented cities or areas TWA served, or were hangovers from past regimes. I think Frye dealt very fairly with them."

Spater saw a lot of Frye. The young lawyer used to come into the ICD offices during the war to help Blackburn with paperwork, and would often pop in on Jack. Both Spater and Bob Rummel have memories of Frye working on the postwar international routes, kneeling on the floor of his offices with maps spread all over the carpet, his broad, almost cherubic face alight with undisguised excitement.

His personnel choices were not always drawn from left field. Shortly after the war ended, he hired as his executive assistant a former Army colonel who had been in charge of security at the first Roosevelt-Churchill meeting. His name was Carter Burgess, and he came to TWA on the recommendation of General Julius Holmes, one of the airline's new vice-presidents. Frye had told Holmes he had engaged a headhunting firm to find him an aide, and when Holmes told him about Burgess, Frye asked the headhunters to check him out.

The firm made an appointment to see Burgess at the State Department, where Carter was working temporarily. Burgess confided this to Fran Schneider, a close friend of his and a minor DOS official.

"I don't think they'll be much impressed," Burgess worried. "This office of mine is kind of small."

Schneider agreed and then had a brilliant idea. He knew Donald Russell, assistant secretary of state, was out of town and propelled Burgess toward Russell's offices. "It was the size of a golf course," Burgess remembers.

"You stay here," Schneider ordered, "and I'll make sure those guys come in here to interview you."

The headhunters arrived and for thirty-five minutes fired questions at Burgess. In the middle of their interrogation, Schneider rushed in.

"I hate to interrupt you, Carter," he announced importantly, "but Secretary Byrnes wants to see you right away about what the hell to do about that problem in Lebanon."

Burgess excused himself while he rushed off to solve the secretary of state's problem; actually, he and Schneider went to the men's room where they stayed a reasonable length of time before Burgess went back to resume the interview. He was hired shortly thereafter as Frye's executive assistant, thus beginning a relationship he was to treasure until Frye's death. He became Jack's friend and confidant, and a close observer of Frye's relationship with Hughes. Another observer was Frye's personal secretary, Jean Phillips, an ex-WAVE who was named his administrative assistant when TWA won its first overseas routes in mid-1945.

Jean and Carter worked in tandem and tranquility. They shared a common loyalty toward Frye, a deep affection for him while admitting his faults and a mutual distrust of Noah Dietrich as they watched him gradually alienate Hughes from Frye. It certainly didn't happen right away, although there were occasional signs of friction between the two young men—each so fiercely independent. They at least had mutual respect, although Frye delighted in relating stories about Hughes to his friends, Spater and Burgess in particular. Spater relates:

Howard would get into some kind of trouble, Dietrich would bail him out, Jack would hear about it and joyfully spread the story. One of his favorites concerned the time Hughes was arrested in Shreveport, Louisiana.

He had flown there in his own airplane and you have to understand first of all that Howard was a nut when it came to food. I had dinner with him once at Chasin's and he sent a steak back to the kitchen three times because it wasn't cooked exactly the way he wanted. Frye used to tell me how Howard would get interested in just one food and would order nothing else for weeks at a time. One day Jack saw him order and eat a dozen chocolate sundaes. Anyway, Howard came into Shreveport this day when he was on a doughnut kick. He got off the plane carrying a brown paper bag crammed with doughnuts and a carton of milk. As usual, he was dressed like a bum and when he walked into the terminal carrying that sack, the police picked him up and started asking questions. Howard refused to give his name so they booked him on vagrancy charges. He called Dietrich from the jail and Noah had to tell the police they had arrested Howard Hughes.

But while Frye could laugh at Hughes, he also could admire him. Overall,

Frye hid mixed feelings about his peers. For example, he once called Pat Patterson of United "just a damned clerk"—a curious appraisal of a man universally regarded as one of commercial aviation's true giants. Conversely, he had great respect for Sigmund Janus of Colonial, a man generally thought of as occupying a somewhat lower status than Patterson.

"You ought to talk to Sig Janus if you want to understand depreciation," Frye once remarked to Spater.

"Janus," says Spater, "didn't know depreciation from a spark plug, but Jack somehow got the idea that he was an expert on the subject."

Of all his airline contemporaries, Frye's favorite was Bob Six. In 1939, Jack had founded an exclusive aviation club called the Conquistadores del Cielo (Conquerors of the Sky); initially membership was limited to senior airline executives but later was expanded to include officials of aircraft manufacturing firms and other related fields. Frye enrolled Six in the group and shortly after the war both Jack and Hughes offered him a job as TWA vice-president. Six declined, largely because he considered Richter to be Frye's eventual successor; without a firm promise that he would become TWA's president some day, Six preferred to remain a large frog in a small pond. But the Continental chief admired TWA to the extent of raiding it occasionally for capable executives—with Frye's permission.

Despite their dramatic transcontinental flight in 1934, Frye didn't get along with Eddie Rickenbacker too well—which wasn't surprising because nobody got along with the Captain. Rickenbacker, in turn, was said to be jealous of Frye. Between the TWA president and his counterpart at arch-rival American, C.R. Smith, existed grudging respect that fell short of affection. Smith considered Frye an opportunist; when Jack heard the Air Force was considering replacing the *Sacred Cow* with a new Douglas DC-6, Frye secretly began lobbying for a Constellation instead. He knew American was ordering the new Douglas transport and he also knew there was a lot of prestige connected with whatever plane would be chosen for the new Air Force One. Smith got wind of Frye's behind-the-scenes maneuvering and sent him a blistering letter that, in effect, told him to mind his own business.

The Air Force picked the DC-6 for Harry Truman anyway, but at least Frye had the advantage of putting the Connie into service more than a year ahead of the airplane that would prove to be the Constellation's toughest competitor. (United and American had ordered the DC-6 in 1944, but Douglas was forbidden to conduct development work until the shooting ended.)

Having conceived the Connie, Hughes followed its gestation, birth and infancy closely. No one connected with the program was totally satisfied with the original 0-49 model. Its range was especially disappointing. Bob Rummel, assigned to the project, informed Frye and Jack Franklin that the plane could barely make it nonstop from Chicago to Los Angeles. Lockheed responded with a number of modifications that improved the range somewhat but still fell short of expectations. A month after V-J Day, TWA signed a new contract for thirty-six 0-49s, with TWA getting delivery rights to the first twelve planes off the assembly line, but even then Frye and Hughes were talking to Lockheed about an improved version.

Howard insisted on testing the new plane himself. He shot so many landings in a Connie at Palmdale that he wore out at least one set of brakes and tires. He also wore out TWA pilots assigned to fly with him, and he was extremely choosy about their selection. Joe Bartles, then TWA's general manager for the western region, was supplying the crews, but Hughes kept complaining, and neither Bartles nor Lee Flanagin, the division flight superintendent, could satisfy him.

Finally Frye phoned Flanagin. "Lee," he said, "Howard just called me and said he doesn't want anyone who's flying the line regularly."

"What's wrong with a line pilot?" Flanagin inquired.

"Well, Howard wants somebody who won't tell him how to fly. Will you do it?"

Lee's first flight with Hughes took place on a calm night. They flew up to Palmdale and with no wind they began taking off in one direction, then turning around and landing in the other direction. They did this from 10 P.M. to 6 A.M. before Hughes finally agreed to call it quits. He hadn't said much during those grueling eight hours but when they landed at Burbank, Howard growled, "This airplane's got too much dihedral. It's unstable close to the ground."

Flanagin didn't agree with him but he kept his mouth shut; if he had tried to argue with Howard, they could have been there another eight hours. But Hughes liked Flanagin and from then on, until Lee had to retire from flight duty after a heart attack, Howard asked for him everytime he wanted to go flying. If Flanagin wasn't available, Joe Bartles usually had to go.

"He was a funny guy," Flanagin says. "I'm sure he spent at least four months pouring over the Lockheed manuals before and during the time he test-flew the Connie. He wasn't a great pilot but he was incredibly thorough."

Frye had insisted on equipping the Connies with berths for both the long-haul domestic flights and the transatlantic operations. Hughes didn't disagree, but he thought Lockheed was overcharging him on the berths, and he kept insisting that they get the price down. While they were still haggling, Hughes finally lost his temper and told Rummel, "I don't want to hear the word 'berth' mentioned again!" But he finally relented at Frye's urging; in those days, he still tended to go along with Jack on most major matters. (During the war, when Frye wanted to buy into a South American airline called Transportes Aereos Centroamericanos S.A. (TACA), Hughes opposed it and so did several TWA officers and directors, but Frye got his way.)

The Constellation itself was another indication of how Frye's judgment prevailed. Not all his technical people, Rummel and Ray Dunn in particular, were that enamored with the plane; they thought the Connie was more complex than necessary. The triple tail simply meant more maintenance and the shark-like shape of the fuselage, while brilliantly aesthetic, actually was impractical because the narrow forward section limited seating. This also was true of the rear section with its similarly tapered streamlining.

The multiple-tail design was a Kelly Johnson speciality; he not only believed it improved directional control but reduced the height of the aircraft so it fitted into virtually any hangar with ease. He also defended the fuselage shape as being aerodynamically necessary. The Connie had large propellers which required a long nose gear for safe clearance. To keep the gear from being too long, Johnson gave the fuselage a slight downward curvature which also reduced drag. The same curved shape was employed behind the wing and the overall fuselage shape gave it roughly the same airfoil as the wing itself, resulting in a further drag decrease.

True, the Constellation was the most complicated transport aircraft of its time, and the more complex, the greater the potential for component failure. Its very size and weight dictated such sophisticated elements as the fully boosted hydraulic controls. On one test flight, the pilots first lost half the hydraulic system and a few minutes later the other half. Hal Blackburn was the captain and succinctly described what it was like to fly a Connie with no boost. "It took the combined strength of myself and two husky copilots to move that yoke," he reported.

While preparing for the introduction of Constellation service, TWA already was operating with an enlarged fleet. By the end of 1945 it had ninety-four airplanes, including forty-eight DC-3s in scheduled service, five more used for pilot training, and seventeen other DC-3s in the process of being converted from military transports to commercial configuration. There were eight DC-4s and five Stratoliners; the latter had been refurbished, but the original pressurization systems, removed for war operations, were never restored. This was strictly an economy move, saving both weight and the cost of reinstallation.

Also on hand were the first ten Connies out of the Burbank hatchery, and being readied for service, and also the most unusual plane TWA ever operated: a B-17 bomber. The airline purchased it for only $13,000 and gave Johnny Guy the job of supervising its conversion into an executive transport, primarily for use of board chairman T.B. Wilson and overseas route surveys. The bomb bay doors were sealed and the bay turned into a cargo compartment. The narrow fuselage housed lounges (purchased from Sears), a desk, small tables and a makeshift galley fashioned by TWA mechanics.

Frye and Hughes flew one of the Connies into Washington for a repeat of the 1944 demonstration visit. This time Hughes didn't object to using hostesses for the brief courtesy flights, but his eccentricities were on full display along with the airplane. Even before they left Burbank, they quarreled over who was to fly the first leg, just as they had in 1944 when they set the speed record. Hughes got in the left seat first but insisted on computing the precise halfway point so Frye wouldn't be flying one second longer than he.

At Howard's request, TWA brought to Washington a small army of mechanics, passenger service representatives and station managers from all over the system so the demonstration flights would be handled smoothly. In charge of the group was Dan Phillips, Washington station manager. Each was given a specific assignment in addition to being on hand at the airport for the flights themselves. Jerry Condon, for example—he was chief passenger agent in Harrisburg—was given the daily job of putting two cheese sandwiches and a glass of milk in the cockpit for Hughes. Each night he picked up what was left—two cheese sandwiches and a glass of milk. During the entire week, Howard never touched the food.

Condon and the others also reported at the end of each day's final flight, going to the hotel where Hughes was staying. It was their hotel, too, but no one was allowed to have a room on the same floor where Hughes had a suite. Phillips would escort the team to the Hughes suite and knock on the door. The transom would open.

"That you, Dan?"

"Yes, sir."

"Got everyone here?"

"All here, Mr. Hughes."

"Okay, start talking."

Phillips, briefed previously on the day's activities by his platoon, would recite everything that had happened at the airport. (Condon recalls, "There we were, a bunch of idiots, talking to a goddamned door.")

When Phillips finished, Hughes would ask, "Is that all?"

"That's all, Mr. Hughes."

"Okay, here's the plan for tomorrow." Then Hughes would outline what he wanted done the next day and would conclude, "Good night, fellas."

The transom would close.

Condon was no stranger to the peculiarities of Howard Hughes. During the war he had been stationed at LaGuardia, and one night he got a call from 7000 Romaine. Mr. Hughes needed four seats reserved for a quartet of starlets wanting to fly to Los Angeles that night. The flight was booked solid with priority military passengers, an apparently unsurmountable obstacle, which Condon dutifully pointed out.

"Get four volunteers," he was told. "Tell them we'll guarantee them seats tomorrow and we'll also contact their commanding officers so they won't get into trouble. And make sure they all have a good time tonight."

Jerry mustered the passengers and explained the situation, adding that TWA would furnish them free hotel rooms and meals plus transportation into Manhattan and then back to LaGuardia the next day. Two sailors, a soldier and a marine volunteered, and greatly relieved, Condon phoned the Romaine office to report total success.

"That's great, Jerry," he was told. "Bring 'em back to the airport tomorrow morning and we'll take care of them."

"Wait a minute," Condon protested, "we don't have a morning flight."

"Just be at the airport. Bring 'em to the TWA hangar."

Condon met them at LaGuardia the next day and escorted them to the hangar as instructed. There was Frye's private Lockheed, with Hughes himself in the cockpit and a TWA hostess standing at the plane's door.

"So I boarded them and Hughes flew all of them to Los Angeles," he recounts. "In all these years I never figured out why we didn't put the starlets on the Lodestar and leave our regular passengers on the scheduled flight. It was just the way he operated."

That second Connie flight into Washington was just a rehearsal for an even greater demonstration of the plane's capabilities. On February 3, 1946, Frye and Lee Flanagin flew a Constellation from Burbank to LaGuardia in less than seven and a half hours, breaking the 1940 Stratoliner record by more than four hours. Aboard were forty-four newspaper, radio and magazine reporters, who were informed that the February 3 date had additional significance: it was on February 3, 1926, that Frye had started Aero Corporation. Now, two decades later, he was on the threshold of his greatest achievement. For the rest of that month, TWA's magnificent Constellations flashed their way across continents and oceans in a series of blazing inaugurals. New York–Paris. New York–Paris–Rome. Los Angeles–New York— this one flown by Hughes and Joe Bartles with thirty-five Hollywood stars aboard. Washington–New York–Paris. New York–Cairo via Paris, Athens and Rome. . . .

The corporate name hadn't been changed yet, but the Connies carried the legend "Trans World Airline" on their silver fuselages. Never mind what it had cost to establish the international routes. After all, TWA's 1940–1945 accumulated profits amounted to more than $10 million, and the anticipated postwar explosion of air travel was just around the corner. TWA's domestic routes fed into the far-flung international system, and above this impressive structure stood the towering figure, not of Howard Hughes, but of Jack Frye.

Almost single-handedly he had won the overseas routes against the formidable opposition of Pan Am and the CAB's own staff. A CAB examiner had recommended against TWA in an initial decision; Bob Buck remembers that black day "when I think all we got was a route to Topeka." When he encountered Frye at the airline's Washington offices on G Street, he expressed his sympathy.

"I'm sure sorry, Jack," Buck said. "I know how hard you've worked for those routes."

Frye nudged the big pilot with his elbow. "Don't you worry, Bob." He smiled. "We'll get 'em."

He had cultivated and courted official Washington with the finesse of a born lobbyist in both the Roosevelt and Truman administrations, never resorting to anything blatant or heavy-handed and obvious, always projecting an image of an airline chief who was personable, ever-helpful and invariably respected, always promoting an image of a progressive air carrier that sought nothing but a chance to prove its worth, always willing to do a favor but never asking one in return. The Frye *modus operandi* was to create a favorable attitude toward himself and TWA, a kind of automatic, sublimal reaction that spelled "Nice Guy" and "Good Airline."

A brilliant poker player, he seldom won in the games he held at the big suburban home overlooking the Potomac River—"Four Winds" it was called. His guests could lose to each other but rarely to Frye. If a government official happened to mention a forthcoming trip, Jack would offer to make the arrangements and provide for special pampering, or he might even off-handedly remark that his private Lockheed was going in the same direction around that time "and we'd love to have you come along."

There was nothing illegal about his technique. It might be frowned on in today's more circumspect environment, but in the context of that era such strategy was an accepted way of political life. Certainly Frye's rather subtle lobbying was effective. He had faced a major obstacle in the person of Pan Am's Juan Trippe, whose vision of postwar international aviation was painted in Pan Am's blue and white colors.

Trippe had fought hard and long for the concept of a single U.S. flag carrier to serve the overseas routes—his own airline being a natural choice because it had pioneered most of those routes. "Chosen Instrument" this policy was called, but the wily Trippe knew Congress wouldn't give him such a monopoly. He argued that Pan Am deserved to be the Chosen Instrument, but he also proposed what seemed like an attractive and logical alternative: form a cooperative venture in which every airline would hold stock, with Pan Am running the whole operation. A so-called "All-American Flag

Line" bill was introduced in two successive Congresses and drew the immediate fire of virtually the entire airline industry; the only carrier to support Trippe was United, which had decided it would stay out of international flying.

Pat Patterson, as early as 1944, claimed it was ridiculous to have competition among U.S. airlines overseas. By 1955, he declared, only twenty-three aircraft would be necessary to carry all the North Atlantic traffic. Trippe's own estimate—admittedly suspect—was even gloomier. He said a dozen planes would suffice. Josh Lee of the CAB scoffed at such predictions, which simply used past history as the basis for forecasting the future.

"It would have been just as logical," Lee said, "to have determined how many people crossed the American desert by stage coach, projected this figure, and announced that this is the number of passengers who may be expected to cross the United States by rail."

Another telling witness against Chosen Instrument was General Harold George, whose Air Transport Command during the war had carried nearly three million passengers. He told the CAB and Congress that the volume of future international travel would "stagger the imagination."

In mid-1944, the Board had announced it would receive applications for international route certificates, and all efforts in behalf of the All-American Flag Line Bill collapsed. Over the next year, the CAB held five separate hearings—the North, Central and South Pacific cases and the South and North Atlantic cases. The last, possessing by far the greatest traffic potential, was the most hotly contested with Trippe insisting that Pan Am deserved to be selected exclusively. But once again, sensing defeat, he proposed another seemingly logical alternative. Despite his previous claim that twelve planes could carry all the North Atlantic traffic for the next decade, he suggested that two U.S. carriers be picked—Pan Am and tiny American Export Airlines, a newly organized subsidiary of the big shipping firm.

Trippe's move was brilliant. He knew that American Export, under the law, would have to divest itself of control by the parent company, and thus would enter the North Atlantic fray against powerful Pan Am as a weak, small competitor. What Trippe didn't count on was that American Export had no intention of feeding itself to the Pan Am wolf. Its president, John Slater, entered into merger negotiations with Ralph Damon of American Airlines, C.R.'s righthand man, and the eventual outcome was the formation of American Overseas Airlines—operated briefly under the old name of American Export Airlines.

Trippe was to find himself faced not by just one flabby little U.S. competitor but a pair of powerful rivals, each with domestic routes to feed into their international systems—something Pan Am sadly lacked. Frye's case for TWA was simple; he merely pointed to ICD's splendid wartime experience and the forthcoming mighty and modern Constellation fleet.

On June 1, 1944, the Civil Aeronautics Board had issued its North Atlantic decision. It authorized American to serve northern Europe and divided the rest of Europe up between TWA and Pan Am; both got rights to India, TWA's via Cairo to Bombay and Pan Am's via Istanbul to Karachi and Calcutta. TWA also got Paris authority and Pan Am, London.

This was the background for a momentous event in TWA's history. On

February 5, 1946, a Constellation christened *Star of Paris,* with Hal Black-burn commanding, took off from Washington, picked up more passengers at LaGuardia, and flew to Paris. Five days later the *Star of Rome* inaugurated the first U.S. airline service into Italy. The third inaugural took place February 15 when the *Star of California* sped from Los Angeles to New York in eight hours and thirty-eight minutes with Hughes and his load of movie stars. (Clancy Dayhoff hated calling the planes *Star of.* . . . He wanted to name the Connies "Thunderbirds.")

Frye went beyond the establishment of the overseas network and the finest transcontinental service (for a while at least) in the U.S. In both 1945 and 1946, TWA began a series of agreements with foreign airlines in which the U.S. company promised to furnish technical aid ranging from pilot training to marketing expertise. In some cases, such as with TACA, Philippine Air Lines and Iranian Airways, TWA bought into the client companies. In others, it contracted services. Ethiopian Airlines was an example; TWA actually helped form that carrier and for years was to guide and supervise its fortunes until Ethiopia was able to stand on its own. Later, Saudi Arabian Airlines enjoyed an extremely close and friendly relationship with TWA and its people that was maintained for many years.

Altruism was not the basis for these foreign projects. Although aid to the tiny, struggling airlines represented little or no profit, Frye saw them as ideal connecting links to TWA's own international routes. Typical was the contract signed with Italian Airways. TWA agreed to help form and operate the carrier (today's Alitalia) over fourteen routes within Italy, connecting with TWA flights at Milan and Rome.

TACA, mentioned previously, was TWA's first foreign client. It had been started by a colorful entrepreneur named Lowell Yerex. A New Zealander by birth, he had fought with the Royal Flying Corps in World War I after learning to fly in the United States. Following the Armistice, Yerex drifted from job to job like most of his fellow airmen—barnstorming, running small airports and operating air taxi services. In 1931 he was hired by two wealthy Americans to fly them around Mexico, Honduras and other Latin and Central American countries. From this venture he amassed enough resources to start his first airline, TACA de Honduras, forerunner of the South and Central American aerial empire he was to build. At the time TWA bought into TACA, it was a loosely knit conglomerate of airlines in Honduras, El Salvador, Costa Rica, Nicaragua, Brazil and the British West Indies.

No one could ever explain why Frye became involved with the Yerez operation. One guess is that he wanted a hedge in case his European aspirations flopped, giving TWA a chance to expand southward if it was blocked over the Atlantic. Eventually Frye lost interest in TACA, which, ironically enough, was acquired later by a wheeling-and-dealing TWA pilot named C.N. "Connie" Shelton, as colorful in his own right as Yerex.

Lowell was a handsome, powerfully built man with an incongruous affliction; he stuttered badly. When Frye dispatched George Spater to examine TACA's books, Spater noticed there were no buildings listed among the assets and asked Yerex why.

"W-w-w-well," Yerex explained, "the w-w-w-w-weather's p-p-p-p-pret-t-t-y m-m-m-ild s-s-o w-we s-s-stand under the t-t-t-t-trees."

The 1943 deal involved acquiring an interest in TACA, but later TWA bought out Yerex's holdings. Frye had made the mistake of wanting to up-grade TACA's operations from the simple service Yerex had been offering. A pair of TWA officials were assigned to TACA temporarily as advisers. Charlie Gallo, an operations man, was sent down there to train personnel, and treasurer John Lockhart was supposed to straighten out the airline's finances. Lockhart, a short-tempered individual, clashed immediately with Yerex and their violent arguments precipitated Yerex's decision to sell out.

Gallo had a rough time, too. He was teaching one cabin attendant how to serve drinks and discovered the employee was working barefooted. Charlie bawled him out and made a point of checking his appearance on another flight. The attendant was wearing shoes this time, but on his head was a battered felt hat.

"The whole thing started to disintegrate," George Spater recalls. "Frye's interest began to wane around the time he got the international routes. He was criticized for getting TWA into the deal, but at the time it was a good investment. TWA bought the stock at about ten dollars a share and it went up to sixty. Time-Life owned a chunk of TACA and so did the Rockefellers and TWA's own board chairman, T.B. Wilson."

Shelton took over TACA later. He restored its simplicity to such an extent that its various carriers became known as "Shelton's barefoot airlines"—this after TWA had disengaged itself from all connections. Yet this was the only unhappy experience of all the foreign airline ventures in which TWA was involved. Eventually these included carriers in Ireland, Greece and Turkey in addition to those already mentioned, and all these projects originally were under the direction of Board Chairman Wilson. The men assigned to run them were of top-drawer caliber. The TWA official sent to Italy, for example, was none other than Otis Bryan, who took a half-dozen C-47s (military version of the DC-3), pilots and mechanics with him and started up the erstwhile enemy's first postwar domestic airline.

The Italian venture was a pushover compared to the job of setting up Philippines Air Lines. PAL was the brainchild of Art Stewart, TWA's regional vice-president in Los Angeles, who had won Hughes' confidence. When the CAB rejected TWA's initial bid to operate a round-the-world route, Hughes confided his disappointment to Stewart. Art said all was not lost; he pointed to Frye's various aid programs with European, Middle Eastern and African airlines and suggested the same thing could be done in the Pacific, where Asian air carriers might operate routes that dovetailed into TWA's. A logical candidate, Stewart added, was Philippines Air Lines, which had just been organized. Its chief backer was one of the wealthiest men in the Far East, Don Andres Soriano, owner of the huge San Miguel brewery and a former wartime advisor to Gen. Douglas MacArthur.

The Stewart-Hughes conversation culminated in contacts with Soriano. Stewart was given permission to pick his own man to head the TWA project team; Bryan was busy not only in Italy but Ethiopia, Saudi Arabia and elsewhere. Art's choice was an unknown youngster whom Stewart had hired away from the Great Northern Railroad in 1944. His name was Frank Howell. Short in stature but long on charm, tact and doggedness, Howell's speciality had been developing good relationships with travel agents. That was an area in which Stewart felt TWA was weak, and he doubled Howell's railroad salary to get him with the airline.

Until the war ended, Howell had little chance to work at his speciality. Stewart put him into reservations to learn the airline business until after V-J Day, when Howell was sent into the hinterlands to line up agencies in medium-size towns where there were no airline offices, concentrating on selling long-haul traffic including TWA's overseas routes, which were just getting started.

One day late in 1945, Stewart summoned Howell and told him he was going to the Philippines.

"Art, I'm very happy right where I am," Howell protested.

"Well, I want you to go."

"Why not get someone with more experience?"

"It's you, Frank. That's all there is to it."

So a few weeks later, Howell headed the 35-person TWA delegation that boarded a liner for the 31-day trip to Manila. They included pilots, mechanics, station agents, navigators, secretaries and clerks. The woman Howell took with him to head the PAL ticket office in Manila was Ruby Williams, widow of the pilot killed in the Carole Lombard crash. She had been working in TWA's Los Angeles ticket office, and Howell recruited her because "she was very intelligent and a great teacher. Later she trained the first eight PAL hostesses."

The ship had hardly docked when Frank began wishing he was back hobnobbing with travel agents. Careless stevedores dropped the cargo nets too fast and smashed about half the typewriters Howell had shipped. Then he discovered the contingent had forgotten to bring an important item: they had loaded TWA manuals, stationery, typewriters, ticket forms, filing cabinets, office furniture and even their own drinking water, but nobody, including Howell, had remembered to bring baggage tags.

The first sight of PAL's flight equipment was dismaying. It consisted of three weary Lockheed Lodestars, which quickly proved to be inadequate to handle the traffic. So many people had been displaced throughout the islands during the war that air travel space was at a premium. Howell began scrounging for airplanes and heard about a number of available C-47s; the U.S. government had decided it would be too expensive to ship them back home. The only trouble was that they had been flown to Guam for scrapping.

Howell happened to meet one of those many Americans who had fallen in love with the Philippines and refused to leave when the war ended. He was an enterprising Texan named Jim Fleming, a former Air Force pilot. When Howell told him about the C-47s on Guam, Fleming came up with a proposal. He'd hitch rides to Guam in military planes and ferry the C-47s back, first rigging them with extra fuel tanks; later he even set up an in-flight refueling system. "He did many favors for us," Howell acknowledges, "but this was the biggest."

"There were many others like him," Frank continues. "Some of them even went AWOL just to stay in the Philippines. I hired one of them, a crack mechanic. The FBI tipped me off that he was wanted on AWOL charges, but they were really decent about it. They said he should just make himself scarce and they'd look the other way."

Thanks to the help of people like Fleming, the TWA group had PAL operating within six weeks after arrival. They added three C-47s to the

Lodestars as soon as Fleming could ferry them to Manila, and soon had ten of them flying. Howell had his mechanics install two-by-fours in the cabin and attached benches to the boards. This provided space for thirty-five passengers with a narrow aisle between the benches.

The customers were wonderfully patient and understanding—even grateful for what passed as airline service—but generally they were also neophytes to air travel. The C-47 model PAL used had a small hole in each cabin window, with a wooden plug in the center of the glass. If a passenger wanted fresh air, he or she could pull out the plug. On one flight, a woman had brought along her small son who had a sudden call of nature. The mother pulled out the plug and held the boy up so he could urinate through the hole. The airstream caught the contents of his rapidly emptying bladder and sprayed half the plane's interior. But the mother was the epitome of *savoir faire*.

"Now you're all baptized," she proclaimed to the drenched passengers.

At first PAL's planes merely island-hopped. Later, as it acquired bigger aircraft, it would extend its routes to Hong Kong and Bangkok. By the time Howell and most of his TWA cohorts left Manila in 1948, PAL had a fleet of forty-two DC-3s and several DC-4s for the longer routes. But in the beginning, it was commercial aviation at its most primitive level. Some of the landing strips were on corrugated mats installed by the Japanese occupation forces. Flights landing at the out-of-the-way airports often had to buzz the field two or three times to scare off the water buffaloes that had wandered onto the runway.

Soriano himself came up with a plan for an extracurricular sales force. He made the mayor of every town serve as a PAL agent. Each received an unlimited pass and a 5 percent commission on every ticket sold. In exchange for the commission, the mayor had to build a hut at the airport and hang a PAL schedule inside. The hut was the terminal building.

"We started with one flight a day to all major island cities and then had to expand it to two," Howell says. "We'd carry any kind of cargo and on Sundays, when most Filipinos didn't like to travel, we'd use the C-47s as freighters—produce, animals, all kinds of goods. Saturday was a very special day; that's when we'd fly the cock-fighting groups into Manila, both the bird owners and the people betting on them. The early C-47s didn't have radios, so every evening we'd count the flights as they came in to make sure nobody was missing."

Howell had expected to use the Manila Airport as PAL's home base, but years before Pan Am had obtained exclusive landing rights there and refused to let PAL in as a tenant. Even the influential Soriano couldn't break Pan Am's lease so he told Howell, "Never mind, Frank, we'll build our own airport." It was called Makati and the terminal was an open quonset hut. Makati is now a large residential area, for the Philippines government finally brought pressure on Pan Am to let PAL use the main airport.

Resourcefulness kept the airline going when all else failed. An American businessman named Stanley sought space one day on a flight from Manila to one of the islands where he had urgent business. The PAL agent reported to Howell, "I have no seat for Mr. Stanley. The airport is full."

"Hold the plane until we figure something out," Howell groaned. "Do you have any great ideas?"

The agent's eyes twinkled. "We have a Mr. Kun on board, one of our regular passengers. He likes beer. Will you pay for the beer if I can get him off the plane?"

"Agreed," Howell said.

Mr. Kun was invited to have a beer. He then was offered a second and then a third, thus requiring a trip to the men's room. As soon as he was inside, the agent locked the door and boarded Mr. Stanley. Once the plane was out of sight, he let the unhappy Mr. Kun out of the men's room with profuse apologies.

"You can go tomorrow," he assured Kun. "I've already got a seat reserved for you and believe me, you won't get bumped this time."

"Okay," grumbled Mr. Kun, "but tomorrow, no free beer, please."

It was Howell who actually wangled landing rights for PAL in Bangkok by trading a Parker 51 pen—an item that somehow had become a status symbol in Asia. Frank always carried an extra one. He showed up in Bangkok for a meeting with the minister of aviation, making sure the official noticed the Parker 51 in his pocket. The minister's eyes gleamed avariciously.

"If you'll make me a present of that pen," he suggested, "I'll sign for your landing rights right now and we can go to lunch."

At the other side of the world, Howell's counterpart was Captain Waldo "Swede" Golien, named by Bryan to head TWA's technical mission to Ethiopian Air Lines. As with all these overseas projects, the object was to install modern operating methods, mostly using American personnel, but gradually hiring and training the nationals until they were qualified to take over even highly technical duties. It wasn't easy. The mechanics Golien was training couldn't read English, so Golien furnished them with books containing pictures of various parts. A mechanic would take a picture and go through EAL's parts bin until he found the component that matched the picture.

"It wasn't ignorance but a language barrier," Frank Busch points out.

The records of such airlines as PAL and EAL today—both operating modern jets with high standards of service—are proof of how well TWA did its job. Furthermore, these missions earned the American airline incalculable goodwill in other nations, friendships that cannot be measured in precise monetary terms. Swede Golien, for instance, became a literal symbol of American efficiency in that struggling, almost primeval African nation. Even Emperor Haile Selassie came to regard Swede as a personal friend; he liked to ride in the cockpit next to the big pilot. "Mr. Golien," as he called him, "has my every confidence." To the Ethiopians, from the emperor on down, Golien represented *all* Americans just as TWA seemed to stand for the United States.

Unfortunately, however, those admirable efforts did not appear on the 1946 balance sheets of an airline that was heading for trouble. To many directors, the foreign projects, combined with the swift implementation of the international routes, added up to overexpansion and a skyful of red ink. The directors that year included Noah Dietrich, who had finally talked Hughes into figuratively shoving him down Jack Frye's throat, and Dietrich viewed all these expansion activities with undisguised alarm.

Some of his alarm, perhaps much of it, was justified. Even Frye's most avid admirers admit he was profligate in his spending, first because it was his nature and second because either subconsciously or deliberately he was sure that Howard Hughes would stand behind any decision he made. Not even Paul Richter could curb Jack's excesses, which ran from expensive service innovations to manpower. During one stage of the war, for example, he had told John Collings to keep hiring pilots at a rate of seventy-two new men every two weeks. Bob Buck went into Collings' office and objected. "It's silly," he argued. "We don't have enough airplanes to justify hiring a hundred and fifty pilots a month."

"I said seventy-two every two weeks and that's the way it is," Collings retorted. But it wasn't Collings—it was Frye who had set or at least approved those hiring goals. "And," Buck recalls grimly, "we had guys sitting around who hadn't taken a flight out for months. Inevitably we had to start furloughing them."

Also inevitable was that all this was going to catch up with the president of TWA some day, particularly with Noah Dietrich perched high on the board of directors tree like a vulture, waiting for something unpleasant to happen.

Something unpleasant did happen, on July 11, 1946, only five months after the Constellations had gone into service. On that day, a TWA Connie on a routine training flight crashed at the Reading, Pa., airport and set off a chain of events that was to doom the Frye regime.

Routine was the word for it. The plane carried five crew members including an instructor. He was Capt. Dick Brown, and in the left seat, undergoing an instrument check ride, was Capt. Art Nilsen. Nilsen had just begun to practice instrument approach procedures when a strong odor resembling burning insulation permeated the cockpit. Brown sent the flight engineer back to find out what was causing the smell; he returned seconds later and shouted, "The whole cabin's on fire."

Nilsen and the flight engineer grabbed hand extinguishers and attempted to enter the cabin, only to be driven back by thick smoke and intense heat. By now, the smoke had seeped into the cockpit in choking clouds and Brown found himself unable to see his instruments or through the windshield ahead of him. In desperation, he opened a side window, stuck out his head, and tried to fly back to the airport in that awkward fashion.

It didn't work. The heat and smoke grew worse, reaching such intensity that neither Brown nor Nilsen could control the aircraft. As the stricken Connie groped toward the ground, Brown finally gave up trying to see with his head out the window. He pulled it back and decided to chance a blind landing. He didn't make it, the plane hit two tall power lines and crashed. Brown was the only survivor and one of his arms was injured so severely that it had to be amputated.

From the evidence, the CAB suspected some kind of an electrical fire, and the investigation centered around the 0-49's electrical system. What was unearthed was devastating. The loophole through which death had passed was a "through-stud"—a tiny metal electrical conductor that allowed electrical power to be brought through the fuselage of the pressurized aircraft without destroying the pressurization seal. To quote the CAB's final report, the through-stud was of a "crudely deficient design" that permitted the stud to come so close to the fuselage skin that arcing resulted. The arcing, in turn, burned both the stud and the skin.

The next link in this deadly chain was the location of the studs, perilously close to high-pressure hydraulic lines filled with flammable fluid. If the stud burned in two, one end would fall on the line and ignite an uncontrollable fire. Why were the studs so vulnerable? Because, the CAB discovered, they were composed of a conglomeration of varying materials. Lugs were made of copper and aluminum. Nuts contained both brass and steel. Bolts were made of brass. All these varying materials spelled out a major fault: each had a different rate of expansion under heat, and this is what caused the studs to become loose, move toward the fuselage skin and produce arcing and pitting.

Immediately after the Reading crash, CAB technicians inspected every Constellation in service and were shocked to find evidence of arcing in nearly half of them. There also were indications of other deficiencies. The board cited inadequate fire and smoke detection systems in the forward baggage compartment, where the fire had started. It also charged that the Constellation lacked fire extinguishing equipment in such remote fuselage areas as the baggage compartment. It criticized the fact that there had been little or no research on the direction of smoke flow in a fuselage fire. In this case, a student flight engineer had opened the cockpit crew hatch, thinking it would draw off smoke; instead, it made matters worse. And finally, the CAB claimed that if TWA, Pan American and American Overseas—the first three U.S. operators of Connies—had more stringent inspection procedures, the Reading accident might never have happened. There had been maintenance reports of leaking hydraulic lines due to faulty studs, and the board felt the airlines should have recognized the hazard. This may be an example of hindsight—noticing the worn studs and leaks didn't mean they could be immediately identified as potentially lethal—but it merely buttressed the CAB's justification for drastic corrective action.

Initial action had been taken within twenty-four hours of the Reading crash. The circumstances surrounding an uncontrollable in-flight fuselage fire had been such that the Civil Aeronautics Authority, upon recommendation of the CAB, ordered all Constellations grounded pending determination of the cause. Once the subsequent probe disclosed the Connie's flaws, the grounding was extended until they were eradicated. That was to take more than two months; the proud Constellations stopped flying July 12 and were not put back into service until September 20—sixty-nine days in which TWA's transcontinental and overseas schedules were demolished. The handful of DC-4s available for the North Atlantic runs were pitifully inadequate and inferior as well. Bob Buck used to dread a DC-4 overseas assignment.

"They could be brutal," he reminisces. "We'd fly the Atlantic with an indicated airspeed of about one hundred and fifty miles an hour, which is the approach speed of a 747. I remember flights when I logged thirty-six hours of flying time between Paris and the East Coast. We'd have three pilots, one for relief, and the captain would make out the bunk schedule. When we'd leave, everyone was rested and nobody wanted to sleep. The hostess always was assigned the top bunk, which was single, but twenty hours later no one gave a damn where anybody slept. If a bunk was empty, you'd crawl into it. In those days pilots couldn't bid equipment, so there I'd be in a DC-4, wallowing around in a storm I couldn't climb out of, and I'd envy the hell out of a crew in a Connie flying at 17,000 feet above the weather."

TWA's troubles went beyond the effects of the Connie grounding on passenger service and revenues, serious as those were. Domestically, for example, the airline had to pit its DC-3s against American's and United's DC-4s because its own DC-4s were committed to the emasculated international schedules. And amid the trauma of the grounding, TWA's management found itself locked in a bitter contractual dispute with the Air Line Pilots Association (ALPA).

It was a family fight that ended in utter disaster.

On October 21, almost one month to the day the Constellations were reinstated, TWA's more than eight hundred pilots walked out in the company's first strike. And in doing so, they drove the final nail into the coffin of the fellow airman who had taken the airline from an also-ran to global glory.

9

Pilots' Strike

The shutdown of an airline already staggering under the Constellation debacle has never been satisfactorily explained. Certainly the pilots didn't want to strike, even though they sincerely believed management had stubbornly rejected what the pilots considered reasonable demands. And Jack Frye himself, painfully aware of his deteriorating relations with Howard Hughes, knew what the consequences of a strike might mean to him personally. Even before the Connies were grounded, TWA was in trouble financially. Establishment of the international routes had cost far more than anyone expected, and the postwar traffic wasn't living up to expectations.

There are some TWA veterans from that era who are firmly convinced the roots of the dispute were implanted deep in Frye's alleged anti-unionism, more specifically in his hatred of Dave Behncke, who headed the Air Line Pilots Association. If Frye hadn't detested the irascible, hot-tempered Behncke, this theory goes, the strike never would have taken place.

That may well be. It was Frye, with Paul Richter's apparent support, who in 1933 had instigated formation of the TWA Pilots Association, which for all intent and purpose was nothing but a company union. ALPA was just getting started at that time and Behncke, an abrasive man with the personality of sandpaper, was making noises about calling an industrywide pilots' strike to dramatize the new union's battle for better working conditions. There wasn't much doubt those conditions warranted improvement, but for his part, Frye didn't think they justified a shutdown of the entire industry. He talked Swede Golien and a few other pilots into forming their own union. Most of ALPA's members in TWA joined it, although some claimed later they joined under duress.

Golien, respected and well liked, was successful in Frye's behalf. But while the TWA defection from ALPA deterred Behncke from a national walkout, some deep resentment festered among those pilots preferring ALPA over an organization presumably beholden to the company. Professor George E. Hopkins of Western Illinois University, a longtime student of ALPA's turbulent history, says the average TWA pilot went along "because he was bewildered, fearful of losing his job and prone to following his local leaders.

"Swede Golien wasn't really a bad guy, and to this day ALPA loyalists refuse to speak ill of him. . . . The idea of directly confronting men like company chief Jack Frye and head of operations Paul Richter was abhorrent to him. . . . He thought of them as his colleagues. Behncke's maneuvering in Washington, coupled with his threat to call a nationwide strike, was too much for Golien and many pilots shared his views."

But one of the several TWA airmen Hopkins contacted while writing a history of ALPA *(Flying the Line)* was a pilot as well-liked as Golien— Howard "Sonny Boy" Hall, Floyd Hall's older brother. Hall told Hopkins that while Golien had led the defecting pilots, he refused to be the new association's president and that the company asked Hall to head it "because they knew I had been a good ALPA man."

"When I said no," Hall continued, "the next word was from Mr. Frye. He said, 'Hall, if you lead a strike against this company, you'll never work for another airline as long as you live.' Now Frye was an excellent pilot, and later I got to be good friends with him. I don't think that Jack Frye was doing anything that any executive would not have done. But if he'd succeeded with that company union, pilots as a *profession* would have gone down the drain. . . ."

Frye did not succeed. In fact, he was largely instrumental in abolishing the company union, and it was the circumstances of the Bolton crash in which Senator Cutting had been killed that changed his mind. As Hopkins wrote:

> The Cutting crash shocked Frye and Richter back to a stark realization of their almost total dependence on the men who actually made the machines go, who controlled the largest part of their corporate assets in the form of a fleet of very expensive aircraft. . . . In short, the Cutting crash helped TWA's higher management accept the necessity of a strong, independent pilot voice in the industry. They might not like that voice. It would sometimes cause frustration and delay. But it was a safeguard the industry needed, and captive outfits like the TWA Pilots Association simply could not provide it.

History confirms this judgment. The company union lasted for only about a year before virtually all TWA's pilots returned to the ALPA fold. But Frye's dislike of Behncke never abated and could have played a part in the bloodletting of 1946. Whether the union president reciprocated in this animosity isn't known. Dave Behncke, intractable and belligerent in his zeal to better the airman's lot, didn't get along with many people, including his own members. There is no reason to suppose, however, that he picked TWA as the battlefront on which to wage a major conflict solely because of Frye. In truth, TWA was an obvious and vulnerable target simply because it was an industry leader.

It was the Constellation that prompted Behncke to declare war on Frye's airline. The ALPA president made an issue out of the trend toward four-engine equipment, in which TWA had led the way since the days of the Stratoliner. Behncke thought the men who flew the sophisticated and complex aircraft deserved higher pay. While that made sense, his professed reasons for increased pay were not as logical. Behncke based his demands on the questionable supposition that because an airplane traveled faster and covered more miles, the hazards it encountered would increase. What he was asking, in effect, was "hazard pay," an argument that few pilots in all good conscience could buy.

Behncke actually had put forth this curious notion when the Stratoliner went into service but had gotten nowhere when he tried to amend TWA's ALPA contract to include hazard pay. The war prevented him from making this a major issue, but when the shooting stopped and the new Connies began taking to the skies, Behncke was back again, arguing this time that a four-engine plane would result in more workload and greater distractions— for example, it was more dangerous to fly than any twin-engine transport. ALPA's rank and file agreed planes like the Constellation were harder to fly and thus justified higher pay, but to most of them the claim of increased danger was a red herring.

Underlying this internal union dispute was the so-called "Decision 83" of 1934, a far-reaching ruling by the National Labor Relations Board that set industrywide pilot pay scales in accordance with aircraft speed. Frye and his fellow airline chiefs had opposed this, but they lost. Decision 83 was to prove an anachronism because it pegged top pay to a 200 mph maximum. When Behncke launched his postwar campaign, the industry embraced Decision 83 as a counterargument; speed, not size, was the proper yardstick they argued, as well they might with that 200 mph limit.

Dr. Hopkins says Behncke then helped foment the TWA strike by insisting that the airlines bargain individually on new pay scales, Decision 83 notwithstanding. The airlines wanted a single agreement embracing all carriers and, adds Hopkins, "had Behncke been willing to compromise on the issue of industrywide bargaining, the companies in turn might have been willing to renegotiate the Decision 83 pay scales."

TWA, Hopkins points out, already had set such a precedent by granting copilots—the low men on the cockpit totem pole—wage increases that took them to $380 a month, $155 above Decision 83's $225 guaranteed minimum, with another $30 a month added for ICD copilots who qualified as navigators. But Behncke wanted no part of an overall industry agreement with its implied Decision 83 limitations. Quite naturally he preferred to be the wolf that cuts a deer out from the pack and runs it down. He merely was faithful to a time-tested labor strategy that bargaining company by company sets off a chain reaction in which each union negotiating committee tries to win a better contract than the one just signed by someone else.

His insistence on individual bargaining set him on a collision course with Frye, who apparently was as intransigent on the issue as Behncke; Frye was under pressure from his peers to stand fast and he did. Even then, there is some dispute over the role Frye played in letting a strike occur. Bob Buck, a stalwart ALPA member, believes John Collings and not Frye was management's version of an immovable object.

"Frye," Buck says, "was devoting all his energies to getting new routes and John Collings was running the airline from Kansas City. John was a rather narrow-minded kind of guy with tunnel vision. I used to go into his office and warn him that the guys were going to walk out, and he'd tell me they'd never strike. He didn't believe anything like that would happen, nor would he give an inch. If Frye had really been on top of things, the strike might have been averted. I emphasize *might* because nobody knows for sure. Moving into the four-engine era meant ALPA had to establish contractual precedents and TWA, being the first [airline to acquire four-engine equipment], had to bear the brunt. Another factor was management's stubborness. Collings was the wrong guy when it came to negotiations—a good operations man but a minor leaguer out of his element in a labor dispute."

Buck seems to have been an astute observer, for when the pilots walked out, no one was more surprised than Collings. He told a close friend, "It was the most amazing thing that ever happened in my life when I saw those guys come out of the bushes carrying picket signs."

But Buck also holds that if Collings and other TWA officials badly misjudged the pilots' unity and determination, ALPA itself was guilty of misjudgment:

I don't think the pilots realized how serious TWA's and Frye's situation was. On the contrary, they thought the company was riding pretty high with all those new international routes. As in most labor disputes, they expected a last-minute settlement—that something would happen to avoid a strike. They were in a shoot-the-wounded mood. There were great animosities involved—bad personnel relationships in which the pilots felt you were either a good guy or a bad guy, and that management was the bad guy, with nothing in between.

Everybody liked Frye, and they never regarded him as being part of the dispute. He was always somewhere else wheeling and dealing, and it was Collings they disliked. I was never aware that the pilots subconsciously expected Hughes to come to the rescue because he owned the airline and could afford anything. No, it was more of an assumption that the future of air transportation looked bright and that the pilots should share in that future.

George Spater agrees with Buck that if the pilots weren't being realistic, they at least were not motivated by greed. And Spater, who was very much a part of the prestrike and poststrike negotiations, also confirms Buck's contention that Frye actually had little to do with what happened.

"Jack wasn't directly involved with the negotiations," Spater adds. "Nor do I believe that Frye's dislike of Behncke contributed to the strike. I don't think Jack liked him but hell, very few people did including the pilots. His own lawyer hated him. Behncke was a very difficult man, a strange kind of fellow. He always carried a dictionary with him. You'd be telling him something and if you used a word he didn't understand, he'd start thumbing through that dictionary while you were still talking. But as for a Frye–Behncke feud being responsible for the strike, I can't buy that. TWA was just a fat target during the industry's transition to bigger planes."

Behncke himself, according to Hopkins, made a last-ditch effort to avert the strike by sending a popular and highly respected captain named Jim Roe to talk with Frye personally. With a midnight walkout deadline only a few hours away, Roe warned the TWA president, "We just can't go on this way. It's going to go unless we change."

Frye replied sadly, "I can't change it—I can't do anything about it."

The pilots, convinced they had done everything to avoid striking, walked out at midnight October 21. They stayed out for twenty-five days. On November 15, ALPA and TWA agreed to binding arbitration. A three-man arbitration board was established, consisting of Buck representing the pilots; Spater, the company; and Frank Swacker serving as the neutral member.

Swacker, who everyone called "Judge," was an elderly, old-fashioned man who knew the law but had some anachronistic views on copilots. One of the thirteen points of arbitration before the special board was copilot pay, and Swacker thought a copilot was just an apprentice undeserving of much attention.

The board convened in Chicago after its members spent three months studying the thirteen issues under dispute. The deliberations took another week with Buck and Spater pretty much settling matters between themselves; they mutually agreed on figures they thought Judge Swacker would accept. Each had moments of difficulty, not with each other but with the two parties they represented. Buck wasn't happy with some of TWA's officials, whose testimony either involved hard-nosed predictions of imminent bankruptcy or an optimistic outlook that invited compromise. "Dealing with TWA was always difficult," Buck remembers, "because there was constant turmoil in the executive suite"—and there is little doubt he was referring to the increasing influence of Hughes and his lieutenants.

Behncke was Spater's *bête noire*. His strident militancy irritated not only George but ALPA's own lawyer. Spater and the lawyer were discussing a minor issue one day. As Spater recalls, it involved how many days a pilot was to have for appeal after a dismissal notice—and during a recess they encountered Behncke in the hall.

"Dave, there's something we can't seem to agree on," Spater said to the ALPA president. He mentioned what the union lawyer was proposing and what Spater thought fair—only he deliberately transposed the two figures, making it appear that Spater's opinion was the lawyer's and vice versa.

"I think his idea is much better than yours," Behncke snapped.

The ALPA attorney didn't say a word.

One major stumbling block was copilot pay. Buck and Spater came up with a new scale they thought Judge Swacker would buy; the judge did but told Buck, "Bob, I'd have never given you that much."

The board members were meeting in a room at the Drake Hotel, and Buck left to report to Behncke and various TWA pilots waiting in the corridor outside.

"Well, I finally settled the copilot thing," he announced. He disclosed the figures and was immediately inundated with cries of "You sold us out!"

Spater made his own report to TWA executives waiting in another suite. He was immediately accused of selling out the company.

"Strikes are like wars," Spater philosophizes. "You get entrenched in a position and it's hard to back out. All sorts of things are said and representations made and the next thing you know, the shooting's started. I remember when the strike was settled, some of the pilots had tears in their eyes. They told us they really loved TWA and hadn't wanted to hurt it. But as usual, both sides had taken stands from which they couldn't back away. It's almost a love-hate relationship. As for TWA, all I can say is that you pay one hell of a price for being an innovator."

Buck's most vivid memory of the strike nobody wanted involves Behncke. It was during the early stages of arbitration, late in December, and Buck came into Behncke's Chicago office one day.

"Dave, I'm going home," he told the ALPA president.

"What the hell for?" Behncke demanded. "You've got too many things to do around here."

"Tomorrow's Christmas eve," Buck reminded him gently.

"We haven't got time for that shit," Behncke growled.

He was a controversial and colorful figure, this founder and first president of the pilots' union. Totally dedicated to his cause, yet often lacking the finesse required by give-and-take compromise, his tenure at ALPA was to end in another five years when a rank-and-file revolt ousted him. He died shortly after he left the presidency, ailing and embittered, but TWA's veterans remember him today more for his dogged determination than his prickly personality—which so closely resembled that of New York's feisty Mayor Fiorello LaGuardia, Behncke's good friend.

Inevitably, the strike left unhappy residues. Old friendships suffered and loyalties strained. As a member of management but also ALPA, Frank Busch approached the picket line the first day of the strike and was accosted by Jim Roe.

"Frank, if you go through the picket line I'll have to report it to Dave Behncke."

"I don't give a shit what you tell Behncke," Busch retorted. "I work for this company and I'm going to work."

Another renegade was Hal Blackburn, who to his dying day will deeply resent the stiff fine ALPA levied against him for ferrying a Connie during the strike. Blackburn argued there were no passengers aboard but the fine stuck. More may have been involved than a technically illegal flight, however. Blackburn testified for the company at one arbitration hearing and made what many considered disparaging remarks about the average pilot's economic background.

Says Bob Buck: "Blackie'd say this one used to be a farmer and that one came out of a filling station and so on. During one recess I got him to one side and told him to take it easier. 'Hell,' I said, 'when you were a kid you used to play a piano in a whorehouse.'"

As is so often the case, the new contract wasn't universally popular. Such is the fate of any compromise, but Buck took plenty of abuse from his colleagues. "Some pilots praised me and some accused me of selling out to management. All I know is that it was the worst period of my entire life, and I didn't enjoy one bloody minute of it."

Yet the long-range effects were far more important than the short-term results. For one thing, by submitting the dispute to binding arbitration, both ALPA and TWA just about abolished industrywide bargaining for airline pilots and also stretched Decision 83's speed yardstick to 300 mph. The status of copilots was forever changed, as well. "It marked," says Buck, "the start of an era when a copilot stopped being an apprentice and became a respected and essential member of the crew, when we finally acknowledged we needed guys who knew what the hell they were doing, when we started a trend that evolved into what we have today—first officers as well trained and responsible as captains."

Another consequence was financial. The final settlement was modest in 1983 terms—captains, for example, were raised to a maximum of $14,550 for a four-striper with eight years seniority. But in 1946, this was a considerable sum and the increased pay scales came out of the hide of an airline already bleeding from the lost revenues caused by the grounding and strike. At the end of the year, TWA was reporting a 67 percent increase in revenues over the previous year but a stunning net loss of more than $14.3 million—the worst showing in its history to date.

The annual report for that year, significantly, was not signed by Frye. Only nine pages long, it bore the imprint of the board of directors' executive committee—Palmer Bradley, Vic Leslie and Paul Richter. The first two were Hughes' appointees and Leslie, in fact, had been forced on Frye by Noah Dietrich. Of the twenty-four directors, at least eight had been picked by either Hughes or Dietrich, and several others could not have been named without their approval.

And Dietrich, with the dismal results of 1946 as armor-piercing ammunition, went relentlessly after Jack Frye—with the reluctant blessing of Howard Hughes.

Prior to the pilots' strike, Hughes and Frye were still working together in relative harmony. There was some friction but nothing so drastic as to fracture their relationship. Hughes was subsequently accused of throwing Frye to the wolves, but there is equal evidence that he remained loyal to Jack longer than anyone could have expected considering the shape of TWA's finances and the pressure from Dietrich. In fact, George Spater says flatly that Hughes wanted to retain Frye on the condition that Dietrich have a greater say in the running of the airline—a condition that was anathema to Frye. If that was true, it could be said that Frye forced Howard's hand.

Certainly, the embattled president could see the axe suspended precariously over his neck. Either just before or immediately after the strike, he called in his administrative assistant, Jean Phillips.

"Jean, will you find out if there's any kind of equipment I can put on my phone so I can record any conversation I have with Dietrich or Hughes?" he asked. "And I don't want anyone here to know about it except you and my private secretary."

Eventually, Frye's handful of loyalists were let in on the hidden recording device, located in a storage closet. Carter Burgess was one, and so were George Spater and his legal associate, Jerry Brophy. When Frye left TWA, he apparently took the tapes with him and their contents were never disclosed. Frye may have destroyed them or thrown them away. But Burgess remembers that some calls from Hughes lasted several hours. He specifically cites overhearing part of a six- or seven-hour discussion that involved Howard's defense of Dietrich and his insistence that Noah should be given greater power.

In the little more than a year he spent with Frye, Burgess himself had only one conversation with Hughes. It concerned a Hughes request that Frye send his personal Lockheed to Indianapolis to pick up one of Howard's girl friends. Frye wasn't in, so Hughes issued his marching orders to Burgess. He not only wanted the plane, but he insisted that color pictures be taken of its exterior and interior so the lady would get some idea of what she would be riding in.

"But that wasn't all," Burgess says. "He kept me on that goddamned phone for almost two hours telling me how to shoot the pictures. That was the first real inkling I had of how he operated. I had to go out to the airport and take shots of the Lockheed from every angle, and it was just a little thing that would have fitted into the lavatory of a 747."

The famous (or infamous) Hughes phone calls seem to have increased during the tense period that marked the approaching demise of the Frye regime. No matter how trivial or vital the subject matter, they taxed human endurance. In self-defense, Frye had installed long telephone extension cords in his Washington residence, so he could walk from room to room while conversing with Howard. Spater used to see Jack answer the phone in the living room and, while still talking, go to the kitchen, mix himself a drink, and return to the living room without breaking oral stride. The duration of the calls and the frequency were in direct correlation with Hughes' progressive loss of hearing. Spater and many others have attributed Howard's love of the telephone to his auditory problems. There was one TWA official who kept a large jar under his desk. Hughes would keep him on the phone so long there wasn't time to go to the bathroom and relieve himself.

No one but Frye and Hughes knew the content or portent of their telephone talks while the TWA president's fate dangled. People like Spater, Burgess and Jean Phillips were aware most of the conversations were being taped, but Frye didn't divulge either details or gists. Jack could gossip unmercifully about Howard's love life, but he kept to himself their discussions about TWA and his own shaky future. Yet one could make a strong case for a theory that Hughes was being pushed reluctantly into a position of demanding that Frye either relinquish much of his authority to Dietrich or resign.

The word "reluctantly" is based on a coincidental time frame which has somehow escaped chroniclers of the Hughes legend.

The key date was July 7, 1946—five days before the Constellations were grounded. It was a Sunday and Howard Hughes went flying in the XF-11, an experimental fighter designed mostly by Hughes himself. The twin-engine aircraft had two four-blade propellers on each engine, one behind the other; Hughes had the idea this unique arrangement, with eight blades biting the air instead of two or four, would be far more efficient.

The test flight lasted only a few minutes. After taking off from a Culver City airstrip, Hughes swung out over the Pacific and was cruising at more than 400 miles an hour when the XF-11 suddenly pitched violently to the right and went out of control. It kept dropping the right wing no matter what Hughes did to counter the maneuver. With airspeed deteriorating and altitude dwindling, Hughes momentarily considered bailing out, but by now the plane had staggered over Beverly Hill, and he refused to risk its dropping on a populated area. As he unsuccessfully tried to regain control, he spotted the Los Angeles Country Club and headed for it. But the stricken XF-11 was dying; it never reached the open fairways. Instead it smashed through the upper roof of one house, clipped an upstairs bedroom of a second, bounced off a garage and after slicing through several trees finally crunched into a third house.

Hughes was so severely injured that doctors gave him only a fifty-fifty chance of surviving; Frye flew immediately to Los Angeles and went to the hospital. He spent that first night in the hallway outside of Howard's room and when Hughes regained consciousness, Frye was the first person he asked to see.

Hughes spent five weeks in the hospital and much longer than that before he recuperated enough to keep full tabs on the faltering airline. And it was during this period that the pilots' strike occurred, with Dietrich accelerating his vendetta against Frye. It could be said that a faulty propeller was one of the links leading to the destruction of Jack Frye. Hughes himself, close to death, had told investigators to concentrate on the right propellers as the source of the crash. As it turned out, he was right; the right rear prop had gone into reverse, literally pushing while the forward prop was pulling. It was a condition that also could have been applied to the Frye-Dietrich feud; by the time Hughes' health was restored, TWA was in a shambles.

Slowly but surely, Dietrich had swung a majority of the directors into an anti-Frye mood. By early 1947, TWA's stock had plummeted from $71 to $9 and the year's financial outlook called for a repeat of disastrous 1946. Dietrich's account of the ensuing crisis, described in his autobiography, has to be challenged on several points but confirms one key conclusion: it was Noah Dietrich and not Howard Hughes who nailed Jack Frye.

According to Dietrich, Frye's biggest mistake was to misuse funds Noah had raised in a loan agreement with Equitable Life Insurance. It was a $30-million loan that, according to Dietrich, contained a provision forbidding TWA to use the money for deficit financing; presumably it was to be earmarked for purchasing the Constellations, but Dietrich accused Frye of siphoning part of it for other purposes, such as paying off debts and meeting the payroll. He further charged that TWA's precarious state was due entirely to "Frye's inept handling of costs, his inefficient operations (and) his extravagance with new purchases of equipment." He claimed that the only way he could keep Equitable from calling in its notes and forcing the airline into bankruptcy was to promise the insurance company he would add eleven new directors to the board, all loyal to Hughes and not Frye, thus providing the leverage he needed to fire the president.

There is some truth to those charges; Frye did technically violate the loan agreement, but it is hard to see how he could have done it without Hughes' permission. Among Jack's faults was *not* a tendency to keep anything from Hughes, and it must be remembered that they were in almost daily contact. But Dietrich's account is of dubious accuracy in other areas.

In his autobiography, he failed to mention two of the major factors that had turned 1946 into a disaster year—the Connie grounding and the postwar recession. Dietrich did mention the third—the pilots' strike—but insisted that this was actually a blessing. According to Dietrich, TWA was so short of cash that it couldn't afford to buy fuel, and that the shutdown thus enabled it to survive. This argument is in direct conflict with the opinion of every TWA official interviewed in the course of researching this history; there was unanimous agreement that the strike shoved the airline close to extinction. It actually cost TWA $8 million, which would have bought an awful lot of gas.

Dietrich wrote that he added eleven new members to the board in 1947, ostensibly as a means of assuring Equitable that he had packed the board with anti-Frye directors, thus assuring the president's dismissal, which the insurance company was supposed to be demanding. Those eleven new directors were named in 1946, not 1947, and at the time they were not anti-Frye nor had they been elected for the sole purpose of firing him. Says Carter Burgess, so deeply involved in those events of 1947:

"When Frye and Hughes had their big breakup in 1947 over the strike and the costs of starting up international service, TWA's board had been pretty much pro-Frye. Remember, he had picked many of the directors himself. Hughes did, too, but their selection was subject to Frye's veto. The trouble was that when everything hit the fan, the board simply deserted Jack."

Thus, Dietrich's insistence that the board was packed against Frye during the 1947 crisis does not bear up. The truth is that when it came to naming new directors, both Frye and Hughes retained some veto power over the other's choices. And in the end, it made little difference who had picked whom; the majority had been infected with Dietrich's incessant warnings that TWA would go down the drain if Frye wasn't deposed.

It may never be known whether it was Hughes or Dietrich who actually fired him; Jack never told anyone, neither did Hughes, and we have only Dietrich's word that Hughes ordered him: "Okay, Noah, I'm fed up. Fire Frye. I don't care how you do it. Throw him out on his big fat ass."

Maybe that's how it happened but those close to Frye doubt that Hughes was as vindictive toward Frye as Dietrich would have us believe. Hughes *was* disturbed over the airline's financial condition, he *was* convinced that Dietrich had made a logical case against Frye, and he *did* believe that Jack should take Noah's advice if he wanted to stay on as president. There is absolutely no doubt that Hughes laid down that last condition and that when Frye rejected it, the two men parted company—yet without mutual malice. As for Hughes telling Dietrich to swing the axe personally, perhaps he did, but the evidence is to the contrary. Ken Fletcher, a veteran TWA public relations man, says Hughes had a face-to-face confrontation with Frye the day before his resignation was announced, and such Frye intimates as Jean Phillips, Spater and Burgess wouldn't be surprised if this had been the case.

While Frye left TWA without malice toward Hughes, he was not without bitterness toward others, starting with Dietrich. Another, apparently, was Lee Talman, the vice-president of administration; Burgess says Frye "felt Lee had given Hughes and the board the wrong picture of TWA's financial problems." Ironically, Dietrich fired Talman shortly after Frye departed, much to Talman's surprise. The Dietrich purge of the upper echelons was to be brutal, as we shall see.

It was brutal for Frye, too, even though he knew it was coming. Shortly before his departure became official, he asked Jean Phillips if she would mind working out at his house instead of the office on G Street. "I'm beginning to feel embarrassed about working here," he explained, "and I don't want to terminate my business from this office."

So in the final days, TWA's presidential headquarters was at the Four Winds. Not only Jean but Burgess operated out of there, although Burgess spent much of his time at the downtown office. When the resignation announcement came, the airline was stunned; there had been plenty of rumors that Frye was about to part company with Hughes but for most employees, it was more comforting not to believe them. One of the last persons to see

Frye as TWA's president was Hal Blackburn. It was a chance meeting and Blackie impulsively asked, "Jack, are you going to leave us?"

"Blackie, I don't know," Frye replied sadly. "Under the circumstances, unless things change, I can't stay."

Blackburn says Frye was terribly depressed. He never saw Frye again, but he did have a curious encounter with Paul Richter shortly after Frye left Washington. Richter, who Blackie thought was harder to know than the gregarious Frye, unexpectedly invited the pilot out to his home and the two of them shared a bottle of bourbon while discussing Frye's departure and what it meant to the airline.

"Are you going to take his job?" Blackie asked.

"No, I'm not," Richter replied. "I'd rather be president of TWA than president of the United States. But what the hell's the use? I couldn't do anything."

Richter's own resignation was announced not too long after Frye's. Spater tried to talk him out of it.

"You can run the company," he told Richter, but Paul shook his head.

"It wouldn't work," he said.

Spater later heard that something happened—an unpleasant incident, possibly—that convinced Richter to leave, but Spater never knew the details. Spater says that in the final months before the roof fell in on Frye, Richter actually was running TWA and, in effect, was offered the presidency.

"He could have done a good job, too," Spater adds. "He was a man of fine character and ability. A little guy but enormously strong."

Daisy Richter says flatly that Hughes, through an unnamed intermediary, asked Paul to become president. She says he turned it down out of loyalty to Frye and the belief that he could not accept the same condition that had cost Jack the job—working under Noah Dietrich. Yet Otis Bryan believes Richter actually wanted to be president and that it was Hughes who decided against it.

Frank Busch says Noah Dietrich had a candidate in the person of Vic Leslie, "who wanted to be president so bad he could taste it." It would have been a disaster because Leslie was disliked and feared as much as Dietrich. They had worked together, Busch discovered, just before Frye was dismissed. There was a board meeting in Kansas City and Busch, who was general operations manager under John Collings, was asked to provide the details of a nonfatal accident involving a Connie that had landed wheels-up at Los Angeles. Collings normally would have handled the briefing, but he was out of town and Busch was chosen to replace him.

"I walked into the board room," Frank relates, "and before I had a chance to open my mouth this little guy sitting on a couch at one side of the room asks me, 'Why are we using more gas in our DC-3s than United?'

"I said, 'you mean gallons per hour or gallons per mile or what?'

"He said, 'I don't know.'

"I got mad and said, 'Well, if you don't know, how the hell do you expect me to know?'"

Warren Lee Pierson, a board member, interceded before Busch could lose more of his fearsome temper. "Frank," he said soothingly, "Tell us about the accident."

When Collings returned to Kansas City, he told Busch, "I hear you tangled with Noah Dietrich."

"Who the hell is Noah Dietrich?"

"The guy you told off at the board meeting," Collings said.

Later, Busch found out that Vic Leslie had fed the question to Dietrich, obviously wanting to embarrass a pilot he knew was close to Frye.

It was the presence of men like Dietrich and Leslie that caused Richter to leave TWA; whether he wanted to be or could have been president is moot. He confided his unhappiness not only to Blackburn but also to another pilot, Lee Flanagin. "I just can't take it anymore," he told Lee. Richter went with another airline for about a year and then was offered a lucrative Coca-Cola franchise in Oakland, California. He accepted the job and was building a new home in the Oakland area when he died suddenly of an aneurism in 1949. He seemed to have had a premonition of death because just before being stricken, he remarked to Daisy that he had lived a full, privileged life and would not be afraid to die. He was only fifty-three, and Frye sobbed openly when he was informed. Hughes sent Daisy a telegram saying, "We had our differences, but I always respected him."

Jean Phillips accompanied Frye to his new post as president of General Analine, a job he was to hold for almost ten years. The most surprising development was that Howard Hughes continued to stay in touch with him. He had been at General Analine for only a brief time when his secretary told Jean, "There's a Mr. Howard Hughes wanting to speak to Mr. Frye."

"I think he'll take the call," Jean said, "but hold it a minute while I check."

She went in to tell Frye. "Sure," he said, "tell her to put him through."

Jean went into an outer office during the conversation. When she saw the light on Frye's private line go out, she went back in.

"Do you mind telling me something?" she asked.

"Of course," he said, trying but not succeeding to look innocent. "What do you want to know?"

"Doesn't that guy have a hell of a nerve calling you after what he did to you?"

Frye's slight smile evaporated. "Jean," he said firmly, "Howard and I didn't have anything but a businessman's disagreement, and don't you ever forget it."

It was the only daytime call Hughes put through to Frye, but Jack told Jean that Hughes often called him at home—the usual marathon sessions. He never revealed what they talked about, and he was always supportive of Hughes. One day Jean said something derogatory about Howard and Frye frowned.

"There's something I want you to remember about Howard Hughes," he said sternly. "No one must ever write that man off. He has without question one of the most brilliant minds I've ever encountered. In fact, I would describe him as being on that fine line between sanity and insanity just because he's so brilliant. That's why so many people just don't understand his peculiarities."

Frye remained loyal to the airline that had discarded him, too. One day he got a surprise call from Juan Trippe, shortly after TWA had applied for a new route through central Europe. Trippe was furious over the planned invasion and asked Frye to support Pan Am.

"I know you were against the Chosen Instrument," Trippe added, "but now that you're no longer connected with TWA, wouldn't you back us up?"

Jean Phillips says Frye's face turned the color of freshly spilled blood. "Just because I've left the industry doesn't mean I've changed my mind," he said with scarcely concealed contempt. "I don't believe in the Chosen Instrument. It's as simple as that, Juan. I can't support something I don't believe in."

Those who knew Jack Frye were only too aware that he had left a large part of himself with TWA. Jean mentioned once that one of his successors was out riding the line, talking to employees, putting on overalls at the Kansas City maintenance base and getting under the planes with his mechanics. Frye looked pensive and then shook his head.

"That was great stuff in the early days of TWA," he said quietly. "We were small enough so you really could know everyone by name. That guy should be sitting on a mountain looking down on the future of that airline, not running around the system saying hello to people."

He almost returned to TWA. In 1956, a period when the airline was floundering without a president and with no leadership, some of Jack's old associates actually started a campaign to bring him back. Otis Bryan was one of the instigators; he called a secret meeting at his home in Kansas City. Present were Ray Dunn, Floyd Hall, Parky Parkinson and Frye himself. They started at 9:00 P.M. and didn't quit until six in the morning, pleading with Frye to let them contact Hughes and make a pitch in his behalf.

Bryan, the ringleader, was no longer with TWA at the time, but he had been approached by several TWA people. "They came to me and said TWA was in terrible shape—that things were awful and getting worse. They said nobody gave them any answers, there was no one to turn to, and that they represented a lot of people who wanted Jack Frye back.

"I asked them what they wanted me to do. One of them said I was a friend of Jack's and could I talk to him? Or would he come to Kansas City and talk to them? Another man said they had heard rumors the directors were considering asking Frye to become president again. So I agreed to contact Jack, and he said he was willing to at least talk."

The meeting was fruitless, largely because Frye wasn't sure he could work with Hughes, but he was tempted. Bryan drove him to the airport to catch an early morning flight after the session broke up. Frye was quiet most of the way but finally blurted, "Otis, I just don't know what to do."

"It's your decision," Bryan reminded him.

"Yeah. Look, you're a friend of Arthur Eisenhower [Ike's brother] and Palmer Bradley down in Houston—he was on the board when I left TWA and he's still a director. I'd trust those two men if you could contact them and ask their opinion."

Otis agreed. Eisenhower was too ill to see him, but he flew to Houston and met with Bradley.

"If TWA's in such bad shape and the employees want Frye back, I think they ought to have him," Bradley declared.

Bryan reported what Bradley had said to Frye, but Jack was still undecided. He consulted George Spater, who advised him to forget it: it would be impossible to work with Hughes. Frye took his advice, and for the last time turned his back on his old airline. A few years after that clandestine Kansas City meeting, he unexpectedly resigned from General Analine, a job that had paid him four times what he had made at TWA. His motive was simple: he had an idea for a new kind of airliner, and he set out to raise development funds. It was a project that had been in his mind a long time. He had even mentioned it to Bryan and the others at the meeting, citing it as one reason why he wasn't sure about going back to TWA.

The aircraft would be a trimotor, vaguely resembling the old Ford Tin Goose but with far more powerful engines and modern systems. Frye envisioned it as the ideal airplane for underdeveloped countries—simple and cheap to operate, easy to fly, and rugged enough to fly in and out of primitive airports. Northrop actually built him a prototype called the Pioneer that Frye flew around the country, demonstrating it to prospective backers.

It was an impressive machine and he raised some $2 million for the venture, adding to that sum every dime he had ever saved. He still didn't have sufficient funds, but he thought he could swing it if he could build an inexpensive factory in an area with low labor costs and good climate. Tucson, Arizona, was the site he picked. He had loved Arizona since the prewar days when TWA had started serving Phoenix and Tucson. He was convinced the Southwest had great tourist potential and he had worked hard to build up good relationships with the resort owners, even to the extent of flying in travel writers free so they could visit the guest ranches.

The site he picked was near the airport and he purchased a home in an attractive desert area just outside the city. One day in February of 1959, he was driving from the factory site to the hotel in which he and his wife were staying until their new home was ready. Out of a side road came a car driven by an intoxicated woman. It was dark and she never saw Frye's car until it was too late. They collided at an intersection and Frye, not wearing a seat belt, was crushed by the impact.

An ambulance took him to St. Joseph's Hospital, thirteen miles from the accident scene, but he lived only forty-five minutes after reaching the hospital. He never regained full consciousness, and the priest who was present when he died said later that Frye kept mumbling "Please help me . . . please help me."

At fifty-five, he was almost broke when he died, but he left Nevada Smith Frye, his widow and fourth wife, a large insurance policy, which he had taken out when he started the new venture; there was a separate policy for their daughter, Neva Jack, the only child he ever had. Nevada, a former Las Vegas showgirl, moved back to Las Vegas after his death and at this writing still lives there. Jean Phillips gets a Christmas card from her every year, the last unbreakable link Jean has to the man whose memory she reveres.

Others have equally fond memories. Stan Phillips, a long-time TWA sales official, was based in Tucson when Frye was killed. "I'd see him walking around town with a briefcase under his arm. His best friend was Bob Smith, the Tucson airport manager then. He didn't know many people because he was new in town and hadn't gotten settled."

Stan's wife told him of Frye's death when he got home, and the next day he got a call from Smith.

"Stan, can you help me?" the airport manager asked. "We need pall-bearers and TWA apparently isn't sending anyone out."

Phillips rounded up some local TWA personnel and a couple of business-men. Joining them at the last minute was Clyde Fullerton, a TWA vice-president who was in town on business and quickly agreed to be a pall-bearer. The initial lack of pallbearers, however, still bothers Stan, who points out, "Here was a man known worldwide as one of the airline indus-try's giants, and we had to go scrounging."

This slur in death was not as bad as the one he suffered after resigning. On someone's orders—and Dietrich was suspected—the March issue of *Skyliner,* the TWA employee newspaper, reported the resignation with a statement as insulting as it was brief:

Jack Frye has not been associated with the Company as of February 22.

But Jack Frye will never be forgotten by anyone who knew him.

George Spater says, "I don't know if he's ever gotten the credit he de-served. He was a great believer in high standards of service. He'd go over the TWA advertising copy word by word to make sure it was in good taste and honest. He insisted that the airplanes be clean. He was a great origi-nator and innovator; it was Frye who thought up the idea of putting a red carpet down between the boarding gate and the airplane. John Collings laughed at this and talked Jack out of it by claiming the carpet would blow away the first time there was a high wind. But later United adopted the idea and so did TWA."

Carter Burgess says, "God, but he was a bright guy. He had two weak-nesses. He couldn't make up his mind about women and he had a habit of always being influenced by the last phone call he got or the last proposal he heard. He'd catch onto a good idea one day and then leave it for one he heard about the next. He was a great writer—a remarkable master of the English language. Some of his memorandums were masterpieces. I remem-ber one he wrote to John Collings about the size of the cinnamon buns on morning flights. 'They look like cow pies.' Frye complained. He could be ruthless yet he was a very decent guy, and he could fly an airplane about as well as any pilot who ever lived."

Bob Rummel says, "Easygoing in appearance but very tough and deter-mined underneath."

Jean Phillips' memories of William John Frye are the greenest of any-one's. Frye was reputed to have Indian blood and Jean believed it. The offices in Washington had rugs, but the corridor floors were a vinyl tile and she always could identify anyone approaching Frye's office by his or her footsteps. Anyone but Frye himself, that is. She once commented on this to Carter Burgess.

"For example," she told him, "when you come down the corridor I know it's you before you step foot in my office. But I never hear Frye coming. I think it's because he walks on the balls of his feet, like an Indian."

"You mean he tiptoes around the tepee?" Carter asked.

A few years after his death, the airline he loved above all else immor-talized his memory. The big TWA training center in downtown Kansas City was dedicated in his name; a plaque at the entrance of the Jack Frye Train-ing Center reads:

THIS BUILDING IS DEDICATED TO HIM AS A TRIBUTE TO HIS LEADER-
SHIP IN THE WORLDWIDE AIR TRANSPORT INDUSTRY.

A leader, he was, and his gambling instinct was part of his leadership even though in the end it betrayed him. Until the cruelties of high-powered finance caught up with him, Frye and Howard Hughes formed one of the greatest teams in aviation history, and their names will be forever linked.

His life had been full of bizarre coincidences; the month of February seems to have been involved throughout his colorful career. He started Standard Airlines in February. His dramatic flight with Rickenbacker was in February. He set a transcontinental speed record in the Connie in February. He left TWA in February. His death was in February. The latter involved one more coincidence. The car that killed him came out of a side road that led from a factory complex. It was called the Hughes access road and the factory was the Hughes Aircraft Company.

10

Our Father Who Art in Hollywood

With Jack Frye's departure came not merely a changing of the guard but virtual abdication of TWA's independence. Now the airline was not only beholden to Howard Hughes but totally under his control.

The reason was simple: Frye left behind him a void that his immediate successor could not fill, however able he was. TWA's new president, LaMotte T. Cohu, had served as a director since 1935 and was no stranger to the airline industry. At one time he had briefly been president of AVCO, American's parent company. But it was evident that Hughes, who apparently chose Cohu, regarded him as an interim chief executive, a president to serve until he could find someone with a far more extensive airline background.

The result was that Cohu's status, unlike Frye's, was that of a figurehead, his ability notwithstanding. He was a stocky, pipe-smoking man, independently wealthy and independent of mind—the latter a distinct handicap if one wanted to establish long tenure working for Hughes. Cohu served less than fourteen months, quitting after a quarrel with Hughes, and of all TWA's presidents, he is the least known. But in that brief period, Cohu at least won respect. Bob Buck describes him as "a pretty smart cookie—hard-nosed, strong and solid. He knew he was a fill-in president and he wasn't overly enthusiastic about the job."

"Hard-nosed" seems to have been an apt description. He got into a rather heated discussion one day with big Walt Hamilton, superintendent of maintenance in Kansas City, and Hamilton made some remark Cohu didn't like. Walt suddenly found himself on the floor, flipped there by a lightning judo hold.

"Never say anything like that again unless you're prepared to do something about it," Cohu said coldly.

Hamilton was one of several members of the "Old Guard," which included Tommy Tomlinson, who left TWA around this time; Hamilton went to work for Boeing. Otis Bryan quit, too, even though Hughes had asked him personally to stay. It was a plea made the day Frye left; Hughes told Bryan, "Jack's leaving but I want to make sure you'll stay on."

Bryan made no promise without talking to Frye first, and Jack advised him not to leave. "TWA's going to need some good people, Otis," Frye urged.

But Otis didn't get along too well with Cohu, nor with the new chairman of the board, Warren Lee Pierson. He resigned and went to work for Don Andres Soriano as his top U.S. aide and representative. Pierson, incidentally, replaced T.B. Wilson as chairman. Affable, with an instinct for survival that would have made a cat envious, Pierson had been Frye's nominee to the board but escaped unscathed from the post-Frye purge.

Wilson, who had done an admirable job helping Frye establish the overseas routes and stations, was a victim of a house cleaning aimed mostly at TWA's Washington office, where he and other members of the pro-Frye cadre had been headquartered.

Col. Fred Betts, an old-time TWAer himself, was the man sent in with a bulldozer-sized broom. For some reason, he asked Burgess to stay but Carter refused; he had been too close to Frye and had a southerner's sense of loyalty. The only survivor in the Washington office was young Tom Taylor, who had worked as Wilson's assistant on route development.

"I had been there for about a year," Taylor says, "when a dapper little guy [Betts] came in one day and fired everyone in the Washington executive offices except me. I was home sick that day and I guess they just forgot about me. Dietrich was the one who dispatched the hatchet man, but I still think the bloodletting was Hughes' idea."

Taylor spent his entire TWA career, three and a half decades, in Washington and served under eight different presidents. In all that time he talked to Howard Hughes exactly once and that was shortly after Frye left. Tom's usual contacts were with Dietrich, who he considered something of a mystery man. "A very tough guy," Taylor says, "but it always seemed to me that he felt he had to act tough."

The Hughes call came in one day when Taylor was the only one in the office; Howard wanted to talk to Warren Lee Pierson.

"He isn't here, Mr. Hughes," Taylor said politely.

"And what's your name?"

"Tom Taylor."

"Oh yes, I know about you, Tom. I just wanted to know how things are going there—nothing important. Do you like your work?"

"Very much," Taylor assured him. Years later, he remembers the conversation as "perfectly rational, sane and friendly." It gave him a memory of Hughes that is at odds with the usual retrospective image of him as a holy terror and impulsive tyrant. Yet Taylor wasn't the only one who holds this sanguine view. In the mid-and late forties and through most of the fifties, the average TWAer regarded Hughes as an eccentric, demanding, but benign ruler whose status was almost that of a patriarch. "Our Father who art in Hollywood" was the way they referred to him in those days. As his hold on the airline tightened—eventually he acquired more than 78 percent of its stock—he could be exasperating, unreasonable and even cruel to his TWA underlings, from the president on down. But he also could display kindness, tolerance and a kind of shyness that seemed to cry out for normal friendships he knew he could never have.

Bill Meador, who would become one of the industry's most respected maintenance and engineering experts, was a young engineer at the Kansas City base specializing in electronic equipment when Hughes flew in one day. He was piloting a converted B-23, a twin-engine bomber developed too late to see World War II combat; Hughes had picked it up from War Surplus. After he landed, he reported his radio compass had malfunctioned and

149

asked that it be fixed. When a supervisor started to summon a mechanic, Hughes objected.

"I want an engineer, not a mechanic," he declared.

Meador was called and diagnosed the trouble quickly. He replaced a vacuum tube and the compass worked perfectly. Meador was just climbing out of the airplane when Hughes walked up.

"What was wrong with it?" he asked.

"Just a tube, Mr. Hughes. It's okay now."

"Where's the old tube?"

Meador handed it to him. Hughes took the faulty part over to a tube-testing machine and confirmed what Meador had told him.

"Yep, it was gassy," he agreed. "Now let's see if the new one really works." With Meador by his side, he tested the radio compass and politely thanked Bill, who started to leave.

"Wait a minute," Hughes said. "Have you had a chance to look at this plane?"

"Well, I've seen the B-23 when I was at Wright-Patterson during the war."

"You haven't seen a B-23 like this one," Hughes said with obvious pride. "Let me show you what I've done to this one."

For the next twenty minutes, he took Meador on a guided tour through the aircraft, happily pointing out every feature from its navigation equipment to the luxurious interior with leather upholstery, a divan and a kitchenette. To Meador, Howard Hughes that day was a lonely man grasping for a little touch of companionship in the prison cell he had constructed himself. It was a cell whose blocks were composed of suspicion, fear, distrust and wariness directed toward anything that remotely challenged his wealth and power. What Meador had witnessed was that rare moment when Howard stepped out of his cell to share with a kindred soul his love of airplanes and flying, the one field in which he seemed completely at ease— with himself as well as with others.

Joe Bartles, who had so much personal contact with Hughes when he was head of TWA's Western region, once commented that Hughes could be Mr. Hyde outside an airplane and Dr. Jekyll when he was in one. "He was, well, just different in an airplane because he really loved to fly."

The truth was that pilots were among the few people Hughes trusted and even so, he didn't cotton to all pilots—as he demonstrated when he told Frye he didn't like line captains because they tried to tell him how to fly. He did the same thing later with Bartles; when Hughes was planning to fly a Connie to the East Coast with those thirty-five movie personalities as his guests, he had asked Joe to get him a copilot and flight engineer. Bartles kept suggesting names and Hughes rejected every one of them until Bartles finally said, "Hell, Howard, you can't fly those people by yourself."

"Well, I don't want any of those check pilots."

"Okay, no check pilots. But I've some good line captains. . . ." He listed some names but Hughes shook his head.

"I don't really know any of 'em," he complained.

Bartles surrendered. "I'll go with you if no one else is acceptable," he offered.

"Would you?" Hughes asked delightedly.

"Sure." That was how Bartles happened to be on that movie star flight as a copilot. "It was a great trip. I think we stayed in New York for about a month, but the flight engineer and I had a hell of a time getting him to pull back on the throttles so we wouldn't run out of gas before we got there."

Hughes and Hollywood—there were times when TWA employees must have wondered how the latter ever succeeded in making travel plans without the help and frequent intercession of the former. The number of times Hughes demanded the airline do special favors on behalf of his motion picture friends and acquaintances would tax the capacity of an IBM computer. Rare was the time he was thwarted, simply because few had the courage to tell him he was being unreasonable. Joe Bartles, however, was one. Hughes called him one day and said a famous movie director was flying TWA to New York.

"I want you to tell the captain to fly low because this guy has a heart problem," Hughes said.

"Howard, I can't do that," Bartles objected.

"You can, too. All you have to do is do it."

"Howard, if I was a captain and Joe Bartles told me to fly a Connie all the way to New York at three thousand feet, I'd tell him to go to hell. You know as well as I do how rough it gets at low altitudes in the middle of the day. You can't make a whole planeload sick for one passenger."

Bartles held his breath, waiting for one of the world's richest, most powerful men to erupt. But after a few seconds of silence, Hughes said calmly, "Okay, Joe, I guess I'll have to fly him east in my own plane."

"That's the only way to go, Howard," Bartles assured him. And, recalling that incident years later, Bartles mused:

"One of the difficulties of dealing with Hughes was that most people were afraid to say no to him. Yet if you explained a problem to him, he could be reasonable and understanding. It was the people who worked for him that gave us headaches."

"The people that worked for him. . ."

As long as Howard Hughes controlled TWA, there was no way of knowing whether a Hughes dictate actually carried his personal "must obey" label or whether that label had been attached by one of his many lieutenants at 7000 Romaine. Dietrich at times was guilty of doing this and so was Johnny Meyer, Hughes' genial press agent, who once caused even the patient Joe Bartles to blow the whistle. Meyer was always calling Bartles and telling him "the boss wants this" or "Howard says you should do that." Bartles usually tried to comply, but there were occasions when he would inform Meyer, "Johnny, I just don't have time; I'm working for TWA." Such protestations couldn't stop Meyer anymore than a ping-pong ball could stop a tank, and finally Bartles had enough. He phoned 7000 Romaine, announced he wanted to talk to Hughes, and waited for the return call. The speed at which a return call was made often was in direct correlation with how Hughes respected or trusted the caller. This time Hughes contacted him relatively fast and Bartles didn't pull a punch.

"Those damned lieutenants of yours at Romaine are after me all the time," he said with undisguised anger. "You want this done and you want that done. Howard, life's too short to put up with that crap. I'm going back to flying airplanes."

151

Hughes was instantly apologetic. "Now you don't have to do anything like that," he said. "From now on, any time one of those guys calls you and you're busy, just have 'em get in touch with me and I'll tell 'em not to bother you."

He lived up to that promise, although Bartles wryly admits, "Of course, it worked for me, but the guys below me, they had to do whatever he wanted."

Bob McKay, for years TWA's public relations chief in Los Angeles after Clancy Dayhoff left, is in full agreement with Bartles' complaint that Howard's underlings often were more of a problem than Hughes himself. The requests invariably were attributed to "the boss" but, as McKay explains, "you never knew whether 'boss' meant Hughes himself or people like Bill Gay, Nadine Henley or Noah Dietrich." (Gay was Howard's most trusted aide and Nadine his private secretary.)

Yet McKay also was a first-hand witness to the fact that Hughes could display kindness. Bob's wife gave birth to a daughter just before a major accident involving a TWA plane sent him to the crash scene before he could get to the hospital. A week later, he returned to his office and was about to head for the hospital when Hughes called, ordering him out of town on another assignment. McKay, tired and depressed, spoke his mind.

"Look, Mr. Hughes, I've got a wife and a brand-new daughter I haven't seen yet. People at the hospital think the kid's illegitimate because the father never bothered to show up."

"Where are they?" Hughes inquired.

"Hollywood Presbyterian."

"You get your ass over there and right now."

Taken back, McKay said, "Thanks, Mr. Hughes, but I couldn't get in now anyway. Visiting hours are over."

"You won't have any trouble," Hughes predicted.

He didn't, and for all the trouble Hughes could give TWA's public relations department, McKay admired him. "I got along fine with Howard," he says. "If you stood up to him, he could be reasonable. It was some of our top brass who gave him the reputation of being mean and tough—guys like Oz Cocke and Gordon Gilmore [the latter became TWA's vice-president of public relations in 1951]. They were scared to death of him."

There isn't much doubt, however, that Hughes could be most difficult when it came to demanding special treatment for his Hollywood friends and compatriots. For particular celebrities, there were certain rituals to be observed, standing orders to be followed. Hedda Hopper, for example, always insisted that TWA provide her with private limousine service from her home to the airport; her arch-rival, Louella Parsons, was no less difficult. McKay's recurring nightmare was that both of them would book the same flight.

Many VIPs patronized TWA because it was the only transcontinental carrier offering sleeper service in four-engine planes during the forties and fifties. The Hughes office required the airline to block out four to eight berths on every eastbound Connie flight out of Los Angeles, releasing them only at the last minute; it was one of the Hughes dictates that the airline's employees resented because the practice was inconvenient for both them and less prominent passengers. That was the main gripe TWA personnel had about Hughes—his habit of interfering with normal operations when he wanted to please somebody he considered important.

Hughes once ordered a TWA flight out of Athens delayed for four hours in order to accommodate several relatives of a Greek-born movie magnate who had died in California. Hughes phoned TWA dispatch in New York and asked that a Constellation be set aside to fly the relatives to Los Angeles when they arrived from Athens that night. He was informed that the only plane available was the one being used for Flight 91, a berth-equipped aircraft, and 91 was booked solid.

"Cancel ninety-one," Hughes ordered, "and use that plane for the family."

"We've got about fifty people holding space on that flight," the dispatcher said desperately. "What are we supposed to do with 'em?"

"Put them up in a hotel at our expense and send 'em out in the morning."

Thus were some fifty passengers inconvenienced for the benefit of a half-dozen relatives of a Hughes friend. And heaven help the airline if one of Howard's VIPs had a complaint about TWA service—they usually griped directly to Hughes, who would insist on corrective action ranging from abject apologies to refunds. Walt Menke remembers the black day when TWA lost Walter Winchell's hat. The columnist had called Hughes personally, and Menke was notified by 7000 Romaine that this heinous crime had to be rectified instantly. "I was told," Menke says, "to go to the best hat store in New York City and buy Winchell a replacement in the exact size, color and style of the one we had lost."

Although Menke was on TWA's payroll, he was on 24-hour daily call to Hughes. He was constantly taking people to dinner or the theater at Hughes' request, or meeting flights to make sure whatever dignitary Howard wanted to impress was transported to his or her hotel. It made no difference whether Menke or any other TWA employee had plans; a request from 7000 Romaine was a command. Manke once tried a sneak end run to circumvent Hughes' demands on his time; he told his wife, "You answer the phone all this weekend and if it's Howard's office, tell 'em I'm playing golf."

Naturally, a call did come. "Walt's not here," Ruth Menke lied dutifully. "He's out playing golf."

"Can you go get him?" the caller asked.

"No, he's got the car."

"Where is he playing, Mrs. Menke?"

She was trapped, and she mentioned the name of the first nearby course she could think of.

"Fine," the Hughes office said. "We'll send a car over there for him."

Menke laughs. "I had to rush to the golf course so I'd be there when the goddamned car arrived."

Hughes always referred to any TWAer assigned to perform one of his chores as "my representative." He would say, for example, "Mr. Menke, my representative, will be at LaGuardia to meet you." His representatives seldom were thanked, but occasionally Hughes demonstrated gratitude. He once sent one of his own employees all the way from Los Angeles to New York with instructions to see Menke. He was ushered into Walt's office and announced, "Mr. Hughes wants me to take you to Abercrombie and Fitch and buy you a new suit."

It was a nice gesture, Menke thought, yet a justified one, for as Walt puts it: "You had to work for TWA in the day and for Hughes at night, but you never got paid for the latter." It also was a gesture somewhat out of focus with Howard's stereotyped image, that of a tight-fisted miser. Hughes definitely was tight, but at times he could be surprisingly generous.

He once borrowed a car from a TWA flight engineer and kept it for weeks. The flight engineer was afraid to inquire as to a possible date for its return, but one day he came home from a trip and found a brand-new automobile in his driveway. That was typical of Hughes. He was always borrowing things he never returned, but he tried to make sure the owner/victim was compensated. Gordon Parkinson remembers that Hughes often would arrive at Burbank for some trip without a hat. He'd walk into the operations department and take whatever hat he found hanging there but would leave a note telling the employee to buy a new one and put it on his expense account.

Art Stewart met him at the airport one chilly winter day when Hughes was about to leave for the East Coast. Hughes was wearing a business suit but had no topcoat, and Stewart warned him the weather in the East was frigid. Hughes nodded absentmindedly and then eyed what Art was wearing—a handsome camel's hair coat.

"Maybe I'd better borrow your coat," he suggested. Stewart handed it over, knowing he'd probably never see it again. He didn't, so after waiting what seemed to be a reasonable length of time, he bought a new one and put it on his expense account. The item was never questioned although camel's hair topcoats are not often found on airline expense accounts.

Hughes borrowed more than clothing and cars from TWA employees. Because he seldom if ever had any cash on him, he was forever chiseling small monetary handouts. He showed up at the airline's LaGuardia medical office once and somehow wandered into the office of Alice Palmer, the chief nurse. He was tieless, wearing sneakers and looking so bedraggled that she almost summoned a policeman, but at the last minute she recognized him.

"Can I help you, Mr. Hughes?" she asked.

"I wonder if you'd loan me a dime," Hughes said. "I have to tip a cab driver outside."

She gave him the ten cents and to this day has wondered what that dime borrowed in 1947 would be worth if it was to be paid back with interest. (Actually, only about ninety cents.)

Howard's penurious habits were often the subject of discussion among his closest associates at TWA. Illustrative incidents were passed around from officer to officer, not with malice but more in a spirit of wonderment—the sheer illogic of a Croesus so apparently insecure that he had to masquerade as a Midas. George Spater tells a story about Hughes he swears is true, one involving a million-dollar settlement in some dispute that had been decided in Howard's favor. The agreement was reached in the morning and the loser in the case was back at noon, bearing a check for $1 million. Hughes looked at it disdainfully.

"It's only for one million," he said.

"But that was our deal, Howard. One million bucks."

"The deal was made at eight this morning," Hughes said coldly. "It's now noon and I want a half-day's interest."

When Hughes was hospitalized after his XF-11 crash, Spater and John Lockhart were assigned the job of negotiating with Glenn L. Martin for the Martin 202, a twin-engine airliner TWA was considering as a replacement for its aging DC-3 fleet. They were under instructions not to conclude any deal without clearing it with Hughes. Out of the sessions at Martin's Baltimore offices came a tentative agreement to buy twenty airplanes, with Martin promising to take back ten if TWA found twenty were too many. The financing arrangements were attractive, too; after a modest downpayment, TWA would pay just under 3 percent interest on the remaining amount. Spater relates:

"The deal was relayed to Hughes, who was in an oxygen tent. He sent back word that he wouldn't accept it unless Martin knocked off another eighth of one percent on the interest. He was always trying to chisel a little bit. If Martin had offered us six percent, Howard would have asked for five and seven-eighths. Like Oscar Wilde once said, Hughes knew the price of everything and the value of nothing. It was characteristic of him to chisel on everything because he never really knew whether he was getting a good deal in the first place."

Yet in many ways, Hughes was like the elephant being described by three blind men—figuring him out depended on who was doing the figuring. Oz Cocke was with Hughes in Las Vegas one night, and they got into a crap game with a wealthy cosmetics manufacturer. The cosmetics man was doing pretty well and made some boastful remark about his skill with the dancing ivories.

"I'll tell you what," Hughes said quietly. "I'll roll you the dice for a million dollars."

Cocke, who loved to gamble himself, held his breath.

"I think I'll call it a night," the manufacturer mumbled.

Much has been written about Hughes and his prowess with women—or lack of it. Some accounts have him rated as one of the greatest studs in history, and others claim he was a bedroom flop despite all the glamor queens he dated. Both views are held among TWAers, but perhaps the most revealing insight comes from Bob Buck. He knew a starlet who had dated Hughes and with the blunt curiosity so characteristic of airmen, asked her how Hughes performed as a lover.

"Well," she confided, "the first time I went to bed with Howard Hughes it was because he *was* Howard Hughes. The second was because he was the best lover I ever had."

Jack Frye used to tell a story about Hughes and his involvement with a very famous actress who we shall describe only as a sex symbol. According to Frye, Hughes wanted to date her and, as usual, assigned Johnny Meyer to the task of arranging it. Meyer reported back that it could, indeed, be arranged but that this particular actress charged for her services. He named the going rate and Hughes balked; even for a night with this beauty, the price was too high.

"Don't worry," Meyer assured him, "just leave it to me."

Frye swore that Meyer got a hotel room directly under the movie star's and late that night climbed a trellis, sneaked into her room and took half the money back.

That was just one Frye story. Another concerns a young starlet Hughes was interested in. She was beginning to make a name for herself in pictures, and Hughes suggested she should have a more attractive apartment.

"As a matter of fact," he said, "I've found a great penthouse for you and if you're agreeable, come along with me tonight and I'll show it to you."

They had dinner first and then drove to the penthouse. The young lady was delighted. "Howard, it's the most beautiful place I've ever seen!"

"I'm glad you like it," Hughes said. "Do you think you can afford it?"

Frye had been privy to the stormy Hughes-Ava Gardner romance and was fond of her, just as she was partial to TWA and well liked, in turn, by the airline's personnel. So this particular tale has a ring of truth because one suspects Frye heard it from Ava herself. It was during the war, when cars were almost impossible to get, that Hughes decided to give Miss Gardner a Cadillac.

"I'd like one, of course," she told him, "but my Mercury's doing fine and besides, where are you going to find a Cadillac?"

That was no problem for Howard Hughes. Somehow he finagled one and drove it to Ava's house, only to discover she was at the studio filming. He asked her secretary for the keys to Miss Gardner's Mercury and was told Ava had them with her. Hughes called her off the set and asked if she could bring the keys back to her house.

"Why are you bothering me in the middle of a shot?" she asked furiously.

"Well," Hughes explained, "I have the Caddie but I need your keys so I can trade the Mercury in on it."

He could be terribly protective of his Hollywood friends. Darryl Zanuck, head of 20th Century, was a particular favorite of his, as TWA found out on more than one occasion and on the following one in particular. Actress Bella Darvi, Zanuck's good friend, had flown into London on a TWA sleeper plane and was met by Stewart Long, then a young European sales representative and today a vice-president. She happened to mention there had been a mixup in her berth assignment; someone had gotten the one she was supposed to have, but she assured Long it made no difference. Lulled by her friendly attitude, Long didn't ask her what he should have asked: had she mentioned this to anyone else besides TWA personnel? The next day he received a cable from Hughes which read:

MESSAGE
SECURE WESTERN UNION BLANK. TYPE DOUBLE-SPACE CAPITAL LETTERS THE FOLLOWING MESSAGE AND DO NOT CHANGE ANYTHING: QUOTE I AM EXTREMELY UPSET WITH INCIDENT AT LOS ANGELES AIRPORT. PLEASE ACCEPT MY PERSONAL APOLOGIES. I HAVE TAKEN THE NECESSARY ACTION WITH THE PERSONNEL INVOLVED, SIGNED HOWARD HUGHES. UNQUOTE. YOU WILL SECURE 72 36-INCH STEM ROSES REPEAT 72 36-INCH STEM ROSES AND DELIVER NOT BEFORE NOON REPEAT NOT BEFORE NOON TO MISS BELLA DARVI AT HER HOTEL ALONG WITH THE TELEGRAM.

"When I read that cable," Long remembers, "I figured she hadn't told me the whole story. Maybe somebody had raped her on the runway or something."

He went to her hotel apartment with the flowers but omitted typing out the telegram that Hughes had requested.

"Here's some flowers," he told her. "Now, what in the hell *really* happened at the Los Angeles airport?"

She was mystified. "I already told you what happened. It was that little business about the berth. Nothing important."

"Did you tell anyone else?"

"Well, Darryl called me when I arrived here and I told him."

Long later found out that Zanuck had reported the berth mixup to the Hughes office, which in turn had distorted the story to Hughes into a major disaster. Neither Zanuck and Miss Darvi were that upset, but unfortunately a TWA reservations agent was fired as a result. Hughes also issued standing instructions that whenever Bella Darvi arrived at an airport on a TWA plane, the airline was to have photographers present. This led to Walt Menke sending to one station manager, alerted to Miss Darvi's impending arrival, the most treasonable instructions in the annals of public relations. "Use lots of flashbulbs but never mind the film," Menke wired.

The late Ingrid Bergman recounted an occasion in New York when she was part of a foursome that included Irene Selznick, Cary Grant and Hughes. Howard had arranged the evening through Grant, who had no idea of the lengths Howard would go in trying to make an impression on a beautiful woman. They went dancing and when Hughes found out Ingrid, Cary and a studio publicist were planning to return to Los Angeles shortly, he offered to take them in his own plane. They accepted but as Miss Bergman wrote in her autobiography: "I learned later that he'd bought up every available seat on planes flying to California that day so if we wanted to fly that day we had to fly with Howard Hughes."

Such a grandiose gesture would not have been uncommon for him; he frequently used TWA aircraft to fly large groups of his friends on special trips, although it must be added that he compensated the airline at regular charter rates. It also must be pointed out that he *had* to pay TWA for the use of the planes; Civil Aeronautics Board rules prohibited any airline from carrying passengers free without specific permission for specific flights such as route inaugurals. And if Howard could display gallantry (albeit rather ostentatious gallantry) on one occasion, he could be tough on others.

Bob Johnson, who was the Wright Engine field representative at TWA for several years, witnessed one Hughes close encounter with a woman that shows he had a less indulgent side. It was his habit to keep one of the airline's Constellations parked at Burbank so he could use it whenever he needed to. The warranties on the engines were valid only if they were run at regular intervals, and Howard was a stickler about warranties and guarantees on equipment.

He would run up the engines himself, invariably in the wee hours of the morning and insisted that someone from Wright be there to certify the tests. One night he brought along an attractive girl who sat in the Connie's forward lounge reading a book while Hughes revved up the engines. Her legs were crossed and, absentmindedly, she started swinging one leg up and down as she read. Her foot kept rubbing against the upholstery on the bulkhead and when Hughes came out of the cockpit, he saw she had worn a spot right through the cloth.

"That," remarks Johnson, "was the last we ever saw of her."

There were times when it was impossible to understand his actions. More than once he called a TWA official in New York and told him, "Come out to Los Angeles. I have to talk to you." The official would drop everything, fly to California, and never get closer to Howard than a phone booth. At one point, he owned a twin-engine Convair 240 which he never flew. After months of gathering dust under 24-hour guard at the Convair plant, he asked Bob Conley of Convair to try to sell the plane for him. Conley dredged up a good prospect and notified Hughes.

"I need the keys and your permission to show this guy the airplane," he said, "so how about clearing us through your guards?"

"Sure," Howard agreed, "but I'd like to remove a few personal things from the plane first. I've got about $200,000 worth of Las Vegas gambling chips aboard, some old laundry and a few letters from my mother. Wait 'til I get everything cleaned out and you can show him the airplane."

Eighteen months went by before Hughes got around to removing his belongings.

Whether this represented Howard's propensity for procrastination or just forgetfulness no one ever knew. Possibly the latter, for as he had once misplaced the DC-1, he did the same thing with an 0-49 that he had flown to San Diego. From there he drove back to Los Angeles and after two weeks went by, the San Diego airport manager contacted TWA Operations.

"What the hell are we going to do with that Connie Hughes parked here?" he inquired.

"Oh, *that's* where he left it," was the reply.

His demands on TWA personnel ranged from the impossible to the incredible, especially the mandatory pampering of his VIP pals. Many celebrities in the early Connie days used to take a sleeper flight that stopped in Chicago enroute to New York. Hughes issued standing orders that his Romaine office notify TWA in Chicago that so-and-so was aboard and should be met to make sure everything was fine. The Chicago welcoming committee consisted of someone from TWA public relations in the Windy City, usually Mac McCollum, the regional sales manager, and Jim Harrigan, then Chicago sales manager. One night Romaine notified McCollum that Walter Winchell was on the flight and should be met as usual. The arrival time was about 4 A.M.

"Okay," McCollum sighed. "I'll go aboard, wake Winchell up and ask him if he's having a good trip."

Nothing was too good for a VIP Hughes liked or felt he needed. It was not unusual for him to order a flight delayed to accommodate one of them. He did this several times for Harry Cohn of Columbia, and TWA agents at the Los Angeles airport were told to allow Cohn's limousine on the ramp area so he could be picked up at planeside. Harry came to expect such favors as his just dessert. He once inquired as to which side of the plane the moon would be on when he flew east on a night flight. "Whatever side it's on," Cohn added, "give me a berth on the other side so it won't be in my eyes."

Yet for all Hughes' incessant coddling (sometimes to the extent of being destructive to employee morale and self-respect), it must be remembered that at this stage of TWA's history, he was not unpopular. If he seemed to need TWA as an outlet for both ego and his love of aviation, the airline needed him for the financial security he provided. He was not impossible to work for, merely difficult at times, and occasionally even fun. Says Al Jordan:

"In those early years, Howard was very interested in the airline. While he did some weird things, he had a vital concern that we were running a good operation. He'd come out and check on us himself. He'd talk to maintenance people and engineering people. He was always wanting to make our airplanes better and safer. Sure, it seemed like every new model we'd get he'd take for his own use. He'd put a guard on that airplane and you couldn't get so much as a spare part off it. But the important thing was that he was interested in TWA's equipment. I think he checked out on just about every type of aircraft this company ever had."

Bob Rummel has these recollections about Hughes' personality and professionality:

I always found him easy to talk to. He was extremely interested in aviation technology, asked the right questions and demanded very detailed information. Before he made a decision he looked at things from every possible angle and even a few inconceivable angles. Yet he had a sense of humor. He was always cracking jokes although he also was a very intense sort of person. I flew with him many times, and he was a different person in a cockpit when he could be his own man and enjoy the freedom of the air.

A lot of the stories I've heard about him may have been true in his later years, like having such fear of germs he refused to shake hands with anybody. Hell, I shook hands with him all the time. He was fascinated by anything technical. I remember once he had me check out the Northrop Flying Wing to see if it had commercial possibilities.

He was hard to reach but I was lucky. I didn't have much trouble but then, I didn't abuse the privilege. His office at 7000 Romaine was really something. Bill Gay headed the operation and a slew of guys worked there—fifteen or twenty. To get into the main office you went through a closet full of brooms, then through a door at the back of the closet. If I wanted to reach Hughes, I'd call them at Romaine and say I wanted to talk to Howard. They'd ask 'What about?' and I'd say 'That's between Hughes and me. All you have to do is tell Mr. Hughes I'm trying to reach him.' The reason for all that was simple: I didn't want anything misunderstood or misquoted. Sometimes I'd say the matter was urgent and that he should call me back in a reasonable time. He usually would.

We had a lot of disagreements, but they certainly weren't heated, although a couple of times I thought I might get fired. But I figured he owned the company and he was entitled to my best judgment. He wanted facts and that's what I gave him. The arguments usually were over technical matters or business [matters] insofar as they applied to airplanes and what you could do with them. I think that gradually through the years he learned to respect me.

Noah Dietrich's book on Hughes was all wrong—a hatchet job full of errors. A lot of people who wrote about Hughes didn't know the man and I did. And no matter his faults, he came to TWA's rescue after the pilots' strike as he did time after time.

Bob Buck was in Howard's company a number of times and recalls this: "One thing that impressed me was how polite, kind and thoughtful he could be. He asked me to come out to Los Angeles once to do some flying for him. I went to his house around midnight, and the first thing he did was apologize for making me take the long trip. He wanted to know if my hotel room was satisfactory. . . . Did the Hughes office supply me with a car and did I have enough cash with me?"

It may have been Hughes who was instrumental in Buck getting an enviable assignment—something far better than his previous extracurricular job flying a B-17 into thunderstorms as part of a weather research mission for the Air Force. The new post involved Tyrone Power, who wanted to do a movie based on the life of South African Prime Minister Jan Smuts, and informed 20th Century he was going to fly to Africa and meet Smuts personally.

Darryl Zanuck liked the idea of the movie but not the idea of one of his top stars flying that distance by himself, even though Power was a Marine-trained pilot. Zanuck offered Power the use of the studio's DC-3, provided that he take along an experienced airline crew. Thanks to Zanuck's friendship with Hughes, only one airline was considered. TWA was contacted and Buck was nominated.

"I wasn't sure I wanted the assignment," Buck admits. "I figured flying a temperamental movie star around would be a pain in the butt, particularly one who thought he was a pilot. But I agreed to meet with Power and at least discuss the trip."

They did meet and Power's first announcement was brief and to the point. "We're all one crew," he said, "not a boss and his hired hands. Whatever I get in the way of quarters, food and all the rest, you get the same. Furthermore, you're the aircraft commander; when we're flying, you're in charge. Any questions?"

"Yeah," Buck drawled. "When do we leave?"

They flew to South Africa along the same route TWA crews had followed during the war—down to Natal and across the South Atlantic in easy stages fitting the DC-3's range. There were five men aboard in addition to Power and Buck—flight engineer Bill Agner, radio operator Bill Ritter and navigator Bob Stevens, all from TWA, plus Bill Gallagher, Tyrone's secretary, and Jim Denton from studio publicity.

Power lived up to his promise. At one stop, the local hotel manager unctuously ushered Ty to palatial quarters and assured him he had been given the finest suite.

"Where's the rest of the crew?" Power asked.

"Oh, we gave each of them a nice single room."

"They get suites, same as me," Power snapped.

When they reached South Africa and showed up for an appointment with Smuts, an aide told Power he could see the prime minister alone, but no one else would be allowed in. Power blew up and announced he was going back to the U.S., and only when Buck calmed him down did the actor agree to see Smuts, leaving the crew waiting outside. Power emerged a few minutes later with Smuts by his side.

"Come in, come in!" the prime minister greeted them. "I don't know why that silly bloke got the idea you weren't welcome."

The same thing happened in Rome, where Power refused to attend a scheduled audience with the Pope unless his crew was with him. But Buck respected him for more than just his camaraderie. "He was one of the best pilots I've ever flown with," Buck maintains.

They came back via a northern route, and over Greenland they flew into an ice storm. The DC-3 was staggering all over the sky and the cockpit was filled with tension until Power remarked soberly, "Boy, if Spyros Skouras [20th Century's board chairman] could see me now, he'd shit!"

Approaching Moncton, Canada, on the return flight, they were warned that the airport was virtually socked in. A Trans-Canada crew radioed that they had tried to get in and gave it up as too dangerous, proceeding to an alternate. Buck turned to Power.

"What do you want to do?"

"Let's make one pass and see what happens."

Buck grinned. "Now you're thinking just like an airline pilot."

With Power flying, they made one pass and sneaked in. The papers the next day carried the story that Tyrone Power had landed when an airliner pilot couldn't. The trip had taken three months and Buck remained friends with the actor until Power died. The TWA pilot has his own epitaph for Tyrone Power:

"I read that sleezy biography some creep wrote about him after he was dead and couldn't defend himself. It was a bunch of crap that he was a homosexual. He was all man. He had a hell of a sense of humor, too. He gave each of the bachelor crew members a wooden cane on which they were to notch every feminine conquest during the trip. We were all betting his own cane would look like an asparagus tip but he didn't win. The quietest crew member—I won't tell you which one—had more notches than Power."

Buck was one of the luckiest TWA employees; in the three months he was away on the Power expedition, he didn't have to witness the post-Frye deterioration of morale, the ineffectiveness of the Cohu regime and the sporadic, spotty leadership of Hughes himself. Hughes could solve a crisis with the usual money transfusion but couldn't prevent the crisis from happening in the first place. In this period, it was not Cohu or Hughes who kept the airline breathing but the people of TWA, who responded to lack of leadership by supplying much of it themselves.

With the typical, traditional resilience of airline personnel, TWAers fought adversity with courage, wit and stubborn optimism. If the occasion demanded, they could even talk back to the brass with the irreverence of frontline troops toward rear-echelon officers. Sales vice-president Clyde Fullerton was holding a pep rally in Chicago, explaining to his staff why TWA had to economize, sell more tickets, live within a budget, go easy on expense accounts and work longer hours without more pay. Finished with a fight talk that would have had Knute Rockne sobbing, Fullerton asked if there were any questions. In the back of the room sat jaunty little Carlos

Belliero, an Italian by birth and a humorist by instinct. He raised his hand, and everyone held their collective breath. Carlos was unpredictable.

"Yes, Carlos?" Fullerton asked.

"Meester Fullerton," Belliero began. "I want to know how come you want us to eat like flies and shit like elephants."

For a time, Carlos was in charge of the Hughes office's travel account, which included handling Hollywood bigwigs who would ask Hughes to make their reservations instead of going through TWA or a travel agent. And to work for Howard Hughes, albeit indirectly, was an achievement for Belliero of such proportions that at 2 A.M. one day he called his colleague Charlie Billerman in Dallas, where he was working on an interchange plan with American and Delta. Billerman was sound asleep and so groggy when the phone rang that he ran into a door on the way to answer it and broke his nose. Bleeding and half-stunned, he finally picked up the phone.

"Charlie, this is Carlos. What you think I did today?"

"Carlos, I don't know what the hell you did, but it damned well better be important."

Belliero dropped his voice to an octave level of sheer awe. "Charlie, I meet the man."

Wounded though he was, Billerman was impressed. "You mean you met Howard Hughes?"

"No. The man who handles everything for him."

"Jesus Christ," groaned Billerman. "Is that all you called me about?"

"Yes. Tomorrow I'll call you about something else."

Belliero also worked in New Orleans for a while and Billerman, visiting the city on business, accompanied Carlos when he made his morning round of sales calls on customers. Billerman noticed that Belliero worked only one side of whatever street he was on and asked why.

"Charlie," Carlos explained, "always I walk on the shady side. I never make calls in the morning if they're on the sunny side."

During the time Belliero was in charge of the Hughes account, National, American and Delta were operating an interchange between Florida and Los Angeles. National took the first leg to New Orleans, where Delta picked up the through passengers and flew them to Dallas. From Dallas to Los Angeles they traveled on American, and one night Belliero phoned Billerman.

"Charlie, got a big deal. I got four people coming from Florida and they can't get space on American out of Dallas."

"When are they coming through?"

"Tonight."

"Jesus, Carlos, I can't do this in one day."

"You gotta," Belliero pleaded. "I got the call from Mr. Hughes' office and they're gonna call you direct."

"What do you mean, they're calling me? It's your problem."

"It's yours now. Goodbye."

Less than a half hour later, Billerman's phone rang. The caller identified himself only by saying, "This is Mr. Hughes' office," and added, "The party of four is traveling under the name Jones and they are to have four window seats on American's interchange flight to Los Angeles. After they are boarded, you're to call me with the number of each window seat they're occupying."

Billerman contacted the manager of American's reservations center in Dallas and explained his needs. He was quickly discouraged. "Charlie, there's no way I can do it. The flight's closed—booked solid."

"Okay," Billerman sighed, "I'll have to call Doc Miller [American's regional vice-president]."

He reached Miller at 2 A.M.

"This sounds like one of your goddamned Hughes deals," Miller guessed.

"It is. Doc, I'm desperate."

"Well, call Bob Blum at the airport."

"I did. He said no."

"So what the hell do you expect me to do?"

"Well, maybe you can put a little pressure on Blum. Maybe he could find four local boardings you could shift to another L.A. flight."

"No way."

"Okay, I'll have to call C.R. Smith."

"You wouldn't have the guts," Miller challenged.

"The hell I wouldn't. Where is he?"

"He's probably in bed by now. He was speaking at some dinner in New York and he's at the Waldorf Astoria. But, Charlie, if you bother him, I'll fix your wagon."

"I gotta, Doc. You said it yourself; this is a Hughes deal."

"Look, Charlie, why don't you come see me tomorrow morning and maybe . . ."

"Tomorrow's too late, dammit. That interchange gets in from New Orleans in a couple of hours."

Billerman hung up, called the Waldorf Astoria and managed to wake up a sleepy C.R. Smith.

"You don't know me, Mr. Smith, but I'm Charlie Billerman of TWA and I have this problem. . . ."

Smith listened to the problem and chuckled. "What kind of a bet do you have with Doc Miller?"

"No bet, but he said if I called you he'd have my ass."

"He will, too," Smith assured him. "Tell you what; I'll give him a call and you just stand by your phone."

By now it was 4 A.M. and Billerman's phone rang—Doc Miller.

"You son of a bitch. Okay, I've got it arranged to get them on the airplane, but there aren't any window seats. So you get your ass out to the airport, meet the flight, and work with our boys even if you have to unload the goddamned baggage."

Billerman expressed his undying gratitude and rushed to the airport. The plane landed and Billerman stood at the bottom of the boarding steps calling out, "Jones—party of four?" Finally, everyone had deplaned, no one had answered and Billerman was dying. Then a passenger turned around and approached him. "Who were you looking for?"

"A party of four named Jones. I'm with TWA."

The man laughed. "That's just like Hughes—tagging us with a fake name. I'm Governor LeRoy Collins of Florida and I have the other three gentlemen with me." (It turned out that they were state officials, accompanying Collins to a meeting with Hughes on some land deal.) Billerman escorted them into a little VIP lounge for coffee while waiting for the interchange flight to be serviced.

"I've still got a problem," he told Collins. "I couldn't get window seats."

"We don't want them," the governor said. "That airplane has a lounge in the back. We sat there all the way from Miami and it was great. The lounge will do just fine."

Billerman found the captain and asked if the "Jones party" could occupy the lounge without being assigned regular seats.

"Well, they're not supposed to sit there during takeoff or landing, as you know, but I'll look the other way this time."

Billerman watched the plane take off and then remembered he had to call 7000 Romaine. The same voice who had issued the instructions answered and Billerman reported that they were on their way.

"Fine. Give me the window seat numbers."

"They're not in window seats."

"What?"

"No. But the governor said he'd rather sit in the lounge and that's where I—"

"The governor? Who told you? How did you find out?"

"Look," said the weary Billerman, "I could hardly spend a half hour with those guys without finding out who they were. As a matter of fact, the governor introduced himself."

Bang went the phone.

"I went home at dawn," Billerman says, "without knowing whether I had a job to go to that day. But I never heard another word, and a few days later it was announced that Hughes had bought all this land in Florida. Eventually it was used for the Hughes Medical Foundation. Today I can laugh about it, but at the time I was in agony. I don't think American would have helped me if they hadn't known it was Hughes, not TWA, putting on the pressure. You could get a lot of sympathy from other carriers, working for Howard."

The airline was thickly populated with characters in ground personnel like Belliero, who later in his career caused an international incident when he was stationed in Rome. Carlos shipped the body of a deceased Egyptian princess on a TWA flight from Rome to Cairo, but a couple of caskets got mixed up. The Egyptians, with great reverence, opened that of the princess and discovered a male corpse.

There also was Mel Warshaw, who seemed unable to make out flight schedules unless he was in a men's room sitting on the john. Another was L.C. Cole, known as "Memphis," who served as station manager in various cities including Burbank and Rome. In the latter post, he worked with Carlos and a regional officer named Dick Mazzarini. The three of them were always feuding. Rod Edwards, a veteran TWA accounting and insurance expert, was sent to establish budgetary controls in Europe and the Middle East but encountered static as soon as he hit Rome.

"Those three guys," recalls Edwards, "had me running from one office to another, denying all responsibility and each telling me, 'that's not my department.' That was some combination—two Italians and a Tennessee hill-billy."

Cole had his troubles with TWA. He was demoted to sales representative in San Francisco and wound up with the same job in Dallas, an off-line city. Jim Harrigan, a well-liked regional vice-president, had the distasteful job of firing him, but as Edwards points out, Memphis couldn't have cared less.

"He drove a specially built Thunderbird," Edwards says, "and he and his brother owned tree farms in Tennessee and North Carolina and also made a fortune packing mud for oil wells. He was so independently wealthy he'd carry around uncashed TWA paychecks for weeks."

Cole was an irreverent type. Someone in the Kansas City hierarchy decided that domestic station managers needed lessons in public speaking so they could sell the international division. Memphis attended the first session in which the speaker was explaining how different sound systems worked.

"Now, can any of you tell me what causes fading?" he asked his audience.

"Cheap dyes," Memphis called out.

Another master of the quick retort was Jerry Condon, who served TWA in many capacities over the years and became president of the Seniors Club after retirement. During his career, not even lordly four-stripers escaped his Irish wit. He once told Hal Blackburn, "You're the only captain whose ring we have to kiss." One of Jerry's favorite targets was a sales official named Milt Chandler, who frowned on any subordinate drinking during business hours. He used to stand downwind so he could smell any whiskey on a man's breath. Condon was in a men's room one day and occupied the urinal next to Chandler. There was an uneasy silence for a moment before Jerry spoke.

"Milt," he said, "I've always wanted to have it out with you."

One of the most popular station managers was Bill Noonan, who ran the Washington base for years and was a good friend of Harry Truman's from the latter's senatorial days to his post-presidential years. Truman was catching a flight to Kansas City one morning, and the TWA Ambassadors Club wasn't open that early. Noonan had a key, however, and offered Truman an eye-opening belt. Drink in hand, the senator proposed a toast: "Bill, here's hoping you live to sixty-five and on your sixty-fifth birthday you'll be arrested for rape."

Noonan laughed but Truman said, "I'm not finished. When they bring you to trial, I hope the judge finds you guilty."

Harry Truman flew TWA frequently to Kansas City, and when he took a flight that had to stop in Chicago enroute, he would deplane, go into the station manager's office and call Bess to tell her where he was and when she should meet him in Kansas City. The airline always had someone from public relations there along with the Midway Airport photographer, Mike Rotunno. One cold winter night, Truman's flight from Washington landed, and John Corris of public relations met Truman with Rotunno in tow. They were making idle conversation about the weather and Truman asked, "How cold do you think it is?"

"Out in Wheaton, it's ten below," the photographer said.

"Wheaton? Where's that?"

Rotunno explained it was a suburb about ten or twelve miles from Chicago. "Colonel McCormick of the Tribune has his farm out there," Mike added.

Truman frowned. "I hope he freezes his balls off," he snorted.

Truman's warm associations with TWA were suspended, naturally, when he became president and acquired his own airplanes—first the *Sacred Cow* and later the *Independence,* the new DC-6 that Jack Frye had tried to derail before it could achieve the prestige status of Air Force One. In a way, Truman's use of a DC-6 was almost symbolic, for it coincided with the model's introduction into commercial service by United and American. It was head-on competition TWA could ill afford to lose, but lose it did—the Connies took a beating.

The DC-6, the first pressurized transport Douglas ever built, was truly formidable opposition. Slightly faster and larger than the 0-49, it bettered the Lockheed's transcontinental schedules by an hour and in both United's and American's configurations carried four more passengers. Simpler to maintain and more economical to operate, the DC-6 also had superior engines; until TWA and Wright finally eradicated a few bugs, the Connie's power plants were disappointingly unreliable. Once the airline suffered ten engine failures in a single day. It was an intolerable situation that strained relations on a broad front; Wright claimed the airline wasn't maintaining the engines properly, TWA blamed Wright for not designing and building them properly, maintenance blamed the pilots for mistreating them and the pilots cursed at everybody.

Ironically, the vaunted DC-6 was to suffer the same ignominious fate as the Connie had. Six months after going into service, all DC-6s were grounded following two internal fuselage fires, one of them causing a fatal crash, that disclosed a major design flaw. During the in-flight transfer of fuel from one tank to another, the CAB discovered, it was possible for an accidental overflow to be sucked into a belly air intake and from there take a path right into the cabin heating system.

For more than three months, all DC-6s stayed on the ground while Douglas changed the location of the belly airscoop. But Howard Hughes already had acted even before the DC-6 got its black eye. With TWA virtually out of cash, he made a time-payment deal with Lockheed late in 1947 for twelve improved Constellations called the 749s, with beefed-up engines and additional fuel tanks to provide New York–Paris nonstop capability.

And, having committed TWA to $15 million worth of new airplanes in a year that had seen the airline lose another $8 million, he began looking around for a new president.

11

Pythias Finds His Damon

Two significant events preceded the selection of TWA's new president. Both involved Juan Trippe's Chosen Instrument concept. Three times the wily president of Pan American had been defeated on this issue, twice in Congress and once before the Civil Aeronautics Board, but Trippe's major strength was persistency. If a front door was locked he went around to the back.

Early in 1947, Trippe got Sen. Owen Brewster of Maine to introduce another Chosen Instrument bill, one which had Trippe's fingerprints all over it. This was not surprising. In Washington, Brewster was known as "the senator from Pan Am," and Howard Hughes himself contemptuously referred to him as "Trippe's mouthpiece." Both Hughes and Noah Dietrich were furious at this latest version of the Chosen Instrument, which they regarded, with considerable justification, as one aimed not only at creating a single international U.S. flag carrier but as a means of destroying TWA.

The legislation once again strove to actualize the concept of one U.S. international airline theoretically owned by a number of carriers but operated by Pan Am. It added a provision, however, that set a retroactive "deadline" for cutting off ownership of international assets—October 1945. It was no wonder Hughes interpreted this as a knife held at TWA's throat; TWA had started its overseas operations after that date, so that while it would be able to hold stock in a flag carrier, it would not be compensated for its international route investments. What infuriated Hughes even more was the fact that Trippe already had made overtures for either a TWA–Pan Am merger, or the sale of TWA's international routes to Pan Am.

Shortly after Brewster introduced the bill, Hughes was summoned to Washington to testify in closed session before the Senate War Investigating Committee, of which the Maine senator was a member. The committee was probing wartime contracts, and included on the agenda were the $60 million worth of contracts Hughes had been granted for airplanes that had never got past the prototype stage. The prime target was the mammoth flying boat *Hercules* Hughes had built largely with government funds. Made of plywood, it had acquired the nickname "Spruce Goose," and Hughes was not only inordinately proud of it but extremely sensitive on the subject of whether it could actually fly.

Before the hearings began, Hughes—apparently seeking to mend some fences (and perhaps on Dietrich's advice)—agreed to lunch with Brewster. The two men met in Hughes' suite at the Mayflower Hotel. Ostensibly, they discussed the giant flying boat, but Hughes claimed later that they also discussed two other topics: the Chosen Instrument bill or a possible Pan Am–TWA deal in which Hughes' airline would sell its international routes to Pan Am. Brewster denied that either subject was raised at the Mayflower meeting, but his denial appears to have been somewhat evasive. The meeting in the suite was not their only contact, for the next day Hughes used his own plane to fly Brewster to an appointment in Columbus and later to Morgantown, West Virginia, and back. If Chosen Instrument and merger hadn't been discussed in the suite, there was plenty of time to bring it up while Hughes was transporting the senator around.

Even before Brewster and Hughes met, Juan Trippe had contacted Noah Dietrich about TWA's bowing out of international competition. Then and on a subsequent occasion, he had talked merger with Dietrich—the second time implying that if TWA didn't go along, it faced domestic competition from Pan Am if the CAB were to approve his application for a transcontinental route linking Pan Am's Pacific and Atlantic operations.

After the Hughes-Brewster contact, Trippe also saw Hughes and made his usual Chosen Instrument pitch. Hughes didn't seem impressed, but from all accounts they parted on friendly terms, and they were to meet again at Hughes' request—secretly in Palm Springs where merger once more was discussed. Noah Dietrich, the only witness, is the sole source of what transpired. According to Dietrich, Trippe wanted to buy out TWA's international routes whereas Hughes talked about a total merger in which Pan Am presumably would have been the surviving carrier. The vague but startling price tag Hughes mentioned was a pretty good indication that Howard had no intention of merging. He told Trippe that TWA's overseas routes alone were worth twice of all Pan Am, a dubious claim inasmuch as the book value of Pan Am's stock was four times that of TWA. Dietrich believed Trippe still had hopes of working out a deal, but Hughes appears to have been toying with his rival. In Noah's opinion, Howard merely was buying time to plan his strategy against the Brewster bill.

That bill was doomed, rejected by committees in both the House and Senate, and never reached the floor of either body. In July of 1947, a War Investigating subcommittee opened public hearings into Hughes' wartime contracts, and Owen Brewster was delighted. The subcommittee had evidence that Johnny Meyer had spent considerable sums of Hughes money entertaining Air Force officers, including Elliott Roosevelt. Here was a chance to tarnish not only the Roosevelt name but the man who had fought so hard against the Chosen Instrument.

The early testimony from Meyer was more damaging to the press agent than Hughes. Gleefully reported by the press, it was a detailed account of the various and voluminous favors Meyer had performed for the late president's son—everything from a $1,000 loan to nylon stockings for actress Faye Emerson who later married Elliott. Roosevelt then took the stand to deny any improprieties and question the accuracy of Johnny's expense accounts, which, indeed, appeared to have been well padded. At this stage, all the subcommittee had was a strong suspicion that Meyer had lived high on Howard's hog, but the Republican members were sounding as if they had a live campaign issue. That Roosevelt had accepted some favors was not in doubt, but at this stage Hughes seemed to have been more of an expense account victim than a cold-blooded briber. He didn't interpret it that way, however. He was in Cary Grant's living room listening to radio accounts of the Washington proceedings and kicked a zebra skin rug across the room.

"They're lying about me!" he exploded to Grant. "And they're not going to get away with it!"

Against everyone's advice, including that of his legal and public relations staff, Hughes issued a statement to the press that should have been typed on asbestos.

Everybody in the aviation industry recognizes that Senator Brewster is lying. The people in the industry are only too familiar with Senator Brewster's relations with Pan American. And the people in the industry know that if Brewster were pushing the investigation of my war contracts for really legitimate reasons, and if Senator Brewster really believed me guilty of obtaining war contracts by improper means, he would not be romancing me on the side, inviting me to lunch, and making appointments over the telephone to see me in California.

I charge specifically that at a lunch in the Mayflower Hotel in Washington, D.C. last February, Senator Brewster in so many words told me the hearings need not go on if I agreed to merge the TWA airline with Pan American Airways and go along with a bill for a single overseas airline.

From the wording, rather awkward in spots, it is evident that Hughes had composed it himself. And having fired this bombshell, he climbed into his B-23 converted bomber and flew to Washington to testify under oath that Owen Brewster, not Howard Hughes, was an attempted briber.

On August 6, he strode into the marble-pillared Senate Caucus Room—some forty minutes late—and proceeded to face his enemies. He was not only tardy but sloppy—tieless, with a soiled shirt he seemed to have slept in and a seedy-looking sports jacket (he had borrowed it from someone). Hughes gave the impression that his careless apparel was deliberate, reflecting his contempt for politicians, Brewster in particular. But to the packed room, heavily populated by women, his appearance was unimportant. As far as public and press alike were concerned, he was Jimmy Stewart challenging the might of the United States Senate in *Mr. Smith Goes to Washington.* The urge to compare him with Stewart was irresistible, for when he was on the stand his slow drawl, faintly tinged with a Texas accent, sounded for all the world like the actor's.

And no actor could have put on a better show nor played a meatier role. Over the next two days, as an admiring Edward R. Murrow put it, Howard Hughes "not only demolished Brewster's charges but almost wrecked the subcommittee established to investigate them." Hughes repeated his accusation that Brewster promised to call off the hearings if Hughes handed TWA over to Juan Trippe. Brewster, also under oath, denied it. One of them, as Hughes himself admitted, was lying. But in the frequent exchanges between these two opponents, it was Hughes who came off as the more believable. He was cool, self-controlled and openly scornful, while Brewster was shrill and frantic. Hughes not only cut Brewster up in little pieces but just about dismembered the subcommittee's chairman, Homer Ferguson of Michigan.

At one point, Ferguson asked Hughes if he had any questions to submit to the subcommittee.

"Between two hundred and five hundred, just about," Howard said.

Ferguson's incredulous stare was matched by the equally disbelieving look on Brewster's face.

The chairman snapped, "I repeat—do you have any questions?"

"Between two hundred and five hundred questions," Hughes repeated. His tone was that of a gunman inviting a bully to draw.

Flustered, Ferguson adjourned the session until the next day.

Many witnesses have been cited for contempt of Congress. Howard Hughes openly displayed his contempt and got away with it. Ferguson, informed that Johnny Meyer had left Washington, demanded that he return for further questioning. Hughes said he didn't know where Meyer was.

"He's not in this room and the staff can't find him at his hotel," Ferguson observed—so petulantly that both Hughes and the audience laughed.

"It isn't funny," Ferguson growled.

"I didn't laugh, Senator," Hughes said. "Somebody behind me laughed."

Angry and frustrated, Ferguson kept pressing Hughes to produce his missing press agent—who, it developed, was in Europe quite legally because his subpoena had expired. Finally the chairman asked, "Will you see that he is here at two P.M.?"

"I don't know that I will," Hughes said defiantly. They exchanged looks that could have been dueling swords. Then Hughes, his voice rising in his first real show of anger, did something few Congressional witnesses have had the courage to do: he went on the attack, challenging that 2 P.M. deadline.

"Just to put him up here on the stand beside me and make a publicity show?" Hughes demanded. "My company has been inconvenienced just about enough. I brought Meyer here twice. You had unlimited time for questioning."

Ferguson warned him of "possible contempt" and once again asked, "Will you bring Mr. Meyer in here at two P.M.?" He had thrown down a gauntlet and Hughes picked it up.

"No, I don't think I will," he said firmly.

There not only were no contempt proceedings, but Ferguson abruptly recessed the hearings—to give the subcommittee ample time to locate Meyer, he explained limply. They were never resumed, and Hughes emerged the clear victor. Brewster subsequently was soundly defeated in his bid for reelection, and Pan Am's Chosen Instrument crusade was dead. Juan Trippe changed strategy. He dropped his courtship of TWA and went after a more receptive bride: C.R. Smith and his American Overseas Airlines. Trippe's timing was excellent; 1948, like 1947, had been a rough year for the airline industry in general, and Smith was unhappy about the red ink gushing from AOA. American Airlines, the parent company, was the nation's biggest and most prosperous carrier, but the overseas subsidiary was a drain.

Pan Am had first sought domestic routes but ran into the unanimous opposition of the entire industry. Rebuffed, Trippe tried mergers, sounding out United, Eastern and National in succession, plus a proposed three-way merger involving Pan Am, National and Delta. Trippe, cold shouldered on these, too, decided his only recourse was to reduce the international competition and in C.R., he finally found a peer willing to listen.

After weeks of negotiations, agreement was reached on a price tag: Pan Am would take over AOA's routes for just under $17.5 million. It was a bargain just for the routes, but Smith threw in AOA's eight new Boeing Stratocruisers, seven Constellations and five DC-4s, plus retroactive mail pay the government owed American Overseas. The government debt amounted to almost $5 million, which exceeded the $4.5 million in debts Pan Am assumed as part of the agreement.

All in all, it was a steal—so much so that Smith's right-hand man, vice-president and general manager Ralph Damon, resigned in protest. Damon had opposed the AOA sale from the first minute it was proposed—without his prior knowledge, it was said—and became even more disenchanted during the negotiations. Publicly, his resignation was said to be more in the nature of a retirement, that Damon was tired and after a rest planned to teach at a small college. But there are few secrets in the airline industry and Damon's real reason for leaving American was well known. The one person who didn't believe it was C.R. himself. He once told George Spater he was positive that Damon made a deal with Howard Hughes to join TWA before American sold AOA to Pan Am.

Whether this was true is unimportant. Damon did reach an agreement with Hughes and most of the evidence points to its having been made after the AOA sale. Hughes contacted him either through an intermediary or by calling him direct—it is not known which—and quickly convinced him to join TWA. The chief selling point was obvious: TWA had the international routes and international potential that Damon had seen go down the drain with the demise of AOA.

Few if any airline executives had a better reputation than Ralph Damon. He had spent a lifetime in aviation and knew every phase of it from manufacturing to in-flight service. At one time he had headed Republic Aviation, one of the nation's leading airframe manufacturers, and at American he had formed a perfect team with C.R., who willingly gave Damon much of the credit for the airline's premier position. Hughes considered himself lucky to land him and so did TWA officials. Their airline was still floundering, with 1948 another red ink year, albeit in a paler shade—just under a half million dollars. That wasn't a bad showing compared to the combined $22 million loss of the two previous years, but it wasn't the whole story.

The trouble was not with the financial picture so much as with the lack of continuity in leadership. For all that has been written about Hughes' interference with the airline's operations, the truth is that he wanted a strong president. In a sense, Howard was the George Steinbrenner of commercial aviation—a well-intentioned owner who picked capable managers and then drove them crazy with second-guessing and unsolicited advice. LaMotte Cohu quite possibly might have made an excellent president, but not with Hughes looking over his shoulder. Cohu's happiest hours at TWA were spent riding the line. He loved to visit the cockpit and some captains let him sit in the copilot's seat and handle the controls briefly.

Cohu resigned June 1, 1948. Damon didn't become TWA's president until January 25, 1949, and in that near-vacuum of almost eight months, the airline's rank and file kept it alive. Leadership at the top was splintered. John Collings ran TWA from the operational side while Oz Cocke provided marketing and sales direction, but there was a sad dearth of cohesion and purpose. The nominal head of the company was board chairman Warren Lee Pierson, described by George Spater in these rather unflattering terms:

"He carried on from one regime to another, kept a low profile, didn't make many decisions or do much of anything except stay out of trouble. Of all the people I've met, Warren Lee did less."

Vic Leslie, vice-president and treasurer, actually wielded more influence than Pierson and enjoyed the support of Dietrich, who had brought him into the company. For this reason, plus his aggressive and domineering personality, Leslie was disliked by most of his fellow officers and a fair-sized proportion of the "troops" who came in contact with him. "He caused a lot of unhappiness in the company," Spater says of him.

For that matter, John Collings wouldn't have won any popularity contests, either. He was an unusual man—as tough as chrome steel, an unrelenting perfectionist, intolerant of human failings. He commanded no affection but he did command respect. The pilots grudgingly admired and hated him in equal proportions. "He could be an unmitigated son of a bitch," Lee Flanagin says. "I never had any problem, but others couldn't get along with him."

Collings' best friend was Frank Busch, one of the few who was totally unafraid of him. Admittedly, Busch wasn't afraid of anybody. Some said it was because he was related to the Anheuser-Busch brewery family but this opinion smacked of envy. Frank's gamecock no-guff personality came naturally and did not stem from financial security. Ida Staggers tells of Busch's early days with TWA when copilots were serving meals:

"Frank used to steal all the beef and cheese sandwiches. All that would be left would be ham sandwiches, and Busch would offer these to Jewish passengers. It's a wonder anybody got fed on a Frank Busch flight."

Busch was always feuding and fighting with Collings, known as "Uncle John" to his associates in operations, although the term carried a connotation of sarcasm rather than affection. Collings had a corner office at 10 Richards Road, a strategic location from where he could see TWA's entire ramp area at the Kansas City Municipal Airport. If a flight was late departing, Collings would run down to the ramp to find out why. He would fine any employee caught without a TWA timetable on his person, and this applied to pilots as well as sales personnel. He was a stickler for detail and very thorough. One cold day Busch was giving some captain a checkride, and they had just taxied to the end of the runway prior to takeoff when the tower summoned them back.

"What the hell's wrong?" Busch demanded.

"Collings wants to see you."

Cursing, Busch taxied back and went to Uncle John's office.

"Yeah, John—what's up?"

Collings glared. "Did you check those wings before you left the ramp?"

"I did. Why?"

"You know damn well what frost on wings can do. It'll keep you on the ground."

"I'm well acquainted with that, John."

"And you checked the wings?"

"Hell, yes, I checked. Not personally, but a mechanic did."

"Okay. I just wanted to make sure."

"Why you goddamned son of a bitch!" Busch roared. "You could have told me that on the radio!"

In person, Collings was tall and slender with a slight, incongruous paunch. He had one idiosyncrasy that puzzled anyone who knew him for his calculating, no-nonsense mind; he was a pushover for the chain letter craze of those days. Parky Parkinson says Collings collected more than $5,000 from chain letters, which seems to have been his only form of gambling.

Oz Cocke, however, would have bet on one of two raindrops descending down a window pane. Dice, poker, roulette or blackjack—it made no difference to Oz, who was gregarious, personable and as popular among employees as Collings was feared.

"A capable guy," says Spater, "devoted to TWA, and likewise the people who worked for him were totally devoted to him, perhaps too loyal. I've come to the conclusion that to be a top airline executive you have to be super-tough, and maybe Oz was too nice a guy. He was very open-minded and knowledgeable, not in the least pompous, either. He'd listen to ideas and he was very nice to his people, probably because he had come up through the ranks himself. He had started as a ticket agent and never forgot it. A hell of a golfer and card player. One thing to remember about him that a lot of people didn't realize—Oz was well liked by foreign carriers who simply trusted him."

Spater raises an interesting point: TWA has always enjoyed good relationships with foreign airlines, even those competing with it. It was one of the plusses that attracted Damon to the airline, for it contrasted starkly with Pan Am, the airline that was absorbing his beloved American Overseas. Stewart Long, overseas for almost his entire TWA career, says the difference was close to being philosophical and describes it this way:

"I don't think there was ever an anti-TWA feeling overseas. If anything, it was pro-TWA and anti-Pan Am because Pan Am always felt they were the U.S. flag carrier, even though they weren't, and acted that way. They've never gone out of their way to be friendly with a foreign government because, historically, they've used our State Department to get what they wanted. TWA went the other way, rightly or wrongly, and made a real, conscious effort to get close to foreign governments, foreign civil aviation authorities, foreign airport officials and even national carriers. If you interviewed foreign airlines, you'd find they're much closer to TWA than any other carrier, even those they pool with."

Pan Am, of course, simply reflected Trippe's own personality—described as "independent" if you liked Trippe and "arrogant" if you didn't. Trippe hated anything or anyone not wearing the blue and white colors of his own airline. TWA once had a Connie grounded in Shannon with engine trouble and Pan Am mechanics there installed one of their own spare engines. Warren Lee Pierson wrote Trippe a warm letter of appreciation and in turn received a polite letter of acknowledgment. Later, TWA officials heard that Trippe fired Pan Am's manager at Shannon for helping his airline's biggest rival.

The TWA Ralph Damon inherited early in 1949 was doing far better internationally than domestically. In the previous year, the International Division actually netted a profit of more than a half million dollars; the Transcontinental Division lost $1.1 million, and there wasn't much doubt that many of the latter's difficulties were attributable to the composition of the fleet. TWA's 0-49 Connies were pitted against American's and United's DC-6s in long-haul markets, and TWA had an aging collection of DC-3s (seventy-two at the end of 1948, twenty-four of them leased) competing with American's brand-new fleet of Convair 240s, the first and most successful of the postwar twin-engine airliners. The Martin 202, intended as a DC-3 replacement, was ostracized throughout the industry when serious structural deficiencies were disclosed following the crash of a Northwest 202. The Northwest plane was brand-new, but on August 29, 1948, it lost a wing in a thunderstorm and the subsequent investigation unearthed metal fatigue—in an aircraft that had compiled less than fourteen hundred flight hours!

The CAB ordered all of Northwest's 202 fleet inspected. Of the seventeen Martins the airline was operating, five had developed fatigue cracks similar to the one found in the severed wing of the crashed airplane, and three of these five had cracks in both wings. All 202s were grounded while the fault, a badly designed wing flange that was supposed to absorb the strains and stresses of flight loads, was eliminated. Made of a new alloy, the flange was vulnerable to fatigue after only eighteen months of operation. TWA, which had ordered twenty Martins and had planned to put the first ones into service by the end of 1948, refused to accept delivery.

One of Damon's first acts as president was to negotiate a new contract with Martin. TWA agreed to lease temporarily twelve modified 202s and ordered thirty Martin 404s, a larger pressurized version of the 202 (the airline later increased its orders to sixty-one planes all told). Nor was Damon satisfied with the long-haul fleet. Even the newer 749 Connie was inferior to the DC-6 in some respects, and there was considerable sentiment within the airline to buy the superb Douglas transport. But Damon opted for an even more improved Constellation—the 1049 or "Super Connie." For years it has been widely believed that TWA kept buying Constellations solely because of Howard Hughes' preference for Lockheed and his friendship with Bob Gross. There was one story that Hughes refused even to consider the DC-6 because Douglas wouldn't demonstrate the plane on a weekend as Howard requested.

Jack Real of Hughes Helicopters, as close to Hughes as anyone who ever worked for him, says he has heard that story many times but was never able to confirm it. But while Real concedes it could be true, he adds that Hughes "wasn't as strong a supporter of Lockheed as some people like to think." Real believes it was his admiration for Gross, not respect for Lockheed airplanes, that kept Hughes buying Connies for TWA despite opposition from TWA technical people like Rummel, Ray Dunn and several others.

In fact, TWA came very close to acquiring a DC-6 fleet after Damon became president, but it was Damon, not Hughes, who decided against it. Howard actually leaned toward the DC-6 after listening to Rummel praise the simplicity of the Douglas design with its single tail, less complicated boost system and "constant width" fuselage. Rummel's main beef about the Connie was its shape—narrow at the nose, widening in mid-cabin and tapering again toward the rear. The DC-6's more conventional shape, with cabin width unvarying from nose to tail, was more comfortable for passengers and provided greater flexibility of interior arrangement.

It made sense to Howard but Damon balked. "He had just come from American," George Spater says, "and simply did not want to buy the same kind of airplane C.R. Smith was operating"—a theory that not only makes sense but is further supported by the fact that United, too, was flying DC-6s.

The decision to buy a bigger and better Connie brought Damon into conflict with Noah Dietrich, who thought TWA's reliance on Lockheed was just bad business. The violent confrontation was witnessed by Spater. Dietrich claimed that Hughes wanted the DC-6 and Damon, who apparently already had talked Howard into the Super Connie, called Noah "a goddamned liar." From then on there was bad blood between the two men, but if Noah had any idea of undermining Damon, it would have been futile. Ralph Damon had Hughes' confidence and respect for as long as he served as TWA's president.

True, there were still the early morning phone calls and the suggestions that were more like orders, the continuing favors for Howard's friends and the occasional bowing to his whims. Sometimes Damon couldn't reach Hughes and would leave a message with Lee Flanagin or Bob Rummel who usually could. Nor could Damon do anything about the VIPs Hughes pampered. Zanuck, for example, used to have five berths blocked out every Monday night on a Paris–New York flight and they weren't released until the last minute. Stew Long remembers one occasion when he deliberately violated that arrangement.

"I knew he couldn't use them every week and neither could his office, so I'd take a chance and sell them. But this once I guessed wrong and oversold the flight. I had to contact Zanuck and tell him what had happened. He understood. The funny thing was that if you could get to him before he got to Hughes, you were safe because the way he'd report it to Hughes and the way it eventually got back to me, it had become an international incident. You can't say this too often; it wasn't always Hughes but usually the people who worked for him. By the time a Hughes request filtered through to TWA personnel like myself, it had been exaggerated into a major crisis, ten times more important than it was to start with. Actually, Zanuck was a nice guy. He used to tell me, 'The United States is a place to make money but Paris is where you get to spend it.'"

Another fond memory is the time Hughes rushed into Long's office in Paris and announced, "Give me five thousand dollars."

"Who the hell are you?" Long demanded.

He found out, in a hurry.

Damon learned quickly to live with Hughes' natural assumption that inasmuch as he owned the airline, he could do anything he wanted with it. But in many ways Damon was his own man, as the Connie–vs–DC-6 decision demonstrated. And there is absolutely no doubt he proved to be a leader. He turned the company completely around in 1949 and kept it in the black for the entire six years in which he served as president. The accumulated profits for that period totaled some $37 million. And beyond that cold if attractive financial achievement was what he did for the morale of TWA's nearly 11,000 employees. They remembered the not-too-distant past when

Tom Taylor in Washington had to run over to the Post Office Department and get an emergency mail payment so the airline could meet its payroll.

No one knew what to expect when Damon came aboard an airline leaking at the seams. A few of the top brass like Cocke had met him at various industry functions, but social contacts are a lot different than working for a man. Rumor started that Damon intended to emasculate the sales department with wholesale firings. On his first visit to Kansas City after he was named president, Damon was scheduled to address the local Management Club and did a double take when he entered the meeting room.

The club president, Jack Burlington, who was assistant sales promotion manager in Kansas City, had rented an old-fashioned bandleader's costume. Over the loud speaker system came the stirring sound of Sousa marches. Hung all over the big room were signs: WELCOME RALPH DAMON . . . HI RALPH . . . WE'RE WITH YOU, BOSS.

Parky Parkinson sighs. "He never felt so welcome and at home in his life. And he didn't fire anybody."

Whether he actually meant to clean out sales will never be known. Damon was promotion-minded himself, and among the things he did at TWA was to beef up a public relations staff that already was highly regarded through the industry. One of his most effective moves was to elevate the head of public relations, Gordon Gilmore, to a vice-presidency, thus giving PR a position of influence that was rare among the airlines.

Gilmore, an ex-sports writer from a small town, was a natty dresser whose sartorial splendor did not quite hide his nervous nature; he could come unglued at any development that did not follow his carefully prepared scripts. A complaint from the news media or a reprimand from an officer higher than himself could put Gilmore into orbit. As previously noted, he was deathly afraid of Hughes. But he was intelligent, innovative and loyal to his own staff. Out of his fertile mind sprang ideas that invariably earned the airline favorable publicity.

It was Gilmore who expanded the prewar Arizona tourist promotion visits into an annual event of far greater proportions—the TWA aviation and travel writing awards competition. Early each January, the airline would fly a large group of aviation and travel writers to Phoenix and Tucson, with an awards dinner in Phoenix climaxing the four- or five-day "Quickie Vacation," as Gilmore dubbed it. It was an event looked forward to avidly by this section of the journalism fraternity. Gilmore even talked his fellow brass into pulling a Connie off regular schedules and flying the press into the sun country, stopping at various cities to pick up the reporters and writers who had accepted invitations. Later the "QV" was extended to Las Vegas where, as was done in Phoenix and Tucson, local hotels or resorts picked up the tab for the rooms and meals.

By all accounts, the favorite QV guest was the late Justin Bowersock, colorful aviation editor of the *Kansas City Star*. He was "Sox" to anyone who was his friend and he had no enemies—even among the various TWA PR men who were assigned to him on each QV solely to keep him out of trouble. Sox was one of the best aviation reporters in the U.S., but he loved to drink and, as a matter of fact, was about the happiest, most inoffensive imbiber who ever got crocked. He once told Gilmore, "When I die, Gordon, I wish I could see a technicolor shot of my liver."

Under the influence, Sox was absolutely unpredictable. He went to a trout fishing farm in Las Vegas one year and was pulled into the water by a fish. On another QV visit to Vegas, he was missing one morning just as the chartered buses were scheduled to take the contingent to the airport. A frantic search failed to locate him, but at the last minute he came weaving out of his hotel, where a TWA PR man spotted him.

"Where the hell have you been?"

"Well," explained Sox innocently, "I was standing outside this hotel waiting for your bus when a wedding party arrived. Naturally I congratulated the happy bride-to-be and her future husband, who confided that the best man hadn't showed up. So I volunteered my services and attended the ceremony—which included a champagne breakfast, I'm pleased to report."

The QVs lasted until well into the jet age, when TWA abandoned them for economic reasons. But while they lasted, they were the envy of other airlines and one of Gilmore's proudest achievements. He was also enormously proud and protective of his staff: Bob McKay in Los Angeles; Tom Bell and later John Corris in Washington; Frank Gillespie in Chicago; Ken Fletcher, Ed Boughton, Dan Kemnitz and Herb Richardson in New York; Bob Helmer, Jerry Cosley and Larry Hilliard in Kansas City, to name a few. But Gilmore could be tough on his troops, too. He insisted that a QV had to be run efficiently according to preplanned logistics. If something went wrong, Gordon climbed walls.

One year John Corris was assigned the job of making sure the QV baggage was picked up at the various resorts and taken to the airport. Corris was aboard one truck that hit a bump so hard that half the luggage wound up in the road. It took time to retrieve it and Corris arrived at the airport late, where an angry and thoroughly upset Gilmore was waiting.

Corris recounted what had happened, adding, "I think we got all the bags, Gordon."

"Thank God," Gilmore said. "But were any damaged?"

"Only one," Corris assured him.

"Jesus," moaned Gilmore. "Whose?"

"Yours," Corris said gently.

Gilmore's passion for adhering to instructions was put to its greatest test when Howard Hughes developed a Terrain Warning Indicator (TWI) just before Damon took over. The TWI projected a radio beam aimed straight down and set to pick up any terrain that rose suddenly. That would activate an alarm in the cockpit, warning the pilot he was approaching a hill or mountain. Originally it had been an Air Force device invented by RCA as a form of tail warning radar; it picked up the echo of an aircraft following in the wake of a bomber. Hughes was intrigued enough to buy it from the Air Force and, with the help of his own engineers, changed the antenna to point downward instead of straight back. TWA's Bill Meador, who was in on the modification project, says Hughes came up with the idea of pointing the antenna down when he learned that 98 percent of the world's topography sloped less than 45 degrees.

It wasn't a bad device but maintenance was a problem, and it gave off so many false alarms that TWA pilots lost confidence in it. Also, it was useless unless the terrain being approached was sloped 45 degrees or less. Bob Buck tested the TWI and reported to Hughes that he didn't like the alarm setting, which called for the first warning bell at 2,000 feet, the second at 1,000 and the final warning at 500 feet. Buck suggested making 300 feet the final setting because 300 feet was TWA's minimum altitude. "Pilots would ignore it at five hundred," he explained, "but they wouldn't if it sounded at their minimum."

Hughes said he'd have to think that over and a few days later, he called Buck, who will never forget the conversation. "It was about two A.M. and he insisted that five hundred feet was better than three hundred. He kept me on that phone for two hours trying to get me to change my mind. I finally agreed to five hundred because I couldn't stay awake. I would have agreed to shooting my mother at that point."

Having won over Buck, Hughes ordered Gilmore to arrange a series of demonstration flights for the press. This was done and the flight got excellent media coverage, but Gilmore learned that one prominent journalist who hadn't been thoroughly briefed on TWI was Malcolm Muir, then publisher of *Newsweek*. Gilmore was informed of this omission while playing golf on a QV in Phoenix. The Hughes office in Los Angeles called him off the course and advised him that while touring the Hughes Aircraft facilities, Muir had expressed an interest in TWI. Gilmore was thereupon instructed to charter a plane to Los Angeles where he was to board Muir's eastbound flight and accompany the publisher to New York on a TWI-equipped Connie.

Bill Meador got into the act when his boss summoned him and told him to catch the next flight to Chicago. "When you get there, Bill, go to operations and wait for our ninety-two from Los Angeles. Gordon Gilmore will get off the plane and meet you to explain everything."

Meador arrived in Chicago and learned that the captain commanding 92 was the one who had written Hughes a glowing letter praising TWI as the greatest aeronautical development since the Wright brothers. When Gilmore showed up, he confirmed that this captain's assignment to 92 was no coincidence.

"You're to sit in the front of the airplane," he continued. "Right after we reach cruising altitude, walk back to where I'll be sitting with Mr. Muir. I will introduce you. Then, Bill, I will say to Mr. Muir, 'By the way, Mr. Muir, Meador was project engineer in charge of installing the TWI on our airplanes, in case you have any questions for him.' He will have plenty of questions, of course, so at that point you will invite him up to the cockpit where he can actually see the device. Is all this clear?"

"Perfectly," Meador said.

The script was followed up to the moment when Gilmore identified Meador as an expert on TWI. "Do you have any questions about it?" Bill asked dutifully.

"No, I don't think so," Muir said, looking out the window.

Gilmore turned pale. "I thought he was going to have a heart attack," Bill adds, "so I decided to save him from one."

"By the way, Mr. Muir," he improvised, "there's a TWI on this airplane if you'd like to see it." The color returned to Gilmore's face, and he gave Meador a look of immense gratitude.

"Well, that might be interesting," Muir allowed.

"Fine," Meador said. "Come with me and just ask the captain if he'd mind showing it to you."

They marched to the cockpit, knocked, and the flight engineer opened the door. The captain turned around and without the slightest prompting blurted, "There's the TWI, Mr. Muir!"

While Hughes dabbled in exotic technology like the TWI, Damon went to work in more prosaic fashion, shoring up what he felt were weaknesses in TWA's domestic system. He encouraged the development of the airline's first coach service, using DC-4s and the old Stratoliners, and later would pioneer the concept of two-class service—first class and coach—in specially designed Connies operating transcontinentally. Never before had a single airplane carried two classes of passengers paying different fares, and it was a brilliant marketing move that set the stage for fare structuring in the jet age.

A great deal of time, money and effort went into fighting the Pan Am takeover of American Overseas—a battle close to Ralph Damon's heart. It turned out to be a case of snatching defeat from the jaws of victory. The Civil Aeronautics Board disapproved the merger that had been opposed not only by TWA but virtually the entire industry. The CAB's vote was a narrow three-to-two, the majority finding that the merger would strengthen Pan Am's dominance of the international market and thus would put undue hardship on TWA.

Tom Taylor, rising fast in the esteem of his superiors, rode shotgun on the case and had every reason to believe it was settled. The board's decision had to be approved by the White House, as did all proceedings involving foreign routes, but the occupant of 1500 Pennsylvania Avenue was TWA's old friend, Harry Truman. Damon instructed Taylor to keep close tabs on Truman's deliberations, an assignment Tom remembers with a great deal of pride because it contrasted with the way Dietrich treated him during the Brewster-Hughes hearings. Noah had summoned him to the Hughes suite at the Mayflower. Taylor recounts: "I had to go through security to get in the room, and I thought I was going to get involved in some really high-level deal. All Dietrich said to me was, 'Do you see those two bags? Take 'em up to New York and check 'em into our hotel there.'"

Taylor commanded much more respect from Damon. He liked the young lawyer who had gone to work for TWA in Washington after a stint as a bomber pilot in World War II. And it was from Taylor that Damon got the news of an incredible turn of events in the AOA case. Truman actually signed the CAB's majority decision but then unexpectedly announced he would approve the merger. Pan Am's effective Washington lobby, plus C.R.'s close friendship with Sam Rayburn, a fellow Texan, had influenced Truman to change his mind.

Taylor was sent to the board to examine the document the president had signed originally and later testified in court that the signature had been erased. "American got it done through its Texas contacts," Taylor believes, "and I'm convinced Rayburn was instrumental in changing Truman's mind."

TWA challenged the legality of the final decision on the grounds that the erased signature represented improper altering of a legal document. The brawl went all the way to the Supreme Court, which upheld the merger, but

TWA wasn't as badly hurt as it seemed. In approving Pan Am's acquisition of AOA, which put Pan Am into Paris and Rome, Truman also gave TWA authority to serve London and Frankfurt.

"In retrospect," Taylor points out, "it probably was a fair switch, although we objected like mad."

Certainly Damon wasn't that bothered, although he went through the motions of voicing abject disappointment. Privately, he welcomed the chance to serve two prime European markets in Britain and West Germany, and he wasn't worried about competing against Pan Am at either London or Frankfurt. Nor did Pan Am's entry into Paris and Rome, both regarded as TWA-dominated cities, concern him unduly. Damon didn't think that much of Pan Am's competitive ability. He had built AOA's service into an operation generally considered superior to that of Trippe's airline, and he figured he could do even better with TWA—particularly when he got the new Super Constellations and an even better version to be called the "Super G" series.

Both the Super C and G Connies were eighteen feet longer than the 049 and 749. Lockheed added nine feet forward of the wing and another nine feet aft of the wing after looking around for an older Connie that could be cut up and then extended to determine if the longer fuselage was aerodynamically feasible. The only one available was the first Constellation ever built, aircraft number 1961, which happened to be owned by Howard Hughes. He had bought it from the Air Force after the war for only $20,000. Jack Real, then with Lockheed, tells the story of that plane.

"It was fully instrumented for test flying with water ballast tanks installed throughout, perfect for our needs. It had been sitting down in Culver City for years, so when we needed a Connie we could cut up and stretch, we contacted Howard. The negotiations lasted three months, but we finally bought the airplane for $100,000. Then the delivery was delayed and delayed, because Howard was trying to strip the airplane. He was removing the wiring, copper tubing and everything he could get his hands on. I knew that for a fact because I was sent over to Culver City to see what was holding up delivery and there was Howard, personally supervising the dismantling!"

As fully important as fleet modernization was Damon's relations with his employees. Few airline presidents have ever had the rapport that Damon possessed—a natural, unaffected charisma that stemmed from his genuine liking of people. Rod Edwards witnessed the "Damon touch" when Ralph was in Boston on a business trip and stopped in at American to see some of his old associates. Edwards says, "They had formed a kind of reception line, and Damon was going down the line when he stops in front of a black skycap. Damon says to him, 'Charlie, aren't you about to get your ten-year pin?' The skycap grins and nods. Damon hands him a twenty-dollar bill and tells him, 'Now you go out tonight and buy your wife a good dinner.'"

Charlie Billerman was in Dallas when Damon came into town to visit his son. His return flight was delayed so he paid a courtesy call on Charles Beard of Braniff, a tough, rather surly man who, according to rumor, wouldn't even say 'Good morning' to his own secretary. While Damon was chatting with Beard, a Braniff official asked him if he'd like to inspect the airline's maintenance base. Ralph, who was fascinated by anything mechanical, accepted, and Billerman accompanied him to the base along with Beard and other Braniff people.

In one hangar, Damon spotted a couple of mechanics working on a DC-3 engine change. "Hey," he called out, "that's an old Pratt and Whitney. Mind if I take a look?" A Braniff vice-president, somewhat mystified, nodded, so Damon took off his coat, climbed the ladder under the engine and started talking to the mechanics.

"The next thing you know," continues Billerman who was accompanying Damon, "Ralph had his hand inside the engine pointing something out to the mechanics. Then he asks for a rag, wipes his hands, shakes hands with the mechanics and climbs down."

The tour went on but Beard came up to Billerman as they walked along. "Does he always grandstand like that?" he asked gruffly.

Billerman stopped. "Look, Mr. Beard," he said. "That man has probably met every employee on our system even if it meant getting up at one A.M. to catch a midnight shift. What you just saw wasn't grandstanding, it was as natural to Ralph Damon as breathing."

One of the mechanics who had been working on the engine caught up to them and said to Billerman, "Hey, who the hell was that guy?"

"That's Ralph Damon, president of TWA."

"You're puttin' me on."

"Nope, that's Mr. Damon."

The mechanic turned and yelled to his partner, "Hey, Joe, that was the president of TWA."

Beard said nothing for the rest of the tour. But a Braniff vice-president called Billerman about a week later. "Charlie, what on earth did you say to Beard? The old man came in the next morning and said 'Hello' to the telephone operator. She damned near had a heart attack. Then he said 'Good morning' to his secretary and she was ready to go home sick."

Fifteen years went by before Billerman saw Beard again. Charlie had been in Hong Kong and after landing in Los Angeles, dropped in at the TWA Ambassadors Club to wait for a continuing flight East. He always checked the club's guest list to see if there was anyone he knew, and this time his eyes fell on the signature of Charles Beard on the register. He looked around and saw Beard standing by a window, staring out at the planes. Billerman approached him.

"Mr. Beard, how are you?"

Beard stared at him. "Do I know you?"

"Does Dallas ring a bell?"

Beard's eyebrows shot up. "You're with TWA?"

"Yes, sir."

The memory circuit whirled and clicked. "Ralph Damon," Beard muttered. "Ralph Damon and that maintenance tour."

Billerman nodded.

Beard smiled. "You know, I learned a lesson that day. I think I should thank you for doing me a favor. Or maybe it was Damon who did me the favor."

One of Damon's greatest admirers was Bob Rummel. He says of Damon:

He was a great man and his relations with Hughes were excellent, at least in the beginning. Ralph was one of those unusual people who was competent in all facets of whatever he did. He was competent as an engineer, as a businessman, as an administrator. He had many unique qualities. His great memory, for instance, and his feeling for people. He made a practice of trying to visit every TWA station once a year. He couldn't do it all the time, but he hit most of them. He'd go through an overhaul facility, for example, and he'd stop and talk to every man and woman in that shop. He'd introduce himself, shake hands, chat and ask questions. Then he might go back to that station three years later and he'd remember everyone he had talked to by name. He'd throw out something like "Hi, Andy. Did your little boy get over those measles okay?"

A very personable man, very straight-forward. You always knew where you stood with Ralph Damon. I think he was one of TWA's two greatest presidents. Jack Frye was the other.

Most top-ranking executives usually bring their own secretaries with them when they change jobs, someone they can rely on and trust in the strange environment of a new post—not Damon. He seemed to trust everyone, Dietrich being the only apparent exception, and he got along surprisingly well with the volatile Hughes. Damon was not an imposing person in a physical sense. Average in height, he invariably wore heavy brown English tweed suits with a vest, even on hot days. On his head would be an inevitable fedora and his overall appearance was that of a somewhat baggy-looking British civil servant. He always traveled light, carrying only a small bag that could fit under a Connie seat. His hobby was astronomy. As an amateur astronomer, his greatest pride was being named honorary fellow of the Harvard Observatory. There was nothing he wouldn't do for the star-gazing profession.

On one occasion, he was informed that a lunar eclipse could be viewed best from telescopes located in Ceylon, on the south end of that island. Damon called Gilmore and told him to arrange a special flight to Ceylon, with the telescopes shipped in advance by boat. Walt Menke was assigned the task of serving as "special projects director." There was some grumbling about this particular junket; George Spater, for one, always thought Damon spent too much time on his hobby and that the "moon mission" was a waste of manpower and money. But then, Spater was one of the few who did not regard Damon with unalloyed admiration. He liked Ralph, but to this day he resents an incident involving Hal Blackburn and Damon.

When ALPA fined Blackie for flying an airplane during the strike, Spater thought TWA should reimburse the pilot. "The company asked him to make the flight and should have paid the fine," he told Damon.

"He agreed with me," Spater says, "but he never did a damned thing about it."

A small matter, perhaps, but one reflecting Spater's opinion that Damon got credit for some decisions that were made by others, like Cocke and Jack Weller, whose somewhat lowly title as "assistant secretary" belied his influence on officers occupying much higher spots in the company. Weller, indeed, was an underrated figure in TWA's history. Spater himself had recruited him from the New Haven Railroad and he considered him extremely capable, even if he was on the dullish, pedantic side—an assessment with which Weller was the first to agree.

"He was so honest and objective about himself," chuckles Spater, "that if you asked him, he'd tell you he was a damned bore. But he was one good man. He never did anything for himself; it was always for the company."

Spater was a decided minority in his less than glowing opinion of Damon. To the rest of the airline, Ralph could hardly do wrong. And if there was an element of blind hero worship toward him, it must be admitted that the years of his regime were golden years. It was a happy airline as well as a prosperous one as Damon's benign influence spread through the ranks, touching all departments and all personnel. In 1950, the corporate name was changed officially to Trans World Airlines, Inc., and almost simultaneously the airplane that had done so much to justify and even make possible that name was honorably retired.

All five Stratoliners were sold to a French air cargo line. They had served TWA faithfully for ten years and compiled a perfect safety record while operating in every part of the world. The closest one came to a crash was the time Capt. Dave Kuhn, a laconic type with ice water in his veins, couldn't get his gear down and had to land at Burbank wheels-up. Bob Word, later TWA station manager in Tampa, was assistant manager at Burbank then and watched breathlessly as the Stratoliner skidded down the runway on its belly. It finally came to a stop and Kuhn, the last one off the plane, smiled at Word.

"Log me on the ground at 0824, old boy," he said calmly.

No one, not even at Boeing, knows whether any 307s are still flying, but no one would be surprised if that were the case. Jerry Zerbone, a former TWA mechanic and flight engineer, saw a couple in Saigon in 1966 and Charlie Billerman came across an ex-TWA Stratoliner in Nigeria about the same time; it was being flown by the same French cargo line. Billerman also spotted one in Cambodia. Rod Edwards was waiting for a flight from Mombassa to Zanzibar and ran across a French crew standing in front of their 307 freighter. Edwards, who knew a little French, couldn't help eavesdropping. The Stratoliner was having hydraulic problems and the copilot didn't want to take off. The captain shrugged.

"*C'est la vie!*" he announced and climbed aboard.

Johnny Guy sums up the sentiment of TWA veterans toward the gallant old bird, perhaps the most underrated transport plane in aviation history. "In many ways," Guy says, "it wasn't just an airplane, it was an epic."

That it was—a 40,000-pound hunk of aluminum that somehow managed to personify the resilience of the airline it served. Resilience is a quality that is never listed in any annual report as a corporate asset, but it was and still is a part of TWA, a kind of intangible component as vital to a company as a wing is to an airplane.

Damon saw the quality demonstrated in July of 1951, when a summer flood hit the Kansas City area, sparing Municipal Airport but flooding the huge TWA overhaul base at nearby Fairfax under fifteen feet of water. The flood trapped six planes in various stages of overhaul—a Connie, a new Martin, a DC-4 and three DC-3s. But it would have been worse if hastily summoned crews hadn't flown five other aircraft out of danger.

Al Jordan, who arrived at the overhaul base two days after the flood, vividly describes his impressions:

"The first real chore was clean-up. The engine shop was completely out of commission, and it took the rest of the year to put it back in shape. All shops on the first floor of the hangars were under at least twelve feet of water. The biggest job was cleaning torn-down engines. They were covered with muck and oil from two nearby refineries that the flood had wrecked. Papers and files were an unholy mess—all our time records on equipment and overhauls. We rented a school swimming pool where papers were washed and then dried and ironed."

Pat Gallup, engineering test director, flew some of the planes out himself with the help of Frank Busch and a few other pilots. With Municipal Airport closed because of fears that the levees might break, the aircraft were ferried to Grandview Airport, eighteen miles south of Kansas City. TWA flew twenty-eight mechanics, foremen and inspectors out of the city to help with the redistributed maintenance load at Newark, New York and Los Angeles.

Saving those five airplanes meant a race against time. At 5 P.M., with most of the day shift on the way home and the twilight shift unable to report because roads and bridges were blocked, authorities informed TWA that the base had to be evacuated. A handful of volunteers from the day shift stayed on duty, trying desperately to put stripped-down aircraft into flying condition so they could be flown out. Five were all they could manage.

The disrupted schedules at Municipal, then TWA's major Midwestern hub, threw the entire reservations system into confusion. Yet scores of employees offered to help the harassed reservations department, and many were pressed into service.

Busch took the last DC-3 out of the overhaul base at 5:15 A.M., approximately twelve hours after the evacuation warning was issued. He left a crew of forty-five weary men behind. They got out via a fire truck and one car. The last person to board the plane was a mechanic. He was still in the hangar and Busch was yelling at him, "For Christ's sake, let's get the hell out of here!"

"In a minute," the mechanic yelled back, and proceeded leisurely to punch his time card.

Such moments of humor were rare and vastly appreciated. The classic line of the flood disaster came from Worth Johnson, Kansas City station manager. He was running around disposing of the contents of two large manila envelopes, one with emergency cash and the other with emergency passes for employees being dispatched to other stations.

"You know," Johnson observed in the midst of these frantic activities, "it's at a time like this that the damned auditors love to show up."

Ray Dunn was then director of engineering and maintenance at the overhaul base. Years later, he remarked, "What I remember the most were all those spare parts, just rusting away."

But more important items didn't rust: the resilience and resourcefulness of airline people that were figurative dikes against adversity. The personnel of TWA, throughout its history, seemed to possess more of those two qualities than most other airlines because it needed them more. During the

Damon regime, the airline's PR staff followed an unofficial but highly appropriate guideline of unknown origin:

> If the circus is coming to town and you paint a big sign saying "Circus Coming to Fairgrounds Saturday," that's advertising. If you put the same sign on an elephant and walk him through town, that's promotion. If the elephant walks through the mayor's prize flower bed, that's publicity. If you can get the mayor to laugh at the elephant, that's public relations.

No one realized it during the general euphoria of Damon's rule, but a lot of elephants were going to walk over a lot of prize flower beds.

12

If the Boss Calls, Get His Name

In 1937, the year the DC-3 became the queen of TWA's fleet, fewer than a million passengers traveled the nations's scheduled airlines and less than 1 percent of the entire adult population had ever boarded a commercial airliner.

By the early 1950s, when TWA was phasing out the grand old lady as fast as it could acquire new Martins, the total annual passenger count was higher than twenty million, or approximately 10 percent of the adult populace. In 1951, domestic air traffic exceeded Pullman traffic for the first time, and over the most lucrative international market, the North Atlantic, the airplane was beginning to challenge the ocean liner. In another six years, the airlines would surpass the railroads as the dominant common carrier of intercity traffic and transport more international travelers than the great liners.

The 1950s were the glory years of the piston-engine airliner which reached its apogee in speed, capacity and efficiency in both short and long-haul operations. Even the comparatively small Martin 404 carried more passengers (forty, all told) than the original 38-seat Stratoliner. As the 404s took over more and more of the short and medium-range routes, the DC-3s were relegated to such mundane chores as carrying cargo or serving low-density cities. The remaining handful of DC-4s became freighters, too, as the airline sought to develop the air cargo market, which was not only in its infancy but held the status of a stepchild in the industry.

While their counterparts in passenger traffic dealt with such glamorous matters as hostess uniforms, in-flight meals and aircraft interiors, the boys in cargo were often hard-pressed simply to turn a buck. Air cargo, traditionally low on the profit side, has always called for ingenuity and imagination. TWA had more than its share of innovators, such as John McCabe, who as an expert in air freight had always fretted over the risky yet potentially viable business of shipping valuable horses by air.

Gene Autry's horse nearly wrecked a TWA DC-3 freighter once when it became frightened and kicked a hole in the side of the fuselage. Expensive horses had been injured on other occasions, and when TWA got a contract to fly some European race horses to the U.S., McCabe went to work. He devised a strap that was placed under the animal's belly in such a way that it lifted his hind legs just off the floor. The horse was comfortable but with all the weight on the front legs, it was impossible for him to kick.

"It was better than a sedative," recalls Fred Spuhler, who had his own share of cargo adventures. "McCabe also thought up the idea of shipping unloading ramps right along with the horses."

One of TWA's big cargo accounts was the Gruen Watch Company of Cincinnati. Gruen had been importing watch parts from Switzerland, shipments packed in heavy lead-lined boxes and sent by sea. If a ship was delayed, Gruen was sometimes faced with expensive overtime to get watches out in time for Christmas sales. Spuhler heard of a Dutch craftsman working for a box factory in Ohio and asked him to design a lightweight yet fully protective box for shipping fragile watch components. The Dutchman came up with a paper box in which the parts could be immersed in wax. It weighed only two pounds, a more practical air freight package compared to the twelve pounds of a lead-lined box.

Spuhler took the new container to Gruen and talked the company into a trial shipment. He flew to Geneva, packed some parts into his sample box and left Switzerland on a Thursday. He landed in Cincinnati at noon on Saturday and by the following Monday, Gruen had workers putting the parts into cases. The sea shipments had taken six weeks. Later, the same Dutch craftsman modified the boxes to hold lobsters and fish.

One of Spuhler's jobs was to sell the concept of shipping by air to various potential customers. One group was assembled in Boston to hear Fred speak on the subject "Boston—Gateway to Everywhere." It was a topic to which Spuhler had devoted hours of research and compiled impressive data, and he confided to Jimmy de Revere of TWA's Boston sales office that he hoped he'd get as large an audience as possible.

"Have no fear," Jimmy assured him. "I've arranged to have Congressman Jack Kennedy there, and he always draws a crowd."

Just before Spuhler was to be introduced, the chairman asked if he'd mind letting Kennedy deliver a few remarks first because he had to return to Washington.

"Sure," Fred said.

Kennedy spoke, was loudly applauded by the large audience, and left. So did most of the spectators. Spuhler's speech on the importance of air cargo to Boston was delivered to a nearly empty room. It was weeks before he spoke to de Revere again.

"Cargo was always a trial and error way of doing business," Fred reminisces. "Once we tried shipping candied cherries and they burst. Another time we flew in a load of brewers' yeast for a new brewery in Newark. The yeast was boarded in St. Louis, all refrigerated, and we were warned not to unload the kegs enroute. Somebody goofed and three kegs were taken off at Columbus. They wound up in our hangar at LaGuardia, all three shaking like they had ten million Mexican jumping beans inside. We got two of 'em staked down but the third suddenly shot up in the air. It missed a Connie wing by inches and hit the hanger ceiling. To this day there's a strip of dried brewers' yeast on that ceiling."

Charlie Billerman was working cargo in New York some years ago when a wealthy woman flying to Phoenix decided to ship her pet cocker spaniel, Debbie, by air so the dog would arrive a few days after she got to Arizona. Billerman told her the dog would have to travel in a crate that would fit into a DC-3's cargo bin. Came the day of canine departure and Billerman was informed that a problem had arisen. The dog's velvet-lined crate, furnished by Abercrombie & Fitch, was of such proportions that it would have accommodated a full-size Bengal tiger.

Billerman groaned and told the cargo handlers to do what came naturally to cargo handlers: improvise. Thus, Debbie was assigned slightly less palatial surroundings—a cardboard box with air holes punched in it. Debbie objected to the downgrading and worked her way out of the box. When the captain boarded, sitting in his cockpit seat was a very happy cocker spaniel.

"Get this goddamned dog out of here!" the captain ordered. But before Debbie could be removed, she broke away and disappeared into the wilds of Long Island. When TWA finally located her, Billerman's boss phoned him.

"How much vacation you got left, Charlie?"

"About a week."

"Fine. You're on vacation as of tonight. And you're spending it taking that bloody dog to Phoenix."

Unfortunately, Billerman was traveling on a pass whereas Debbie had confirmed space in the cargo bin. Charlie was bumped off the plane in Chicago and Debbie continued her trip, getting as far as Albuquerque where all flights were grounded by weather. It was a weary Billerman who finally got to Albuquerque, where he was greeted by the sight of an empty dog crate on top of a mountain of unclaimed luggage. Feeling sick, he asked the station manager where the dog was.

"Oh, she's outside playing somewhere."

"There she was," Billerman recounts, "chasing gophers or something. We went after her in a food truck and caught her, all covered with mud. I took her to a hotel where I gave her a bath, and then got on a train with her all the way to Phoenix."

Such anecdotes are part of an airline's way of life—a major crisis at the time, yet in retrospect something to remember with humor. Tragedy is also part of that way of life, however, and the very airport at which Debbie had culminated her brief but hectic association with TWA was the scene of an unusual accident—one involving a captain accused of deliberately deviating from course and a fellow airman who fought to clear his name.

At 7 A.M. on February 19, 1955, a TWA Martin 404 operating as Flight 260 from Albuquerque to Baltimore, left the ramp area of Kirtland Field and waddled toward its assigned runway. In command was Capt. Ivan Spong, 44, an introvert whose joy was his 4-year-old adopted son. Standing 6'3" and handsome in a rugged way, Spong was one of the airline's most popular and respected captains. He was a native of Wichita, the son of poor parents of Swedish decent, and his entire life had been wrapped up in flying.

Spong literally had taught himself how to fly, hanging around the Wichita airport, watching planes and talking to pilots. He soloed at 14, in a plane he had built from discarded scrap. With only a high school education, he had taught himself such skills as celestial navigation, engine maintenance and instrument flying. After working briefly for a small plane manufacturer in Wichita, he was accepted by TWA for pilot training and rose to captain after serving in the Army Air Corps during World War II.

When he was just a copilot, his colleagues had tagged him as certain material for a captain. His gentle demeanor was a velvet glove around a steel fist. Spong hated to argue with anyone, even subordinates. There were times when he walked away from a discussion rather than contradict someone. But if asked for an opinion, he'd give it, bluntly and briefly. On the ground, when Spong was talking to a copilot, it was hard to tell which was the four-striper; he often deferred to the views of subordinates, considered their opinions gravely and treated them as mature men. But there was no democracy on a plane Ivan Spong was commanding. He flew by the book and expected his copilots to do likewise.

This was the man in the left seat of Flight 260. He had just completed his twelfth year as a TWA pilot and had logged nearly 13,000 hours in the air. On the morning of February 19, he was about to make his twelfth trip of that month over 260's route. He knew it well, including the dangerous terrain between Albuquerque and the first scheduled stop at Sante Fe.

Albuquerque's elevation is one mile above sea level. Sante Fe, a thousand feet higher, lies just forty-five miles away on a course straight to the northeast. Directly between the two cities, like a great stone wall, Sandia Ridge rises abruptly from the valley floor to nearly 11,000 feet above sea level. Instrument flight on this direct course was unauthorized, but if a pilot wanted to ignore the rules or fly visually, the minimum safe altitude over Sandia would be 13,000 feet. The approved air route, only nine miles longer, was a dogleg running north-northwest out of Albuquerque and then east-northeast into Sante Fe. The flight plan Spong filed called for the dogleg course, on which the minimum prescribed altitude for instrument flight was 9,000 feet—the altitude at which they planned to fly.

Just before boarding Flight 260, Spong and his copilot, Jim Creason, discussed the weather with the crew of a TWA Connie that had just landed. A storm had gathered over Sandia, and the pilot could see only the foothills. By the time Spong and Creason started their pre-takeoff checklist, snow had obscured the upper ridge. The first item on the list was to erect the fluxgate compass—the instrument on which they would rely to follow the required dogleg course, away from Sandia.

In the early days of navigation, pilots steered by a magnetic compass similar to the ones used in boats. But airplanes, unlike boats, bank, climb and dive; an ordinary magnetic compass reads incorrectly when an aircraft is not level. So to overcome this difficulty, the fluxgate compass was developed. Located in the wingtip, it is perpetually stabilized by a spinning gyroscope; no matter what the attitude of the airplane, the gyro holds the compass steady and level. Its readings are transmitted to the cockpit electrically and appear on an instrument panel dial called the Radio Magnetic Indicator (RMI).

The fluxgate compass is a reliable, generally trustworthy instrument, but some TWA pilots had expressed concern about it. One of them was a young captain named Larry De Celles. During a checkride prior to his earning his fourth stripe, he was flying a Martin into Dayton and was given approach clearance along with the proper compass heading toward the assigned runway.

De Celles banked until his RMI showed the required south heading and came out of the overcast. There were no approach lights ahead of him. The city of Dayton, which should have been off his left wing, was off his right wing.

"What the hell's wrong?" he asked the check captain. The latter reached down and flicked a switch; the RMI spun around and showed the plane heading southeast instead of south, the direction displayed when De Celles had completed his bank. It had been a blatant example of compass error, and later De Celles discussed what had happened with the check captain who explained that the fluxgate compass can malfunction—usually from dirt in the gyro bearings or a short circuit.

"If that happens," he added, "when you recover from a bank as you did tonight, the gyro's still spinning in what *was* a level position but in reality is tilted. That's what gave you a forty-five-degree heading error. To correct it, you do what I did: cage the gyro [bring it back to level]."

De Celles frowned. "I'm just wondering how you can tell the gyro's tilted. I didn't know it until we came out of the overcast and saw Dayton off to the right instead of the left. What did your RMI show?"

"Same heading as yours. Both RMI's are hooked to the same circuit. If a captain gets an erroneous heading, so will his copilot."

Six months later, De Celles was working his way through a squall line and had just emerged into the clear when he felt something was wrong. The storm area had appeared huge, yet the Martin had gone through it quickly— "Too quickly," De Celles thought. The plane was flying in bright sunlight. Ordinarily, the backside of a squall line is forbiddingly dark. De Celles, remembering that Dayton approach, caged his gyros. His RMI's swung around from the westerly heading they had been showing and were now indicating east. Somehow they had developed a 180-degree error while De Celles was trying to get out of the storm.

On January 16, 1955, De Celles wrote TWA Engineering pointing out a potential hazard in the Martin's fluxgate compass wiring. There were two fluxgates on the 404, but both RMIs were hooked to the same one; the second compass was a standby unit. De Celles suggested that the captain's RMI be wired into one fluxgate and the copilot's to the second, so any erroneous reading on one would not appear on the other. TWA called him in for a meeting with an engineer who was impressed by his warning that a fluxgate compass malfunction could steer an innocent pilot right into a mountain. De Celles later received a cash reward for his suggestion. But before TWA could implement it, somebody did fly into a mountain. It was Ivan Spong.

After erecting (activating) the gyros, Spong asked the Kirtland tower for clearance. It came back promptly: "TWA Two-sixty, cleared for an approach to the Sante Fe airport, cruise nine thousand feet by way of Victor Airway number one-nine. Climb northbound on the back course of the Albuquerque ILS localizer."

The clearance required him to take off on Runway 11 toward the southeast, and then make a right turn away from the mountain, continuing the turn until the aircraft was heading north. At 7:05 A.M., Flight 260 broke ground and a minute later, Spong requested permission to make a right turn. The tower operator obliged and his last view of the flight was a normal right turn. His attention was directed elsewhere but a ground service employee two minutes later saw the Martin rolling out of its turn, and then, instead of heading north as he had seen so many other flights do, proceeding east-northeast directly toward Sandia Mountain.

The last person to glimpse Flight 260 was an Air Force colonel about to leave on a hunting trip from his home, located about a mile and a half north-northeast of the airport. As the plane passed overhead, he thought to himself, "If he's eastbound, he's too low; if he's northbound, he's off course."

He watched the plane through binoculars as it flew in a shallow climb toward Sandia and disappeared into the clouds. The time was 7:09. Four minutes later, the 404 crunched into a cliffside, impacting in a left bank, nose high. Spong must have seen the cliff at the last second and tried desperately to avoid it. Spong, Creason, hostess Sharon Schoening and all thirteen passengers died instantly.

Eight months after the crash, the Civil Aeronautics Board issued its report—a damning indictment of Captain Spong. It stated there was no evidence of instrument failure and emphasized that Flight 260 had followed a course on which visibility was good. Only the top of Sandia had been obscured, the CAB insisted, and even if some unsuspected instrument failure had occurred, ". . . all the captain had to do was look outside to determine that he was not following the airway. Therefore," the report added, "from all available evidence and the lack of any evidence to the contrary, the Board can conclude only that the direct course taken by the flight was intentional."

The last word stood out like braille. It meant that Spong had deliberately left an assigned course, flew at an altitude of 9,000 feet toward an 11,000-foot mountain he could see in his path, and made no attempt to climb until the last split second before disaster. In effect, the CAB had come close to accusing at least the captain, and possibly the copilot as well, of committing suicide and taking fourteen innocent victims with them.

It is not unusual for the wives of dead airline pilots, particularly after a crash in which pilot error is suspected, to receive crank calls and letters. The CAB's implied verdict of suicide meant agony for Jean Spong, the captain's widow. She began getting countless anonymous calls and mail, mostly accusing Spong of murder. One woman kept phoning her and each call was was identical.

"Is this where that TWA pilot lives that got killed?"

"Yes," Jean would whisper.

The woman would just laugh and hang up.

Another caller would phone in the early morning hours. When Jean picked up the phone, all she could hear was heavy breathing. The mail was heavy and vicious, all from perfect strangers. Jean opened one envelope and found a torn piece of brown paper with Spong's picture attached. There was no message.

The telephone call that almost tore Jean Spong from sanity was from a sadistic person who told her, "Now don't stop me, but they brought all them bodies off the mountain in chunks and none of them had any heads."

The dirt rubbed off on little Mike, their adopted son. He came home from school one day in tears and Jean asked him what was wrong. He sobbed, "The kids say Daddy's in Hell because he killed people."

Mother and son used to take long walks. If Mike saw a plane overhead, he would ask, "Daddy sly [fly] right?"

"Yes," Jean would say softly, "he always flew right."

During the eight months that elapsed between the crash and the CAB's verdict, the Air Line Pilots Association did little to clear Spong. The pilots never dreamed the CAB would find him at fault. When the findings were published, the airmen closed ranks. Captain Bob Adickes, chairman of the TWA Central Safety Committee, asked all crews to notify him of fluxgate compass malfunctions. Adickes was succeeded by Dave Halperin who brought De Celles into the case. De Celles, by then, had become a recognized expert on fluxgate compass troubles and was telling anyone who'd listen that Spong must have had a compass malfunction.

Halperin, De Celles and Ted Linnert, ALPA's safety and engineering director, met with CAB officials to discuss the possibility. At this point, they didn't have much of a case; if the CAB had convicted Spong on purely circumstantial evidence, the pilots were trying to clear him with purely conjectural evidence. All they had were a few previous cases of fluxgate compass errors, and their absolute conviction that no pilot in his right mind would intentionally fly northeast from Albuquerque for five minutes at 9,000 feet. All the CAB could do was point out that if Spong was encountering instrument trouble, he just had to look out the window and see the mountain in his path.

The CAB had based its findings on the visibility evidence. The pilots brought up testimony from another airline crew that had taken off just behind Flight 260 and reported Sandia completely obscured by a snowstorm. The Board countered with the evidence of the Air Force colonel who had seen the Martin only four minutes before the crash; the report had quoted him as saying that only the top of the ridge was cloud-covered.

Board officials did tell the ALPA delegation it hadn't meant to imply suicide. They felt Spong was taking a short cut—although it made no sense that a pilot of his background and reputation would risk sixteen lives just to save nine miles. And a supplementary report, while it deleted "intentional," still blamed Spong entirely.

Larry De Celles spent a total of four years investigating the circumstances of the Sandia Mountain tragedy. Slowly, laboriously, he tore the CAB's case into shreds. He read and reread the transcript of the accident hearing and discovered that both CAB reports had badly misquoted or ignored actual testimony. For example, the reports said the colonel had noticed that "the upper portion of the Sandia Ridge was obscured by clouds." What the colonel had really said was that the "upper third" was obscured—a not insignificant difference. On another page of the transcript, De Celles found that the colonel had testified specifically that the visible portion of the ridge was only 500 feet, while the height of the cloud-covered portion was approximately 3,200 feet. In other words, about 86 percent of the ridge was obscured, not just the upper third or upper portion. Furthermore, the CAB's reports totally ignored sworn testimony from other witnesses that contradicted the Board's claims of good visibility.

". . . the clouds were right down to where the terrain starts leveling off. . . . All you could see was just little parts of the foothills. . . . The mountains were completely covered but the base could be seen. . . . The height of the base of the [cloud] layer over the mountains was approximately eight thousand feet and it lowered as you went south along the mountain. . . ."

Spong's own point of observation had been several thousand feet above those of the ground witnesses. He would have encountered even more obscurity than they saw.

The CAB claimed that the flight just behind TWA 260 flew through instrument flight conditions for only about a minute after takeoff. De Celles' study of the transcript showed that the Board had quoted only that small portion of the crew's testimony. What they had added, and what was omitted in the reports, was that within four minutes after leaving Albuquerque, they were just above the storm overcast at 10,000 feet. If that flight was barely clear of clouds at 10,000 feet, how could Spong have enjoyed clear visibility at 9,000 only a few minutes earlier?

The CAB had insisted that Spong could see the ground during the turn around the airport and for the next five minutes before entering the overcast cloaking Sandia Mountain. De Celles, reconstructing the flight from the evidence in the CAB's own transcript, showed that the Martin disappeared into the clouds within two minutes of completing the turn, not five minutes, and was on instruments from the time Spong rolled out of the turn.

Having shot down the Board's "clear visibility" findings, De Celles turned to other evidence contained in the transcript but unmentioned in either report. The tower had asked Strong to report passing a certain radio navigation checkpoint, the "Weiler intersection." The name had been changed recently and was not on Spong's air charts, so he asked the tower to define its location. Just before takeoff, he again asked the tower to confirm that his understanding of the Weiler location was correct. No pilot would have gone to this trouble if he did not intend to follow the prescribed course.

Much of the time De Celles spent on the case was devoted to demonstrating the possibility, if not the probability, of fluxgate compass malfunction. He continued to fly his regular trips but virtually every off-duty hour went into the Spong accident. On one occasion, he even climbed Sandia Mountain to visit the crash site. At every turn he had TWA's cooperation; the airline even loaned him a Martin 404 for a series of test flights to check out fluxgate data and reenact the Albuquerque accident with a professional movie cameraman in the cockpit filming the simulation.

The cockpit movies, along with films De Celles shot himself, were part of an elaborate presentation before the CAB when ALPA and TWA formally requested reconsideration of the Board's findings. De Celles alone testified for a day and a half and Bill Meador represented the airline as they offered in evidence slides, graphs, depositions, photographs, charts and statistical tables all designed to show how a fluxgate compass error could have led Spong to the point of impact.

On June 15, 1960, the Civil Aeronautics Board issued its third report on the accident at Albuquerque. It conceded that Spong could not have flown intentionally toward Sandia, called the probable cause of the accident "unknown" and admitted the possibility of fluxgate compass malfunction. For the first time in history, the CAB had reversed itself in an accident probe.

Years later, Fred Spuhler and his wife were on a ski tram going up Sandia Mountain and were startled to hear a recorded voice pointing out the accident site. "If you look over to the left, you see part of the tail from the TWA plane," the voice intoned. Spuhler marched into the ski lift owner's office a few hours later and demanded that the recorded descriptions be stopped. In the end, TWA had to spend $6,500 renting a large helicopter to remove the last of Flight 260's wreckage.

Larry De Celles could never get the Spong accident out of his mind. One clear day, flying out of Albuquerque in a Connie with a new copilot, he reached down and tripped the fluxgate compass to induce a deliberate error. The youthful first officer, intent on his instrument, didn't notice anything was wrong until they rolled put of a turn. The RMI was still showing a north leading, but Sandia Mountain was directly ahead.

"My God," said the copilot, "what did I do wrong?"

"Nothing. I tripped the fluxgate compass. Just wanted to show you something."

"A guy could get killed that way," the copilot observed.

"One did," said Captain De Celles.

TWA came close to not buying the Martin 404; that it did was, ironically, due to none other than its former president, La Motte Cohu. After leaving TWA, Cohu became president of Convair, which was successfully peddling its new C-240, and the airline was very much interested in the plane.

Hughes had Bob Rummel look into the 240 design. Rummel reported back that it was fine but inferior to the 404 Martin was planning as a replacement for the discredited 202. But, Rummel added, with certain improvements the 240 could be turned into a transport markedly superior to the 404. TWA thereupon entered negotiations with Convair. As usual, the Hughes Tool Company would purchase the planes and sell them to the airline.

Cohu was about to leave on a European vacation just as the negotiations got underway. Rummel, Hughes and Convair engineers had agreed on the necessary modifications by the time Cohu returned. The improved version would be called the 340, but just as TWA was ready to sign, Cohu pulled the rug out from under everyone. He wrote Damon a letter to the effect that Convair had decided not to build the 340 but would be happy to sell TWA the standard 240.

"Cohu," says Rummel, "had this idea that airlines should buy airplanes off the shelf instead of always insisting on something special. We didn't really want anything special; we just wanted certain things done in the interest of safety and economy. When Cohu refused, we began seriously negotiating with Martin for the 404 and so did Eastern, which also had been interested in an improved Convair. When Convair lost both TWA and Eastern, it started negotiating with United. The airplane United bought was at least ninety percent of the airplane we wanted, and Cohu was fired."

Second choice notwithstanding, the 404 was popular with TWA crews despite a few idiosyncrasies. The flap settings were confusing. There was no identation for three-quarter flaps, and the flap handle was so close to the landing gear handle it was possible to push one or the other by mistake. Both Eastern and TWA had incidents where a pilot meant to raise his flaps and raised the gear instead. But the 404 was rugged and dependable. It served TWA for more than a decade with an almost perfect safety record. The Albuquerque crash was the only fatal 404 accident.

If the fifties were a kind of "last hurrah" for the piston transports, the same was true for some of TWA's pilots—the rugged individualists, mavericks and unpredictable characters whose escapades became famous. Many graduated into the jet age, but this would be an era when individualism, carefree camaraderie and practical jokes had to give way to the fly-'em-by-the-book dictates of enormously expensive and demanding turbine aircraft. In a 600-mile-per-hour jet, there was no time for much besides workmanlike demeanor. Thus did the pilot stories of the 1950s became treasured nuggets of memory.

There was Charlie Davis, a tall gangling captain everyone called "Black Dog." Why, no one is sure, but one theory is that he owned a huge black Labrador. Another source for his nickname may have been the big black mustache he sported, giving him the appearance of a predatory pirate. Davis called every copilot "boy" in a loud tone implying total lack of respect and trust. A young copilot named John Mitchell drew Black Dog on a Martin trip and arrived at the plane and parked in front of a hangar to find the captain already there. It was snowing hard and Mitchell began reading the checklist prior to taxiing toward the gateway. Black Dog looked at him sternly.

"Boy!"

"Yes, sir."

"This is one of those flights you read about."

"Sir?"

"I said, this is one of those flights you read about."

"Captain, I don't understand."

"Ill-fated from the beginning!" Black Dog bellowed.

Mitchell was his copilot on another occasion when Black Dog delayed a flight for thirty minutes. He had wandered over to a hangar where an antique plane buff was restoring a World War I Spad and became so engrossed that he lost track of time. But unusual happenstances were routine for Captain Davis. On his final flight as a TWA four-striper, he let his copilot make the landing and the tailskid hit the runway—an embarrassing event for a final flight before retirement.

"He gave away his last landing," Capt. Russ Derickson muses sadly, "and his copilot screwed it up."

Possibly due to Black Dog's influence, Mitchell came to be regarded as something of a character himself; the fearsome Davis was the only captain toward whom Mitchell displayed politeness. Mitchell was flying copilot one day and in the left seat was Walt Gunn, who held several college degrees and was scholarly in speech and manner. They were approaching St. Louis at 12,000 feet and Gunn intoned solemnly, "John, do you see the confluence of the Mississippi, Missouri and Illinois Rivers?"

"Do I see what?"

"The confluence of those rivers, on your side."

Mitchell glanced out the window.

"You mean where those three fucking rivers come together, Walt?"

Another of Mitchell's favorites was Capt. Frank Jones. They were on a 749 Connie before TWA equipped all its aircraft with storm radar and were getting bounced around enroute to St. Louis. They cleared the storm area and Jones informed the passengers they could expect a smooth flight the rest of the way. He was being over-optimistic; they hit turbulence again and Jones decided he'd better explain his erroneous prediction.

"Well, folks," he announced on the PA, "it was smooth for awhile, but I'm letting my copilot fly now."

Throughout the industry, TWA pilots had a reputation for good looks. There was a widespread belief that this was due to Howard Hughes' influence, but while there were a number of captains who appeared to have gotten their jobs through central casting, the general reputation was exaggerated. No Greek god was Mitch St. Lawrence, a colorful captain whose sense of humor was in direct proportion to the size of his bulbous nose. Compared to Mitch, W.C. Fields' famed proboscis resembled the aquiline profile of John Barrymore. St. Lawrence's appearance, however, had no effect on his popularity. He was loved by all, including those who were victims of his practical jokes.

On one flight, he had two new hostesses, and he overheard them talking about getting back to their Kansas City homes on time because they each had a heavy date. The plane landed in Pittsburgh and St. Lawrence went into the teletype room.

"I need a message typed out," he requested politely, and then proceeded to dictate the following.

HOSTESSES SMITH AND JONES: IMMEDIATELY UPON RETURN TO DOMICILE YOU HAVE BEEN ASSIGNED TO VICE-PRESIDENT NIXON'S CHARTER FLIGHT.

He reboarded the Connie and handed the message to the two hostesses without saying a word. A few seconds later they were in the cockpit pleading for his intercession.

"We can't do it," they wailed.

"You have to," Mitch said firmly. "You don't have any choice. Besides, you don't realize what a privilege it is—serving the vice-president and all those famous people you'll meet. Also, the first stop on that charter trip happens to be San Francisco. You can go to I. Magnum's and charge anything you want to TWA. Believe me, this will be the greatest experience of your lives."

He kept up this propaganda for the rest of the trip, emphasizing the unlimited expense accounts, until both girls were fairly panting to get back to Kansas City and the charter. "Luggage, clothes—all on the company," he assured them.

On the return flight, they stopped in Pittsburgh again and St. Lawrence told the teletype operator, "I need another message." This obtained, he returned to the Connie and handed it to the girls.

HOSTESSES SMITH AND JONES: CANCEL ALL OF THE PREVIOUS.

Mitch did some heavy braking on a Connie one day and some food trays fell on the floor. He got out of his seat after landing and shook his head as he passed the galley area.

"Honey, you've got salad oil all over this floor," he told the hostess.

"I know, Captain, but I'm going to wipe it up."

St. Lawrence frowned. "Didn't they tell you about salad oil spilling on a linoleum floor during training?"

"No, sir."

"It'll eat its way right through the floor in two hours if you don't get it cleaned up fast. Do you have any strong fluid?"

The hostess was almost in tears. "I was going to use water," she said. "Is there something else I should use?"

"Prop wash," Mitch told her.

She ran into TWA maintenance, which informed her they were out of prop wash and to try Allegheny. There she hit a sympathetic mechanic who gave her a small bottle. "It's prop wash," he assured her, "but use it sparingly because the stuff's really potent."

When St. Lawrence returned to the airplane, the hostess was on her hands and knees scrubbing the floor with the contents of the bottle. Mitch always figured the Allegheny mechanic gave her some kind of detergent.

St. Lawrence was based in Boston through most of his TWA career, and he was a great lover of steamed clams. Dick Kenny, who was to rise to vice-president of flight operations, flew copilot with Mitch on numerous occasions. He remembers this about St. Lawrence: "He'd pick up steamers on the way to the airport and if the galley wasn't being used he'd cook the clams on a hot plate. I'd fly the plane, smelling those clams cooking, and pretty soon Mitch would bring them to the cockpit all buttered and everything. The trouble was, he didn't have any place to put the shells. The Connies had a weather radar you'd pull out of the floor for servicing or inspection, so during the winter Mitch would open the door and put the empty clam shells in the radar compartment. In a few weeks, every Connie he flew was being written up for strange odors in the cockpit."

After St. Lawrence retired, a fellow pilot ran into him at a Seniors Club meeting and commented how great he looked.

"Yeah," he sighed. "If I had known I was gonna live this long, I wouldn't have misused my body so much."

"The thing to remember about some of the guys," says Russ Derickson, "is that most of them were great pilots as well as characters." Certainly fitting that description was Tex Butler, admired by everyone, from mechanics to fellow four-stripers. The copilots worshipped him because he was one of the few veterans who would let them get in flying time.

Where he got the nickname "Tex" is a mystery; Butler was born in North Dakota and as far as anyone knew, the closest he ever got to Texas was flying over it. Mick Martinez, now a TWA pilot on Lockheed 1011s, once asked him where he got his name.

"Well," Tex explained, "I was born in North Dakota but it would sound pretty damned silly calling me 'North Dakota Butler,' wouldn't it?"

Tex himself never could remember anybody's name, not even pilots with whom he flew regularly, so he called everyone "Coach." He was as friendly as a puppy with everyone, including federal inspectors. One of them gave Butler an oral quiz and was asked later how Tex did.

"Well," the inspector confessed, "I don't know how much he knows about the airplane but I sure learned one hell of a lot about duck hunting."

Tex was flying a trip through Cairo during the 1967 Arab-Israeli War and the purser informed him there was a frightened elderly Jewish woman aboard.

"She's afraid the Egyptians will take her off the airplane," the purser said.

"No trouble," Tex drawled. "Just before we land, bring her up to the cockpit."

She sat in the cockpit jump seat as they landed, and when they taxied to the gate, Butler saw that Egyptian troops were surrounding the plane. "You just stay right where you are, honey," Tex told the frightened woman.

He left the flight deck, locking the door behind him, and stood in front of the door as the soldiers and security police boarded looking for anyone vaguely resembling a Jew. Butler greeted them all with a broad grin and called some of the police by name (he seems to have known airport personnel at every TWA station). When the Egyptians left, Butler took off and not until they reached cruising altitude did he summon the purser to escort the old woman back to her seat.

Butler died a few years ago after a heart attack and was mourned by the entire airline. "Tex remained a sixteen-year-old boy all his life," Russ Dickerson says. "He was really something. So was Jake Simmons—everyone called him 'Jake the Snake' for some reason. He'd be telling you something in the cockpit and when he finished, he'd say 'Now ain't that right?' and he'd smack you on your shoulder. His hands were huge and by the time you landed, you couldn't move your arm."

Being an international carrier, TWA crews had frequent contact with their brethren on foreign carriers. Thanks to the airline's various airline advisory missions, they had a hand in training many of them—Lufthansa employees, for example. When the German airline was allowed to resume international operations after the war, it acquired some Constellations, and TWA was picked to help train Lufthansa crews.

The first contingent to reach Germany was in the charge of Ernie Pretsch, who looked like a Prussian general himself. Pretsch, a check captain out of Kansas City, had close-cropped blondish hair, jug ears and features that could have been chiseled out of solid granite. He had a slight German accent and could speak the language fluently. For the training mission, he recruited only pilots who weren't deathly afraid of him—a criterion that eliminated about 99 percent of the TWA pilot corps. Hal Blackburn was one and Howard Hall was another. A pilot asked Blackie why he was going. "You must be nuts, flying for that bastard," the pilot added. "He's just taking his friends."

"That's what I'd do," Blackburn replied.

The TWAers thoroughly enjoyed their assignment, so much so that some were suspected of extending the training more than was necessary. John Corris ran into Hall one day and inquired how the Germans were doing.

"They're real sharp," Sonny Boy said. "Excellent pilots."

"So I guess you'll be releasing them for line duty pretty soon," Corris observed.

"Oh, no," Hall protested. "We're being very thorough because they've got so much to learn."

They did have a lot to learn. Many were ex-Luftwaffe pilots who hadn't flown for ten years and had little if any instrument training. The younger ones had only a few hundred hours on small planes before they were turned over to TWA. They were scrupulously polite, correct and respectful to their superiors. The TWA pilots got used to having doors opened for them and even having their cigarettes lit. More important, the Americans began to respect them as professionals. Blackie remembers flying one Lufthansa trip—the TWA captains commanded the earlier overseas flights—and it was a long one, from West Berlin to Hamburg, Paris, and across the South Atlantic to Natal. At one point, Blackburn suggested that his young copilot get some sleep on the next leg, with a relief copilot sitting in for him. The German refused.

"Captain," he said, "if I stay up here I might learn something."

Dick Beck was one of the dozen or so TWA captains sent to train the Lufthansa crews and confirms that they refused to take naps on the long ocean flights.

One night Beck was flying into New York with a German copilot who was making the landing. Beck had a pair of fake false teeth in his nav kit. The Connie bounced pretty hard on the runway and Beck surreptitiously pulled out the false teeth, holding them accusingly in front of the Lufthansa pilot.

"Can'th you make a dethent landing?" he lisped.

The German turned pale. "Oh, my God, sir!" he blurted.

"I felt sorry for the poor guy," Beck relates. "If he hadn't had his seat belt fastened, he would have stood up and saluted. Actually, they were excellent pilots and so polite we free spirits couldn't believe it. I'd stand there in operations, pull out a cigarette and there'd be five Zippo lighters in front of my face."

Blackburn, a stickler for cockpit discipline himself, got along well with the Lufthansa crews. They respected him for his toughness and bluntness, two qualities that a handful of Blackie's American subordinates sometimes resented. Legendary is the check ride report Blackburn wrote on one TWA captain who was making the transition from the DC-4 to the Constellation—and not succeeding very well.

"Captain———," Blackie remarked, "was one of our best DC-4 pilots—and still is."

TWA's own international schedules were crippled in the summer of 1953 when the airline's navigators staged an eleven-day strike. Coming in the heart of the busy North Atlantic travel season, it was a walkout that hurt but also one that was a Pyrrhic victory for the tiny Air Line Navigators Association, the union calling the strike. Stung by the walkout, the airline began studying electronic means of navigation that would some day be adopted and abolish the navigator's job in the jet age.

TWA's "Magellans" were a clannish lot that included one navigator with an unusual phobia; he hated to wear socks. When TWA finally ordered him to don this item of apparel while on duty, he responded by painting his feet and lower calfs black. He didn't last long enough to be punished for this ruse. The transgression that nailed him was far more serious than sockless feet. On a night flight across the Atlantic, the navigator kept giving the captain a series of erratic course changes that made no sense.

They reached such a stage of unexplainable turns that the captain became worried and went back to the navigator's station to find out what was wrong. The navigator was placidly eating dinner.

"What the hell's going on?" the captain demanded. "Why all those course changes?"

The navigator pointed to his map and the captain leaned over, his eyes following the course the navigator had been directing. The path led to a stray string bean, circumvented the bean and continued a few miles until it encountered a small piece of uneaten dinner roll. This had necessitated a sharp turn to the left, with another 90-degree turn back on a course after the roll had been bypassed. The path then resumed a straight course until the navigator's pencil faced imminent collision with a piece of chicken, the evasive action consisting of a 70-degree course change.

That was the last TWA flight the navigator worked. The captain relieved him of his duties immediately and reported him to the company after they landed.

The strike had no effect on domestic operations, where the new Martins were proving highly efficient and the Super Constellations competed effectively against the DC-6s, although not as effectively as Hughes or Damon wanted. The Connie still wasn't fast enough or long-range enough. It had a slight speed advantage over the DC-6, but neither plane possessed nonstop transcontinental ability in either direction.

The Super G, perhaps the best all-around Constellation ever built, had more powerful engines and true transcontinental range. But so did the DC-6B, an improved version of the DC-6 that could get from Los Angeles to New York seven minutes faster than the new Connie. For Howard Hughes, it was a long seven minutes. Jack Real of Lockheed recalls that "it was a terrible disappointment to Howard. He would have paid anything to have the G two or three minutes faster than what American or United were operating. We tried everything to make it faster. We even got rid of the paint catwalks on the wing—anything to reduce drag and make up that seven-minute bulge the DC-6B had, but we just couldn't do it."

Speed, of course, was Howard's obsession. He was intrigued by any technical development promising a faster airplane. Lockheed began experimenting with a prop-jet engine (a turbine hitched to a conventional propeller) in 1953, installing one on Aircraft 1961, the original Connie. With Hughes unhappy over the Super G's speed, Lockheed was thinking about building an even bigger Constellation with turboprops. But even before the design work was really underway, Hughes became fascinated with the concept of jet propulsion. The year 1952 had witnessed the introduction of Britain's Comet, the world's first production jetliner, and one destined for a tragic future.

Sometime during that year—exactly when is not known—Hughes either wrote or called de Havilland, the Comet's manufacturer, asking that an engineer fly to Los Angeles with the jet's design plans. One was sent, arriving at the Beverly Hills Hotel, where Hughes was staying. He met Hughes in his suite and stretched out on a sofa while Howard studied the plans. The examination lasted all night. Early in the morning, with the dawn just beginning, Hughes handed the plans back to the de Havilland engineer.

"It isn't safe," he declared.

He didn't go into any detail nor explain his unfavorable opinion; whether he really knew what was wrong with the ill-fated Comet is impossible to ascertain. It would not be surprising if he did grasp the Comet's weakness, however. Hughes, for all his foibles, was a brilliant, if instinctive, engineer. The British jet's weakness turned out to be structural—inability to withstand the stresses of repeated cabin pressurization and depressurization. The Comets began carrying passengers in May of 1952, shortly after the Hughes–de Havilland meeting is believed to have taken place. In less than a year, Comets were grounded after two were destroyed by explosive decompression. The jet age had gotten off to an abortive start, but Hughes remained interested in the potential of the turbine engine.

Ralph Damon was interested, too, but like his contemporaries, he believed safe, viable jet travel was a long way from reality, and the sad fate of the Comet, after a brilliant start, seemed to confirm this conservative outlook. Of all the U.S. international carriers, only one had actually ordered the British jetliner. That was Pan Am, and Juan Trippe had options on an improved version that wasn't even off the drawing boards yet. The options were never exercised.

By 1955, however, the picture had changed; in the three years following the Comet's grounding, aeronautical science had solved many of the problems that the de Havilland experience had raised. The Comet's weakness was more than technical, it was economic, too. The airplane was simply too small to be profitable. On July 15, 1954, America's first jet transport, the Boeing 707, made its first flight—a 160,000-pound rebuttal to all the doubts and fears raised about jet transportation. With the structural strength of a battleship and the speed of a fighter, it was designed to carry more than a hundred passengers at altitudes far above the domain cruised by the pistons.

Douglas, too, announced it would build a huge new jetliner called the DC-8. On October 13, 1955, Pan Am revealed it had ordered twenty-five DC-8s and twenty 707s, thus pulling the trigger for the great jet race—a massive struggle involving virtually every airline in the world as well as the titans of the U.S. aircraft industry. For TWA, the timing couldn't have been worse; the Pan Am order came on the heels of what was unquestionably a major equipment mistake by Hughes—a $50 million commitment for the purchase of twenty-five Lockheed Model 1649 Constellations.

In fairness to Hughes, there were reasons for buying another piston-engine transport, even when the jet age was just around the corner. First, "around the corner" was at least three years away, and in 1955 no one could really predict with certainty the impact of the jet revolution. Second, Hughes was disturbed over what the competition was flying; Douglas had developed the DC-7, a long-range stretched version of the DC-6 that American and United were operating transcontinentally with great success, and Pam Am had bought the DC-7C which had an even greater range than the domestic model. Third, any decision made by Howard Hughes had to be judged in the context of his fierce competitiveness. In the 1649, Hughes saw an airplane capable of flying nonstop between Los Angeles and London via the polar route; one that cruised some thirty miles per hour faster than the DC-7, one that promised to be the most luxurious, roomiest airliner ever created, and yet a transport not so radically different and unconventional as to invite teething bugs and lack of public confidence.

Against these reasons and this logic must be weighed the almost unanimous advice of the TWA technicians on whose judgment Hughes supposedly relied. TWA's engineering department was virtually unanimous in opposing the 1649, and this included Bob Rummel, whose expertise Hughes admired more than anyone else's. When Hughes persisted, Rummel tried to talk Kelly Johnson into giving the 1649 a constant width fuselage, but he never got to first base. That would have meant new fuselage dies and unacceptable development costs.

Yet there is a curious sequel to the 1649 story, one never before told. It comes from a man who was extremely close to Hughes in his later years. According to Jack Real, Howard actually had second thoughts about buying the airplane. In Real's words:

> We discussed the 1649 many times. He claimed he never really committed himself to the airplane, that he had a verbal agreement with Bob Gross and not an actual contract. He told me he simply didn't have the heart to tell Gross the 707 would catch up to the 1649 faster than anyone expected and that the TWA deal was a mistake. One night Gross called Hughes and said, "Well, Howard, we've started to cut metal on the 1649." It was years later that Hughes said to me, "That's when I didn't have the heart to tell him I never signed a paper, that it was a mistake and I wanted out."
>
> Hughes used to point out to me that going through with the 1649 deal was a matter of honor with him. He felt that Gross, a true supersalesman, honestly thought he had a commitment from Howard even though nothing had been signed. So Hughes went ahead with the 1649. Deep in his heart he knew it was wrong because the 707 was coming, but to him it was a moral obligation.

There is a ring of truth to that story. Many disparaging things have been written about Howard Hughes and most of them are probably true, but it is hard to find anyone who would not admit that Hughes was a man of integrity who always kept his word. During the donneybrook with Senator Brewster, when it was apparent that either Brewster or Hughes was lying, Hughes faced up to the issue of integrity squarely.

"As for me," he told the subcommittee, "I have been called capricious, a playboy, eccentric, but I don't believe I have the reputation of a liar. I think my reputation in that respect meets what most Texans consider important."

After that speech, uttered in tones of sincerity that impressed even the cynical Washington press corps, one might as well have challenged John Wayne's integrity. It may seem incredible that Hughes threw away $50 million on an airplane nobody wanted just to honor a verbal obligation. But Jack Real believes it and, unlike many of Hughes' critics, he knew the man.

If the 1649 story is true, it is highly unlikely that anyone at TWA, including Damon, was aware of the facts. As usual, Hughes bought the airplane in the name of Toolco; all Damon knew was that TWA was getting twenty-five of them and would have to pay Toolco back. How much of a role Damon played in the controversial acquisition is uncertain. Some TWA veterans say Damon opposed the deal just as Rummel and so many others did. Others claim Damon went along with it willingly, convinced as Hughes originally was that the 1649 was the epitome of piston transport design and would serve TWA well until the jets were fully proved and established.

TWA did order jets after the Pan Am announcement, but the initial agreement called for only eight 707s to be delivered starting April 1959. The huge new Connies were scheduled to go into service early in 1957, giving TWA at least two years in which to operate what it hoped would be the finest piston airliner ever built.

Whether Damon objected to or supported the 1649 purchase is moot; time was running out for the president of Trans World. He was tired and ailing, and much of his decline was his own fault. A slender man to begin with, he insisted on dieting against his own doctor's orders. One diet consisted of nothing but ginger sticks and coffee. Bob Rummel ran into him at a meeting during this particular weight reduction program and was shocked.

"You could see the guy shrinking down to nothing," Rummel remembers. "He was at the point where he had no resistance to anything."

On a cold night late in December of 1955, Oz Cocke had arranged a lighting ceremony for a new TWA sign on top of the old Astor Hotel on Times Square. It was quite a sign—a replica of a Super G Constellation that was startlingly realistic. Damon went up to the roof of the hotel to take part in the activities and didn't bother to wear an overcoat. The next day he was ill with a bad cold that developed into pneumonia. On January 4, 1956, Ralph Damon passed away in a New York hospital, leaving TWA a legacy of six magnificent past years and a future temporarily devoid of real leadership.

"A lot of people at TWA felt they had lost a friend," says Bob Rummel, "even though they may not have met him more than once or twice." This was even more true of those who did know Damon well. One pilot who had been close to Ralph was Dave Richwine, then a young captain with the unusual ability to work well with management even though he also was very active in ALPA. To this day, Richwine expresses bitterness at Damon's death, which he considered tragically premature.

"Just before he died," Richwine says, "he had gotten the results of a management morale survey which depressed him. It reflected the absence of any real management training and development program. There was no leadership and no effort to train an heir apparent. Damon really needed about six more months to really straighten out the airline. He was subject to the same old influences, people in management were trying to protect their own skins, and nobody was worrying about TWA."

Richwine is on target when he speaks of the failure to train a successor to an obviously sick Damon. Hughes himself was stunned at his death. For a long time, industry gossip snidely hinted that Damon's poor health was due largely to Hughes' incessant phone calls at ungodly hours, his constant badgering and interference. Such gossip belonged in the category of fiction, cruel fiction at that. Hughes did make inconsiderate and inconvenient phone calls and he did interfere, but Ralph Damon had more autonomy as president of TWA than people supposed. Damon almost certainly ruined his own health. Hughes' respect for him is better appreciated when it is realized how long it took to find a successor.

That task was to consume almost an entire year—a ten-and-a-half-month period during which time a three-man committee ran the airline. It consisted of board chairman Warren Lee Pierson, Oz Cocke and John Collings. Of the three, Collings perhaps had the most real authority; he had been named executive vice-president in 1951. But while the title alone gave him the status of an unofficial acting president, Hughes never gave him the authority to go along with it. As board chairman, Pierson enjoyed a titular top role, but he didn't have any more actual say than anyone else. A handsome, imposing man, he tried hard to live up to his formidable physical appearance, but he was badly cast for the part of a true leader. He was a two-fisted martini drinker who wasn't renowned for the ability to hold his liquor. His main forte was the stock market, at which he was something of an expert, and international finance. (He had come to TWA from the Export-Import Bank.)

Walt Menke tells of the time he was in charge of international in-flight service and Pierson intercepted a service bulletin advising pursers how to mix a martini. Pierson was even better acquainted with martinis than the stock market, and he took immediate umbrage at Menke's formula—three parts gin to one part dry vermouth. Walt got a memo from Pierson asking "Who the hell is the martini expert?" Menke continues: "As a result of further consultations with the chairman of the board, the martini ratio was increased to ten-to-one."

Pierson once got on a TWA Connie and found J. Fred Muggs, the famous chimp from the Dave Garroway show, sitting in a seat. "What's that goddamned ape doing on this airplane?" Pierson yelled.

From his wife came an answer. "Maybe they've decided to name a new board chairman," she suggested.

If Pierson lacked both the stature and savvy to run the airline, he had plenty of company in this deficiency. Collings was unpopular if capable in his own area of operations. Cocke, a brilliant marketing man, was well liked and there were quite a few in the company who wanted to see him become president, but Oz was too afraid of Hughes to have been effective. And the main trouble with the triumverate was that the three men were constantly subject to the influence of others, starting with Hughes. Vic Leslie, the pipe-smoking, mustachioed senior vice-president of finance, threw his weight around, and both Cocke and Pierson relied frequently on Jack Weller, by then vice-president of planning and coordination, whose office was right next to Pierson's. The committee that ran TWA after Damon's death was a reminder of the bureaucratic definition of a camel—"a horse designed by a committee." George Spater, who had long since gone off the board but still served as TWA's legal counsel, describes this period as "a terrible time."

"Someone once compared TWA to Belgium," he remarks, "because it kept getting invaded but somehow managed to survive. The three who really ran the airline were Weller, Cocke and Collings."

Yet TWA had some able executives on the roster, most of them promoted by Damon. Ray Dunn was vice-president of maintenance, Tom Taylor had become vice-president of the Washington office, Woody Thomas was vice-president of civic affairs and Frank Busch had succeeded Collings as vice-president of operations. There was Rummel in engineering, Gilmore in public relations and many others—capable men, respected throughout the industry. But just as in the brief period before Damon took over, there was no cohesion and direction at the top.

The fault was Hughes', of course; he simply procrastinated while choosing a new president. Some felt he could have picked one from the ranks. Cocke's name comes to mind first, but if Hughes chose from within the company, he also might have selected Vic Leslie, which would have pleased only Noah Dietrich.

Hughes does appear to have seriously considered one person whose name was familiar to all in TWA, and that was Jack Frye. Shortly before Frye was killed, he confided to Bob Buck that Hughes had approached him to come back as Damon's successor. Buck recounts: "Jack told me the whole story. Hughes wouldn't sign the contract Frye was insisting on, and Jack wouldn't return unless he did. He didn't reveal the exact terms, but the gist was that Frye would be allowed to run the airline without any interference."

If Howard couldn't talk Frye into coming back, he finally landed a man who had been Jack's good friend, and someone who knew both TWA and Hughes very well. On December 17, 1956, TWA's board of directors elected a new president. His name was Carter Lane Burgess.

13

The Short but Eventful Reign
of Carter Burgess

It *was* a short reign. Carter Burgess was president of Trans World Airlines for exactly eleven months and nine days—the briefest tenure of any TWA chief executive.

But in that time, Burgess ruffled more feathers, bruised more egos and stirred up more hornet nests than all his predecessors and successors combined. Hughes hired him without ever meeting or talking to him, and Burgess never. laid eyes on Howard even after he became president. Yet the long-distance sparks that flew between these two strong-willed men would have ignited asbestos.

Conversely, Burgess got along with Noah Dietrich; it was Dietrich, in fact, who put his name before the board of directors at the suggestion of George Spater. The lawyer had watched Burgess' career with interest and admiration during the post-Frye years. After Frye left TWA, he took Burgess with him to General Aniline as his executive assistant for a brief period. Then Burgess became assistant to the president of the University of South Carolina, and executive vice-president of a life insurance company. He left this post when President Eisenhower asked him to serve as assistant secretary of defense, the job he held when TWA directors contacted him to offer him the airline's presidency at an annual salary of $60,000, considerably less than the $100,000 the press claimed he would get.

Hughes knew virtually nothing about him, despite Carter's earlier service with TWA. He simply took the assurance of Dietrich and Spater that Burgess was a tough, able administrator, highly regarded by President Eisenhower, and was not averse either to hard work or banging a few heads together. Burgess tells one particularly illuminating story about his appointment and Howard's rather supine acquiescence to it. Carter was in Seattle visiting Bill Allen of Boeing, shortly after joining TWA. He had been inspecting the 707 project and the Boeing president invited him to his home for dinner. Midway through the meal, Allen was summoned to the phone.

He didn't return for an hour and a half, and apologized to Burgess.

"It was Howard Hughes," Allen explained. "I finally had to tell him I couldn't talk to him anymore because I was entertaining TWA's new president."

"What did he say then?" Burgess asked curiously.

"Well, he said, 'size the guy up for me, will you, Bill? I've never met him—what's he look like?'"

It didn't take long for the airline to size up its new leader. Burgess started cracking heads even before he became president. The day the board elected him, a number of TWA officials and Carter's friends held an impromptu reception for him at the Chevy Chase Country Club in surburban Washington. Present was Gordon Gilmore who made the mistake of offering the president-elect some unsolicited advice—how to handle a certain congressman who had been critical of Burgess' National Guard policies.

"Goddamn you!" Burgess roared. "When you know as much about dealing with the Congress as I do, I'll let you give me some advice. But that happens to be my field and I don't think it's yours. I don't want to hear another goddamned thing about it!"

Years later, in an interview on the lawn of the same country club, a mellowed Burgess grinned as he recalled that incident. "Gordon never knew how close he came to getting fired that night," he chuckled, "and I hadn't even become president yet."

TWA saw another side of the explosive Burgess, however. He needed a few weeks to clean up his desk at the Pentagon and it was agreed he would not take over TWA until January 23, 1957. But on Christmas Day, he went out to National Airport and spent the afternoon introducing himself to TWA employes on duty. He didn't have Damon's finesse and charisma, but he could be as considerate and caring as he was fearsome. Someone asked his Pentagon boss, Defense Secretary Wilson, how he thought Burgess would get along with Howard Hughes.

Wilson smiled wryly. "You mean, how is Hughes going to get along with Burgess?"

Actually, they got along fine at first, largely because there was virtually no contact between them for several months. Significantly, Hughes made no real effort to block some of Burgess' more controversial moves, chief of which was his sudden and unexpected axing of John Collings only a few days after Carter took over. Officially it was announced that Collings had resigned but would remain as a TWA director and "senior consultant" to both the board and the president. But it appears that announcement was typed in face-saving ink.

"I fired him," Burgess says flatly. "Hughes wasn't happy about it and tried to reverse it but I refused. Collings was a lost cause by the time I got there. Whatever TWA's overall status was at the time, it had a lousy reputation for on-time performance and a lousy record for service."

The blunt truth is that Burgess considered the airline overloaded with deadwood from top management all the way down through the ranks. He took a dim view of the fact that in 1956 the airline's payroll had climbed to some 19,000 employes while the bottom dropped out of profits—from six consecutive black ink years under Damon to a $2.3 million net loss that would have been twice as bad except for a tax credit. Burgess didn't stay around long enough to do much more upper-echelon pruning. Collings was his major victim, but he terrorized the entire airline with his frequent station inspections, some of which cost middle management personnel their jobs.

No one knew where, when or whom his wrath would strike. He had a habit of riding many TWA flights at night because he suspected that their multi-stop schedules were costing the airline plenty. He took one plane from New York to Kansas City and it stopped eight times between tte two cities. When he returned to New York, hc called dew executives and announced he wanted a cost analysis of multi-stop flights between New York and both Kansas City and St. Louis. Recounting his own experience, he added, "Hell, when I got off at Kansas City I was the only one on the goddamned airplane!"

The man assigned to the analysis was a young financial wizard named Al Damm. When Bob Six visited Burgess at TWA's Madison Avenue offices one day, Burgess showed him Damm's work. Not too long after that, Six hired Damm away from TWA and Damm eventually became president of Continental. TWA under Burgess seemed to be a breeding ground for future airline presidents. Among his underlings at the time were Frank Lorenzo who went on to head both Texas International and Continental, and Bob Crandall who became president of American.

Burgess not only enjoyed but invited contact with the troops in the field. He sent out a memo to the effect that "if you can't get your boss to act, call me." One commissary employee in New York took him up at his word. He phoned Burgess at his home in Pelham, N.Y., around 1 A.M., waking him out of a sound sleep.

"Mr. Burgess, this is Charlie Blssk [he deliberately blurred the pronunciation of his last name]. Do you know what happened to Flight ninety tonight?"

Burgess, thinking it had crashed, was instantly wide-awake. "My God," he said hoarsely, "what happened?"

"It went out with no cream for the coffee."

Burgess, possibly because of his long military career, had an absolute fetish for cleanliness. He actually wore white gloves on station inspections and kept Ray Dunn's phone off the hook with complaints about dirty airplanes. "Dunn," he'd yell, "are you ever gonna get this goddamned airline cleaned up?"

Dunn would retort, "Yes, if you'll give me the people to do it."

"You can do it with the people you already have!" Burgess would shout back.

Their vitriolic exchanges didn't hide the fact that they liked one another—and this was true of a lot of TWA officers whom Carter would lambaste one minute and invite out for a drink the next. Frank Busch was a favorite and frequent target. One of Burgess' moves was to transfer Operations from Kansas City to New York—something Busch opposed because he didn't feel he had his fingers on the airline's pulse sitting in a Madison Avenue office. It was about 10 P.M. one night when Busch, working late as usual, got a call from Burgess.

"Frank, do you know we've got a ship out of commission in Chicago?"

"How the hell would I know it?" Busch growled. "You moved me here where I have no control over anything."

"Well, there's a ship down and I want to know what you're going to do about it?"

"I'll tell you what I'm *not* gonna do about it!" Busch shouted. "I'm not gonna get a set of wrenches and go out and fix the fucking airplane myself. I'll tell you that!"

"Well, maybe you should!" Burgess shouted back. "Somebody has to do something about those airplanes."

"You've got the wrong boy," Busch retorted, and hung up. A few minutes later, Carter called again. "Frank, I'm in my office. Come up."

Burgess had moved from Damon's large office to a much smaller room—

"just to show off," Busch chuckles, "which indicates what an egotistical son of a bitch he was. Anyway, he was sitting there twirling a big fat cigar and giving me a dirty look."

"Busch," Burgess said coldly, "what makes you such a tough little bastard?"

"You started the fight," Busch declared.

Burgess laughed. "So I did. Come on—I'll buy you a drink."

Busch accepted the vice-presidency—it was offered to him by a Hughes emissary who told him Collings was out—"only if Collings knows I had nothing to do with his leaving." Still loyal after all these years, Busch insists Collings wasn't really fired. "Nobody fired John. He fired himself when he refused to go to New York, and not even Hughes could budge him."

Collings went downhill fast after leaving TWA, drinking heavily. The last time Busch saw him was at a 1965 Seniors Club meeting in Wickenburg, Arizona. Parky Parkinson told Busch that Collings was in bed, refused to get up and wouldn't eat. Busch went to his room with a sandwich and coffee. "Eat something and get out of that damned bed," he ordered Collings.

"I'm not hungry," John muttered.

"You're gonna eat, you old son of a bitch, if I have to stuff it up your ass!"

Collings, the man so many at TWA had feared, smiled faintly. "All right, you little bastard," he whispered, "I'll eat."

For Busch, it was a sad way to remember John Collings, who died shortly after the Wickenburg reunion. Frank's own epitaph for the man who had devoted most of his adult life to the airline sums up that life poignantly.

"He wasn't a brilliant man," Busch says, "but he got things done because he worked at it."

There were no plaques for John Collings, no buildings dedicated to his memory. But in a sense, his memorial is the huge TWA maintenance installation at Kansas City's Mid-Continent Airport. When TWA completed its move from Municipal to the new airport in 1957, it culminated years of effort on Collings' part. He knew every city official in Kansas City and had lobbied hard for the new field.

It is undoubtedly true that Collings began slipping in his later years at TWA. Busch himself says John was spending too much time at the Kansas City Club. It is a fact that the airline's on-time and reliability record deteriorated badly in 1956 and this was perhaps Burgess' top priority. He was satisfied with the irascible Busch, who always spoke his mind. Once, when a captain who had been training Lufthansa pilots commented that they were too regimented and didn't think for themselves, Busch shook his head derisively.

"Bullshit," he snorted. "I can show you a hell of a lot of B-17 pilots who think otherwise."

But Burgess knew that Busch, as vice-president of operations based in New York, inevitably was hamstrung by paperwork and Carter wanted more of a handle on day-to-day operations. Frank's nominee was a young TWA captain he not only respected but had nurtured. His name was Floyd Hall, and Busch started keeping an eye on him the day Floyd walked into his office in Kansas City. Hall was a pilot and Busch was general manager of the domestic division.

"Mr. Busch," Hall said, "I want to get somewhere in this company. What do I have to do?"

Busch eyed the tall, dapper captain whose suave manner went well with his William Powell-type mustache. "It's pretty simple, Floyd. Work. Nobody else does, so you'll be outstanding."

Hall did more than work; he studied. While still flying the line, he spent almost all his spare time taking management courses at both UCLA and the University of Michigan. When Burgess asked Busch to recommend someone as the new general manager of domestic operations, Frank suggested Hall, whose gratitude was diluted somewhat by his sudden exposure to the Burgess temper.

With his appointment as general manager came a series of confrontations with Burgess. The new general manager found out that Burgess had inherited a Hughes trait. "He loved to get you out of bed," sighs Hall, "particularly if something had gone wrong."

Hall remembers one stormy scene in his office in Kansas City. At 5 A.M. that day, Burgess had phoned him from New York. "Floyd, get that goddamned Ray Dunn and both of you meet me in your office—I'm catching our first flight to Kansas City." Dunn and Hall were present when Burgess came charging in. He threw an oily engine part on Hall's spotless desk.

"Look at this goddamned thing! Do you know why pilots are complaining they throw a rod everytime they turn around?"

"Where did you get it?" Dunn asked.

"Never mind where I got it," Burgess yelled, and then turned to Hall. "Any general manager should know where I got it. You tell me where it came from, Floyd."

"Damned if I know," Hall confessed.

"Well, it came off one of your goddamned airplanes. And I want both of you to make sure this kind of thing stops immediately!"

At three o'clock one morning, Floyd's hotel phone rang. He had been in New York for some meetings and was staying at the Waldorf, where TWA employes got a $23-a-day rate.

"Floyd, this is Carter. Do you know what the hell's going on at La Guardia and Idlewild?"

"No," Hall said sleepily. "Is anything wrong?"

"A good general manager should know. Find out and call me back."

Hall, fearing the worst, phoned both airports and was assured all flights were departing on time and everything looked routine. He started to call Burgess back but had second thoughts. By now it was 4 A.M., there was nothing to report and he had a meeting that day in Boston. So he shaved, dressed and caught a 7 A.M. flight to Boston, where he was greeted by an agent at the arrival gate.

"Mr. Hall, you're to call Mr. Burgess immediately."

Hall did. Burgess yelled, "Why didn't you call me?"

"Because there wasn't anything going on," Hall said patiently.

"I told you to call me and, by God, you should have!"

"Look, Carter," Floyd told him, "I work for you and you're the boss, but this kind of bullshit has to stop or you can stick this job up your ass and I'll go back to flying."

He slammed down the phone but just before he left TWA Operations for his meeting, Burgess' secretary phoned him. "Mr. Burgess says you're to be in his office at two o'clock today."

Hall showed up on schedule, figuring he was fired. Who was sitting in Carter's office but La Motte Cohu. Burgess got out of his chair, put his arms around Hall and turned to Cohu.

"La Motte, do you know Floyd Hall? This is one of the nicest, most capable young men I have. But he has the worst goddamned temper I ever saw. He loses it every time he turns around."

Adds Hall, "Carter and I got along just fine from then on."

It was hard for anyone to keep up with Burgess, who worked long hours, and expected everyone else to do likewise. To Burgess Saturdays, Sundays and holidays were no different from any other day of the week. Walt Menke remembers that Carter had acquired a list of especially knowledgable people in various departments—ticketing, reservations, scheduling, etcetera. He sent them on survey trips with instructions to report back on any ideas for improvement—a noble plan but the trouble was that all survey trips were scheduled on weekends and were universally dreaded.

Burgess insisted that staff meetings start at eight in the morning. Says Menke, "That was before any commuter trains got in, so we'd have various officers arriving on milk trains at 6 A.M. just to make an eight o'clock meeting."

He was a fountain of ideas, some good and some bad. One of his suggestions involved a special award for passengers whose initials happened to be T.W.A.—like a "Thomas William Atterbury," for example. Burgess instructed Menke to have a tie clasp designed carrying the initials; Walt had a prototype manufactured, but by the time it was ready, Burgess had left the airline and Menke comments, "Thank God, we didn't order fifty thousand of the damn things."

For some obscure reason, Burgess became hooked on a biography of a Civil War general named Dan Sickles—a Northern general, at that. Sickles had won more notoriety than fame. While serving as a congressman before the war, his wife became involved with Philip Key, the son of the "Star Spangled Banner" author. The angry husband shot Key to death, but was found not guilty by a jury that set the precedent for the so-called Unwritten Law. Burgess read and re-read the biography, *Sickles the Incredible* by W.A. Swanberg, published in 1956, and kept sending Menke out for copies which Carter gave away as gifts.

But Burgess took a dim view of Menke's occasional chores on behalf of Hughes. He told Gordon Gilmore one day, "I want a detailed report on what Menke's doing for the West Coast" (meaning Hughes). When Gilmore broached the subject to Menke, Walt suggested that Burgess talk to Bill Gay or Hughes himself. Gilmore insisted, so Menke finally composed a log of the various assignments he had performed for Hughes. Burgess called him in, threw the log at him, and growled, "Not satisfactory!"

"I thought for awhile I was going to get fired," Menke says, "but it blew over. I think somehow Carter got the idea I could get through to Hughes while he couldn't, and he resented it."

As we've seen, in the early months of his regime Burgess had little occasion to contact Howard. In fact, Carter at first dealt more frequently with Dietrich, who, even before Burgess officially became president, tried to get

211

him to promote a certain officer to senior vice-president. The man in question had the reputation of being a boozer, which Carter didn't know at the time. But he refused anyway, telling Dietrich, "Noah, I don't like Christmas Eve appointments and I want that clearly understood." That same night, the spurned vice-president called Burgess; he had been drinking and asked Burgess if it was true he had been rejected as a senior vice-president.

"Yes, goddamnit!" Burgess told him. "And when you're sober, I'll tell you why."

Some weeks later, Burgess got a report that the vice-president had gotten drunk on a plane and hit a passenger. Burgess called him in.

"You write out your resignation right now," he said. "I'm going to put it in my desk and the next time anything like this happens, I'll pull it out and accept it."

It did happen again and Burgess fired him. There was no intercession by Dietrich, either; Noah already had plenty of indication that the explosive Burgess wasn't afraid of him. Dietrich had urged him to hire a certain Los Angeles caterer to take over TWA's food service; the caterer's wife was a good friend of Noah's spouse. Burgess agreed to meet the caterer and taste his food at a dinner in Dietrich's home. Carter didn't think he was as good as the caterer he liked himself, Dave Chasen, and informed Noah his candidate was out.

"Interestingly enough," Burgess adds, "Hughes didn't want this guy either. But he didn't have the guts to tell Dietrich to lay off."

Not even Carter, however, was immune from Hughes' favor-dispensing proclivities. Burgess best remembers an incident involving—who else?—Darryl Zanuck. Hughes personally called Burgess and informed him Zanuck was going to Paris on a TWA sleeper flight out of Idlewild that night.

"I want to really fix him up in good shape," Howard said. "Darryl would like to come to the airport two hours before flight time, and I want you to have the plane at the gate ready for him to board as soon as he gets there. Also, Zanuck doesn't want anyone in the upper berth above him—he needs the whole compartment. Now, I want the hostesses on duty when he arrives and his berth all made up by five o'clock."

As usual, he then repeated the instructions. Burgess grumbled, "Look, the plane doesn't leave until seven. What the hell's he going to do for two hours sitting in an empty plane?"

"Oh," explained Hughes, "he's gonna take sleeping pills and go to bed before the rest of the passengers load."

Burgess issued the neccesary orders but at 6:15, Operations called him. The aircraft had a major mechanical and departure would be delayed indefinitely.

"What do we do with Mr. Zanuck?" Operations wanted to know. "He's sound asleep."

"Roll him in the hangar with the plane," Burgess suggested.

When Zanuck awoke the next morning, he was still at Idlewild. Before departing for Paris, he made a call to Howard that Burgess would just as soon forget.

"God Almighty," he admits, "Hughes ate me alive."

But Burgess wasn't averse to standing up to the moody millionaire, even though he didn't always win. He lost one battle involving an addition to the Kansas City maintenance base that Ray Dunn was recommending strongly.

Because the money would be loaned by Toolco, Burgess had gotten them to set up an engineering group to evaluate the project. Hughes heard about it and stopped the proposal right then and there—why, Burgess could never understand unless Hughes resented his going to Toolco without consulting him first. Yet generally, Burgess and Hughes weren't that much at odds and Howard, no softy himself, had to respect what Burgess was trying to do for the airline.

And he *was* trying, although there were times when the troops wished he wasn't trying so hard—and with so much noise. Once he ordered all the corners in a hangar painted white so it would be impossible to sweep dirt into them without showing it. He was especially tough on commisary inspections when the white gloves would move ominously over upper shelves and behind refrigerators. One commissary had been damaged by a flood. When Burgess arrived to inspect the premises, he didn't know about the flood and there hadn't been time to clean the place up. He assumed the condition was permanent and almost fired the manager.

Ed Frankum remembers an occasion when he was chief pilot at La Guardia and Burgess showed up at 6 A.M. with the usual white gloves.

"We went on a tour of the hangar facilities and we finally came to a padlocked locker. Burgess asked what was in it and was told, 'stationery and office supplies.' Burgess says, 'Unlock it.' Nobody had a key so Carter got suspicious and demanded that somebody get a hacksaw. It took twenty minutes to saw through the padlock and when we opened it, that's all there was inside—stationery and other office supplies. Burgess actually seemed disappointed but we went onto the commissary. There he took a broom handle and poked around under the refrigerator and stoves. Pretty soon he hits paydirt, so to speak, and pulls out a dead mouse. All hell broke loose. But then a funny thing happened, which makes me wonder if he was mostly bark. There he was chewing out the whole commissary staff and he didn't use the same four-letter word twice in a ten-minute tirade. Right in the middle of his yelling, he turned around and sneaked me a wink."

Of all TWA employee groups, the pilots were Burgess' favorites. The admiration was mutual. He socialized with the flight crews and went out of his way to make them feel each was as important as any executive, including Carter himself. Much to the resentment of not a few TWA non-pilot employees, he made all captains members of the Ambassadors Club. Then he came up with stand-mounted placards to be placed at the foot of the boarding stairs before every flight. They were white with red lettering.

TWA FLIGHT 22
CAPTAIN SO-AND-SO COMMANDING

Under the name would be four red stars.

Actually, it wasn't bad showmanship and the pilots ate it up. To such an extent, it must be added, that most of them took the signs with them when they retired. Several captains put the placards on their front doors and one, Reg Plumridge, hung it over his bed until his wife made him shift it to his den.

Only once was Burgess thwarted in his zeal to demonstrate his pride in the pilot corps. He proposed to buy each one a pair of white kid gloves and a white scarf, but a few of the officers talked him out of it. Today, Burgess defends his pro-pilot attitude vigorously, explaining first that he made them Ambassadors because they could buy VIP passengers drinks in any Club they were visiting. Frankum thinks his liking for airmen stemmed from his association with Frye, but Burgess himself goes beyond this.

"I suppose some of my predecessors and also successors thought I was too pro-pilot. You have to understand, and I've never changed this opinion, that they're the finest group of men I've ever known. They're exquisitely unusual; I never ran across a bad one. They have a certain elegance that shows in their faces.

"Sure I admired them—guys like Don Allen, Don Terry, Fletcher Grable. That Grable, he was flying a Connie when he lost one engine and had a second one about to go. He was over the Atlantic and I sent him a message that the first voice I wanted to hear when he got on the ground at Shannon was his own. By God, I stayed in my office until I got that call and I was proud of him, proud that we became good friends. I once made a speech in which I pointed out that when you're at thirty-five thousand feet with a couple of hundred people aboard a machine that cost seven million bucks and something goes wrong, you can't call a meeting of the board of directors."

The pilots tried to play ball with Burgess, too. TWA was having a lot of trouble with the Constellation autopilot and the pilots' contract contained a provision stipulating that they didn't have to fly transcontinental if the autopilot was inoperative. At Carter's request, they agreed to waive that provision until TWA could get a better autopilot. Burgess, informed that the best one available was a model developed by Bill Lear, arranged its installation on a Connie for test purposes.

"Hughes heard about it and stopped it cold," Burgess said. "He was tipped by someone in the company. There was more than one TWA officer reporting to Hughes everything I did."

His two leading candidates were Rummel and Gilmore; Rummel denies it and Gilmore, ailing after a stroke, was unavailable for interviewing, but such a "spy" system was not necessarily unfair or unusual. Hughes did own more than 70 percent of the airline and naturally wanted to know what was going on. It was simply unfortunate that he didn't try to obtain information directly from Burgess or any other president. One of Burgess' difficulties with Hughes was the fact that often he couldn't even get in touch with him and had to use people like Rummel and Lee Flanagin as go-betweens.

Rummel is the first to admit that for a time he was on two payrolls: TWA's and Toolco's. It was not the most comfortable situation for Rummel, who made no secret of the unique arrangement.

"I was very thankful I had a good understanding with TWA management because there were a lot of things going on that were secret. I told TWA what I dared and what I thought they had to know, and I always leveled with Hughes. Burgess, for example—I honestly enjoyed working with him. There were times when he seemed to encourage me to talk to Hughes, when he couldn't reach him, and there were other times when he didn't like the idea at all and I didn't blame him. There were a few cases which I could have handled easily for Hughes but I refused because I wasn't sure what Carter would have liked. So I'd call Carter and say, 'Here's the situation. Now what do you want me to do?' Sometimes Burgess would just ask what I'd do, and a few times I never did get out of him what he wanted."

This is why Burgess, at a time when TWA was only two years away from the jet age and in the midst of crucial equipment decisions, had incredibly little say in those decisions. He didn't know as much about future aircraft acquisitions as Rummel, and even Rummel often was kept in the dark or saw his advice ignored.

Burgess was occupied mostly with improvements in service and the introduction of the 1649. He was not involved with the decision to name the plane "Jetstream." From all accounts, that was Howard's idea and it was a controversial one. Hughes claimed the name was appropriate for a transport that cruised high enough to take advantage of the upper-altitude winds, which was true. But TWA caught a lot of flak from other airlines, which charged that "Jetstream" was misleading advertising because it implied the 1649 was jet-powered. It almost was; Lockheed originally planned the 1649 as a turboprop but couldn't get a satisfactory engine/propeller combination developed in time to meet TWA's delivery schedules. Lockheed, which discreetly stayed out of the controversy, called the plane "Starliner."

So the 1649, the last piston-engine airliner to be developed, joined TWA's fleet in mid-1957. It may not have been the best of the pistons, but it quite possibly was the most beautiful. It combined the Super G's graceful fuselage with a wingspan fully 27 feet longer than the G's. The elongated wings not only provided more fuel space and a range of more than 6,000 miles, but enabled the engines to be located farther away from the fuselage, making the 1649 the quietest of all piston transports.

For passengers, its outstanding feature was a TWA-developed "Siesta seat," largely Oz Cocke's idea. It reclined almost to a flat position, was deeply upholstered and cost some $2,500 per unit. TWA had it exclusively, much to the envy of competitors who admitted, albeit privately, it was the most comfortable airliner seat ever designed. Another passenger-oriented item was the Jetstream's interior; the cabin was broken up into compartments which eliminated the tube-like effect of a long fuselage.

Some TWA pilots loved the 1649; others preferred the Super G. Bob Buck, who flew both, always thought the 1649 would have been a better airplane if Lockheed had lengthened the fuselage as it did the wings. "As it was," Buck says, "you had to land it with a lot of power or it would fall out from under you. The biggest drawback wasn't the airplane, but the engines. They were turbo-compounds and if you operated them with full blower, you'd get the altitudes you wanted, but a terrible engine failure rate. To cut that rate, we started flying them at low blower and this put us in lousy weather."

Buck, incidentally, was one of the few pilots who thought Burgess was wrong in catering to the flight crews as much as he did. "I think he decided that the company's strength would be the pilots and they did love him—they even had a slogan: 'Work Harder For Carter'—but frankly, it pissed off everybody else, including mechanics and hostesses."

It was true that Burgess' bluntness and temper could alienate people. His sarcasm was bitter. If anyone walked into an 8 A.M. staff meeting five minutes late, Burgess would greet him with a "good afternoon." Ronnie Duckworth, corporate secretary when Carter was president, had a transparent vase and upon Burgess's departure, he put a bottle of tranquilizers into the vase, draped it in in black and hung a sign reading: "In Memoriam to Carter L. Burgess."

But no one could criticize Burgess for not working at his job. No phase of TWA's operations escaped his attention. He bumped into Captain Russ Black at a dinner and remarked, "By the way, I saw your log write-up on your last trip—I'd like to know what the hell it was all about." Black told him, but thought to himself, "Now how could he have time to read pilot aircraft logs?"

Ironically, Burgess in some ways was like Hughes. He could be unreasonably demanding and inconsiderate—with early morning phone calls for example—but also impulsively kind. Fran Moran, for years TWA's station manager in San Francisco, was exposed to Carter's inspections and had been warned to wear a uniform jacket—seldom done at the major stations. He did this time, however, and after walking around TWA's facilities for an hour or so, Burgess invited Moran and the base chief pilot, Bill Townsend, back to his hotel suite for a drink.

They were in the suite for a few minutes when Burgess announced he was taking them to dinner at Ernie's, one of the city's best restaurants.

"Mr. Burgess," Moran said, "I appeciate the invitation but I can't go. I'm in uniform."

"The hell with that," Burgess beamed. "I'll take care of everything. Just go into my closet and you'll find a dinner jacket you can put on."

Moran donned the jacket and went to dinner—one he will never forget. Burgess was 6'1" and the jacket came down to the 5'7" Moran's knees. The next day, Burgess was heading back to Kansas City and told Moran he wanted to inspect the airplane before the passengers boarded. With Moran accompanying him Burgess walked up and down the aisle. Then he turned to Fran, whom he had been calling by his first name all the previous evening.

"*Mr.* Moran, I want you to call Kansas City right now. Upon arrival in Kansas City, I want every piece of carpeting in this airplane ripped out and new carpeting installed."

He could be brutal in actions as well as words. A crack that went around the industry at the time defined an optimist as "a TWA employee who brings his lunch to work." But it must be remembered that Carter Burgess took command of TWA at a time when an airline whose fortunes were sagging really needed a tough guy. There were many who hated his guts. Those who really knew him were fond of him—Busch, for example, who fought with him constantly. Frank showed up at a dinner one night sporting a crutch and a cast on one leg. He was asked what happened.

"Carter said jump," Busch said jokingly, "and I was on the third floor at the time."

Burgess' greatest accomplishment was to shake TWA out of its doldrums and lethargy. The airline lost money during his regime ($1.5 million in the red in 1957) but it was an improvement over 1956. And Burgess at least laid the foundations for a return to profitability. He launched the advance planning for jet operations even though he was operating almost in the blind as far as specific jet purchases were concerned—he wasn't even sure how many jets TWA would be acquiring. Most of all, Burgess was like a tough football coach who puts pride back into a team that was beginning to feel sorry for itself.

Nowhere was that "maybe we're jinxed" attitude more prevalent than during the six months that preceeded Burgess' assuming the presidency. For on June 30, 1956, TWA had been stunned by one of the world's most spectacular air disasters—the collision of a TWA Constellation and a United DC-7 over the Grand Canyon.

All 128 persons aboard the two planes were killed in a supposedly impossible accident—the aircraft collided in literally empty airspace at a high altitude in clear weather. They had both left Los Angeles heading east and were flying "off airways," or in uncontrolled airspace. This was common practice in the fifties when Air Traffic Control's approved routes were congested, or when those airways were not very direct. But when pilots chose to fly in uncontrolled airspace, they assumed the responsibility of avoiding other aircraft.

Grand Canyon was not an "accident that couldn't happen"—it was bound to happen. Pilots flew off airways because ATC centers were undermanned, the airways they controlled were inadequate and the air traffic regulations were obsolete. TWA's flight, originally assigned to a lower altitude, had been given permission to climb "one thousand feet above the clouds"—a dangerously imprecise clearance. To get above the overcast, the Connie had to reach 21,000 feet, which was United's assigned altitude.

ATC informed TWA that United was at 21,000 feet, but controllers were too busy with traffic on controlled airways to advise United of the TWA clearance. One controller told investigators later he had noticed that the estimated arrival times of both flights over a checkpoint near Grand Canyon were identical. But the harassed controller, busy with flights directly under his jurisdiction, gave no further thought to the deadly coincidence and the two airlines raced toward their fatal rendezvous at 300 miles per hour.

For TWA, it was a family tragedy: on board the Connie was the wife of John Brock, TWA's popular district sales manager in Washington. Lois Brock was on the way home after visiting relatives on the West Coast and Brock was napping on his patio. Later he would drive to National and pick her up. He awoke with a start at 12:45 P.M.—the exact moment the collison occurred. He had an unexplainable feeling that he should go to the airport and meet two people—why two, or who they were supposed to be, he never knew. A couple of hours later, TWA notified him that Flight 2 out of Los Angeles was overdue and unreported.

When word got around that Brock's wife had been on the plane, Brock's airline friends rallied around the grief-stricken man. Herb Ford, his counterpart at American, called him. "John, we'll help you in any way we can. If you want to go to Arizona, you have a positive space pass on American—just let me know. We'll take you either to Los Angeles or Phoenix and we'll make arrangements to get you to Flagstaff."

Bob Six was another caller. "I just want you to know we'll arrange passes on any Continental flight that'll help you get to Flagstaff, John."

Brock had decided to go when a TWA official phoned.

"There's no point in your going," he said as gently as possible. "Everything's in bits and pieces. There's nothing you can do."

Frank Busch and Ray Dunn went to the crash site and were taken by helicopter to the bottom of the Canyon where they found the Connie's tail—with red, white and blue paint marks from a United propeller. When the chopper tried to pick them up, it was too windy for it to land and they spent the night on the cold Canyon floor.

Those markings were the first indication that the DC-7 had hit the Connie. Other searchers located a rear cargo door from the TWA plane which also had the telltale red, white and blue gouges. Bob McKay of TWA's Los Angeles PR office phoned this finding to Gilmore, who told him to contact Howard Hughes immediately. McKay reached Hughes and offered his opinion that "it looks like United was at fault."

"Knock that shit off," Hughes said angrily. "I don't want either United or us blamed."

Ten months later, the CAB issued a report that agreed with Hughes. The collision was blamed on the inadequate ATC system, not the pilots or their airlines. The subsequent aftermath of Grand Canyon was the creation of the independent Federal Aviation Agency in 1958 with the authority and funds to modernize air traffic control. And there were other aftermaths of a more personally poignant nature.

About a year after the accident, John Brock remarried. His new bride, also named Lois, was a widow and had been a United reservations agent. One night they had identical dreams: both their dead spouses were talking to each other about them.

Eighteen months after the accident, a TWA official in charge of tracing lost personal effects notified Brock that a gold ring had turned up. Inscribed "from John to Lois," it carried the date of their wedding twenty-four years before.

Any fatal accident has terrible effects on an airline, but Grand Canyon was especially bad because of the circumstances. TWA itself was as innocent a victim as the unfortunate passengers and their families. Carter Burgess sensed the low morale that was the residue of the tragedy, still in evidence when he took over. Some of his bombast was a deliberate effort to erase all vestiges of this down-in-the-mouth feeling, but it was his personality and not his intentions that caused resentment.

On his desk he kept a clenched fist made of brass. It was funny, but in a way it also was frightening. It seemed to symbolize a kind of ruthlessness that was partially a sham, but occasionally became only too real. Burgess could blow up over relatively minor accidents. He had, for example, a hatred of parsley. He was on a TWA flight and the meal entree of turkey was served with a sprig of the decorative vegetable. At a general staff meeting the next day, Burgess chewed out the vice-president of passenger service, John Clemson. His opening remark set the mood for the rest of the tirade. "I'm amazed," he said sarcastically, "that you're not wearing parsley in your lapel."

Petty, yes, and also unwarranted because his criticism was based on a personal prejudice. But most strong executives can be that way. Occasional unreasonableness goes with the territory. More important was Burgess' overall dedication to improving TWA, and there is no doubt he did achieve improvements. Perhaps he might have even mellowed if he had stayed on the job longer, but this was not destined to happen.

With the delivery of the 1649 Jetstreams, Burgess and Hughes embarked on their own collision course.

14

A Little Trip to Nassau

Hughes regarded the big new Connies as airplanes that would keep TWA competitive until the jet age arrived, but his obsession with speed as a competitive weapon resulted in a design mistake.

To make sure the 1649 could whip any DC-7 flying, he had insisted that it be equipped with hollow-blade propellers as a means of saving weight. Rummel and Dunn advised him against it and so did Lockheed's own engineers. They all pointed out that while such blades were lighter, they also were less durable. They had a spongy material inside, a batting that could work loose and shift to the prop tips where the imbalance caused blade chips to fly.

But Howard refused to listen, just as he had refused to listen when Frank Busch, urged on by Floyd Hall and others, begged Hughes not to buy the 1649 in the first place. The new plane went into service with the hollow props and on a flight out of Paris, one lost a blade tip that flew into a lavatory, slightly injuring a passenger. The incident was reported to Burgess, who feared the government might ground the airplane. On his own initiative, he asked Lockheed to install solid props on a 1649 still at the Burbank factory, and then get a CAA regional inspector to certify the modification after a test flight. His fast action, taken fairly soon after the 1649 started carrying passengers, probably saved the plane from a grounding order and Hughes expressed his gratitude to Carter.

Until all hollow-blade props could be replaced, they had to be inspected frequently to make sure the batting hadn't shifted. This was a simple process: a mechanic or flight engineer merely tapped the prop with a spoon, coin or metal prong. "If it sounded like a watermelon," Burgess says, "we knew it was okay."

By now, however, Hughes already had become convinced that the 1649 was not really the ideal interim airplane. He was intrigued with two British propjets, the short-range Vickers Viscount and the much larger Bristol Britannia, which could cross the Atlantic nonstop. Both Bristol and Vickers had aircraft in Canada for demonstration flights and Hughes, shortly before the 1649 actually went into service, had decided to fly to Montreal where he could inspect the two planes firsthand.

The mode of transportation he chose was a brand-new 1649, the second one off the assembly line. It was scheduled to be used on a so-called "provisioning" flight to Europe prior to its going into regular service. (A provisioning flight involves the delivery of material such as schedules and maintenance manuals relative to the inauguration of a new airplane.) When

Hughes left for Montreal in the Jetstream, the provisioning flight had to be postponed and Burgess heard about it immediately. He happened to be in bed with a case of mumps when he got a call from 7000 Romaine that Hughes would phone him at eight that night. Operations already had advised Carter that Howard had the airplane.

"That was one thing about Hughes," Burgess said. "If you were told that phone would ring at eight, it would ring at eight. If it wasn't Howard, it would be some one explaining that he was unable to make the call and a new time would be set."

So Burgess moved to a dressing room telephone adjacent to his bedroom, mumps and all, and awaited the call, which came promptly. Continues Burgess:

"It was Howard. He called me Mr. Burgess and I called him Mr. Hughes—all very respectful. He had a voice I'll never forget. I can't remember my own father's voice but I'll always remember his. A little high-pitched, very courteous, very methodical. He said he had heard about my illness and felt very upset about it. He wanted to fly in a mumps specialist from Los Angeles. I told him thanks, but no—I already had a good doctor."

Then, Burgess adds, the following conversation ensued.

"Now, Mr. Burgess, you live in Pelham?"

"Yes, in Pelham."

"You, know, I went to school up that way. Is Mt. Vernon the stop before Pelham and is New Rochelle the stop after Pelham?"

"I believe that's right, Mr. Hughes."

"I don't want to talk to you too long because I know you're in bad shape and I want you to get well. I've heard you're doing a great job at TWA."

"Who told you?" Burgess asked suspiciously.

"Gene Sarazen," Hughes said, mentioning the name of the famous golfer—a questionable judge of an airline president's performance, Burgess thought wryly.

Hughes added a few more compliments and then got to the point. "I'm up in Montreal. Mr. Dietrich and I have come to a parting of the ways and I wanted you to know that. The sole reason of my call this evening is that I want to find out if you can be loyal to me."

(That Dietrich and Hughes had parted company came as a complete surprise to Burgess. In his autobiography, Dietrich said the break occurred March 17, 1957. Either Dietrich was mistaken in the date, or Hughes managed to keep it a secret for several months. The consensus of those interviewed on the reason for their estrangement was that Dietrich demanded a greater financial reward for his work and Hughes thought he was being greedy. Jack Real says Hughes told him he was paying Dietrich a half-million dollars a year plus a $250,000 annual expense account, but that Noah demanded a piece of Toolco as a condition for his staying with Hughes. Real says Hughes likened it to Adam and Eve and the apple—that Noah could have had everything in paradise but the apple, and that apple was a piece of Toolco. "I think," Real says, "Noah killed the goose that laid the golden eggs.")

Startled by the question and the news that Dietrich was out, Burgess still didn't hesitate.

"Mr. Hughes, I can be loyal to the airline."

"That's me," Hughes drawled. He was about to hang up when Burgess said quickly, "Mr. Hughes, just a minute—you've got me in a hell of a spot. We've literally worked our tails off to get those goddamned airplanes you bought for us out of the factory and into service. The one you've taken to Montreal is one we vitally need and we need it tonight. We've got provisioning schedules set up for London and Paris and we're going to neutralize the delivery gain we've made from Lockheed by your having that plane up there. I'd like to send a crew up there to get it. When you want to leave, I'll send another plane to Montreal and take you wherever you want to go. I need that airplane, I need it tonight and it'll help my mumps a lot if I can get it."

"Well," Hughes hedged, "I'll talk to you about that tomorrow."

Adds Burgess, "Tomorrow never came—it was always tomorrow with him."

Hughes appropriated the 1649 in late June. Carter's decision to replace the hollow-blade props came the following fall. That one 1649 stayed in Hughes' possession until the end of December and it was the direct cause of Burgess' resignation.

Hughes had flown it from Burbank to Montreal with TWA Capt. Ted Moffitt as his copilot; also aboard were Bill Gay and Johnny Meyer. Joining Hughes in Montreal later were Bob Rummel and actress Jean Peters, whom Howard had just married. The group stayed in Montreal for a month, looking over the Viscount and Britannia and using the Connie for occasional test flights. Moffitt and his flight engineer returned to Los Angeles almost immediately and Hughes wanted another TWA crew sent to Montreal.

The replacements were Capt. Jim Rappatoni and flight engineer Bill Bushey—the latter an instructor who was one of the few FEs checked out in the 1649. Bushey was based in Los Angeles at the time and was called in by the chief pilot along with two other flight engineers who were informed Hughes needed a qualified 1649 crew in Montreal.

"You'd be gone about three days," the chief pilot assured them. He finally chose Bushey who accompanied Rappatoni to Canada, where they reported to Hughes. They were checked in at the Ritz Carlton, told to be on call at all times, and to charge everything to Hughes. Their main job was to accompany Hughes on a number of 1649 test flights. On one occasion they flew to Ottawa, where Hughes shot landings all night long.

Rappatoni tired of all this and asked Gay and Rummel if he could go home. They called Bushey, wanting to know whether he'd be willing to fly with Hughes alone. Bushey, who was thoroughly enjoying himself, said "Sure." He had no idea of what was going to happen. On August 1, Bushey was informed they were going to fly to an unnamed destination about 1,500 miles from Montreal. Bill guessed Houston, but he was way off—they went to Nassau.

Before leaving Montreal, the 1649 was fueled with about 7,000 gallons. Bushey suggested they should take on more but Hughes refused. "Where we're going," he said, "gas is two cents cheaper."

They stayed in Nassau for three months. Bushey's chief duty was to accompany Howard when he wanted to fly the Connie, parked at Oates Field under 24-hour guard by special security men. Bushey got a day's notice before every trip. Gay would tell him, "The boss wants to go flying tomorrow," but otherwise his time was his own. The whole party, not more than eight or nine persons as Bushey remembers it, was quartered at the Emerald Beach Hotel where Hughes had leased the entire fifth floor. When the hotel management wanted to shut down for some pre-winter remodeling, Hughes refused to move. He was paying about $8,000 a day just for rooms and meals. He even charged the plane's gas to his room.

Exactly what he was doing in Nassau, why he went there in the first place and the reason he stayed so long was never explained. On some of their flights out of Nassau, Hughes would fly over neighboring islands in the Bahamas at low altitudes. Bushey suspected he might be scouting some property, but Hughes didn't say anything to him unless it involved the airplane. Bill also noticed that while Hughes was hard of hearing on the ground, he had no trouble communicating in the cockpit, where he was invariably friendly and considerate.

"What's on my side is mine and what's on your side is yours," he'd tell Bushey, who considered him an above average pilot—"good, although not in the same class as an airline pilot."

"We'd be up around twenty-one to twenty-three thousand feet and he'd say, 'Bill, this airplane's no ball of fire up here, is it?' Occasionally he'd be bothered by a nosebleed, maybe because he had only one lung left from that fighter crash."

Jean Peters went along on a few flights. Once Hughes asked her, "Honey, how do you like the airplane?"

She said, "Fine, but the armrests on the seats are too narrow—it's like putting your arms in your lap." (Hughes ordered the armrests changed when they returned to California.)

Bushey liked Jean. "I was invited to have dinner with them a few times, always in their suite. First time I was introduced to her, Hughes asked me to call her Jean. She was a very nice girl with absolutely no airs. Everytime I saw her, she wore no makeup, her clothes weren't one bit fancy and she kept her hair tied up in a bun."

Shortly after they arrived in Nassau. Hughes suggested to Bushey that he invite his wife to the island at his expense. "Do you have children?" he asked. "A boy and a girl," Bushey said. "They're in kindergarten and first grade."

"Bring them, too," Howard offered.

"I appreciate that, Mr. Hughes, but they're too young and anyway I wouldn't want them to miss school."

"Well, bring their teachers," Hughes proposed. "I'll pay all their expenses and their salaries, too."

Bushey called his wife with this surprising offer, but they decided she would come alone. She was with Bushey for two weeks and Hughes picked up the entire tab. But on just one flight, Bushey earned whatever generosity Howard displayed. They were in the air for nearly nine hours, beyond their estimated fuel exhaustion time, and at Oates Field they were making bets the Connie was down in the ocean. On final approach into Nassau, the fuel gauges showed empty, Bushey lowered the gear and didn't get a "down" light. Hughes said calmly, "This is a hell of a mess, Bill—no fucking gear and no gas. We're not going to get much older in this kind of a situation, are we?"

Bushey suddenly remembered he previously had pulled a circuit breaker for some kind of a check. He flipped it back and the gear light came on. One reason they had almost run out of fuel was Hughes' insistence on flying low much of the time, often only a hundred feet above the ocean. But Bushey didn't complain. By now he was used to Howard's strange ways. The only order he gave Bushey on the ground was to not swim in the hotel pool.

"The water's not recirculated," he told Bushey, "and these islands are full of t.b." Bushey wasn't surprised at this remark. He had noticed that all Hughes' food was flown in just for him and brand-new silverware was used at every meal. Bushey always remained philosophical about such eccentricities. He figured Hughes could afford them and he obviously wasn't in good health, not with only one lung.

"I never did see him in a restaurant," he says. "He had that whole fifth floor and they wouldn't let anybody past the fourth. My own room was on the second floor."

The Connie arrived in Nassau August 2 and didn't leave until October 27, when Hughes flew it out alone. Why he decided to fly back to Los Angeles solo, Bushey never could understand. They had been discussing the return trip and Hughes suggested that Bushey might as well go home. Apparently he wasn't sure of an exact departure date and didn't want the flight engineer to be away from his family any longer. During that stay of almost three months, Burgess kept phoning Hughes in Nassau—first pleading and then demanding that he return the 1649 so it could be put into service.

According to Bushey—and he was on the premises as a first-hand witness—Carter made one too many calls. There was another Constellation based at Nassau and at Hughes' disposal—an older model owned by Resort Airlines. One day, Hughes remarked to the flight engineer, "Well, Carter's on me again about this airplane, Bill. Let's get it back to him and we can use that Resort plane."

But a day or so later, Hughes told Bushey that Burgess had phoned him again and apparently had gotten tough about the missing 1649. Bushey never found out what was said, but Howard was extremely upset and angry. Says Bushey, "I guess he decided right then and there that that Connie was going to stay in Nassau until the tires went flat."

Bushey is a TWA captain now, based in Kansas City, and his son is a Delta flight engineer. Few people have ever gotten as close to Howard as Bushey did in that four-month period, even though his contact with Hughes was limited almost entirely to the cockpit.

We never had any social conversation, not really. I gathered from that long time with him he liked three things—airplanes, TWA and girls. Before I left, we talked about the 707s we were going to get and he asked me if I'd go with him sometime on a flight. It didn't work out and I never heard another word from him. While I was on the trip, I got my regular TWA salary as a flight engineer instructor. If I needed dough— and Hughes told me always to tip fairly—I sent Bill Gay a note.

In leisure time I'd rent a boat. I got to meet a lot of people, but I'd never tell them what I was doing in Nassau. They'd ask me what I did for a living and I'd tell 'em I was a car dealer from Newark on vacation.

They'd ask how I could afford to stay at the Emerald Beach for so long and I'd just say, 'I sell a lot of cars.' There was never any strain on my marriage. My wife's an understanding gal and anyway, I'd call her every night. Hughes told me I could talk to her all I wanted. I didn't get to say goodbye to him in person. I talked to him on the phone just before I left. Why he didn't ask me to wait until he was ready to go back is a complete mystery to me—he damned near killed himself flying back alone.

That he did. He had radioed ahead to have Lee Flanagin meet him at Los Angeles International. Lee was waiting in the hangar—it was a rainy night, about 10 P.M.—when the control tower called. Hughes was trying to contact him for advice on what to do. The airport was almost socked in.

"You guys can see better up there than I can," Flanagin said. "Tell him to circle until it clears here."

Hughes complied, circling the Long Beach airport for almost two hours. When LAX finally cleared, Flanagin told the tower, "Tell him he can get in here now." Hughes, almost exhausted, landed after midnight. But he perked up when he saw Lee.

"I wish you'd go over to your office," he said, "and get the Long Beach tower on the phone. Tell 'em I'm sorry I had to circle them for so long."

Burgess, advised that Hughes was back, resumed his requests for the 1649. Howard didn't like to be pressured by anyone and he was bristling. The Connie stayed in his possession throughout November and most of December, and when Burgess tried to reach him, Hughes wouldn't return his calls. Finally Carter began sending messages through Ray Dunn and Flanagin, but neither could budge Hughes. Flanagin, in fact, kept making excuses for Hughes and Burgess was frantic with frustration. Once he told Flanagin, "I don't like being president of a company in which I have to take my orders from an underling."

"It isn't my fault," Lee retorted. "I take my orders from the guy who owns it."

Late in December, Hughes asked Flanagin to call Burgess at home. "Tell him I'm ready to turn the airplane back to him."

It was one o'clock in the morning, Los Angeles time, and Flanagin balked. "Howard, I'll call him if you insist but he's quite quite obstreperous and he doesn't want to talk to me. Frankly, I think it's about time you talked to him yourself."

Hughes made a call, but at first it was not to promise the 1649's return. He had been tipped that Burgess was in Washington, about to testify before the CAB the next day. It was a tariff case, but Hughes was told Burgess might be asked about the missing Connie. Howard's appropriation of the airplane had been well publicized. He reached Carter at the Carlton Hotel, where Burgess was staying, and he wasted no time on pleasantries.

"Carter, I hear you're going to appear at the CAB tomorrow."

"Yes, sir. Looking forward to it."

"What are you going to tell them about the airplane?"

"Howard, if they ask me I'll tell them the truth."

"And what is the truth?"

"The truth is that you've got the airplane and the airline can't get it back.

It's under illegal insurance, it hasn't been helpful to our bottom line and it's been a goddamned lousy morale symbol for our pilots, flying lesser aircraft into Los Angeles and seeing that damned thing straddled there at the L.A. airport. Howard, I'll tell 'em the truth!"

There was an uncomfortable silence for a moment and then Hughes said, "Well, you can tell the CAB the airplane is back in service."

The next day, Burgess appeared before the Board, which didn't bring up the matter of the missing Connie at all. Burgess, who had asked Ray Dunn to check Los Angeles on whether the plane actually had been turned over to TWA, put through another call to Dunn. Then he flew to New York where George Spater met him at La Guardia. Burgess drew him to one side, away from any eavesdroppers.

"George, I'm quitting TWA tonight," he said. "I just called Ray Dunn again and the plane's still sitting there under guard."

Spater didn't even try to talk him out of it. Burgess went home, got his wife, and drove back to his Madison Avenue office. He took personal papers out of his desk and left.

"I wasn't going to live in dishonesty over the thing," he says. "I made no effort to bring up the plane before the CAB but hell, they knew about it. There were pictures of it on the front page. Stories out of Nassau that its gas had been charged to Hughes' Nassau hotel bill. In fact, the hotel manager told me later it was the first time he ever saw ten thousand gallons of gas on a hotel bill."

To Burgess, the airplane was a matter of principle and personal honor. Hughes held that 1649 for about half the eleven months Burgess served as president. It ate at him constantly even as he tried to run the airline. Not everyone thought he should have resigned over the issue, arguing that Hughes owned the airplane and had the right to do anything he pleased with it. Burgess disagrees with this thinking.

"The point was that while Hughes Tool did own it," he insists, "it didn't need the airplane and TWA did, especially during the Christmas holidays. The whole incident didn't exactly prove I was president and chief executive officer."

Burgess' resignation was made public the day before Christmas, effective on December 31. Some of Hughes' lieutenants spread the word that Burgess had been fired, although the official announcement cited resignation due to the differences over policy. Burgess vigorously denies being fired.

"That just isn't true, he says. "I can't prove it and I've never tried to prove it, but dammit, I was the one who pulled the linchpin, not Hughes. My conscience bothered me about that airplane so I quit and I could ill afford to quit. I had five daughters and I was making the grand sum of sixty thousand a year and I hadn't even finished the year.

"I made a lot of mistakes at TWA, I'll admit it, but that airplane wasn't one of them. I should have asked for Warren Lee Pierson's resignation the day I walked across the threshold. George Spater would have made a great chairman for TWA. Pierson was an elegant guy, but he drank too many martinis. I had to tell him to stop it, too. Once I challenged one of his expense accounts and I thought he was going to have a heart attack."

On Christmas day, twenty-four hours after Burgess notified Hughes he was leaving, he received a final telephone call from Howard.

"Carter," he said, "what is it going to take to keep you?"

"Howard, it's a price you won't pay."

"Name it."

"I'm not asking you for one goddamned cent, Howard. All I wanted is to get a job done at the airline. But I'm not gonna run it in accordance with your last phone call. That's got to stop. I want a board with some representation on it. Men of unchallenged integrity and position with some geographical spread. I don't want you to appoint them and I don't want to appoint them. But we'll get some person you have reliance in, and someone I have reliance in, and he'll get us three or four or five directors on this board who are not your captives. Then you tell that board what you want done and if those sons of bitches vote it, I'll execute it!"

"I won't pay that price," Hughes murmured.

"I didn't think you would," said Carter Burgess.

Twenty-five years later, he expressed no regrets and no hard feelings toward Hughes, who in his own way tried to make amends. Several months after Burgess left, Toolco attorney Ray Cook paid a call on Burgess and handed him a check for a sizeable amount. Carter doesn't remember the exact sum, but says it was at least $60,000 and may have been as high as $100,000. Cook got along well with TWA officials. Spater, for example, thinks it was Cook's influence that led to Hughes' dismissal of Dietrich. But Burgess took one look at the check and shook his head.

"Ray, I won't take it," he declared.

"Carter, you might as well know that Howard feels very badly about what happened. He didn't settle with you when you left and he feels we owe you something. And if that's not enough, just let Howard know."

Burgess took the check and wrote on the back, "Endorsed to the order of Trans World Airlines."

He was soon named U.S. Ambassador to Argentina and while serving in that post he had an ex-FBI agent on the embassy staff. One day they were discussing Carter's TWA experiences and his stormy relations with Hughes. "You know," the former agent said, "when I was with the Bureau I saw the FBI file on you right after you were nominated for this job. It included a report from Hughes."

"Oh? Favorable or unfavorable?"

"He said, and I quote, 'Burgess is the most honest man I know.'"

For a long time, Carter missed the airline business—TWA's people, his industry peers and the excitement and challenge of taking Trans Word into the jet age. He got along well with most of his contemporary competitors, especially those of the so-called Big Four—American's C.R. Smith, Eastern's Eddie Rickenbacker and United's Pat Patterson. He says both Smith and Rickenbacker offered him the presidencies of their respective airlines after he left TWA, but he is proudest of what Patterson said.

Burgess recalls:

The guy who really complimented me when it was all over was Pat. He told me I scared the balls off him. We were stealing his transcontinental business with those Dave Chasin meals and Cocke's Siesta seats. There were some interesting chief executives around when I was with TWA— guys like C.R. and Eddie, Pat and Bob Six. They had great instinctiveness. It petered out after a time, but they did something right for a long, long time.

Hell, I didn't get along with all of them. Don Nyrop of Northwest was the tighest guy in America. Everytime I flew his airline I felt like leaving a five dollar tip in the seat. And Juan Trippe—he was busy kissing my ass because he wanted our international routes. He kept having me over to his Sky Club for lunch. I never forgot what Frye used to say about him—that Trippe had the worst case of injured innocence of any man he ever knew. Trippe would just fawn over me, but the minute I left TWA he wouldn't recognize me.

Although Burgess served TWA for less than a year, he will always be one of the best remembered presidents. That, too, is something he has in common with Howard Hughes. Much of the resentment he invited during his brief but turbulent regime has mellowed into wry recollections of the kind of leader he was.

It was during Burgess' tenure that TWA hired its first black hostesses. All the airlines were under pressure from civil rights groups to break the color barrier. Although Burgess was a Southerner by birth and breeding, he was not prejudiced against blacks. His father, a Norfolk and Western Railroad official for more than fifty years, had a black employee named Charlie Fisher and used to admonish Carter when Burgess was working temporarily for the railroad: "Now you be nice to Charlie, first because he's a very able man and second because he might be your boss some day."

When the New York Anti-Discrimination Commission began pressuring TWA to hire a black flight attendant, Burgess balked—not because he didn't want to hire one but because the commission insisted on a specific woman.

"You may have to send me to Sing Sing," he informed the Commission, "because while you can tell me to hire blacks, you can't tell me which ones I've got to hire. And don't accuse me of being prejudiced because I have a very superior record in this area. If you don't believe me, just ask the Pentagon."

This was a potentially explosive situation, but it was resolved when Burgess suddenly hired a black personnel advisor—Jim Plinton—on the recommendation of Bob Buck, who knew Plinton and admired him. Plinton, a remarkable man, had started a small airline in Haiti, but left the country when its political upheavals discouraged him. Buck, TWA's system chief pilot, was one of the first persons Plinton saw when he returned to the U.S. He walked into Buck's office with a typical Plinton remark: "Don't worry, Buck—I'm not gonna ask you for a job." Buck couldn't have given him one anyway, but he happened to be at a meeting with Burgess and Spater on the hostess situation. Burgess was complaining that the girl TWA was being pressured to hire was unnattractive and surly.

"I've got a black friend who might help us," Buck suggested. He mentioned Plinton and subsequently arranged for Plinton to meet both Burgess and Spater. Plinton agreed to talk to people he knew in various civil rights organizations and the result was the hiring of some very personable black women. Burgess was so impressed that he hired Plinton as a staff assistant.

He not only handled Burgess' correspondence, but did sales and promotion work among black and minority groups.

A few years later, when Floyd Hall left TWA to become Eastern's president, he took Plinton with him and made him a vice-president.

"He did one hell of a job for us when he was with TWA," Buck says. "Africa was an example—he knew every government leader in Africa and wound up shutting out Pan Am in Nigeria. Once Juan Trippe called TWA and pleaded for Jimmy to let Pan Am into Nairobi."

It is hard to find a senior TWA pilot who doesn't miss Burgess. They threw a party for him after he left and their gift consisted of a model of a 1649 at which he laughed . . . but not very hard. Later, Ray Dunn sent him a memento that he still treasures and has hung in his Roanoke, Virginia, home. One of Hughes' ideas for the 1649's cabin decor was a mural for the plane's cocktail lounge area—a different mural in each Jetstream. Hughes commissioned an artist to do twenty-five portraits of women Howard admired, each posed against a background depicting a city TWA served. The mural installed in the Connie Hughes flew to Nassau was that of Anna Kashfi, the Indian actress who married Marlon Brando; the background of her portrait was the Taj Mahal.

When the Jetstreams were converted into freighters, Dunn made sure this particular mural was not damaged or thrown away. He had it wrapped and mailed to Burgess as a final reminder of the plane that had cost him his job, but not his sense of integrity.

It must be realized that it was more than just an airplane out of service and far more than merely an unpleasant, friction-generating incident between Hughes and Burgess. That 1649 starkly demonstrated TWA's real Achilles' heel—the airline's total dependence on Hughes for its flight equipment. All other airlines financed their own aircraft purchases. TWA, almost totally subservient to the unpredictable, procrastinating Hughes, surrendered what had to be one of its most precious perogatives: the right to decide which airplanes it needed, in what quantity and how they were to be used. In a technical sense, maybe TWA had no legal right to that Jetstream. Bill Gay once said it was a Toolco-owned airplane with no guarantee it would ever go to the airline. But morally, Burgess has a point when he says the airliner was painted in TWA's colors and had been earmarked for TWA's fleet.

"Hughes didn't call Toolco and tell 'em don't deliver it to TWA," Burgess adds bitterly.

Carter Burgess is remembered by TWA's people for many things. The Coca-Cola machine he insisted on keeping in his office, for example. The white gloves and the invective. The early-morning awakenings of officers who were bawled out before they could get their eyes opened—an ironic habit on Carter's part because he was the only TWA president who figured out how to stop Hughes from doing the same thing to him. He told Bill Gay after one such call:

"I sleep in the same bed as my wife. My telephone is now by my bed and she can hear everything that's being said. Now I don't want my wife to go around the neighborhood tomorrow morning telling everyone what I was talking to Howard Hughes about the night before!"

The night calls ceased—for Burgess, anyway.

Most of all, however, he should be remembered as the president who first exposed TWA's almost fatal weakness—its dependence on the moody, mercurial man who owned its airplanes.

Yet if dependence on Hughes was the airline's most vulnerable part, it was also the Achilles' heel of Hughes himself. The 1649 he had appropriated first on a whim and then retained out of sheer stubbornness was symptomatic of what was basically wrong with this one-man control—it was too restrictive and potentially destructive, not only to the airline but to himself.

Burgess had no illusions about the job when he accepted the presidency. He knew what Hughes was like from the Frye days in Washington. But he also figured that TWA was Howard's first love and everyone he talked to assured him that Hughes' only desire was to help the airline.

"It was in such disarray that they felt he was ready to make it right," Burgess says. "I think if Howard had remained friends with Dietrich, we might have made it. I could do business with Noah. He was a reasonable man and he never pushed me. Of course, I could never tell from talking to him whether it was Dietrich's idea or Howard's; you had to be very careful."

But Hughes ditched Dietrich and even those who thought little of Noah are agreed Howard made his biggest mistake. Dietrich could be as arrogant and vindictive as Hughes, but he was brilliant in finance and capable of saving Howard from himself.

Hughes was to find this out too late. He learned it from the man he picked to replace Carter Burgess.

15

Beginning of the End

Once again, it took a long time for Hughes to choose another TWA president.

Six months elapsed between Carter Burgess' dramatic exit and the selection of a successor. In that period, history repeated itself—TWA stumbled around aimlessly, losing nearly $12 million in the first half of 1958.

The problem was not entirely, however, a repetition of Howard's notorious vacillation and indecisiveness. Reportedly, he approached several able and experienced airline executives who turned him down. Recruiting within the industry was difficult—nobody thought the job was worth putting up with his interference, haphazard ways of doing business and ironclad control. Recruiting within TWA itself collided with his apparent belief that the airline hierarchy lacked anyone with presidential stature.

The third reason for the delay was the reluctance of the man he finally chose to take the job. The nominee, like Burgess, was an experienced administrator, with solid government service credentials. Hughes began wooing him three months after Burgess left. Not until July 2, 1958, did the board elect Charles Sparks Thomas as TWA's new president. Thomas, just retired as Secretary of the Navy, was an industrial troubleshooter before going into government. He had saved a chain of clothing stores (Foreman & Clark) from bankruptcy with a textbook corporate reorganization. That association generated a nickname for him at TWA—"Two-Pants Charlie"— but it was more a term of good-natured affection than derision. In truth, he looked more like a haberdashery clerk than an airline president. Very short in stature, totally bald and pleasant-mannered, he offered quite a contrast to the towering, fiery Burgess with the look of a southern aristocrat and the vocabulary of a dock worker.

But Thomas was tougher than he appeared, as both TWA and Hughes were to discover. He owed his appointment to Lockheed's Bob Gross, who recommended him to Hughes as early as April of 1958, after hearing that Thomas had decided to leave his Navy post. When Gross brought up his name, Hughes remembered him. They had played golf in California years before, while Howard was still married to his first wife, Ella Rice.

Thomas and his wife Julia were at a Republican fund-raising dinner in Washington when Hughes phoned him. It was close to midnight and the Thomases were just about to leave the hotel. After recalling their golfing days, Hughes said suddenly, "Charlie, I want you to be president of TWA."

Startled, Thomas' immediate reaction was one of horror. He was planning to retire soon and the prospect of heading an airline appalled him. "I just can't do it, Howard. I'd have to spend quite a bit of time in a job like that and I'm planning to go back to California."

"I won't take no for an answer," Hughes told him. "I'll be in touch with you later. You think it over."

Thomas did think it over—when he had time to think. Hughes courted him, pressed him and pestered him for the next two months. When Charlie and Julia traveled, they found a Hughes-rented limousine waiting for them at every airport. "I don't even know how he found out what flights we were on," Thomas marvelled later.

They had a face-to-face meeting in the Beverly Hills Hotel—"it was the biggest damn suite I ever saw," Thomas remembers—but once more he resisted Howard's courtship. In May, however, just as Thomas was getting ready to leave the government, Hughes contacted him again and he began to weaken. "Well, I'll keep thinking about it, Howard," he hedged. "I'll give you an answer shortly."

He talked it over with Julia, who was intrigued with the perks of being an airline president's wife—free first-class travel all over the world. Sometime late in June, Thomas gave in, but says he laid down the rules in a final conversation with Hughes that, to his recollection, went like this: "All right, I'll reorganize your airline. I'll do it for two years and no longer. If, within that time, you're not completely satisfied with what I'm doing, all you have to do is say it and I'll get out. At the end of those two years, Howard, neither you nor I have any commitment. We'll just see what happens."

Hughes quickly accepted those terms. Strangely, neither man brought up the question of salary. Thomas had been on the job for two weeks when he got his first paycheck and was somewhat disappointed at the amount. It figured out to $60,000 a year, which is precisely what Hughes had paid Burgess. Typically, Thomas made no fuss about it—for one thing, he was independently wealthy—and never did as long as he was president. He was too busy learning the airline industry, branding TWA with his own methods and business philosophies and worrying about something that no longer was just around the corner. The jet age had parked on TWA's doorstep.

He was a much stronger president than anyone expected, despite his inexperience. Thomas may have known little about the airlines, but he knew a great deal about corporate management structure and he found TWA's a shambles. There were thirteen vice-presidents reporting directly to the president. It meant that the chief executive was at the narrow end of a funnel through which were pouring the day-by-day activities and troubles of the company. No president, he realized, could concentrate on long-range policies and problems if he had to function on a day-to-day basis.

He also was appalled at TWA's slipshod attitude toward aircraft utilization and scheduling. Burgess had realized this to some extent when he unearthed so many inefficient night flights that went everywhere and carried nobody, but Carter hadn't been around long enough to do much about it. Thomas did, largely because he was listening to lower echelon management that for years had been hamstrung by the feuding cliques and factions within the upper echelon.

His first act was to establish five task forces, composed of senior executives, to look into every aspect of TWA's operations and find out what was being done right or wrong. But to make sure those task forces weren't "preaching to the choir" or merely protecting their own flanks and rear, he also asked the chief of each department to pick two capable subordinates who weren't afraid to speak up about the company's faults. Out of this came a ten-man middle management task force. Each member was summoned to Thomas' office and given the same earnest message. Dave Richwine, a line check pilot, was picked for the committee by Frank Busch as one of the pilot representatives, and has a vivid memory of what Thomas told him.

"Dave, if you're betting I won't be around here very long, this won't make much sense. But if you have the nerve to tell me what's wrong with this company, and can offer good suggestions, you're going to have a great future."

Richwine was impressed. After Damon died and the airline had gone to seed, Richwine had written Hughes, pleading that he hire a real administrator as the next president. He didn't get an answer from Hughes, but Nadine Henley, Howard's personal secretary, told him Hughes had appreciated his letter. Burgess, the pilot felt, might have been a good administrator, but he wasn't around long enough to accomplish much. In Thomas, Richwine saw an earnest, sincere man who seemed to mean what he said.

The peppery, engaging little guy did, Richwine discovered. Thomas set up a joint meeting between his senior executives and the lower echelon task force. Richwine and his fellow lesser lights took chairs against the wall of the conference room. Most of them were nervous and felt a little out of place, like a group of cockneys in Buckingham Palace. Then Thomas came in. He walked up to Richwine, shook hands and said, "Captain, it's so nice to see you again." He did the same with the other junior officers. "Oz Cockes and Vic Leslie nearly fainted," Richwine recalls gleefully.

They weren't reassured by Thomas' opening remarks, either.

"Gentlemen," he started off, "we have a difficult job to do. If you do a good job, you have a brilliant future at TWA. If you do not do a good job, you have no future at all." His eyes roved over the tense faces of every vice-president in the room. "It may well be," he added dryly, "that when we get through with this program, some of our senior members will no longer be with us."

Fortunately for those present, there was no general purge of the executive ranks—not because Thomas was bluffing, but because his message had gotten through. The junior task force produced recommendations and reforms that saved $12 million a year in operating costs. The five senior task forces overhauled scheduling and aircraft utilization and helped Thomas reorganize their own departments into more efficient lines of authority and responsibility. The funnel had become a series of interconnecting pipelines, with Thomas looking down on each instead of standing at one end and catching everything in his face.

And Charlie Thomas turned the company around. After losing $12 million in the first six months, TWA ended the year with a modest deficit of $700,000 and was back on the apogee of its perpetual economic and emotional roller coaster. The financial achievements of the last six months were especially gratifying, for in addition to a general business recession that year, TWA had been shut down for seventeen days by a mechanics' strike that began just before the busy Thanksgiving weekend and wasn't settled until the second week in December.

Even in that dark period, Thomas kept his sense of humor. When Ray Dunn broke the news that a strike was inevitable, Charlie gave him a pixie-ish grin. "Gee," he commented, "Hughes didn't tell me there would be times like this—I should have asked for more money."

He was tremendously fond of Dunn, although their first meeting was a near disaster. Thomas had come out to Kansas City to inspect the maintenance base and was shown around by Dunn and his top assistant, Al Jordan. They went to the main hangar, an immense structure three stories high with offices in the middle and hangar bays cantilevered on each side.

Thomas walked down one aisle and frowned at the sight of about a third of the work force smoking, playing shuffleboard and gabbing. He walked down the other aisle. Same thing. He proceeded to Hangar 2. Ditto. Thomas said nothing to either Dunn or Jordan and he was so pleasant that neither realized he was seething. Dunn drove him to the airport to catch a flight back to New York and late that day he called Dunn.

"Ray, you've got some serious problems at that base. I've already talked to my friend Harlow Curtice at General Motors and he's sending you a couple of efficiency experts to help you get it straightened out."

"Wait a minute," Dunn protested, "we don't need—"

"Ray," Thomas interrupted, "believe me, I'm not mad at you. I'm just trying to help. Now those GM people will be coming down from Detroit on our flight. . . .

Dunn, in shock, informed Jordan of the forthcoming invasion. Both knew what had happened. Contractually, TWA mechanics were allowed regular ten-minute breaks at staggered intervals. Thomas had staged his inspection in the middle of one of those breaks and unfortunately, without asking the reason for all the leisure activity, had assumed the mechanics were goofing off. Recounts Jordan:

"Those efficiency experts from Detroit got in about ten A.M. the next day and we had everything lined up for them. We figured they were more mechanically-minded than Charlie, so we took 'em on a tour, showing them stuff they were interested in. They spent the whole day with us. They were cold characters at first, looking down their noses at us and hardly cracking a smile. By late afternoon they had softened up and we had a debriefing with them in Ray's office before they got on a plane to go back to Detroit. By then they were telling us what a fine operation we were running. We had explained what had happened with Thomas and they understood."

TWA veterans from the Thomas years remembered him as a bright, personable little man who seemed to get along with everybody, from senior vice-presidents to skycaps. Unpretentious and informal, he privately regarded board chairman Warren Lee Pierson as "a stuffed shirt" (his own words), but generally speaking they had a live-and-let-live relationship, largely because Thomas refused to take any guff. Pierson once demanded to know why Thomas hadn't done something or other and Charlie snapped back, "You're the chairman of the board—why didn't you do it yourself?"

Thomas even managed to put a stop to Howard's 2 A.M. phone calls. He simply told Hughes, "Howard, you might as well know I don't take any telephone calls after midnight." Hughes didn't believe him and kept calling. Charlie turned down the volume on his bedroom phone so he couldn't hear it ring. Several times he and Julia heard the phone ring in another room between midnight and 3 A.M., but neither would answer it. Eventually Hughes stopped calling.

The disappointingly low salary didn't bother Thomas (although he had expected to be making more than $100,000 as TWA's president) because Hughes was generous in other ways. He gave Charlie and Julia a beautiful apartment on Fifth Avenue in New York, and Thomas' expense account was virtually unlimited. It took him a little while to get used to an airline's occasionally informal way of doing things. While Thomas hated red tape, he half expected it after all his years with the government. This was brought home to him once when he mildly suggested that something should be done to improve TWA's facilities at Idlewild. The magnificent new terminal designed by Eero Saarinen hadn't been completed and the temporary quarters consisted of a dingy quonset hut with abysmally inadequate ticket counter space. It was so dismal employees called it "The Sheep Roundup."

Floyd Hall had just named Capt. Ed Frankum the new general manager of the eastern region and Idlewild was under his jurisdiction. Like all pilots, Frankum detested paper work so when he got word that Thomas wasn't happy about the Idlewild facilities, he took direct action.

"Actually," he admits, "I was so new at the job that I didn't know what procedures I had to go through—the authorizations, requisitions and so forth. There was a vacant counter somewhere else around the airport so I went over to the New York Port Authority, signed some papers and in twenty-four hours we had a new ticket counter. Then I got some paint crews to spruce the place up and called Floyd to come over and inspect it."

Hall showed up and gaped at the results—new lighting, with bright, cheerful colors on the plasterboard walls used for the remodeling.

"Jesus, Ed, it's beautiful," Hall admitted. "Who did it?"

"I did."

"Where did you get the money?"

"The hell with the money. I got it done, didn't I?"

"Fine, but who's gonna pay for it?"

"You are," Frankum declared.

Hall threw up his hands and called Thomas, suggesting that he come out to Idlewild and see Frankum's "new" terminal.

Hall relates: "Frankum really made a hit with Charlie by getting that done. Up to then you needed twenty pieces of paper to get a light bulb changed. Vic Leslie probably got another ulcer from that one incident."

Both Hall and Frankum liked Thomas and it was reciprocated. And they worked well together themselves, enjoying the banter and mock disparagements that come so naturally to airmen. They were always criticizing each other for a mutual tendency to put on weight and one day Floyd remarked to another TWA officer, "Have you seen Frankum lately? He looks like a Goodyear blimp." Thirty minutes later, the same official encountered Frankum.

"Have you seen Hall lately?" Frankum inquired. "He looks like a Goodyear blimp."

It was during the Thomas presidency that Frankum began moving up the executive ladder—a climb that would be culminated by a senior vice-presidency. He never changed—he was a tough disciplinarian with everyone, and his fellow airmen were no exception. At one meeting, he couldn't hear what was being asked from the floor and bellowed, "Speak up!" Someone murmured, "It's hard to talk in a baritone when your balls have been cut off."

Floyd Hall once summed up Frankum's relationship with the pilot ranks. "If he's not exactly beloved," Hall commented, "it's because he doesn't believe ALPA created the whole airline industry with its bare hands on a Friday afternoon."

It was his association with men like tough Frankum, solid Dunn and erudite Hall that convinced Charlie Thomas TWA was an airline worthy of his best efforts, one whose characters gave it character. If running TWA had been the only responsibility facing Thomas, his would have been the happiest of regimes. It had done a financial about-face, it had acquired a new domestic route with great potential—St. Louis-Miami via Nashville, Atlanta and Tampa—and international traffic, TWA's great profit source, was booming. For the first time in history more people were flying across the Atlantic than were crossing by ship. And when the jets started flying, this ratio would tip even more sharply in favor of the airplane. Eventually twenty-three out of every twenty-four passengers would fly.

But *that* was the fly in Thomas' otherwise smooth ointment—the forthcoming jets.

For before 1958 had ended, he learned that Howard Hughes had ordered more than $400 million worth of jetliners and engines without the means to pay for them.

Hughes' inability to make up his mind about airplanes—and then sometimes make it up in the wrong direction—was the biggest cross TWA had to bear as long as he owned it. It was the key element in the whole unhealthy relationship. He would not take the airline into his confidence. He foisted equipment on it that TWA neither wanted nor needed, and he insisted on one-man control in an area begging for consultation.

When Hughes was in Montreal, he called Burgess one day and announced that TWA was getting twenty-two Viscounts. Where they were supposed to be operated or how they were to be scheduled, neither Burgess nor anyone else knew. Carter was still fretting about this out-of-the-blue acquisition when Hughes phoned him from Nassau—he was buying TWA twelve Britannias.

"What about the Viscounts?" Burgess asked.

"Oh, don't worry about the Viscount," Hughes said airily. "Just worry about the Britannias. There's a demonstration aircraft in Montreal. You have Frank Busch take you and some other officers up there and fly it."

Burgess told Busch, who balked. "I've never been checked out in one of those wagons," he pointed out. "I don't even know what the hell one looks like."

"I don't care about that," Burgess sighed. "Hughes said to bring you and that's that."

As Busch remembers it, he and Burgess were accompanied by Cocke, Leslie and Rummel, with Leslie objecting strenuously. "If we crash," he complained to Busch, "you'll kill every top executive in the whole damn airline."

They didn't crash, but Busch didn't like the huge British prop-jet—he thought the controls were too heavy—and told Burgess to forget it. Carter was willing, but not Hughes. He kept insisting the Britannia was perfect for TWA's overseas and transcontinental routes, an excellent interim airplane between the 1649 and the 707. Burgess talked to Bob Buck about it and Buck was intrigued, largely because Bristol claimed TWA could break even on a transcontinental flight with only a 37 percent load factor (load factor is the percentage of total aircraft seats occupied by revenue passengers). The key question was whether TWA could get twelve Britannias delivered in time to provide at least a year's service before the jets arrived; British aircraft manufacturers were notoriously slow on their production lines.

"Go over and look at the airplane and their factory facilities," Burgess ordered.

Buck went.

"I hung around there for awhile, waiting to fly one. The weather was lousy and they were having some problems with the plane. So I went up to London and said I'd be back in a couple of days. While I was gone, the weather cleared and they took a Britannia up for a test flight. It crashed, killing everyone aboard—a near-miss for me because I would have been on that plane. Anyway, I saw their assembly line and knew there was no way we could buy that airplane—not with all those tea breaks and their leisurely production methods. I came home and told Carter to forget it."

Hughes soured on the Britannia, too. He had now become enamored of the promising new Lockheed Electra, a four-engine prop-jet roughly about the same size as the Britannia. Hughes was convinced TWA needed an interim pre-jet transport, an opinion he seemed to hold exclusively. Charlie Thomas was against it and so were Rummel, Dunn and the rest of TWA's engineering brain trust.

It was the Electra that first brought Hughes into direct contact with the man who became one of his best friends—Jack Real. In December of 1957, just before Burgess and Hughes parted company, Hughes and Bob Gross had a falling out over a joking remark Gross had made. When Hughes asked him if he'd be willing to sell TWA some Electras, Gross said, "Well, we've sold forty to Eastern and thirty-five to American, but maybe we could find two or three for you."

He meant it as a joke but Hughes, who was not known for his sense of humor, took him seriously and was furious. With a friendship of years apparently fractured, Gross asked Real to repair the damage. Real was a highly rated engineer in the Electra test flight program and had taken Hughes with him on several occasions. From then on, he was involved with Hughes on an almost daily basis and when he retired from Lockheed in 1971, he not only went to work for Howard Hughes, but lived with him.

It is Real's contention that Hughes was serious about buying the Electra, even though by then he was up to his armpits in a financing morass. According to Real, Hughes verbally committed TWA to forty of the big prop-jets, but not one was ever delivered. Gross himself released Hughes from any obligation when Howard found he was unable to pay for the $315 million worth of pure jets he had ordered.

It would later be charged that Hughes lacked the foresight to anticipate the impact of the jet revolution, that first he didn't order enough jets, then ordered so many he couldn't swing the financing and thus almost ruined TWA competitively. In one sense, this was a bum rap. It wasn't technical foresight that Hughes lacked, but financial foresight. He had a far clearer vision of what the jets would mean to commercial aviation than most people realized. True, he initially ordered only eight 707s but a short time later he increased this to thirty-three—eighteen of them long-range Intercontinental models for TWA's overseas routes. And it may well be that Howard Hughes came close to giving TWA the honor of being the first U.S. airline to enter the jet age, not Pan Am.

The story is that Hughes went to Bill Allen of Boeing sometime in the mid-1950s and offered him a deal: he would underwrite the entire $16 million in 707 development costs in exchange for a six-months-to-one-year exclusivity on the jet. In other words, TWA would get enough preferential assembly line positions to make sure that no one else would be flying the 707 for at least six months after TWA had put it into service.

Allen was tempted—$16 million represented more than one-fourth of Boeing's entire net worth at the time. But he turned Hughes down, remembering how Boeing had become hoisted by its own petard when it gave United the first sixty delivery positions on the 247. "We made that mistake twenty years ago with the 247," Allen is said to have told Hughes.

The authority for that story is Johnny Guy. It was told to him by someone who knew Bill Allen well. Unfortunately, it is an account that cannot be confirmed. But Guy, so closely associated with both Boeing and TWA for years, believes its authenticity. Surely it is exactly what Hughes would have tried to pull off, for later, after ordering both the 707 and smaller Convair 880 jets, he made a deal with Pratt & Whitney for 300 jet engines valued at $90 million—in an obvious effort to corner that market. If he couldn't tie up the airframes for TWA, he could do the next best thing and tie up the supply of powerplants. It was an abortive effort, but he *tried* to give TWA a leg up on the fast-approaching jet age and when he failed it was not because he didn't grasp the import of the turbine revolution.

The 880 was a case in point. As early as 1955, when everyone else was thinking in terms of giant jets like the 707 and DC-8, Hughes was considering the feasability of a smaller plane for TWA's shorter routes. He even toyed with the idea of building in the U.S., under a licensing agreement, the new twin-engine French Caravelle jet, which first flew in 1955. Then he debated whether he would design and produce his own medium-range jet, an idea he abandoned when he became interested in a scheme to link up with Convair and build a versatile jetliner tailored for both TWA's medium and long-haul routes. Convair, by then part of the General Dynamics combine, wanted badly to compete against Boeing and Douglas and welcomed Hughes' input.

Howard was fascinated with a preliminary Convair design the company called Model 18. It had been conceived in 1954 and was a four-engine giant slightly larger than either the original 707 and DC-8 and longer-ranged than either. It was still on the drawing boards, however, when Boeing decided to build its Intercontinental 707 with true nonstop trans-Atlantic capability. Model 18 would have it, too, but with the 707 prototype already flying both Hughes and Convair knew Boeing had too much of a head start. Bob Rummel, who at Hughes' request was working closely with Convair, says the Model 18 "was a better airplane than either the bigger 707 or DC-8, but not enough better to justify a third manufacturer."

"We sort of picked up the ashes of the 18 and made a much smaller airplane," he continues. "I can tell you that Hughes and Convair had the specs written and the contracts drawn for the 18 when both Boeing and Douglas announced their international versions."

What finally evolved into the 880 started out as the "Skylark"—Convair's initial choice for a name—and then the Convair 600 to denote its 600-mph speed. Hughes didn't like either name; he wanted to call it the "Golden Arrow" because he had conceived the idea of actually building an all-gold airplane. Theoretically, this could have been done through a process known as anodizing. A gold shading would be anodized into the aluminum skin as it went through milling, which meant the airplane would never have to be painted or re-painted.

Rummel told Hughes gold might be a great aesthetic idea, but it was impractical from an engineering standpoint. For one thing, no one was sure the anodizing would produce the same shade of gold on every piece of aluminum plating, nor was there any way to keep the gold on the rivets, which had to be shaved to keep the airfoil clean.

But Hughes refused to abandon that "Golden Arrow" concept, and he even got C.E. Woolman of Delta, the only other airline ordering the jet, to go along with the idea. One day Dick Maurer, Delta's vice-president of finance, was meeting in Atlanta with Toolco attorney Ray Cook. They were discussing the Convair contract when Maurer got a frantic call from Delta's representative at the Convair plant.

"We've got troubles with the airplane," he reported. "Convair sent about two dozen plates through anodizing and they all came out a different shade of gold. The goddamned plane's gonna look like a checkerboard. Convair wants to drop the whole idea and go back to regular paint on the skin."

"I'll call you back after I talk to Woolman," Maurer said. He excused himself and went to see Delta's president. Woolman said, "Well, if they can't, they can't. Tell Convair we'll amend the contract and use the same paint scheme we've ordered for our DC-8s."

Maurer returned to his office and told Cook what had happened. "The thing is," he pointed out, "we can't change our contract unless Hughes changes his. Would you call him and get his okay?"

Cook smiled sadly. "You don't understand. Nobody calls Howard Hughes. You call one of his secretaries and leave word for him to call you."

"That's reasonable. How long before he returns the call?"

"Up to six weeks," Cook confessed.

He did agree to phone 7000 Romaine. It was three weeks before Maurer was notified he could change the contract.

Howard encountered a further obstacle to his "Golden Arrow" plan when he was informed that Bob Six had obtained a copyright on the name "Golden Jet" for Continental's 707s. Six's idea was far more practical—only the tails of his jets would be painted gold—but Hughes was ready to do battle with him until Rummel finally convinced him that anodizing just wouldn't work on a whole airplane.

"It looks like a crazy quilt," Hughes admitted when he inspected the different shadings of gold on the test plates.

"Convair 880" was finally picked as the name, one supposedly derived from the plane's ability to fly 880 feet per second. Another theory is the

"880" stood for the eighty-eight passengers it could carry, while Convair's official explanation was that the jet was twice as good as its last piston transport, the 440. Jack Zevely, Convair's vice-president of sales, had the best explanation. He insisted the 880 designation stood for the 880 meetings held with Hughes before the final contract was signed.

It was, incidentally, an unusually restrictive contract, one reflecting Convair's eagerness to get into jet competition. Hughes got Convair to waive the usual progress payments. He made only a downpayment with a promise to pay the remainder upon delivery. It also hamstrung Delta, which agreed it would not put any of its ten 880s into service until after TWA got started with the first of the thirty Hughes had ordered. This was a provision destined to lead to an angry confrontation between Woolman and representatives of Toolco.

The 880 looked promising, but Rummel wasn't happy about its engines and Ray Dunn was downright pessimistic. The jet had been designed around the General Electric J-79, a successful military powerplant, but one that had never been tried commercially. Dunn was of the opinion it wouldn't stand up to the rigors of airline service. "It just wasn't made to fly eight hours a day," he kept insisting.

Rummel suspected he was right, but could do nothing about it. The J-79 was the only engine that fitted the 880's airframe. "Structurally and systemswise," he says, "it was an excellent airplane, but the engine wasn't much good and GE would be the first to admit it. The J-79 was troublesome, expensive and difficult to maintain. GE cut their eyeteeth commercially with that engine."

Floyd Hall, who at the time heard Dunn warn over and over again that the engine would be a disaster, says that because of the J-79 the 880 never did meet its specifications. TWA couldn't even overhaul the J-79 itself and had to farm out the job to a GE plant in Southern California. But all the admonitions fell on the deaf ears of Hughes who had put much of himself into the 880 and refused to admit it might be a failure. It was the Constellation project all over again: he didn't design the jet, but to a great extent the concept was his and so were its ambitious specifications. He wanted a plane at least thirty-five miles an hour faster than either the 707 or DC-8. He was way ahead in his belief that the airlines would need smaller jets. Unfortunately, he combined this farsightedness with the propensity for interference. Mostly, he kept insisting on design changes aimed not so much at improving the airplane, but delaying its production. As Hughes ran into increasing financial difficulties, he wanted badly to stall the whole 880 project.

He didn't have nearly as much to say about the 707's construction, but he did manage to nearly wreck the program inadvertently by almost crashing the Dash-80, the 707's $16 million prototype. It was in the late fall of 1958, a few months before TWA was scheduled to take delivery of its first 707s, that Howard asked Boeing to fly the Dash 80 down to Los Angeles. He wanted to check out in the jet himself and also, he informed Bill Allen, to convince all the bankers then crowding him that it was good business to buy the plane.

Boeing sent the plane to L.A. with one of its best test pilots, Brien Wygle, today a Boeing flight operations vice-president. His instructions were simple: Don't alienate him. "All pilots were told this," Wygle adds.

The very first flight was the one that almost ended in disaster. With another Boeing test pilot, Harley Beard, serving as flight engineer, they took off at night and flew around the Los Angeles area for about an hour while Hughes, sitting in the left seat, familiarized himself with the plane. Returning to Los Angeles International, with Hughes flying, they ran into trouble because Hughes ignored Wygle's warnings to keep his airspeed down on final approach. The Dash-80 had a strict speed limit for every flap setting, particularly with full flaps (40 degrees), because excessive speed could damage a fully extended flap.

"We had full flaps and he kept flying it too fast," Wygle relates. "I reduced flaps from forty to thirty when he exceeded speed restrictions for the forty-degree setting, but I was too late. One of the flap sections failed and fell on an automobile just short of the runway."

With Wygle's help, Hughes landed the 707 safely and in one piece except for that section of flap—about eight feet long and eighteen inches wide. The car it hit happened to belong to an employee of the newly created Federal Aviation Agency. Hughes might as well have dropped that huge piece of metal on the roof of the control tower. There were FAA inspectors waiting for the Dash-80 when it taxied up to the TWA maintenance hangar. They wished to discuss the situation with Mr. Hughes.

As he did so often, Howard insisted that Lee Flanagin be at the airport for the demonstration flight. Before Hughes took off, he had asked Lee, "Now, how do I tell the tower what we're going to do?"

"All you have to say is that you're going to make a local flight around Los Angeles," Flanagin instructed. Lee could never figure out why he had to figuratively hold Howard's hand when he flew. "The Boeing pilot knew what to tell the tower, but Howard had to hear it from me," Flanagin says. It was a strange insecurity that manifested itself through most of Hughes' life—a desperate need to have certain people around him under certain circumstances. Flanagin and Joe Bartles were his TWA crutches when he flew.

And it was Flanagin who tried valiantly to get him out of the wing flap scrape. As the crippled 707 rolled to a stop, Flanagin grasped instantly what had happened and steered the FAA inspectors to the rear of the huge wing where they could see the damage. While they were looking, Hughes slipped away unseen via a car that was waiting for him at the hangar.

He didn't get away with it, of course. "They knew he was on that airplane," Flanagin says—but he was never fined although Wygle, held responsible as the aircraft commander, finally was. But for Wygle, the experience of working with Hughes was worth far more than the modest fine he paid. His recollections offer a fascinating insight into the mind of Howard Hughes, a troubled, lonely man to whom a cockpit seemed a place of blessed refuge and a relatively strange copilot a treasured friend in whom he could confide.

After we repaired the plane, we flew it five or six times. He always said he was going to fly in the morning, but we never went up until late afternoon or evening. We'd go over to the Mojave airport and do touch-and-go landings until we were almost out of fuel.

I was staying in a cottage at the Beverly Hills Hotel. Harley and a Boeing ground crew were in another hotel. If Hughes was going to be late, his office would call and warn me and they'd have everything worked out to the split second. They'd say, "Brien, the car will pick you up at your cottage at eight-fifteen, so leave your room at eight-eleven because you need four minutes to get from the cottage to the curb." Hughes kept a close rein on me. His driver warned me never to leave my hotel in case Hughes wanted to reach me. One day he cancelled the flight so I went over to the other hotel to have a few drinks with my crew. I hadn't been in Beard's room for fifteen minutes when the phone rang. It was the front desk telling me I was wanted in the lobby. I went down and there was the driver, all upset. "Mr. Hughes is very distressed that you left your hotel," he told me. I was a little miffed so I said I'd go back as soon as I had one drink. The driver said, "Mr. Wygle, my orders are to get you back to your hotel immediately so I'd very much appreciate it if you come along."

I'll never forget the way Hughes looked. Very thin, even gaunt. He wore shoes with holes for laces but there were no laces and he never wore socks. Sometimes he'd take off his shoes in the cockpit and fly in his bare feet. His trousers looked new and were well pressed; He had a belt, but he didn't put it through the loops—he tied the belt around his waist with a square knot.

He didn't fly badly except that he had no discipline whatsoever. He was very stubborn about flying and didn't like to be told anything. The tower would give us headings and he'd refuse to fly them. I had to make up stories on why the non-compliance. It was like threading a needle to keep the FAA off his back. In some ways he flew very well but he was out of his element in a jet. He was a seat-of-the-pants pilot and things like clearances and checklists meant nothing to him. Once we taxied out and were fourth or fifth in line for takeoff clearance. Just as the tower gave us a green light, Hughes decided to take a leak and walked out of the cockpit. The tower's screaming at us to take off and I finally told them we had a mechanical. They sent us back to the rear of the line and Hughes couldn't understand why.

He loved to talk to me because I was a pilot. One time he told me stories for four hours before we started engines. Stories about airplane designs, his dealings with Kelly Johnson and how he'd argue about everything. One story I remember in particular involved the time he flew a Connie solo from New York to Los Angeles. He stopped in Wichita to refuel and then took off again, climbed to what seemed to be a good cruising altitude, set the autopilot, took out a briefcase and started working. Two hours went by and all of a sudden he saw something flash by the cockpit window. "Brien," he says to me, "I suddenly realized those things going by me were trees—I didn't have enough altitude to go over the mountains."

One night he announced we weren't going to Mojave to shoot landings, but were heading instead for San Francisco. He did all the flying and he had Jean Peters with him. He was very attentive to her, but he kept her out of the cockpit. We landed in San Francisco about one A.M. and taxied over to the TWA hangar where some banker got on board. Hughes asked me to leave while the banker and he sat in the cockpit, talking. After about a half-hour, Hughes called me back and we took off with the banker in the jump seat and went back to Los Angeles. He was board chairman or president of some big West Coast bank—I never did know exactly who he was.

It was quite an experience, those few days with Hughes. He made me nervous flying because it was so difficult to control him, but I did enjoy the conversations and camaraderie. He was always very polite and friendly, and I got the feeling that was because I *was* a pilot.

The trouble was, of course, that Howard didn't get along as well with bankers and financiers as he did with fellow airmen. His trust of the latter was in direct contrast to his distrust of the former and it was a fatal attitude. With his staggering orders for thirty-three Boeing 707s and thirty Convair 880s, he had left himself exposed to the very men he feared.

Catastrophe at Kansas City. The 1951 flood that hit TWA's maintenance facilities.

The size of the 747 is clearly demonstrated in this aerial shot of TWA's Flight Wing One at JFK. It was the first terminal in the world specifically designed to handle jets.

Pope Pius XII just before boarding his TWA 707

Above: Will the real Joe Patroni please stand up? Roy Davis (left) with George Kennedy.

Right: John Collings with Howard Hughes. The aircraft is unidentified but is believed to be Hughes' converted A-23 bomber.

Secretary of Commerce Jesse Jones (third from right) greets Howard Hughes and Jack Frye after their record transcontinental flight in 1944. The War Department owned the Constellation and didn't like the TWA paint scheme.

Above: A never-before-published snapshot of Howard Hughes. It was taken either just before or just after Howard's demonstration of his Ground Proximity Warning System aboard a TWA Connie in May 1947.

Below: Hughes at the controls of the Connie.

A few of the memorable people who have molded TWA's history:

George Spater   Ray Dunn

Bob Rummel

Bill Meador   Johnny Guy

Daisy Richter and Parky Parkinson

Bob Buck

Hal Blackburn. His TWA flying career included more than 6.5 million miles and 750 ocean crossings.

In the left seat is Floyd Hall, and just behind him, Ed Frankum.

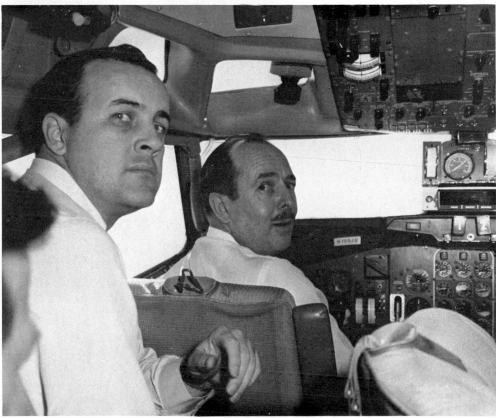

Left to right: Ed Smart, Tillinghast and Ed Meyer. The picture was taken shortly after Meyer assumed the presidency.

16

For the Want of a Dietrich, an Airline Was Lost

The trouble really started as far back as 1954. That was when Hughes established the Howard Hughes Medical Institute, a non-profit research foundation to which he had transferred ownership of his aviation electronics firm, Hughes Aircraft. Ownership included the company's profits, modest at the time but destined to mushroom over the next ten years as the electronics industry boomed.

It was a generous gesture that came back to haunt him, for by assigning Hughes Aircraft to the foundation, he eliminated it as a source of funds when he needed money later. He still owned Toolco, of course, but while the electronics firm was prospering, Toolco ran into great difficulties. Just when the Boeing and Convair plants were beginning to hatch their giant new birds, Toolco's earnings went into a sharp decline. Every airline except TWA had entered into long-range financing plans with various banks and insurance companies. Hughes had wanted to buy jets without outside help. He couldn't; for the first time in his life he was cash-short.

This didn't stop him from taking a deep interest in the jets under construction. Jerry Zerbone, an ex-TWA flight engineer who wound up working for Boeing, remembers Hughes sending Ray Cook to Seattle. Cook would tell Zerbone, "Now Jerry, I know you'll do your job, but I want to remind you Mr. Hughes will insist that these airplanes be perfect."

Howard made sure Johnny Guy was on the premises while the 707s were being built and Guy didn't disappoint him. He insisted on the development of an acrylic paint to prevent the planes from skin damage during production. Air Force inspectors on hand to monitor construction of KC-135s, the military version of the 707, saw the TWA planes and accused Boeing of having a double standard. In typical Guy fashion, Johnny put them straight.

"You guys sit on your asses drinking coffee instead of being on the assembly line keeping your eyes open," he told them. "If you're not getting quality, it's your own damned fault!"

Hughes faced his first financial crisis in the summer of 1958, long before TWA's first jet was ready. He tried to negotiate extension of a $12 million short-term loan to TWA that had just fallen due. The money had been borrowed to meet the airline's payroll toward the end of 1957, and it had come from a variety of lenders, including Equitable Life and Irving Trust. When the notes fell due, Equitable informed Hughes it would give TWA an extension only if Hughes agreed to arrange long-term financing for the $405 million commitment he had made for TWA's jet-age entry—$315 million for planes and $90 million for engines.

As expected, Hughes refused to be pushed. He scraped up the $12 million himself, thus depleting his own ready cash. And there was no Noah Dietrich around to tell him what to do in the next and inevitable crisis: paying for the jets. Bob Gross of Lockheed came to his temporary rescue by lining up a prominent banker, George Woods of the First Boston Corporation, who agreed to work out a financing blueprint. This was in October of 1958 and before the end of the year, Woods reported to Hughes he was ready to sit down and discuss specifics. Hughes said fine, but it would have to be discussed by phone—he didn't hold personal conferences. Woods, understandably miffed, refused. "That's not the way I do business, Mr. Hughes," he said. "I am accustomed to dealing with a face, not a voice."

Exit Mr. Woods. Enter Boeing. An increasingly impatient Boeing.

Hughes had been failing to meet the required quarterly progress payment but had wangled extensions that were due to end in January 1959. His overdue payments on the 707 fleet amounted to some $15 million that he didn't have. In desperation, he asked the investment firm of Dillon, Read & Company to draw up a financing plan and include two other prestigious Wall Street giants—Lehman Brothers and Lazard Frères. When Dillon, Reed accepted the assignment, Hughes was able to pry another extension out of Boeing with the promise that the new plan would assure past and future payments.

There was a plan established. It called for creation of the Hughes Aircraft Leasing Company (HALCO) as a kind of middle man between Toolco and TWA. Hughes Tool would buy the jets (with borrowed money) and through HALCO lease them to the airline. The lenders would be repaid from the lease payments and Toolco would be able to apply aircraft depreciation charges against its dwindling profits. In essense, it was much the same arrangement Hughes had been working for years—buying TWA's aircraft through Toolco and leasing or selling the planes back to the airline.

Charlie Thomas was informed of HALCO and was angry. He wanted no part of any financing plan in which TWA wouldn't have legal title to its own jet equipment, the most important, crucial and expensive airplanes it had ever operated. It must be understood that at this point, TWA owned most of its aircraft. It had borrowed the money to buy them from Toolco and was thus flying a heavily mortgaged fleet with Equitable holding the bulk of the notes.

So not only was HALCO unacceptable to TWA, it also was anathema to Equitable which told Dillon, Reed that the plan had one huge drawback: if the airline didn't own it jets, they could not be listed as assets used to secure the loans held by TWA's army of creditors. So HALCO foundered on the rocks of unyielding opposition from both Thomas and TWA's lenders.

The hard-pressed Hughes swung delivery of TWA's first jet by borrowing the money from Irving Trust and Bank of America. He used the plane itself as collateral and leased it to TWA on a day-to-day basis. It was not only a jerry-built, shaky way to finance the aircraft, but cast doubt on how he was going to deal with the remaining sixty-two jets under contract. When the second 707 was delivered a few weeks later, Equitable stepped in and prevented the airline from operating it. To Equitable, day-to-day leasing fell way short of a truly stable financing structure. For months it had been pressing Hughes to come up with a solid financing plan and the stubborn Hughes hadn't bothered to answer the insurance company's letters.

Equitable had no power to stop Hughes from leasing the second 707, but as TWA's chief creditor it had enough muscle to stop the airline from making any payments—a decision that grounded the jet as effectively as if it had been delivered without engines. So on March 20, 1959, TWA gallantly entered the jet age with exactly one jet—the only operational one it was to have in its fleet for the next month.

The one-plane jet fleet was assigned to the San Francisco-New York route and flew it for twenty-one consecutive days with no "down time" (mechanical delays) and a load factor of 100 percent. Fran Moran, the San Francisco station manager, is prouder of that record than any other achievement in his long TWA career. "I think the way we operated that one airplane for almost a month was one of the greatest moments in TWA's history. I remember it was off-again-and-on-again as to when we would start service. The inaugural was finally scheduled for March 20 and Gordon Granger was the captain—Flight Twelve as I recall it. Actually we had more than a hundred percent load factor; the early 707s had a forward lounge and that's where we put our oversales."

The second delivered 707 was used for crew training until Hughes worked his way out of his cash dilemma—and he displayed some fancy footwork. He swung a complicated deal with Pan Am, trading delivery rights for six of TWA's eighteen Intercontinental 707s to the rival airline, which then refunded to Hughes the $6 million downpayment he had made on the six planes. Hughes, in turn, applied the $6 million to overdue payments on the Transcontinental 707s. With this kind of shuffling, plus fresh short-term personal bank loans, Hughes finally squeezed out enough cash for TWA to take delivery on all fifteen of its shorter-ranged Boeings.

These were the so-called "water wagons"—the early model 707s with a water injection system on the engines. On a hot day, those first Boeings lacked the power to take off safely with a full load. The solution was the injection of cold water into the engine air intakes during the takeoff roll. The water lowered the engine temperature, making the air within denser, so more fuel could be burned. This provided about a thousand pounds of additional thrust just when it was needed the most.

Even so, TWA's first jet captains remember almost every "water wagon" takeoff as marginal. They brought back to Ed Frankum memories of taking off from Chicago's bandbox Midway in the then-new Connies, when "you'd head for San Francisco nonstop with a full load and you could barely get it off the ground. You'd go screaming over a shopping center adjacent to the airport and then over a schoolhouse just beyond." It was an experience repeated for Frankum and his fellow pilots, for even at Idlewild, with a 9,500-foot runway, a water wagon used up all 9,500 feet before breaking ground on a hot summer day.

But power deficiencies notwithstanding, the 707s were money machines from the start. TWA was grossing more than $17,000 per transcontinental 707 flight, almost double a 1649's or Super G's revenues. Still, it was lagging behind Pan Am internationally and American domestically in its jet services, with both these rivals receiving their new planes on schedule. Only

United was in worse shape than TWA; Pat Patterson had opted for the DC-8, which was running almost a year behind the 707 in deliveries.

Gradually, TWA begn to catch up with Pan Am and American. Hughes kept borrowing throughout 1959 to free the airline's 707s for delivery and simultaneously kept digging a deeper hole for himself. Equitable continued to block the airline from making lease payments to Toolco. Deprived of this cash flow, Hughes' debts to various banks increased beyond his immediately available cash. Incredibly, the airline was prospering even while Hughes was hurting—ironic, yet a situation whose significance Howard failed to grasp. If ever there was a time for him to arrange suitable long-term financing, it was now—TWA was enjoying the stability and efficiency of the Thomas regime, it was making money and its future seemed solid.

But not Howard Hughes. First he committed himself to another $85 million worth of new airplanes and engines—thirteen Convair 990s, a slightly larger and faster version of the 880. Nobody at TWA wanted the 990, but Hughes apparently ordered it as part of a new strategy. He evidently thought Convair might put pressure on its own lenders to help bail out Hughes, its biggest customer, and the Convair outlook was gloomy indeed. Only TWA and Delta had ordered the 880 and the sole 990 customer, other than Hughes, was American. Hughes had the same strategy in mind when he told Bob Gross he was ready to buy a fleet of forty Electras. Gross knew very well that Hughes couldn't afford the planes and that Lockheed would have to help obtain financing.

But Gross himself was under terrible pressure. Charlie Thomas, who was once on Lockheed's own board of directors, told Gross TWA didn't want or need the Electra. For the first time in over two decades, a TWA president was openly and angrily defying the man who owned the airline and Gross was shaken. Hughes really did want the prop-jet; he had flown it even before he flew the 880 and once told Jack Real he preferred the Electra. "The 880 flies like a truck," he said, "but maybe I expect everything to fly like the Electra."

In March of 1960, Gross called in Real and asked him to talk frankly to Hughes. Real followed the script to the letter.

"Howard," he said, "forget the Electras. You've got your hands full with the 880 and 707. There'll be another day and another battle."

Hughes shook his head. "No. I've made up my mind I'm going to put the Electras into TWA's fleet and we'll sink or swim with 'em."

Real fired his biggest gun. "I'm authorized to tell you we want you to back off or you'll lose the airline."

"No, I won't," Hughes insisted.

He was tragically wrong. Charlie Thomas did more than object to Bob Gross over Howard's Electra intentions; he informed Equitable and the rest of TWA's lenders that the deal was insane. It was a tough decision for Thomas to make, too; Gross had been instrumental in his getting the TWA job and Charlie felt a lot of loyalty to both Gross and Lockheed. Yet he also wanted to show he could stand up to Hughes.

The Electra sale fell through when Hughes failed to arrange the financing; so did the 990 order—Hughes couldn't pay for those thirty 880s. By March of 1960, TWA had taken delivery of only twenty-two 707s—fifteen water wagons and seven Intercontinentals. That left forty-one jets still on order, thirty of them the Convairs that Hughes himself blocked the airline from receiving. If they weren't delivered, he wouldn't have to pay for them. What followed was a bizarre invasion of the Convair plant by Toolco security personnel who took the first three 880s that had come off the assembly line, towed them to a field on the edge of the plant grounds and put them under 24-hour guard.

Delta officials, headed by president C.E. Woolman, arrived in San Diego to accept the first of their own 880s. Hughes at first insisted that Delta contractually couldn't fly the 880 until TWA did and it took some angry words on the part of the usually mild-mannered, courtly Woolman before Howard's representatives agreed to reverse this dog-in-the-manger attitude and let Delta fly away its first 880.

It was an episode more tragic than comic, for it demonstrated how badly the whole TWA-Hughes situation had deteriorated. Ailing and aging, Hughes was beginning to lose control of himself even as he fought to maintain control of the airline. It was a savage, debilitating struggle raging inside this complex man who wanted so badly to retain TWA that he seemed willing to ruin it. If he was keeping the lenders in turmoil, he was doing the same thing to the airline. Floyd Hall has this grim memory of the days when TWA was trying to get ready for jets it wasn't sure would ever be delivered:

"It was a bad time. We had a group of pilots training at Boeing and others at Convair. One of Hughes' lawyers would call me in Kansas City at two A.M. and tell me to bring 'em all home. They'd be home for two days and we'd be told to send 'em all back again. We finally stopped sending pilots to Convair altogether. At Boeing, however, we started to ignore the messages and kept the crews in training. We hoped we'd get the airplanes eventually and this on-again, off-again schooling was driving us nuts."

On March 5, 1960, Howard's own banks cut off his credit—he already owed them $125 million and could borrow no more. It was a worried Charlie Thomas who summoned the TWA board, still largely controlled by Hughes, and informed the directors that TWA had to get financing for its undelivered jets or go down the drain. Even the Hughes-appointed directors were jolted. After days of almost continuous meetings, the board accepted Thomas's proposal to resurrect the old Dillon, Read plan, but in a modified form. The latest version called for raising $260 million, $160 million from banks and insurance companies and the rest from Toolco in exchange for TWA subordinated debentures that would repay Toolco for the money it already had spent on jets.

Thomas added one final word: he informed Hughes, through Ray Cook, that if Howard didn't accept the plan, he'd resign. He meant the warning, for TWA's lenders were pressing for more stability in management. Hughes could not ignore the possibility that one more resignation by a TWA president could sink the airline, and Ray Cook so advised him. Hughes accepted the Dillon, Read plan—on principle, that is. When it came down to the nitty-gritty, he balked again and threw the whole affair into another crisis.

For what the lender threw into the Dillon, Read refinancing program was a provision requiring Hughes to put his TWA stock—representing slightly more than 78 percent of outstanding shares—into a ten-year voting trust if there were any alarming change in TWA's management that he did not correct within ninety days. In between the lines of all the legal language was a simple directive: Don't mess around with Charlie Thomas' administration. It was the kind of ultimatum Howard Hughes understood—and resented.

His relations with Thomas already had worsened to the point where he was refusing to accept calls from the TWA president. Hughes told his aides Thomas was plotting to take the airline away from him, although Howard himself seemed bent on taking the airline away from Thomas. In mid-1960, he started negotiations for a merger of TWA with Northeast Airlines and never informed Thomas in advance. Charlie was livid and his opinion of Hughes took another nose dive when he worked out a jet fuel contract that needed Howard's okay. Thomas was orderd to fly to Los Angeles and see Hughes for the necessary approval. He did, only to have Hughes fail to show up for the scheduled meeting.

Instead of immediately accepting the new Dillon, Read plan, Hughes thrashed around in other directions. One abortive effort was to merge TWA with Bob Prescott's small, but profitable, Flying Tiger line. He called Prescott at 2 A.M. but before discussing what was on his mind, he asked, "How many phone extensions do you have in your home?"

"Hell, I don't know," Prescott said. "Why do you want to know?"

"I want to make sure nobody's listening. You go around and check 'em all."

Prescott put down the phone and sat there for five or six minutes. Then he picked it up again. "It's okay, Howard. Nobody's listening."

But Prescott wanted no part of such a merger, which for some reason Hughes believed might stave off the financial crisis. He was still groping for some kind of solution when Charlie Thomas cut the ground out from under him. On July 28, 1960, Thomas resigned. He wrote out a brief statement to the effect that the two years he had agreed to serve were up and he wanted to return to California. He also wrote a personal letter to Hughes accusing him of never taking him into his confidence, never being available when he (Thomas) wanted him, and hurting TWA by not providing it with the jets it had been promised. It was a letter to which Carter Burgess could have added "amen."

Thomas could not have picked a more devastating time to resign. It came the day before Hughes had to decide whether to accept the Dillon, Read proposal. The lenders had set the next day as the deadline for finalizing the plan; they regarded Thomas' resignation as an unfavorable change in management and refused to go ahead with the loans. Hughes then made what was, for him, a desperate concession—if they gave TWA the money, he promised within ninety days to find a new president acceptable to the board. If he failed, he pledged, he would turn over his TWA stock to a voting trust. In effect, he had adopted the plan's most distasteful condition, but by now the lenders were fed up with his delaying tactics. Their answer: the only way TWA would obtain jet funding was for Hughes to surrender his stock immediately.

Hughes, cornered, still wouldn't give up. He staved off surrender to a voting trust by proposing a series of new deals, each one rejected, but succeeded by a fresh proposal that kept the pot boiling. All the time this Brobdingnagian struggle was going on, TWA was waging its own battle against increasing competition. It had not received any new jets for five months, but its outnumbered fleet was holding its own, managing to keep the airline in the black. The modest profits, however, were not enough to keep the creditors happy. On October 25, the banks seized the accounts of TWA and Toolco for debt default, putting both companies on the brink of bankruptcy. Only one thing saved the airline—no one wanted to destroy TWA by blowing the final whistle on Howard Hughes.

Hughes used this temporary and very unofficial "grace period" to attempt another deal. Col. Henry Crown, a wealthy Chicago industrialist and the largest stockholder in General Dynamics, had offered to arrange new financing if Hughes agreed to commit TWA to buy more Convair jets for an unspecified period in the future. Crown had part of the funds just about lined up and Hughes was convinced he had saved his control of TWA. The whole plan, however, hinged on the public sale of $165 million in TWA debentures to supplement the financing Crown had arranged with the Bank of America. If these debentures could be peddled, Hughes would name as TWA's new president Crown's own candidate—Frederick Glass, vice-chairman of the Empire State Building Corporation, which was one of Crown's properties. So confident was Howard that he announced he would move TWA's corporate headquarter from New York to Los Angeles as soon as the deal was consummated.

It never was. The underwriter of the debentures issue received such a lukewarm reception on Wall Street that it declined to guarantee their sale. Hughes reluctantly abandoned the Crown deal and in doing so lost his last chance to retain control. His next action was almost suicidal. He fired Ray Cook, whose law firm had been representing Hughes in all the negotiations with the lenders and who had won their respect for his skill and patience under trying circumstances.

Cook's replacement, Hollywood attorney Greg Bautzer, had an impossible task. At Howard's direction, he tried to revive the Crown plan, but was shot down in fast order by the Civil Aeronautics Board. The CAB said it would never approve any arrangement whereby an aircraft manufacturer (General Dynamics/Convair) would have a sizable interest in an airline. And Bautzer's next problem was a revolt brewing among the respective directors of TWA and Toolco. Led by Thomas A. Slack, a Texas lawyer and a long-time friend of Hughes who served as a director in both companies, the rebellious board members informed Bautzer he'd better accept the Dillon, Read plan if Hughes wanted to save the airline and Toolco itself.

Under that plan, one of the three voting trustees would be named by Toolco. The directors of that company chose board member Maynard Monrose, but Hughes was to have his final, if rather empty, revenge. He demanded Slack's resignation from both boards and named Raymond Holliday, vice-president of Hughes Tool, as Toolco's voting trustee. But while Hughes got even with Slack, he was helpless to stop the Dillon, Read plan itself.

The absolute deadline was set for Friday, December 29, 1960—the last business day of the year. On the day before, the lenders picked their own trustees: Irving S. Olds, former chairman of United States Steel, and none other than Ernest R. Breech, who had just retired as chairman of the Ford Motor Company.

Wall Street held its breath as the hours ticked away through that Friday. The tension was even worse at TWA, where every officer and employee knew the boom was about to be lowered if Hughes did not sign over his stock. Not until 7:15 that night did Holliday hear from Bautzer—Hughes had given the go-ahead for Holliday to sign all necessary documents.

Ten minutes later, one of the lenders telephoned the Federal Aviation Agency that TWA's aircraft were to be registered in the name of the lending institutions.

For the first time in twenty years, Howard Hughes no longer controlled TWA's destiny. There is no way to escape the conclusion that it was his own fault—a fatal mixture of stubbornness, insecurity and fear. This is admitted by the person who admired him to the day Hughes died—and still regards him as a truly great man. Says Jack Real:

Howard would not have liked to hear me say this, but he would never have lost TWA if he hadn't fired Noah Dietrich. Noah didn't know anything about airplanes, but he knew how to put a financing deal together. Howard didn't. He was afraid of bankers. He'd dream up some financing plan and Noah would tell him, "Howard, I know it's a good idea but let's back off a bit and let me put it together." Without Noah, Hughes was helpless to deal with the lenders. In any banking plan, they want decisions and Howard's one failing was procrastination. He had a distrust of bankers all his life and when it came to financing he was in an area he actually feared.

Years later, when we discussed his losing TWA, he'd tell me: "There are only three people who know why I lost the airline—you, Bob Gross and me. It was because you both insisted on my buying the Electra."

It just wasn't true. We talked him out of that. He lost TWA because he didn't have Dietrich around to advise him how to get out of the mess. In spite of all the criticism that has been voiced about Noah, he could have put a financing plan together.

Charlie Thomas returned to California and became head of the Irvine Company, a giant land development firm. He was the last president to serve under Hughes. Retired at this writing and, like Burgess, considerably mellowed by the passage of time, Charlie's memory of the 1960 crisis is almost totally at odds with what others have recalled, written and even documented.

According to Thomas, he parted company with Howard on friendly terms and says Hughes even offered him "a top job at Toolco."

"He said I could have a desk alongside him there," Thomas insists. "There never was any trouble between us—we had a very nice association. I think wanting to go back to California was the main reason. I didn't fight with him over the jet delays. They were his airplanes and it was his money. I didn't kowtow to him, though. Basically he was a decent man and a good engineer. Of course, you're asking an old man to go back a good many years. . . ."

Thomas honestly remembers it that way, although the letter he sent to Hughes when he resigned says otherwise. The overthrow of Howard Hughes was cataclysmic in scope and emotion, with a strange sense of *déjà vu*. For at the end, there stood the physically tiny, but intellectually towering, figure of Ernie Breech. For the second time in two decades he had come into the life of an airline fighting for its very existence.

Part Three
(1961 - 1983)

17

". . . A guy from a brake and bearing company?"

Ernest Breech's re-entry into the friction-generating atmosphere of the airline world came just after he had completed twenty-one successful years at Ford.

It was mid-December 1960, and he was looking forward to a life of semi-retirement—Ernie Breech could never totally retire—when he got a call asking if he'd meet with Grant Keehn, executive vice-president of the Equitable Life Assurance Society. Breech agreed and Keehn came to his office two days later with an invitation to join the TWA voting trust.

Keehn, a pleasant, persuasive man, briefed Ernie thoroughly on TWA's planet-sized problems and what had led to creation of the trust. Breech, with his usual directness, said the job didn't appeal to him. "It sounds to me," he told Keehn, "that my responsibilities would be no more than those of any large stockholder. I wouldn't be participating in the business and I wouldn't have anything to do with running it."

Keehn quickly suggested an alternative. When and if the trust agreement was signed, he explained, the lenders would be able to place their own men on the TWA board—that was part of the deal. Would Breech consider becoming a director?

He had cannily tweaked Ernie's weak spot. Breech was still very proud of his association with TWA during its formative years. "I might be interested in something like that," he admitted, "but only if the voting trust goes through and TWA can be run properly."

Keehn probed deeper. "Well, if we get a good board of directors, would you consider becoming chairman?"

"That's something for the board itself to decide," Breech said. "If I came on the board, we could consider the other matter later."

Keehn left with Breech's promise to serve as a director and also his suggestion that retired Gen. Lucius Clay would make an excellent trustee. But a few days later, he called to report that while the CAB had approved Irving Olds, it had rejected Clay because he was a director of a shipping firm and could have no connection with an airline. "The CAB says it would have no objection to you," he added, "so would you help us out for an interim period?"

"All right," Breech replied. "I'll help you out temporarily, but only temporarily—just long enough for you to get someone else."

The "someone else" didn't show up for quite awhile. Breech found him-

253

self getting deeply involved with TWA only a week or so after he became a trustee and returned to his winter home in Phoenix. Keehn called him to advise that Floyd Hall had received an attractive offer from a rival airline and was about to resign as a TWA vice-president. Keehn was no airline man himself, but he knew what Hall meant to TWA—more than anyone else, he had prepared it for the jets under extremely difficult circumstances. That the airline had managed to remain competitive amid all the turmoil of the Hughes financing controversy was the talk of the industry, and most airline officials credited Hall with being largely responsible. Keehn insisted that Breech talk to Hall before he made his move (the offer had come from American, it can now be revealed).

Breech demurred, pointing out that he wasn't even a TWA director yet. "I'm not the person to talk to him," he argued.

"There isn't anyone else," Keehn pleaded. "The damned company hasn't had a president for months and there's nobody in authority Hall can consult."

Ernie finally agreed, but he wanted a question answered first: he had to have something to offer Floyd, so would the voting trustees have the right to approve a stock-option and incentive compensation plan for TWA's executives? Keehn said he'd have to consult lawyers; he phoned back a few minutes later and informed Breech he could make Hall such an offer.

Ernie invited Hall to spend a day in Phoenix with him. They had never met, but Breech broke the ice by recalling he had known Howard Hall, Floyd's brother, years ago. Then for the next two hours, Breech made his pitch. How, he asked, could Hall have worked under all the terrible conditions of the past months and then leave just when TWA was getting a fresh start? He told how he had helped reorganize Ford from an archaic, feudal monolith into a modern and efficient competitor. TWA was no worse off than Ford had been, Ernie said, "and if I'm going to have anything to do with this situation, we're going to revitalize this company and above everything else, if the company makes money you fellows who run it are going to make money." He went on to explain what he had in mind in the way of stock options and incentive pay. After two hours of this, Hall was ready to charge a locomotive bare-chested; he stood up and said, "Mr. Breech, I'll stay."

Having solved this crisis, Breech found himself embroiled in another, this one involving the Toolco member of the voting trust, Raymond Holliday. The three members had met January 20, 1961, and agreed on how to reorganize the board of directors, a move to be announced at a board meeting scheduled for January 26 in New York. In accordance with the loan agreement, six Hughes directors would resign and be replaced by six new men, including Breech. The night before the board meeting, Breech had dinner with Holliday and assured him that Howard Hughes didn't have to worry about TWA.

"We're going to run it, as long as I have anything to do with it, for his benefit and the benefit of all stockholders," he promised Holliday, who, in turn, expressed his heartfelt gratitude and assured Ernie he would so advise Hughes. They planned to breakfast together before the board convened, but Holliday was late. He had been on the phone with Hughes.

"I've got good news and bad news," he said, "The good news is that Mr.

Hughes has agreed to release all those Convairs to TWA. The bad news is that I've been instructed that our men are not to show up at the board meeting today, so you and the other new directors can't be elected because there won't be a quorum present."

"What the hell are you trying to pull?" Breech demanded. "You agreed to our program. You said Hughes had been informed of how the trustees had voted to constitute the new board and had agreed to it—Toolco will have four members and the six new people, including myself, will represent the public. All six of us are in the city right now, ready to take our places."

"All I can tell you," Holliday shrugged, "is that Mr. Hughes changed his mind."

Breech went to the meeting anyway and, as expected, it was a farce. Breech went into a huddle with Olds who called Holliday.

"I want a meeting of the voting trustees immediately," Olds said grimly.

"I'm sorry," Holliday replied, "but I can't come."

"That's fine with me," Olds snapped, "because we're going to hold a meeting without you!"

Acting as a majority of the trustees, Breech and Olds called a special stockbrokers meeting in Kansas City to elect new directors. The subsequent election on March 1 left only four directors on the board beholden to Hughes but at the very first meeting of the new board, those four signified their intentions of serving as an out-of-step quartet. They voted no to all but one proposal—a resolution wishing Ray Dunn, who had suffered a heart attack, a speedy recovery. Breech snorted later that they were about to vote against it until a Hughes lawyer in the room signalled them to approve it.

The opposition was more symbolic than effective; the outnumbered Hughes contingent could not stop passage of three key resolutions which asked TWA to: (1) determine if it needed additional jets, (2) set up a directors' committee to look into a stock option and bonus plan and (3) find a new president.

Breech headed the search committee and by the time the directors held their next meeting, March 20, he had a candidate—a lawyer with a superb track record for corporate management and one who, from personal experience, considered TWA a long way from being a good airline.

He was a tall, long-faced, ex-football player from Brown University named Charles Carpenter Tillinghast, Jr.

Tillinghast was vice-president of international operations for the far-flung Bendix Corporation when he was approached about the TWA presidency. Up to then, his only contact with TWA had been as a passenger—and a not too satisfied passenger at that. His most recent prior experience with the airline had occurred on New Year's Eve of 1958 when he had booked space on a TWA 1649 Jetstream from Paris to New York. The Connie had mechanical problems and the passengers were finally bussed to a hotel for the night with departure scheduled for the following morning. Tillinghast showed up at the airport the next day and discovered that the 1649 was still *hors de combat*. He called the Paris office of Bendix.

"I'm getting a little fed up with this," he complained. "Is there any alternative?"

"Let's see if we can get you on a Pan Am jet," he was told.

That afternoon he flew back to New York on one of Pan Am's new 707s, thoroughly enjoying his first jet trip. He refused to try TWA again, using Pan Am whenever his business took him to Europe. He was still clinging to this anti-TWA bias when Francis Reed, an old friend and counsel to the voting trust, phoned him.

"How would you like to be president of an airline?" Reed asked.

"I don't know. What airline would I be president of?"

"TWA."

"I'd have to think *that* one over," Tillinghast said.

"Would you be willing to talk to some people?"

"Sure, I'd be willing to talk."

Over the next few days, he talked to several persons about the job— mostly Ernie Breech, whom he had known since 1942 when Breech was with Bendix and Tillinghast was a young lawyer with a firm representing the company. Breech filled him in on what was good and bad about TWA. Its strength, he emphasized, was in its technical operations—good crews, maintenance and a long history of engineering excellence. It lagged behind American in marketing, Eastern in efficiency, and United in achieving an image of solid, conservative reliability. Its chief weakness was lack of modern equipment, Breech added. TWA as of March 1961, had only twenty-eight jets competing against Pan Am's forty-six, United's forty-four and American's thirty-four. American's standing would improve even more, however, when it received the new fan-jets it had ordered—707s with quieter, more powerful and economical engines.

George Spater, another old friend of Tillinghast, also briefed him, supporting Breech's views and then arranging a meeting at his home with Carter Burgess, who gave the potential president an honest appraisal of the airline he had once headed. By now, Tillinghast was intrigued, but he also was concerned over what Burgess had told him about the pitfalls of working for Howard Hughes. While the voting trust would last ten years, Tillinghast worried about what would happen if the admittedly vindictive Hughes should regain control of TWA before the trust expired.

"If you didn't argue with Hughes about airplanes or money," Carter Burgess had said, "you could have your job for the rest of your life." But that was precisely what had defeated Burgess and Thomas: money and airplanes. Tillinghast had no illusions so he insisted on a contract that would continue his income even if Hughes came back and fired him. His salary was set at $122,000 a year.

On March 20, 1961, TWA's directors elected Tillinghast president and chief executive officer; a little more than a month later, Breech agreed to become chairman and Warren Lee Pierson finally stepped down, retaining only his directorship. At long last, the airline had the management stability it so badly needed; it remained to be seen, however, whether stability was synonymous with acumen.

In Charlie Tillinghast, some 20,000 TWA officers and employees saw an unknown quantity who was as much a lawyer as a businessman—and the legal background bothered a lot of people. Only twice before in airline history had lawyers become airline presidents: Terry Drinkwater at Western and Malcolm MacIntyre with Eastern. But both had possessed considerable airline experience before they headed their respective airlines; Tillinghast had none. And even his business background was suspect, devoid as it was of much aviation knowledge—"What the hell does a guy from a brake and bearing company know about running an airline?" was the question one employee put to Jerry Cosley, then a youngster in Gilmore's public relations squadron.

He didn't know a hell of a lot. But for a "new boy on the block," he learned fast. Faster than anyone dreamed.

In spite of all the briefings from Breech, Spater, Burgess and the TWA officers he talked to, Tillinghast actually was unprepared for what he found at the airline.

"It was in terrible shape," he recalled many years later. "Ernie really didn't warn me how bad things were. If I had known before I said yes, I wouldn't have said yes. At the time I joined TWA, I was told that the airline was profitable, which was true in the sense that it had been profitable for the last twelve months. But by mid-1961, I thought we were looking at bankruptcy. If there was any airline that would have thrown in the towel, it was TWA."

He wasn't kidding. First quarter losses in '61 hit nearly $10 million. The long delays in jet acquisitions were finally taking their toll competitively. Ten days after he took office, Tillinghast—with board approval—ordered twenty-six 707 fan-jets carrying a $150 million price tag. Breech carried the ball for him with the lenders. "You've got bad money in there now," he told them. "You have to put some good money after bad money, or this thing can't be saved."

But ordering jets for the future didn't solve the hemorrhaging of the present. Two months after Tillinghast became president, the directors asked him to prepare a frank analysis of TWA's weaknesses. He approached the task with the detached objectivity of a lawyer preparing a case for a client he didn't know very well. The thirty-page report he submitted to the board toward the end of 1961 amounted to a surgical dissection of the airline.

Tillinghast conceded that many of TWA's troubles were due to "absentee management"—his polite term for Howard Hughes—which, he said, "reflected itself in a turnover of chief executives unique in the industry, thus depriving the company of consistent leadership or, at times, of any presidential leadership at all.

"This, combined with inadequate financing and repeated periods of financial stringency, have delayed and impeded orderly planning and have prevented the taking of needed action. Deteriorated interdepartmental relationships have been another result of the lack of leadership. Most importantly, the inability of TWA management to plan and execute adequate and long-range equipment programs has prejudiced the company's success."

Tillinghast was sharply critical of TWA's long-standing reliance on Constellations. They were slower and more costly to operate than the oppositions' DC-6s and DC-7s because they were heavier, and when TWA tried to match its rivals in speed, the result was frequent engine troubles and disrupted schedules.

The report noted that up to 1958, TWA had the highest rate of advertising expenditures in the industry but, Tillinghast felt, this resulted in TWA relying more on advertising than on performance and reputation. TWA's public image, in fact, did not correspond to what a 1961 *Chicago Tribune* survey described as "the ideal airline." In the mind of the public, the survey found, "the ideal airline is visualized in terms of dependability, safety, speed, efficiency and service." TWA was visualized as "a large and powerful airline that emphasized speed, style and glamor over personal attention and efficiency."

The image problem—and it probably stemmed largely from the Hughes/Hollywood influence—had harmful consequences, according to Tillinghast. It attracted more tourist than business traffic, even though TWA's route structure embraced the nation's commercial and industrial heartlands. There was nothing wrong in serving non-business passengers, yet traditionally TWA had attracted the greatest percentage of first-time fliers in the industry—a worthy achievement, yet a flimsy one on which to base all-important repeat traffic: consistent, frequent passengers with a sense of loyalty toward one airline.

The report admitted that TWA had enjoyed great success in obtaining new routes, domestically and internationally. But new routes, it pointed out, are useless unless an airline has the equipment to exploit them. TWA was serving such important cities as Cleveland, Denver and Detroit but was being battered by the competition in all three. Its schedules were weak and its flight equipment generally obsolete.

Tillinghast tagged TWA's international routes as its strongest asset. Significantly, they were being served by jets whereas domestically the airline was still relying mostly on obsolete Connies and Martins for the short and medium-length routes. He considered fleet modernization the airline's highest priority, one that could not be solved merely with additional 707s and the expedited delivery of the 880s.

The first Convairs had finally gone into service three months before Tillinghast joined the airline. Enormously strong and easy to fly, they were popular with passengers and pilots alike but not with Ray Dunn's mechanics. Ray always considered the 880, a fuel guzzler, TWA's worst equipment decision. The GE engines gave them fits and the airplane itself, although well designed, was plagued with minor but annoying ailments—systems that developed malfunctions, cabin equipment that didn't always work and various components that often went haywire. TWA's hostesses referred to the 880 as "our Japanese Boeing"—remember, these were the days when Japan hadn't yet acquired a reputation for assembly-line perfection.

Captain Ted Hereford, senior enough to bid the 707, was one of several pilots who insisted on checking out on the 880 instead. He thought it flew like a fighter. On his first Convair flight out of Chicago, the galley oven caught fire an hour after takeoff. Hereford's initial awareness came from a hostess who burst into the cockpit yelling, "The fucking galley's on fire!"

Her voice carried through the whole cabin and one passenger complained to TWA about her obscene language. In fact, the passenger had announced to all aboard that he was writing the president of Trans World Airlines. Fortunately for the hostess, also on the plane was Tex Thornton, head of Litton Industries, which made the 880 oven. Three days later, Tillinghast received a letter from Thornton.

"Before you discipline that hostess for her language," he wrote, "I want you to know that the fucking galley *was* on fire!"

Twenty of the thirty Convairs Hughes had originally ordered were in service by mid-1961 and that completed the 880 deliveries. One of Hughes' last-ditch moves to ward off the voting trust had been to cancel ten of the jets. Tillinghast eventually latched onto another six—planes General Dynamics had repossessed from Northeast when the small New England-based carrier ran into a financing crisis of its own. But he knew the 880 was too big and too expensive for TWA's short-haul markets and he was looking hard for a smaller jetliner.

The only one immediately availably was the French-built Caravelle. Tillinghast signed a contingent contract for twenty, with deliveries scheduled to start in early 1963. The deal, however, was predicated on TWA's engineering department approving the twin-jet, on financing, and on the possible availability of a U.S.-made medium jet before the Caravelle contract was finalized.

The negotiations were held in secret. Floyd Hall says the Caravelle contract "came as a complete surprise to practically everyone—Ray Dunn nearly had another heart attack because all he needed was one more strange bird in his house."

Hall continues: "They showed up one day with a Caravelle and we were supposed to fly it and see what we thought of it. It was a nice airplane to fly. It had some oddball characteristics, but I'm not sure but what some of these weren't due to our own built-in apprehension as to the operating procedures. We were told to fly at twenty thousand feet and then descend with the spoilers on the wings pulled up. The damned thing came down about four thousand feet a minute, rattling and shaking like hell. Our feeling was that it just wasn't a suitable airplane for TWA."

The airline would never find out whether Hall's judgment was right. First the Caravelle financing fell through and then Boeing announced it was building the 727, a tri-jet that was to prove the most successful commercial transport in history. Versatile, viable in both short and medium-haul markets and economical to operate, the 727 was destined to become the true successor to the DC-3 as the airlines' most widely used workhorse. (United was the only U.S. carrier to buy the Caravelle, which turned out to be too small for its needs. The pioneering French twin had one unique feature—its cockpit section was built in England and was the exact replica of the original Comet's nose section.)

TWA had a direct hand in the 727's design. Boeing was under pressure from United to build a small four-engine jet; Eastern preferred two engines for economy reasons. Bob Rummel was urging a tri-jet as being safer than a twin and cheaper to fly than a four, and his counterpart at Eastern, Charles Froesch, went along with that concept, provided that the plane could operate at short-runway airports like LaGuardia and National.

The breakthrough in the 727's five-year development program came when Pratt & Whitney designed the JT8D engine, a fan-jet with 15,000 pounds of thrust. That provided ample power even for Denver's mile-high airport, a key United hub, and UAL backed off its demand for four engines. When Eastern and United ordered or took options for eight of the new planes, Boeing decided to go ahead with production. TWA's initial order was for a modest ten, but eventually the airline would operate more than seventy of the tri-jets, half of them the stretched 727-200 version. As the remarkable jet proved itself, TWA kept adding 727s to its fleet and no airplane ever served it better.

The 727's success, of course, was far down the line; it wouldn't go into service until 1964. Tillinghast's most immediate problem was stemming the airline's losses, which at the end of 1961 showed a $14.7 million deficit. Yet considering a more than $9 million loss in the first quarter alone, it was obvious Tillinghast was achieving some results. For one thing, he had shaken up the top brass in a swift series of promotions, demotions, responsibility shifts and job changes.

Tillinghast came to TWA with an open mind toward the executives who would be serving under him. True, he had been influenced somewhat—and quite naturally—by what men like Spater and Burgess had told him. He knew Spater had severed all relations with TWA by 1961. Fed up with the Hughes mess and the constant turmoil, he had gone over to American and would eventually become its president. Burgess had been particularly specific in warning him that Hughes had spies among TWA's officers who seemed to be more loyal to Howard than to the airline. It didn't sound like a case of sour grapes, either—the spiteful admonitions of a man who resented losing his job. Spater was one of Tillinghast's oldest friends—they had known each other since 1937—and when Spater told him he had great admiration for Burgess, Tillinghast was willing to at least listen. Carter, as Tillinghast remembers it, mentioned only one top officer by name as being loyal to Hughes, and that was Vic Leslie.

He may have mentioned Rummel, [Tillinghast adds], but I'm not sure and I don't remember Gilmore's name being brought up at all. Whatever Burgess told me, I confirmed on my own. Right from the start, I sensed a morale problem at TWA, stemming from the Hughes influence. There was chaos at the top, with that triumverate of Leslie, Warren Lee and Cocke running the airline. On the upper managment level, each was tending to his own little garden and jockeying with the others.

The possibility of having people around who were still loyal to Hughes was a lurking question—and a particular question in the case of Leslie, which is perhaps one reason he didn't stay very long. Rummel was a different case. I was never concerned about his loyalty. He was very able, but he worked too long for Hughes and I think from Hughes he developed the attitude that being different was being better. Our equipment was different, yes, but whether our planes were better than American's and United's is highly debatable.

I found a lot of dedicated professional people in TWA and also, in some areas, incompetents. The fact that I made a number of changes at the executive level indicates that I didn't regard everybody as a genius. A lot of devoted people held the airline together but there were a lot of devoted people who weren't conspicuous geniuses. Indeed, the constant churning had taken its toll of some of the more gifted ones. There were exceptions—Floyd Hall, Ray Dunn and Rummel—come to mind.

Hall was a great tower of strength at TWA in '61 and '62. He was always pretty much of a white-gloves man . . . a spit-and-polish guy. He had ambition, too. One of the troubles at TWA during all the chaos was that a lot of people had nothing but a survival instinct. Not Floyd.

He had the ambition not just to get by, but to be superior, and he had the personality to get by with it. He played a big part in getting people to climb off their survival mat. He provided the stability we needed. Everybody knew him and respected him.

Ray Dunn was a good fellow. Except for his health problems, he might have eventually become president. One of the rumors I found going around TWA was that you had to be a graduate of an Ivy League school to get anywhere in management. Hell, Ray virtually was self-taught and enormously capable.

Oz Cocke was a good head salesman. I never worried about Oz and the Hughes problem. I didn't know and didn't care how many pipelines he might have had into the Hughes headquarters. In my dealings with him he was always cooperative.

Jack Frye? It was tragic that someone who had so great a part in creating the business and creating the route structure had to work for somebody who repeatedly failed to follow up with a fleet that could exploit this potential, and finally ended up cashiering the guy who put this together. It's also tragic that TWA always had about half the fleet it needed for a route structure of its size. People were always telling me that TWA had the greatest route structure in the industry, but the problem was that the fleet hadn't been provided to serve it. In market after market we were second man or third man, trying to cover both domestic and international with a fleet just about adequate for domestic. Remember, in the early years of the jet age we had a piston fleet feeding international jet routes!

Those frank comments about his TWA associates were borne out by his actions. Vic Leslie departed the scene. Floyd Hall became senior vice-president and system general manager—in effect, Tillinghast's right-hand man and heir-apparent. Cocke was named senior vice-president of industry affairs. The title implied a promotion but it was more of a tribute to Oz's long and honorable service. His crucial marketing duties were put into the hands of a man Hall recommended, Tom McFadden, a former NBC executive. Frank Busch's job changed from flight operations to vice-president of equipment retirement; Ed Frankum replaced him in operations, sporting the title of vice-president of transportation. Ray Dunn was promoted to vice president of technical services with all of maintenance and engineering under him.

Tillinghast had begun to form his own team, one of new independence and initiative. Nowhere was the latter trait more amply demonstrated than when TWA introduced one of the greatest marketing gimmicks of them all: in-flight movies on its jets. As we already have seen, airborne motion pictures were not new, but TWA's jet age rebirth involved first-run films complete with sound. It was a motion picture theater 35,000 feet in the air traveling 600 miles an hour.

The idea was not the airline's, but came from a young entrepreneur named Dave Flexer. He wangled an appointment with Hall and Cocke while Charlie Thomas was still president and told them he had invented an in-flight movie projector. "I don't have the money to develop it," he admitted, "but if TWA will back me I'll give you five years exclusivity."

Hall and Cocke took the proposal to Thomas and didn't try to hide their enthusiasm.

"It'll be worth four or five extra passengers on every transcontinental and overseas trip," Oz predicted confidently. And Floyd added, "It would be worth more than that if we can get exclusivity for five years."

Thomas agreed to let Flexer proceed. The development costs were modest, but the equipment would cost $60,000 per aircraft to install. This fish-or-cut-bait decision was placed in Tillinghast's lap shortly after he became president. Hall and Cocke lobbied hard in favor of the expenditure, at least for one or two 707s to see if the public liked it.

The public did, even though the system had plenty of bugs at first and flight engineers spent as much time fixing wayward projectors as monitoring engine instruments. Choice of films was another major headache. "We had a hell of a time finding movies that wouldn't offend anybody," Floyd Hall recalls.

It was decided to form a movie selection committee, and Gordon Gilmore appointed John Corris as the public relations representative on the committee. The other members were two men and a woman from other TWA departments and they relied heavily on films approved by the Catholic Legion of Decency and *Parents' Magazine,* logically assuming that if these two upstandingly conservative groups liked a movie, it had to be safe.

Both the Legion and *Parents'* had praised Alfred Hitchcock's new film, *The Birds,* and the screening committee cleared it for in-flight presentation. "The roof fell in," Hall remembers. "People complained they had been locked in a cabin and forced to watch a scary movie."

As a member of the screening committee, Corris was frequently invited to previews of the latest films. When Gilmore tried to reach him, he was told on several occasions that "Mr. Corris is screening a movie." Gilmore finally got tired of this and asked Corris, "What the hell are you doing spending all your time watching films?"

"You put me on the committee," Corris pointed out. "How can I pick a movie without seeing it first?"

"Well, okay," Gilmore said, "but do you have to see 'em all in the daytime?"

Flexer's projectors initially were installed in the first-class sections of three domestic and nine international 707s. The biggest drawback, outside of the system's early unreliability, was the bulky, uncomfortable earphones needed in order to hear the sound track. But the headsets and films were free and a little discomfort was a small price to pay for this time-killing device. So popular were the in-flight movies that American and United rushed to develop their own systems and foreign carriers beefed that TWA, by showing the movies free to first class passengers, was engaging in unfair competition. There were hints of retaliation, such as suspending TWA's landing rights, and Tillinghast finally agreed to a compromise—the airline began charging overseas passengers $2.50 for a headset.

The policy of running the films only in first class inevitably led to resentment on the part of the less-fortunate riders in the back of the plane. TWA pursers would draw a curtain between first class and coach so passengers in the aft cabin couldn't peek at the screen suspended from the ceiling in front of the forward lounge; they couldn't hear, of course, but even a soundless film could relieve the boredom of a long flight.

Buddy Ledger was the purser on one trans-Atlantic flight when a coach passenger, an elderly lady, kept parting the curtain so she could see the movie. Buddy kept yanking it closed and she kept yanking it open. Finally Ledger stood firmly in the center of the aisle, holding the curtain in place. The angry passenger crawled underneath and bit his leg.

Magazine cartoonists had a field day on the subject of in-flight movies. One had a drawing of a hostess telling a passenger, "Don't worry, sir—the captain says he'll keep circling until the movie's over." Another showed a smiling pilot standing at the front of the plane, and a smiling hostess by his side. The caption read: "While the flight engineer repairs the projector, here's our own Peggy Johnson to sing 'Mi Chiamano Mimi' from *La Bohème.*"

Later, when American, United and others got their own film systems, there were reported cases of passengers basing their choice of flights on what movie happened to be playing. There even were instances of people switching from one airline to another at the last minute because they preferred the latter's picture. The novelty wore off, of course, particularly when in-flight motion pictures were made available to all passengers, but TWA's brief competitive advantage helped create a fresh image of aggressive, smart marketing. For a while, the airline had film producers riding its flights so they could get passenger reaction to their latest movies.

In-flight entertainment was just part of the new TWA. Floyd Hall's magnificent Royal Ambassador service, featuring Rosenthal china and silver tableware by Reed and Barton, also helped woo passengers away from rival carriers. Some of his peers on other airlines either sneered at or criticized Floyd's innovations in airborne opulence: one official remarked that all he knew about Hall was that "he has the reputation of creating a passenger service that uses eleven napkins between New York and Los Angeles."

Floyd wasn't as extravagent as some of his opposition claimed. He happened to be one of the first airline executives who thought passengers, especially those paying premium fares in first class, deserved more than bland, uninspired food served in a bland, uninspired way. "I always felt we should give them something for their money and not just something to fill up their stomachs," he explained. "Royal Ambassador service came out of that. I think I got a bum rap for supposedly going overboard with things like Rosenthal china. Actually, we used real Rosenthal China only for a couple of months, for the publicity. Then we switched to an imitation made just outside Philadelphia—if you held a cup or plate up to the light, you couldn't tell the difference. All I wanted was something that *looked* expensive."

As TWA's reputation for in-flight service improved—and internationally, it was ranked by impartial observers as equalling or even surpassing the best any European carrier was offering—so did its traffic, to the point where TWA began to dominate the trans-Atlantic market. It raced past not only the foreign competition, but entrenched Pan Am, as well. It was a resurgence with an ironic twist—it wrecked what Tillinghast himself thought for a time was TWA's only hope: a merger with Juan Trippe's airline.

Merger possibilities were first raised at a directors' meeting in St. Louis in the summer of 1961, a time when TWA's outlook resembled the inside of a coal mine. The first suggested merger partner was Eastern, and Tillinghast was authorized to initiate discussions with Eastern's president, Malcolm MacIntyre. They met several times, but negotiations ended when MacIntyre sadly informed Tillinghast that Eastern was going to merge with American—a marriage, incidentally, that never took place.

One day Tillinghast ran into Trippe, who apparently couldn't have encountered a TWA baggage handler without singing his Chosen Instrument aria. Over an impromptu drink, Trippe voiced his opinion that while TWA was doing fine domestically (which it wasn't), it was hurting internationally (which it wasn't), so why not turn over the overseas routes to Pan Am? In exchange for those routes, TWA would get all the stock Pan Am held in National Airlines—400,000 shares plus an option for another 250,000 shares, which if exercised would give TWA control of the Miami-based carrier. If Tillinghast didn't read between the lines, it looked like an attractive deal; those 650,000 shares added up to a TWA-National merger, and National had some excellent routes including New York–Miami.

Fortunately, Tillinghast was capable of reading between the lines. Pan Am had acquired its National stock in exchange for leasing National two 707s for the 1958-59 winter season, thus enabling tiny National and its wheeling-and-dealing president, George Baker, to claim the honor of introducing domestic jet service. Baker, who had ordered DC-8s that wouldn't be delivered until late 1959, wanted to beat Eastern with the first New York–Florida jet service and had offered Trippe the stock along with a modest lease fee.

"National's stock will strengthen you domestically and you can get out of this international mess," Trippe argued.

Tillinghast said that he didn't want to be suckered as Baker had suckered Trippe. The 707 lease agreement with National was the worst deal Juan Trippe ever made; he was so anxious to get his hands on National's domestic routes that he apparently refused to consider the chance that the CAB would never allow one airline to acquire control of another without formal hearings. Tillinghast recognized this possibility would exist for TWA as well as Pan Am; without CAB approval, the National stock was virtually worthless to Pan Am as a means of acquiring routes and would be equally worthless to TWA if the CAB decided it amounted to illegal acquisition of control.

"The CAB would approve TWA's acquiring the stock," Trippe predicted confidently. "They're mad at me and they're pressuring me to get rid of it."

But Tillinghast smelled trouble and, as it turned out, the CAB subsequently did force Pan Am to divest itself of National's shares. Whether the Board would have ruled likewise in TWA's case will never be known, for Tillinghast did not accept Trippe's initial proposal.

"It would not be to our advantage," he told Trippe politely. "I think the only thing we could possibly discuss with Pan Am is a complete merger."

There followed a number of negotiating conferences, described wryly by Tillinghast as having the atmosphere "of an Armenian rug merchant trading session." Trippe, as secretive and difficult in his own way as Hughes, refused to meet with Tillinghast in either of their respective offices, which he considered too public. Where they usually convened was the coffee shop in the old Commodore Hotel, not far from the Pan Am Building. Tillinghast would be getting ready to leave home for work in the morning and Trippe would phone him. "Charlie, I'd like to see you for a few minutes. Could you stop and have a cup of coffee on your way to the office?"

Out of this coffee shop haggling, which went on for the rest of 1961 and through most of 1962, came a tentative merger agreement subject to stockholder approval and the blessing of the Civil Aeronautics Board. A formal merger petition was filed with the CAB December 21, 1962, but Tillinghast was already having second thoughts. He knew TWA's future looked brighter, despite 1962 losses of $5.7 million. The deficit stemmed from reverses in the first half of the year; TWA netted more than $6.7 million in the last two quarters, a remarkable turnaround reflecting the airline's down-the-line improvement—on-time performance, for example, was the best in the industry, thanks in no small part to Ray Dunn's superb operation. Dunn was rising fast in Charlie Tillinghast's estimation. One of his most impressive achievements had been a constantly moving production line for piston engine overhauls, similar to an automobile assembly line. It wasn't adaptable to the turbine engine, but as long as TWA flew pistons Dunn's procedure saved thousands of dollars and hundreds of hours.

Shortly after Tillinghast arrived, Dunn invited some three hundred of the airline's vendors and suppliers to a symposium in Kansas City. He dubbed it "The Price is Right"; it ran all day, and was followed by a dinner that evening. During the working session, Dunn pulled one of the smartest and most effective stunts ever staged at an airline technical meeting. He had women bring to the platform various parts that TWA was buying for its aircraft. Each component carried the price TWA was being charged. Next to every component was an identical part Dunn had purchased from regular retail sources, such as Sears. He held up a 707 toilet seat for which Boeing was charging the airline $120. Then he held up an identical seat he bought from Sears—for $3. By the time he finished, he had the vendors squirming. They saw an electric razor plug for which TWA was paying $278; Dunn showed them the same plug he had bought in a hardware store for eighteen cents. He told how he had asked one supplier for a manual TWA needed to repair an air-conditioning unit. No manual was necessary, he was informed, because the unit was so simple.

"I took the thing apart myself," Dunn related. "The damned thing had a hundred and nineteen separate parts. Some of you guys won't sell us individual component replacements—we have to buy a whole new unit. Here's a small timing motor, gentlemen. It cost us two hundred and thirty dollars and all it needed was a part worth not more than ten bucks."

The result of the "Price is Right" meeting: supplier prices came down to a more realistic level. Ray Dunn, says Al Jordan—Dunn's own protege—was "a stickler who could drive you up a wall. He got his best ideas when he was shaving. Compassionate and fair, but a tough taskmaster. He had a penchant for getting his staff out on his patio on a nice Saturday afternoon, talking business, when you'd rather be home with your family. But everyone loved him."

Dunn was one of the "professionals" Tillinghast was talking about. So was Bob Buck. He got the assignment to flight-test the new Doppler navigation system on TWA's overseas jets. Doppler was a form of radar, a fully automated means of overwater navigation more precise than any human calculations could provide. Its development enabled TWA to eliminate navigators from the international crews, all of them getting severance pay that was amortized over a few years of Doppler operations. Another crew complement change was made in 1962 when TWA helped settle a bitter feud between pilots and flight engineers—a jet-age controversy.

ALPA had insisted that the complex, unforgiving jets required the third cockpit crew member to be pilot-trained; a flight engineer, it argued, really didn't have much to do in a jet except watch the instruments and help hostesses fix something in the cabin. The Flight Engineers International Association claimed that any large airplane needed the services of a "Mr. Fixit"—a kind of super-mechanic who knew the jet's systems to a degree no pilot would.

It was an extremely touchy situation for all airlines. They realized that ALPA was trying to become the bargaining agent for all flight crew members. Yet they also conceded ALPA was right. The flight engineer's role, so vital in the piston era, had diminished with the jets even as the need for a third pilot increased. At the same time, no carrier wanted to fire loyal and skilled flight engineers.

The first solution came from TWA, American, Eastern and Pan Am. They all signed contracts agreeing to operate their 707s and DC-8s with *four*-man crews: three pilots and a flight engineer. The compromise, at best, was temporizing and at worst uneconomic—"featherbirding" the FAA itself called it. The fat went into the fire when United refused to go along with the other big carriers, and the ALPA-FEIA dispute wound up in the hands of the National Mediation Board, which ignited dynamite. It ruled that all crew members in a jet cockpit should be represented by a single collective bargaining unit, a body blow to the small flight engineers union that stood no chance of winning any representation contest with ALPA.

Infuriated, the flight engineers struck TWA and seven other carriers in February of 1961. With virtually the entire air transportation system facing chaos, newly elected President Kennedy appointed a special fact-finding commission to investigate the dispute, a move that ended the short-lived strike. Headed by Wisconsin professor Nathan Feinsinger, the commission months later ended the controversy for good. It recommended that jets be manned by three men, that the third man be pilot-qualified, and that flight engineers either be given pilot-training or, if they preferred to resign, be awarded liberal severance pay.

It was a decision that pleased TWA, which already had reached a similar agreement with its flight engineers prior to the Feinsinger Commission's announcement, and may well have influenced its findings. Thus ended a dispute that had plagued Tillinghast almost from the day he took office. It was no wonder that Breech at first felt guilty about getting him into a constant can of worms.

"It was kind of a dirty trick," Ernie confessed to Jerry Hannifin of *Time*, "taking him out of Bendix where he was doing well and putting him in a business he knew nothing about."

But Charles Carpenter Tillinghast, Jr. thrived on both challenge and controversy. Long before he learned about flight engineers, in-flight movies, executive loyalties, 880 engine problems, equipment needs and 707 contracts, he had taken TWA into multimillion-dollar litigation against the airline's one-time master: Howard Hughes.

18

All the King's Lawyers
and All the King's Men

It was inevitable that Tillinghast and Breech were exposed to stories about life with Howard. Every officer had them, even Vic Leslie. He was discussing Hughes' *modus operandi* with Tillinghast one day and mentioned an incident that occurred during the Burgess regime. Carter had been president for several months and hadn't met or talked to Hughes yet. Leslie happened to be in Europe discussing the Viscount with Vickers and Hughes was on the phone to him daily.

On one call, Hughes suddenly changed the subject from airplanes to presidents. "By the way, how's this fellow Burgess doing?"

"I think he's doing fine," Leslie assured him. "He's a great addition to the company and you know, it would be nice if you'd call him and tell him."

"Tell him what?"

"That you've heard he's doing a good job and that you appreciate it."

"I'll do it," Hughes promised.

How soon he did it, or whether he did it at all on Leslie's advice, isn't known nor it is important except that it was part of an unpleasant mosaic forming in Tillinghast's mind and Breech's too—rightly or wrongly, a portrait of an eccentric egomaniac who had no business dictating his whims to an airline, even his own.

Stories like Leslie's were relatively mild. Al Jordan had a worse one involving the problems of overhauling the engines on the first 707s. Hughes wouldn't let TWA build and equip its own overhaul shop; he gave no reason for the refusal—it may have been that he was simply strapped for cash or was just being ornery—but it made no sense. The alternative was to contract with Pratt & Whitney to do the overhauls in its Connecticut factory.

"They knew how to build engines, but they didn't know how to overhaul them," Jordan says. "This went on for quite a while and it cost us a fortune. We were getting parts we didn't need and the labor hours were out of control. We kept preparing proposals for Hughes, begging him to let us install our own overhaul facilities. Every proposition we made had to be approved by Hughes. We'd prepare one and send it out to Los Angeles and, believe it or not, every revision on our plan would go on a string up to a second-floor window at 7000 Romaine. He'd sent it back, usually with the message 'too many words—put it on one sheet of paper.' We finally convinced him, through some devious means, that we had to overhaul our own engines to

267

save money and get a better product, but it took at least a year to get it through his head."

Tillinghast listened to tales like that and knew they weren't fiction. They came from men like Bob Buck, for example, who sympathized with the new president because he knew what Thomas and Burgess had gone through. He told Tillinghast: "We had contracted for all these jets with no provisions for overhauling them, for spares, ground support equipment, fuel contracts—there were major decisions to be made and Hughes wasn't around to make them. Carter and Charlie really suffered with that damned Hughes. They were presidents of TWA and they couldn't even get him on the phone."

It began to dawn on both Tillinghast and Breech, as they surveyed the airline's sad state, that a legal case might be made of Hughes' actions. At the very board meeting that formally elected Tillinghast president, the directors authorized an independent study of possible legal claims against Hughes. The study was put into the hands of Cahill, Gordon, Reindel & Ohl, a prestigious law firm, which two months later informed Tillinghast there seemed to be a basis for an antitrust suit.

Tillinghast, a lawyer himself, wasn't sure. Cahill, Gordon based its conclusion on the possibility that Hughes may have violated the antitrust laws by forcing TWA to buy all its equipment from Toolco. Tillinghast considered this "interesting and novel" (and, he insisted later, sound) but he still hestitated. He was busy trying to get the airline straightened out and it seemed foolish to get it involved in bloody and lengthy litigation; the voting trust was TWA's fortress against any Hughes intrusion for the next ten years.

But it was Howard himself who precipitated the opening barrage of a legal battle. The minute he heard that TWA had ordered twenty-six more Boeings, to be financed through a $90 million loan arranged by Equitable, Metropolitan and Prudential, he challenged the right of TWA's board to authorize the deal. He was angry for two reasons: first, he had assumed the voting trust would at least discuss future aircraft purchases with him since he technically still owned 78 percent of the airline's stock; and second, he didn't like a covenant in the insurance companies' new loan that demanded immediate payment if the voting trust were to be terminated. Hughes interpreted this as one more attempt to prevent him from regaining control before the trust expired.

And Hughes was giving every sign of staging a counterattack within the trust's ten-year life span. Toolco's profits had begun to climb once more and the Dillon, Read plan had reimbursed Hughes for what he already had spent on TWA's jets. He was solvent again, he wanted his airline back, and he had different ideas as to what additional jets TWA needed. Hughes wanted TWA to accept those eight additional 880s and thirteen Convair 990s he already had ordered and when Ray Holliday expressed doubts that the airline would ever take delivery on them, Hughes said that was his worry. "Most likely the Hughes Tool Company will control TWA when the matter comes up," he added tartly.

He was confident of that, too. TWA was a long way from getting out of the woods although this was hardly the fault of Tillinghast and the new directors—they hadn't been around long enough to execute reforms. But their very newness worked against them and for Hughes; it diminished employee confidence and made the entire management corps jittery. It was one thing to be loyal to Tillinghast, but suppose Hughes did regain control and took revenge on those who supported the new administration? When Burgess and Tillinghast talked about some officers having more loyalty toward Howard than the airline, it should be remembered the officers were walking a thin tightrope. Vic Leslie once remarked that it was like being the ham in the middle of two slices of bread: no matter what happened, you were going to be bitten.

At this point, a Cahill, Gordon attorney named John Sonnett recommended to TWA that TWA sue Hughes on antitrust grounds—a strategy designed mainly by Sonnett himself who had once been with the Justice Department's antitrust division. And even as Sonnett entered the unfolding drama as a principal character, so did another lawyer—tough, relentless and frequently abrasive Chester Davis, hired by Hughes to represent him in his fight to regain control. Davis's first move was to carry an olive branch into TWA's executive stronghold. He was an unlikely bearer; Floyd Hall once described him as "one of the most obnoxious men I've ever seen."

In a preliminary meeting with Tillinghast, he expounded on the virtues of the Convair 990—far superior to the new Boeing fan-jets TWA had ordered, he insisted. Tillinghast wasn't impressed and neither was anyone else he consulted on the subject. As it turned out, the 990 would have been a disaster for TWA. American was the only U.S. carrier to order it and it was the worst equipment decision American ever made. The jet fell woefully short of its promised performance and proved even more expensive to operate than the 880. Tillinghast, supported by TWA's entire engineering corps, told Davis that he wasn't interested in the plane. Davis then held out the olive branch.

If TWA would agree to dissolve the voting trust, he promised, Hughes would be willing to invest $100 million in the airline. Davis also proposed that if TWA accepted the thirteen Convair 990s, Toolco would buy an additional $11.2 million in TWA subordinated debentures. And finally, the lawyer revealed that Hughes was willing to sell TWA every one of those eight 880s and thirteen 990s *at cost*.

Tillinghast said he wasn't interested. To him, the olive branch was covered with hidden thorns; the whole package Davis had offered appeared to be nothing but a scheme to put Hughes back in control of the airline. Then in June of 1961, TWA public relations vice-president Gordon Gilmore received a tip that Hughes was preparing to file a lawsuit against the airline and its lenders, charging that the voting trust represented illegal seizure of the Hughes stock. Gilmore immediately relayed the report to Tillinghast; Gordon may or may not have been totally loyal to Burgess, but by now he was firmly on the side of the new management.

On June 29, the board's executive committee unanimously authorized Tillinghast to take legal action against Toolco, Howard Hughes and Raymond Holliday, following Sonnett's antitrust strategy.

The battle had been joined.

There was one final attempt at mutual conciliation. No one was more against litigation than Hughes' personal lawyer, Greg Bautzer. Even before TWA filed suit, Bautzer had flown to New York and talked frankly to

Breech and Olds, urging peaceful settlement of all differences. Bautzer did not come strictly on his own; he had Howard's blessings on that trip, and the lawyer knew why—a court fight would strike at Hughes' greatest weakness: his obsession for privacy.

When the suit actually was filed, Bautzer's need to protect his client from the spotlight's glare became even more urgent. Sonnett's initial moves were aimed at forcing Hughes to testify in person against TWA's charges. He not only demanded that Howard be the first witness, but made no secret of his intention to keep Hughes on the stand for up to six months. It was a horrifying prospect for a man who was not only ailing, but had withdrawn even further into his impenetrable shell; he had always cherished his privacy, but at this stage of his life, Hughes would have made a hermit seem gregarious.

He thus empowered Bautzer to offer what seemed to be a reasonable and generous compromise: call off the suit, and Hughes would put another $150 million into the airline through the purchase of additional stock and subordinated debentures, and promise to leave the voting trust stand over the established ten-year period, which added up to a pledge not to interfere with the airline's management as long as the trust existed.

Hughes asked only one thing in return for these major concessions. He wanted TWA to use about $63 million of the $150 million fresh investment to take those 990s off his hands. This would still leave the airline enough cash to buy additional aircraft if necessary.

Tillinghast and the TWA directors were tempted. The lawsuit claimed $115 million in damages; the proposed settlement would give the airline $35 million more that what it could collect from a successful legal action—actually more than $35 million because the court fight would be expensive.

But there were arguments against accepting Hughes' offer. First, the fact that an offer was made at all indicated that Hughes was afraid of fighting it out in court. Second, no one really trusted Howard. If he had an obsession for privacy, he also had one directed toward TWA, his proudest possession. It was hard to believe his promise to keep hands off the airline for the next nine and a half years.

In the end, the directors voted to make a counter-offer. They accepted the terms of the proposed agreement in every respect but one—instead of dropping the lawsuit entirely, they would keep it in limbo for the rest of the voting trust's life. Legally, this would be done by Hughes signing a consent decree, a kind of armistice in which Hughes would not plead guilty to TWA's charges, but would agree to refrain from his alleged illegalities while the consent decree was in effect. Such a decree would keep the TWA lawsuit inactive unless Hughes violated his promise not to interfere.

The peace plan collapsed over that one provision. Hughes was unwilling to leave a sword hanging over his head in the form of that consent decree. He felt that TWA, at any time, could reinstate legal action if he so much as innocently inquired about a management decision. He was still the majority stockholder, he had an abiding interest in the airline's welfare, and yet he was being told that even by exercising that interest he could expose himself to the lawsuit's revival.

The TWA suit became official August 1, 1961, in the U.S. District Court for the Southern District of New York, thus launching a war that was to last for years.

In one corner was TWA, charging that Hughes and his corporate alter ego, Toolco, had seriously harmed its ability to compete in the early years of the jet age by monopolizing control over purchasing and financing of jet aircraft. The airline claimed it could have bought and financed its own jets at a time when financing interest was as low as 4½ percent; it wound up paying at least six percent because of the Hughes-dictated delays. TWA accused Hughes of preventing it from obtaining the number of jets it needed, citing such instances as cutting the 880 order from thirty to twenty and diverting six of TWA's intial 707s to arch-rival Pan Am. Finally, the suit mentioned constant interference by Hughes with the airline's management, not only before the voting trust agreement, but after it was established.

In the other corner was Howard Hughes with a pretty good case of his own. How could a man owning 78 percent of an airline be accused of unfairly monopolizing it? What legal justification was there for forcing a man to surrender control temporarily over his own company, and then conspire to prevent him from ever regaining control? The latter was a touchy issue, for when the details of the proposed TWA-Pan Am merger were made public, unwrapped for all to see was Juan Trippe's plan to get rid of Hughes once and for all.

Trippe wanted to avoid any share-for-share swap in which Hughes would wind up owning up to 35 percent of the merged airline. His idea, which Tillinghast reluctantly accepted, was to establish Pan Am as a holding company controlling most of the shares of a separate company—namely, the new airline. Pan Am's stockholders would own shares of the holding company, but not the airline. The bottom line was that Trippe, as chief executive of both the holding company and the airline, would be able to outvote Hughes.

Tillinghast had agreed to this devious end run only because he feared TWA, at the time, was about to go bankrupt. And Hughes seemingly had every right to consider the Trippe strategy as an underhanded way of robbing him of TWA while the voting trust controlled his stock. The ramifications of the Pan Am-TWA merger deal became public after the Hughes-TWA litigation was well underway, and go far to explain why Hughes was so determined to end a voting trust he had agreed to under duress and which now threatened to take TWA away from him altogether. Even the TWA lawsuit bore out those fears—it asked not only for damages but demanded that Hughes sell all his TWA stock. It was obvious that the airline's new management wanted an end to the one-man control that had taken TWA from one crisis to another. It also was obvious that Hughes considered TWA *his* property, one he was trying to save either from cold-blooded lenders or death in the form of that Pan Am merger.

The tide of legal battle kept shifting; it was, for all the world, like a wrestling match in which one opponent seemed to have the other hopelessly pinned, only to have him squirm out of danger and apply his own crippling hold. Yet what was going on outside the ring also was affecting the course of events in the court struggle.

Late in 1961, the CAB was faced with the prospect of Northeast Airlines going under unless Hughes saved it by acquiring control. With his TWA stock still held by the voting trust, this would be legal except that Hughes refused to come to Northeast's rescue unless the CAB came to his. He'd pay off Northeast's debts if the CAB would then let him buy off the loans that had put the hated voting trust into existence. This would mean Hughes would control two airlines—forbidden under the law—so Hughes would simpy merge TWA and Northeast. This was his master plan, and under the pressure of Northeast's impending demise, the Board agreed to let Hughes provide financial assistance even though it knew that having gone this far, it couldn't prevent him from actually acquiring control anytime he wanted to. He had saved the damsel from a cruel landlord and it wouldn't do to prevent the hero from marrying her. Only a year earlier the CAB had so sharply criticized Hughes for letting TWA get into such precarious shape, that its statement was part of TWA's lawsuit as evidence of his harmful influence. Hughes' strategy, while only partially successful, was working; the CAB would have to let him acquire Northwest, thus negating its previous criticism; if he was fit to control one carrier he had to be fit to control another.

About a month after the CAB let Howard into the Northeast chicken coop, District Judge Charles M. Metzner began hearing the first of the sworn testimony in the case of TWA-vs-Howard Hughes. Chester Davis already had won the first skirmish when Metzner agreed to let him question his witnesses first; Sonnett wanted to get Hughes on the stand immediately, and it became clear right from the start that Davis was ready to keep Hughes off the stand indefinitely. Thus, the first witness, on January 5, 1962, was Charles Tillinghast.

Davis had announced his intentions of questioning four TWA executives, starting with Tillinghast, over a four-day period. At the end of four days, Tillinghast was still testifying. In fact, he was to be on the witness stand off and on for a total of forty days that added up to some 180 hours of ruthless interrogation. The transcript of his testimony covered more than 6,000 pages. How he ran TWA during this period—from January 5 to June 30—remains one of the most remarkable jobs of corporate management under stress in the history of American industry.

He managed to establish some kind of schedule; there were no hearings on Mondays and Fridays, so he could put in a full day's work at TWA. Usually, the hearings were held Tuesday, Wednesday and Thursday. On those days, he would come to his office early, attend the hearings from about 9:30 A.M. to 3:30 P.M., and then go back to work at TWA until six or seven. Many nights he would have to take work home and he saw as much of John Sonnett as he did his wife—they lunched together almost daily.

Being questioned by Chester Davis was an ordeal in itself. "Chester," Charlie recollects with typical Tillinghast understatement, "did not evoke warm feelings in a person." They clashed frequently and heatedly, for Tillinghast had a sharp tongue and Davis could be insultingly sarcastic and exasperatingly obtuse in his questions. He was capable of convoluting sentences so badly that no one in the room could quite understand his point. And in back of everyone's mind, Tillinghast and Sonnett in particular, was the knowledge that every day Davis kept the TWA president on the stand was another day of delay in warding off Hughes' appearance. The long, involved questioning became so drawn out that Judge Metzner—at Sonnett's suggestion—finally appointed a special master to take testimony so the judge could concentrate on other cases. The special master was James

Lee Rankin, former Solicitor General of the United States under the Eisenhower administration. His selection required a month's recess, during which time it was possible for him to appraise the course of the battle thus far.

The general feeling was that Tillinghast had proved to be an effective, forceful witness, but not entirely a persuasive one. His vulnerability was identical to that of Sonnett's whole case—it was extremely difficult to cite chapter and verse of how Hughes had damaged the airline, and how that damage supported an antitrust conclusion. In terms of dollars-and-cents amounts, of specific time lost with statistical evidence of reduced traffic and revenues, Tillinghast could offer no real proof during the first few days of his testimony.

And when Rankin took over, it became quickly apparent that Davis had used the one-month recess wisely. Rankin first ruled that the Hughes lawyer could question Tillinghast as long as was necessary. Then Davis broke the news that he had filed, in behalf of Hughes, a counter-suit against TWA's lenders and individuals representing both the airline and the lending institutions.

In one respect, the Hughes suit followed the line of defense Davis had established from the day Sonnett first fired his antitrust charges—namely, that the antitrust laws hadn't been violated because Toolco didn't fit Sonnett's definition of it as a company engaged in the development, manufacture and lease of aircraft used in interstate and foreign commerce; that the Civil Aeronautics Board, not a U.S. District Court, had exclusive jurisdiction over issues involving control and management; that the same CAB had approved Toolco's control of TWA, thus immunizing Toolco from antitrust prosecution; and that Toolco's efforts to overthrow the voting trust represented perfectly legal efforts to protect Toolco's interests.

Defense against the antitrust charges constituted only the first part of Davis' 68-page counter-suit. The second part sent eyebrows soaring. First, it sued institutions and individuals not only on behalf of Toolco but TWA itself, thus putting the airline into the novel position of being the plaintiff in two opposing lawsuits. The counter-suit named as defendants the Metropolitan and Equitable insurance companies, Irving Trust and Dillon, Read—the four financial groups that had forced Hughes into the voting trust arrangement—and five individuals: president James Oates of Equitable, vice-chairman Harry Hagerty of Metropolitan, senior vice-president Ben-Fleming Sessel of Irving Trust, Breech and Tillinghast. They all were guilty, Davis charged, of damaging TWA—which, in itself, was a surprising admission, one that conceded the airline *had* been hurt.

But not by Hughes or Toolco, Davis claimed. No, the damage was done by TWA's new management (Tillinghast and Breech) and the lenders. He not only agreed with Sonnett that TWA had suffered, but said the suffering was even worse than Sonnett claimed. Whereas the TWA suit against Hughes called for $115 million in damages, the Davis counter-suit demanded $135 million for the airline and another $308 million for Hughes and Toolco.

The audacity of Hughes' lawyer surprised even those who knew Chester Davis. He accused his opponents of being the ones who violated the antitrust laws, conspiring to restrain interstate commerce by forcing TWA to obtain loans only from the named defendants, and forcing Hughes to sur-render control of the airline by denying him access to other lenders. Estab-lishment of the voting trust, Davis continued, was not only part of the antitrust conspiracy, but also violated the Federal Aviation Act of 1958, which made it illegal for any individual or firm already engaged in any phase of aeronautics to obtain control of an airline without CAB approval; Equita-ble and Metropolitan, the counter-suit argued, had loaned other airlines millions of dollars and thus, through the voting trust, had acquired control of TWA illegally.

Finally, Davis made the astounding claim that TWA's jet delivery delays, the higher interest rates it wound up paying and the inadequacy of its jet fleet all were the fault of the lenders and the present airline management. Except for the voting trust conspiracy, the counter-suit charged, TWA would have received its Boeings and Convairs on schedule.

Sonnett thought the counter-suit was a phony, an opinion shared not only by all of his colleagues in the case, but also by a large portion of the fasci-nated legal profession following the duel. The general feeling was that it was not a legitimate counter-suit; it named as defendants the lenders who hadn't sued Hughes at all, and it didn't name TWA, which had. Furthermore, its attempt to tag Hughes' opponents as the antitrust villains was almost univer-sally regarded as extremely weak—far weaker than the case Sonnett was trying to make.

But if the counter-suit wasn't legitimate, what was it? Sonnett and his fellow lawyers knew. A rather capricious yet clever smokescreen behind which Davis could hide his real intent: to delay, delay and delay. To keep Hughes from having to testify long enough for him to win the battle he was waging on another front—at the CAB. All of Davis' brilliant legal maneu-vering, it must be emphasized, was predicated on his argument that only the Civil Aeronautics Board had jurisdiction over who should control TWA. He had hung his hat on that hook and every ploy he pulled, every delaying tactic he dreamed up, was aimed at letting the CAB decide the case, not any court.

The next round of legal brawl centered around Sonnett's dogged efforts to overthrow special master Rankin's decision that gave Davis first crack at the witnesses and no time limit on his questioning. What Sonnett feared most of all was that Davis would demand the same right for interrogating witnesses called to testify on the counter-suit—at the rate Davis was questioning Tillinghast, TWA's turn to ask questions might never come.

On March 5, Judge Metzner gave Sonnett a partial victory by ruling that while Davis could continue to question the witnesses he had scheduled, their evidence had to be limited to TWA's charges against Hughes and not the counter-suit. But Davis was not easily thwarted. He kept Tillinghast on the stand day after day, often with repetitious questions, and simultaneously extended his delaying tactics to another area.

Both sides had agreed to exchange documents that might be relevant to the case—tax statements, correspondence, inter-office communications, even personal diaries and notebooks. TWA turned its files over promptly. Davis kept stalling and delay wasn't the only motivation. The secretive Hughes wanted no exposure of what he always kept confidential, however legitimate and aboveboard his dealings might have been. But not even Chester Davis could hold out forever. Metzner finally gave him an irrevocable deadline for letting TWA examine the files it was demanding.

The exchange and examination consumed more time—TWA alone turned over a million pieces of paper—but Sonnett, too, was conducting a war on more than one front. On April 18, he filed a second suit against the same defendants—Hughes, Toolco and Raymond Holliday—in the Court of Chancery in Wilmington, Delaware, the state where both TWA and Toolco were incorporated. This latest action did not charge violation of the antitrust laws, but instead accused Hughes of mismanagement and breach of fiduciary responsibility. It was just one of the legal fireworks that continued to explode as TWA-vs-Hughes plodded on.

Hughes scored a victory on June 19 when the CAB approved, by a four-to-one margin, his acquisition of control of Northeast. But Sonnett continued to aim his shells in the direction of Howard himself, trying one legal maneuver after another to force his appearance. Sonnett was convinced of two things: if he got Hughes on the witness stand, he could tear him apart, and if Hughes refused to appear, he could lose the whole ballgame by default.

It had become apparent to Sonnett that his antitrust strategy was risky. Tillinghast's testimony had fallen short of proving the antitrust allegations. At one point, Tillinghast had even conceded that not buying the Electras Hughes wanted may not have been a wise decision. Sonnett knew that Davis would be questioning TWA officers like Leslie and Rummel, both of whom might testify adversely against TWA—the former out of resentment toward Tillinghast and the latter because he had been close to Hughes.

Slowly but relentlessly, Sonnett began backing Chester Davis into a corner from which there was no escape. Both the special master and the judge gave Davis plenty of leeway, extending one deadline after another for Hughes' appearance. Rankin was particularly tolerant and more than once ruled in Davis' favor and against Sonnett. But even ths special master became impatient over Davis' persistent and obvious delaying efforts. As 1962 drew to a close, the court had ordered that Hughes appear on February 11 and Rankin bluntly told Davis, "I don't want to leave any doubt in your mind or anybody else's—I expect to proceed with Mr. Hughes on February 11."

The year's final witnesses were Oz Cocke, Vic Leslie and Bob Rummel. Under Davis' skillful verbal manipulation (he asked only the questions whose answers would help Hughes and hurt TWA), all three generally refused Sonnett's antitrust claims. In some respects, however, their testimony was misleading in that it was incomplete. For example, Leslie was never asked about a 1960 document he had written blaming TWA's financial condition entirely on Hughes. Rummel's evidence was decidedly pro-Hughes—as far as Davis allowed it to go. He brought out that Hughes didn't have the complete control over TWA's aircraft purchases that the lawsuit alleged. Hughes preferred twin-engine Convairs, not Martins. Hughes would have switched to the DC-6 instead of buying more Connies, but Damon prevailed. Hughes had wanted to buy both the Viscount and Britannia, Rummel pointed out, but was talked out of it by TWA's management.

Cross-examination wasn't allowed in these deposition hearings so Sonnett had no chance to ask Rummel about aircraft that Hughes *had* forced down the airline's throat, such as the 1649.

With the start of the new year—a time when the idea of a Pan Am-TWA merger was still very much alive—Davis kept up his efforts to keep Howard Hughes away from John Sonnett. He tried one legal twist and turn after another in a series of masterful and occasionally ingenious diversions. His chief argument was that TWA should be required to produce certain facts before Hughes appeared; Sonnett retorted that 75 percent of TWA's evidence would come out of Howard Hughes' own mouth.

Desperately, Davis asked Judge Metzner to allow TWA's questions to be submitted to Hughes in writing so they could be answered in the same way. Metzner refused. The legal skirmishing was in full swing when the United States suddenly gave Davis what appeared to be an unexpected reprieve. In a separate case unconnected to the TWA-Hughes litigation, the Court ruled that Congress had given the CAB the right to grant the airlines and their owners immunity from the antitrust laws if such immunity was in the public interest.

The opinion, handed down January 14, 1963, was exactly what Davis had been arguing. Now, pressed by Metzner to produce Hughes on February 14, Davis instead moved to dismiss TWA's case entirely or surrender jurisdiction to the Civil Aeronautics Board.

At this point, Davis was juggling two sticks of dynamite: Howard's appearance and a TWA demand that Toolco turn over certain tax records that Sonnett believed would prove that Hughes manipulated the airline for personal tax gains. Davis had repeatedly refused to produce either Hughes or the tax documents, and either refusal could lead to a default judgment. The Supreme Court decision had given him a hoped-for out via the granting of his dismissal motion, but Metzner would not be budged.

The judge ordered the tax records to be delivered to TWA by January 22 and he refused to let Hughes be questioned in writing. Davis appealed that ruling to the Court of Appeals and was turned down. Rankin warned him he stood a good chance of being found in contempt if the tax documents and some additional tax papers were not produced, but Davis was harder to pin down than mercury—and at least escaped a contempt citation largely because neither Rankin nor Metzner appeared willing to lower the boom without giving Davis every chance due him under the law.

He grabbed at every chance, relying mostly on the Supreme Court decision and even filing a complaint with the CAB against the same defendants named in the Toolco counter-suit plus Juan Trippe and Pan Am. Having opened up this latest can of worms, he went back to Metzner and argued once more than Hughes should not be forced to testify until the CAB investigated and ruled on his complaint. Metzner wouldn't buy it. There followed several more days of intense activity both public and private, the latter involving conferences between Hughes and his lawyers, at least one of whom (Bautzer) was advising him to appear. At least he didn't have to go to New York—Sonnett had agreed to let him testify in the Los Angeles Federal Courthouse.

Metzner's final order was that Hughes appear in person at 10 A.M., February 11, Los Angeles time. At that precise hour, a court clerk called out, "Is Howard R. Hughes present?"

There was no answer. The clerk repeated the question three times. The only sound was the ticking of the courtroom clock.

Howard Hughes had defaulted.

Why? It is a question that remains unanswered. There probably was no single reason. One theory is that he didn't expect to be fined an exorbitant amount and preferred to swallow a little medicine rather than appear in public. Certainly seclusion was an all-important factor—reportedly emaciated, almost totally deaf (an earphone was in the Los Angeles courtroom for his use) and in poor health, there is no doubt he did not want people to see him. His deteriorating physical appearance had increased his phobia of public contact.

Whatever the reason or reasons, he deliberately blew a case he might have won; proving those antitrust charges was at best a fifty-fifty shot. For the next two and a half months, the lawyers argued over the consequences of his default—how much he should be forced to pay, if anything. Sonnett had upped his own ante. He took the damage figure mentioned in the Toolco counter-suit and added a demand for another $10 million for damage incurred after the voting trust was established.

On May 3, Metzner found Hughes in "deliberate and wilful" default and tentatively imposed the maximum penalty: $145 million, subject to review. At the same time, he dismissed the Toolco counter-suit with prejudice—which meant it couldn't be re-filed. Davis began the laborious appeals process, first taking his plea to the U.S. Court of Appeals, which upheld Metzner. But only five weeks after this defeat, Davis scored an incredible victory at the CAB. The Board approved his motion to return control of TWA to Hughes. It was an action taken without any hearings or investigation, the CAB ruling that it wasn't necessary to investigate an ownership it already had approved. The only stipulation was that if Hughes wanted to reacquire TWA, he had to sell Northeast: no one man could own two airlines.

Sonnett immediately asked the Court of Appeals to review the CAB's decision and the case was put down for argument during the September 1964 term. Not only did this prevent Hughes from immediately regaining control of TWA, but he was not out of the woods yet at the CAB. It was one thing for the board to tell him to get rid of Northeast first; it was another to find a buyer for this very sick airline.

Ray Cook, who had gotten back in Howard's good graces by aiding Davis during the antitrust litigation, came up with an intriguing plan: put Hughes' 55 percent stock interest in Northeast into the hands of a trustee, with complete authority to dispose of Northeast any way the trustee wanted. Cook's nomination for the trustee was one of the most respected men in aviation: former CAB chairman Louis Hector. When Hector accepted, Hughes asked the CAB to approve the arrangement.

But before the CAB could act, the Court of Appeals ordered the Board to hold full evidentiary hearings on whether return of TWA to Hughes was in the public interest. The still-existing default judgment, the court noted, raised serious questions that the CAB had ignored.

Hughes suffered another defeat when the Supreme Court first agreed to review Metzner's findings and then changed its mind and decided to let the default judgment, plus dismissal of the counter-suit, stand. Not even the unexpected purchase of Northeast by the Storer Broadcasting Company, a deal arranged by Hector, could help him; the CAB still had to hold a public hearing on his resuming control of TWA. That Court of Appeals ruling had been upheld by the Supreme Court and it was anathema to Hughes. A public hearing meant a public appearance, for TWA was certain to insist that Hughes testify.

Reluctantly, then, Hughes abandoned his plan to get the airline back through the good offices of the Civil Aeronautics Board. All that remained was a final decision on the damages he would have to pay for defaulting, and the outlook on that score was dim, too. The damage hearings opened May 2, 1966, almost five years after the original lawsuit was filed. Sonnett didn't have to prove that antitrust violations had occurred; the default made that point moot. But he did have to show how TWA had been specifically damaged, and his chief witness was none other than Rummel.

This time it was Sonnett asking the questions, not Davis, and Rummel gave facts that Davis had deliberately avoided bringing out. The brunt of his testimony was that if TWA had received on time the sixty-three jets Toolco had ordered, the airline's financial picture would have changed drastically and for the better. Instead, by the end of 1960, after two full years of jet operations, the airline had received only twenty-eight aircraft, far short of its competitive requirements.

One might be tempted to wonder how Hughes felt about Rummel doing a 180-degree turn. It is very likely that Howard couldn't have cared less.

By the time his most trusted technical advisor started testifying that Toolco's domination of TWA's aircraft acquisitions had inflicted grievous harm on the airline, Howard Hughes no longer owned TWA.

TWA-vs-Hughes was one of the most prolonged conflicts in American legal history, and its very length had an inevitable consequence: it went on so long that the conditions under which it had been instigated changed completely.

When Tillinghast and Breech decided to recoup what they felt Hughes had cost the airline, TWA seemed about ready for the last rites. It was still in trouble during the first year of the litigation, but the turnaround had started in mid-1962 and accelerated from that point on. TWA made almost $20 million in 1963, netted $37 million the following year and showed a $50.1 million profit in 1965. The greatest irony of a period loaded with ironies was that the Tillinghast regime, castigated by Davis as bringing TWA to the brink of ruin, was making Hughes richer by the day.

TWA's stock stood at $7.50 per share through most of 1962. By 1965, it had climbed to a record high of $96.84, an incredible increase that did not go unnoticed by the man who owned more than 6.5 million shares. On May 3, 1965, with the stock standing at $86, Hughes did the one thing the voting trust could not prevent him from doing: he sold all 6,584,937 shares, netting him, after deductions for underwriters' fees, slightly over $546.5 million. He may have lost most of the battles, but in monetary terms, at least, he had won the war.

The shock waves reverberated not merely through TWA, but the entire industry. Disbelief was a common reaction and "why?" a universal question.

The simplest explanaton is that he was tired of the endlessly drawn-out court battle and saw a glittering chance to come out ahead no matter what the final outcome of the damage claims. They certainly weren't going to add up to over a half-billion dollars. He honestly had loved TWA, but it also had brought him controversy, frustration and grief; his health and mental state had faded markedly from the time he lost control of the airline.

"After that," Bob Rummel says, "he seemed to lose his marbles. Something happened to him. I had no direct contact with him after he lost the airline but the reports I heard about him were horrible. I don't think his real love was for TWA. His real love was for the dollar. But I have to add that of all the dollar opportunities he was involved in or created, TWA was the closest to his heart."

The sale of his TWA stock was not the end of the Hughes-TWA story. The damage hearings, conducted before former U.S. Attorney General Herbert Brownell, Jr., dragged on for another two years, compiling more than 70,000 pages of transcribed testimony and exhibits. Both sides produced expert witnesses who contradicted one another. It was said that they cost both TWA and Toolco a total of about $3 million in fees and, in the end, the verdict rested on which experts Brownell believed most convincing.

He believed, it turned out, TWA's. After more than five months of deliberation, Brownell issued a report upwards of 300 pages that added up to a stunning defeat for Toolco. The special master awarded TWA just under $138 million. Three months later, Judge Metzner upheld Brownell's decision.

As might be expected, Toolco appealed and TWA-vs-Hughes once more wound its weary, complicated path through the labyrinth of the nation's judicial system. Toolco, which continued to lose at every lower court stage, finally convinced the Supreme Court to hear the case. It was argued on October 10, 1972. Exactly three months later, the Surpreme Court overturned all previous findings and found Toolco not guilty of antitrust violations. It was a six-to-two opinion with Justice William Douglas speaking for the majority. Douglas agreed with Chester Davis' original contention that the CAB had immunized Hughes from the antitrust laws.

Tillinghast was disappointed, but not entirely surprised. One of TWA's board members at the time was former Supreme Court Justice Arthur Goldberg; he had warned Tillinghast, "it's a very independent bunch—you never know what's going to happen."

Ulrich Hoffmann, today TWA's vice-president of legal, was the company's assistant general counsel at the time and remembers ruefully that "everyone thought it was a piece of cake—no one expected it to be overturned.

"I thought we'd win and certainly I don't think anybody expected us to lose on the basis we did. It was a decision that could have been made ten years earlier, namely that the CAB had granted Hughes antitrust immunity. I'll always remember that the Supreme Court said in its decision TWA might have had a mismanagement suit, but not antitrust."

Sonnett wasn't around to ponder whether he had used the wrong strategy. He died of brain cancer before the case went to the Supreme Court for the second time. Tillinghast doesn't believe the Court's decision was Sonnett's fault one bit; he thinks it was largely the work of Douglas, an admitted unpredictable maverick.

"In the final analysis," Tillinghast says, "it was an oddball justice who had a love and affection for fellow oddballs, who thought it was terrible to do this to an oddball like Hughes, taking away his property."

Thus ended eleven years of litigation that cost TWA at least $10 million in legal fees alone, not to mention the loss of nearly $150 million it almost had in its pocket. For that matter, it is not quite ended. At this writing, TWA's $35 million mismanagement suit filed more than twenty years ago in Delaware is still pending; it would have been resolved long ago, but disposition was held up by the estate proceedings that followed Hughes' death in 1976.

There may never be another case like TWA-vs-Hughes simply because there may never be another man like Howard. In the end, he was the most tragic figure. He won the war, but lost his airline, defeated by the man who taught Hughes TWA could exist and prosper without his one-man rule.

During the early stages of the litigation, when Davis was asking Tillinghast the same question in fifty different variations, Sonnett pleaded with him to hurry up. "Let him go back and run the airline!" he finally shouted in total desperation.

Which is what Tillinghast did—running an airline that, for all the world, was like a child being buffeted between two divorcing parents, never quite sure which to obey, love or believe. Even in normal times, an airline's daily existence is composed of one minor crisis after another. Under Tillinghast, TWA also had to contend with major crises, one right after the other—from the morale-draining merger with Pan Am to the aftermath of another mid-air collision, from the gigantic problems of jet age expansion to the loss of the airline's most able young executive.

Out of all this adversity, trauma and tension, Charles Tillinghast and his team—from ship cleaners to senior vice-presidents—rebuilt Trans World Airlines.

19

Life After Howard

There were times when Charlie Tillinghast must have wondered if his career at TWA was to be forever entwined with legal incriminations and accusations.

Almost four months to the day before he joined the airline, a TWA Constellation had collided with a United DC-8 in the murky skies over Staten Island, New York. The date was December 16, 1960; the Connie was about to complete a routine flight from Columbus, Ohio, and was flying at 5,000 feet, approaching LaGuardia.

Its radar blip was moving steadily on a LaGuardia Approach Control scope when the controller spotted another blip.

"Unidentified target approaching you . . . six miles . . . jet traffic," he informed TWA.

"Roger. Acknowledged."

The controller watched the two blips carefully, frowning as he paged TWA again. "Unidentified object . . . three miles . . . two o'clock."

"Roger. Acknowledged."

The two blips moved unerringly toward each other, like a pair of tiny bugs scurrying for the same piece of food.

At 10:33 A.M., they merged.

The second blip was the United jet, a nonstop Chicago–New York flight, getting ready to land at Idlewild. An outboard engine sliced into the Constellation's fuselage with the force of a giant meat cleaver and the smaller plane dove earthward. It smashed into a field only a hundred yards from a public school, where the children pressed against classroom windows staring at the destruction outside.

The jet, mortally stricken, staggered through the sky while its captain fought to keep it aloft long enough to make a landing. Lower and lower it wobbled, over the rooftops of Brooklyn, until one wing tilted as the plane surrendered to its wounds and crunched into the roof of a four-story apartment house. From the roof it bounced into a street, cartwheeled and rammed into the Methodist Pillar of Fire Church. Aircraft and house of worship burst into flames and burning debris exploded in every direction, setting ten more buildings on fire. The crash site was only one block away from two parochial schools occupied by 1,700 students and teachers.

One hundred and thirty-four persons died, eight of them bystanders and the remainder on the two planes. Only one passenger survived the immediate crash, an 11-year-old boy riding in the rear of the jet, but he suffered burns over 80 percent of his body and all efforts to save him failed. He died the day after the collision, the 135th victim.

Both history and death had repeated themselves—the airlines were the same ones involved at Grand Canyon and, like at Grand Canyon, the accident at Staten Island was "not supposed to happen." Only one month before, FAA administrator Elwood R. (Pete) Quesada had proudly told the National Press Club in Washington that jets were being monitored by radar "from takeoff to touchdown." Since Grand Canyon, more than a half-billion dollars had been spent on air traffic control projects.

The "takeoff to touchdown" boast turned out to be an overconfident bit of hyperbole. Two minutes before the collision, the Idlewild Air Route Control Center (ARTC), monitoring United on radar, advised the flight that if it had to hold at Preston (a radio checkpoint), it was to execute the usual "racetrack" pattern for holding at an assigned altitude until cleared for final approach.

UAL confirmed these instructions. One minute later, the flight informed ARTC it was descending from 6,000 to 5,000 feet. ARTC acknowledged and added these key words: *"Radar service is terminated.* Contact Idlewild Approach Control. Good day."

At 10:33, seconds before the collision, United informed Approach Control, "Approaching Preston at 5,000."

That was the last communication from the jet. Approach Control advised UAL to maintain 5,000 feet, reported that no traffic delays were expected, and gave the flight a weather report and landing instructions. The collision occurred while Approach Control was transmitting this information that took exactly sixteen seconds to complete.

It had been just sixteen seconds earlier when UAL reported it was approaching Preston, yet the collision took place over Staten Island. To fly from Preston, where United said it was, to the point of the collision in only sixteen seconds would have required a speed of more than 1,000 miles an hour!

In actuality, the timetable established two facts:

1. United was not where its instruments showed it was. When it radioed "approaching Preston," it was eleven miles beyond that point and racing through the buffer zone that separated Idlewild from La Guardia traffic. It literally had run an aerial red light.
2. Radar could not have been monitoring UAL very closely. Only eighty-eight seconds before the collision, ARTC had advised "radar service terminated." The DC-8 at that moment already was far off course and the discrepancy should have been spotted and UAL warned. There still was nearly a minute and a half to avert tragedy.

The CAB put the blame for the disaster entirely on the United crew, which had failed to report that one of its two key navigation instruments was inoperative. At the speed the jet was making, the crew had been unable to determine its exact position soon enough. If the malfunction had been reported, the CAB declared, ARTC would have handled the flight more carefully.

It was not one of the CAB's fairest verdicts. United *was* partially at fault, but the air traffic control system had to share the responsibility. While the FAA refused to admit any culpability, the actions it took almost immediately after the collision indicated otherwise. The agency drastically reduced speed limits for aircraft entering a terminal area and began assigning extra controllers at high-density traffic centers. Their specific duties were to watch radar scopes for any planes straying from terminal area clearances and holding patterns. It was an indirect admission of involvement and one that could not be ignored when the lawsuits began pouring in. The claims from 115 individual suits totaled $77 million, filed against United, TWA and the FAA as co-defendants.

President Tillinghast found himself in conflict with Lawyer Tillinghast. The former felt that in no way had TWA been responsible, but the latter recognized the unpredictability of juries in air accident cases. The most blatant example occurred shortly after World War II when a fighter plane manned by a Bolivian pilot rammed into the top of an Eastern DC-4 at National Airport. The CAB spread the guilt equally betewen the fighter pilot and the control tower; Eastern was cleared completely. Yet Eastern wound up paying all the damage claims, with jurors in the case explaining that they knew the Bolivian couldn't pay, the government was too hard to sue, and the airline appeared to be the easiest target for collection.

So Tillinghast went along with a compromise settlement of the Staten Island claims. United agreed to pay 60 percent, the federal government 25 percent and TWA 15 percent. As a lawyer, Tillinghast felt the airline had gotten off as cheaply as could be expected.

The trauma of post-crash investigation and litigation was just one of the aspects of airline life to which he found himself exposed. He had brought to the job the twin handicaps of inexperience and a somewhat stern, forbidding personality that TWAers could not help comparing with the warm-hearted Damon, free-wheeling Burgess and likeable Thomas.

It wasn't quite fair, of course. Tillinghast was his own man and he was far from being insensitive and unfeeling. Because he was rather hard to get to know—some officers thought he was something of a loner—not everyone realized he had a dry sense of humor and a quick wit. His greatest asset was his uncanny ability to grasp so quickly the intricacies of the rough-and-tumble airline business. That he could do this despite the time-consuming distractions of the Hughes litigation makes his feat even more remarkable. Almost overnight he went from neophyte to expert in virtually every phase, from equipment to route structure, from marketing to maintenance.

Practically every big airline has been stamped with the personalities of its leader. Continental, brash and innovative like Bob Six. American, efficient and businesslike, reflecting C.R. Smith. United, solid and conservative in the image of Pat Patterson. Northwest, tightly run and economy-minded, which described Don Nyrop. Pan Am, confident and domineering, in a mirror image of Juan Trippe. Eastern, no-frills and no-nonsense, Eddie Rickenbacker's own philosophy. Delta, warm and friendly with the homespun southern hospitality of C.E. Woolman.

Almost from its inception, TWA had been the glamor airline, the "big name" carrier—from the days of the Lindbergh Line right through the two decades of Hughes and his Hollywood influence. As we already have seen,

Tillinghast was not only aware of that image but wasn't very happy with it. Yet he also realized that under all the flashy chrome and glitter was something solid. Glamor, yes, but also a touch of style and class. A willingness to innovate, experiment, gamble. A lode of daring and dash. An inner streak of know-how and professionalism. It was no accident that so many foreign carriers emulated and imitated TWA, from in-flight service to pilot training and aircraft maintenance.

Tillinghast never had to brand TWA with his own personality and philosophy, as did the Rickenbackers, Smiths, Woolmans and Trippes, and he was intelligent enough to realize it. Trans World already had all the ingredients of its own individualism. Once freed of the Hughes influence, glamor was subordinated to a kind of professional style that began to emerge in the post-Hughes years and still exists today.

The much-admired gimmick of illuminating the TWA logo on aircraft tails with an ingeniously mounted spotlight, is one example. Ray Dunn is said to have conceived the idea and Bill Meador's engineering department carried it out. Sam Mead was the engineer assigned to head the project and he had the devil's own time trying to figure out where to hang the spotlight. He worked with a manufacturer who finally came up with a small, but high-intensity floodlight that could be mounted on a 707's horizontal stabilizer.

The intention at first was to turn on the light only when the aircraft was on the ground; it was conceived more as a stationary billboard than anything else. But after the first one was installed on a test 707, several TWA pilots suggested it could be used in flight as an anti-collision light. Meador checked with the FAA, which said it sounded fine, but would it really work?

A TWA crew took up a Boeing one night with an FAA plane flying alongside. They switched on the floodlight and the FAA inspectors were ecstatic. "It's great," they proclaimed. "You can see the airplane better than you can with rotating beacons."

Test flights showed that the light mounting didn't interfere with the jet's flying characteristics and the floodlights went from stationary billboard to flying billboard status. They not only provided extra visual anti-collision protection, but passengers and spectators at an airport could spot a TWA flight five miles away. TWA held a patent on the device briefly but other firms developed similar and improved models. TWA, in fact, wound up using a different light on some of its later aircraft.

Not so successful was the paper uniform disaster of 1969. TWA's advertising agency had come up with the idea of matching hostess uniforms to the airline's prime overseas routes, and the job of transforming the concept into a workable plan was given to Larry Stapleton, then a vice-president of advertising and now general manager in Spain.

The uniforms really were made of a tough paper material with a high fiber content for added strength. Four basic outfits were designed: a dress modeled after those worn by serving wenches in British pubs, a white, gold-trimmed Roman toga, a French gold lamé cocktail dress and the "Manhattan Penthouse"—actually black lounging pajamas. The idea was to tie in the uniform with special ethnic or national menus; hostesses assigned to a New York–Rome flight, for example, wore the Roman toga and served Italian food specialties. The serving wench outfit went with English dishes like kidney pie. Bill Borden, a former purser who was an in-flight manager when the uniforms were introduced, says they worked well for about ten days but after that "everything fell apart."

The first headache was that we couldn't always match the uniform to the menu. We'd have hostesses assigned to a London flight and the only uniforms available when they checked in were Roman togas. Then we got into an even bigger problem. The initial supply of uniforms was well-made, but we were using them up so fast, they didn't last. They were all the same size but could be altered with a pair of scissors. Next we ran out of the original material and had to substitute a different, lighter paper. This resulted in complaints that the new material wasn't fire-resistant. It went from bad to worse. The original uniforms lasted less than six months and from then on it was a nightmare—we were lucky to get more than one flight out of each outfit, and most of the girls were afraid some clown would touch a match to the paper. Some of the hostesses looked great—the Penthouse pajamas were the most popular because they were the most comfortable. But other girls hated the whole idea, particularly the older ones. Ida Staggers absolutely refused to wear them.

We finally dropped them after seven or eight months. Stapleton developed the only other specialized uniform we ever had, the 'blue chip' motif. It was worn only on New York–Chicago flights—a white knit outfit with blue circles representing blue chip stocks. Some circles had bears and others bulls. A cute idea, but too expensive. Through the years we've had hostess input on uniform design. We didn't want them unhappy and it finally was written into the union contract that the airline had to take their suggestions into account. We used to change uniforms every three years when there was a heavy turnover, but now they're changed when the current stock starts wearing out. Remember, it costs as much as seven hundred dollars per person to switch to a new uniform or a total of about four million.

(It is generally conceded that TWA's most popular hostess uniform was worn in the 1940s: One lapel on the jacket formed the letters "TWA" and in slightly modified versions, this design lasted more than ten years. Helen Frye, Jack's wife at the time, conceived the idea for a lapel that formed the airline's initials. Ida Staggers remembers that originally the lettering was on the left lapel but says, "John Collings didn't like the location and moved it to the right side. The overall designer took one look at the lapel and jumped over sofas screaming, 'That's not my uniform!'")

The paper uniform idea may have laid a dinosaur-sized egg, but it still smacked of originality—the same kind of flare TWA's public relations troops had demonstrated so often. Tillinghast acquired a great deal of respect for Gordon Gilmore's efficiently effervescent crew. Gordon himself was a fountain of promotional and publicity ideas, some of which required the logistics of a moon shot to carry out in accordance with his perfectionist demands. He was especially good at arranging inaugurals—and there were plenty of them throughout the years of route expansion. Veteran aviation writer Wayne Parrish, who probably went on more airline equipment and route inaugurals than anyone else in aviation history, always thought TWA ran the best show.

"They were number one in handling inaugurals," he says, "and you had to credit Gilmore with the organization. United came close once, but they took months to organize it and even then it was on the basis of how TWA staged theirs."

The compliment is sincere, for Parrish was not always enamored of airline public relations efforts—including those of TWA. He came to New York once on a business trip and was startled to find his name up in lights on Broadway; Carter Burgess had the TWA sign on Times Square rigged to carry any message desired. On this occasion, much to Parrish's embarrassment, it read "NEW YORK WELCOMES WAYNE PARRISH" and Wayne never forgave him.

One of Gilmore's best and most publicized stunts, an affair in the honored tradition of Clancy Dayhoff himself, was a 1963 transcontinental Ford trimotor flight commemorating the twenty-fifth anniversary of the Civil Aeronautics Act of 1938. Gordon loved to dredge up anniversaries as an excuse for some publicity gimmick. It was once claimed that he could have somehow connected TWA with Custer's Last Stand if he had really tried. But the reincarnation of the Tin Goose may have been his masterpiece.

He managed to locate a still flyable trimotor owned by an Indiana barnstormer named John M. Louck and hired Louck, a copilot and the ancient airplane—N-414-H—for a month. The feat of finding the airplane and a qualified crew was only slightly more difficult than the feat of talking Tillinghast out of the money to stage the event. Gilmore also sold Lee Flanagin on the idea of coming out of retirement and acting as an advisory captain.

Gilmore thought of everything, such as pilot uniforms circa 1930 for Flanagin, Louck and copilot Jack Marshall. The aircraft itself carried "TWA" on its fuselage and wings. Gordon insisted that the commemorative flight travel TWA's 1930 transcontinental route: Los Angeles to Newark via Winslow, Albuquerque, Amarillo, Wichita, Kansas City, St. Louis, Indianapolis, Columbus, Pittsburgh, Harrisburg, and Philadelphia. The first hostess TWA hired, Thelma Jean Harman, was brought out of retirement to "work" some segments of the trip—wearing, naturally, her old white uniform of the trimotor/DC-2 era.

Gordon lined up seven intrepid writers willing to take the entire trip, coast to coast. The three remaining seats on the Goose were occupied by TWA public relations men who changed off on different segments, or by local reporters who flew one segment from their own respective cities to the next scheduled stop.

In due consideration for the age of the airplane, Flanagin and Louck agreed it would be prudent to conduct a few test flights. On one of them, they were flying from Burbank into Los Angeles International and the LAX tower became impatient over the speed of their approach.

"Do you have omni?" LAX inquired.

"Negative," Flanagin replied.

"Do you have a directional finder?"

"Negative."

"N-414, what are you using for navigation?"

"A compass," Flanagin admitted.

"A compass? How are you going to find LAX?"

"Well," Lee growled, "before you started asking all these goddamned questions, we were gonna follow Sepulveda Boulevard right into the airport."

That incident was a preview of a flight back into time. *N-414-H* left Los Angeles at dawn, June 21, and arrived in Newark early in the afternoon of June 23—a 72-hour ordeal that included two overnight stops in Wichita and Columbus. The crew needed rest and so did the time-travelers, all of them almost temporarily deaf. A reporter for *The New York Times,* one of the seven scheduled to make the entire flight, got off in Wichita and refused to re-board.

"I covered the Normandy invasion," he explained, "and it wasn't as bad as what I've just gone through."

It hadn't helped that the trimotor had to make a forced landing between Los Angeles and Winslow. An outboard engine developed an oil leak—one writer said it looked "like a chocolate sundae"—and Louck landed on a dirt strip just outside Parker, Arizona. The only witness was a startled policeman who agreed to wake up the local Ford dealer just in case he had something that would stop the leak. The dealer sent out a mechanic who disclosed that he had once worked on the Ford assembly line building the Tin Goose—"I haven't seen one of these things since," he added wistfully.

The mechanic finally came up with an oil plug off a Model T and it fit perfectly. A United Press reporter on the flight wired the story of the forced landing to his nearest bureau, which almost refused to use it. The local editor thought TWA had staged the whole thing, ex-trimotor mechanic and all.

At Albuquerque, one of the passengers deplaned and rushed into the airport newsstand. He was gone quite awhile and Flanagin, trying to keep the trip on schedule, asked what had taken him so long.

"I was looking for a Bible," he confessed.

N-414-H truly was a kind of time machine, transporting its occupants back to the days when TWA and the industry were young and struggling toward respectability. The passengers, particularly the six who made it all the way, got a real glimpse of what air travel was like in the trimotor era. The seats were wicker, with very inadequate pillows. The plane's lavatory was so primitive and dimly lit that everyone refused to use it; one writer swore it had to be haunted. Over a Kansas superhighway, when the Goose was encountering a stiff headwind, the passengers noticed that the trucks below were going faster than the plane. The highest altitude reached was 3,000 feet; on one occasion, they flew so low over a village that people enjoying a barbecue in a backyard waved an invitation to come down and join them.

This was what Gilmore was trying to achieve through pictures and words—how far commercial aviation had advanced. Leased chase planes provided vivid shots of the old transport with modern 707s and 880s in the background; the contrast was not only startling, but impressive. After the Newark finale, the trimotor toured several cities for sightseeing flights and almost came to grief on one of them. The plane got caught in the wake turbulence of a 707 and went into a spin from which Flanagin and Louck were barely able to recover. But overall, it had been a spectacular public relations venture and a dramatic demonstration of aviation's progress.

It also was one more reminder to Tillinghast that the airline, given the right leadership, had the courage, ability and determination to survive on its own. Except for those qualities, the photographs of *N-414-H* and its escorting jets might have been the last ones taken with TWA letters and logos on the fuselage hides. The Pan Am merger was still alive at that point and Pan Am would have been the surviving carrier.

But by the end of 1963, Tillinghast was most willing to let the merger agreement expire without further action. The jets were making money and TWA was back on course, even though one of the men most responsible for flying it out of trouble had left. Since mid-summer, a selection committee representing Eastern Air Lines had been wooing Floyd Hall intensely. Hall resisted at first but began to weaken, largely because he was not getting along with Tillinghast's choice as Vic Leslie's successor, vice-president of finance James Kerley.

One night, according to Hall, he found a Kerley subordinate going through his desk drawer and Floyd went right to Tillinghast who managed to calm him down. Not sufficiently, however, to quell Floyd's resentment entirely. His relations with Kerley were such that the Eastern offer was beginning to look more attractive, and he finally met with Tillinghast and Breech to disclose he had been talking with certain EAL directors.

Tillinghast reminded him that he was in line for the TWA presidency. In about two years, Breech expected to resign as chairman and Tillinghast would move into Ernie's spot. It was more of a hint than a flat promise, but Breech said the future could well be the way Tillinghast had outlined it.

Hall wanted to know if they were prepared to "muzzle the guy giving me fits." They would give him no such assurance and Hall understood why. "If they had given in to me," he admitted later, "they would have been captive to me." There was more discussion about Hall's future at TWA, but the blunt Breech suddenly ended it.

"Floyd, you know what's the matter with you?" he said. "You've arrived! Goddammit, nothing is going to satisfy you until you get a chance to take some downtrodden company and put it on its feet. As badly as we'd hate to see you go, and believe me we don't want you to leave, take Eastern up on its offer."

Tillinghast nodded in silent agreement. Floyd Hall's brilliant career at TWA had ended, much to everyone's regret including his own. He was to admit many years later that if he had followed his heart, he would not have left. "I should have stayed and worked with Tillinghast—he was one of TWA's best presidents. We would have gotten along just fine if he didn't have so damned many committee meetings!"

Hall left behind him his administrative assistant—none other than Frye's "Girl Friday," Jean Phillips. She had been with him since he was made vice-president and they had become friends as well as business colleagues. She stayed to become manager of customer relations before retiring.

"He brought a whole new management approach to the airline industry," she recalls. "He expected his department heads to establish goals in their own fields, spell them out, put dates on them and submit accomplishment charts by specific deadlines. I had to keep master charts on each staff member. It may have been a very common management technique, but it was brand-new to TWA, which had never been very sophisticated—we sort of grew like Topsy. Jack Frye would have laughed at all this. He would have asked, 'Would this have helped me deal with Dietrich and Hughes?' Yet they were alike in many ways."

Hall left TWA in December of 1963. He was cleaning out his desk when Ken Fletcher of Gilmore's staff stopped in to say goodbye.

"Floyd, I just want you to know I'm sorry to see you leave," Fletcher told him. It was a remark Hall appreciated because Ken was an iconoclast when it came to most brass hats.

Hall smiled. "Ken, once in a lifetime a man gets a chance to save a company. I'm getting two chances. I can't turn it down."

That he helped save TWA there is no doubt, and his contributions went far beyond holding the airline together while Tillinghast was both learning and litigating. Hall gave the airline pride and motivation, a sense of superiority and confidence in what it was delivering to the public. And he made sure TWA realized exactly *what* it was delivering: a product.

This, in his own mind, was his major achievement. He installed what may have been the airline industry's first real marketing organization. All carriers, for years, had departmentalized into two categories: traffic, which handled passengers directly, and sales, which dealt mostly with travel agents and usually advertising. Hall's own observations:

In the airline industry, we never really considered the fact that we were selling a product. We didn't try to find out who the customers were and where they were located, how much of our product and of what quality they wanted and how much they were willing to pay for it. In other words, what's the market for your product? That's all marketing is.

For example, we never had a Kansas City–New York nonstop. We operated Kansas City–Chicago–New York. We did our first real market research and found there was a big demand for Kansas City–New York direct. We put in a nonstop and within a year we had enough traffic for three nonstops. Then we began looking at St. Louis and the potential was enormous. We wound up dominating the city. After I became president of Eastern we tried putting all first-class DC-9s against TWA between St. Louis and New York. We offered fancy linen, the best steaks, free booze and all for the same price TWA was charging. Hell, we couldn't even make a dent in that market—TWA owned it. After awhile we decided we couldn't get a foothold there if we gave tickets away. Same thing happened to United when they tried to invade Kansas City. After one year, they just gave up.

Hall firmly believes that the marketing strategy established at St. Louis, and to a lesser extent in Kansas City, actually were examples of the "hub-and-spoke" concept followed by virtually all U.S. carriers today. In simplest terms, it is a system by which an airline funnels virtually all its traffic through a single point so that it controls the bulk of connecting traffic. Delta first did it at Atlanta, and it was a textbook operation the entire industry copied—Eastern also at Atlanta, American at Dallas, United at both Chicago and Denver, and TWA at St. Louis. For years, the standing industry gag was that "if you die and want to reach heaven, you have to take Delta through Atlanta."

But Tillinghast doesn't agree with Hall that TWA recognized the value of the hub concept as early as 1962. In fact, Tillinghast says the St. Louis hub really wasn't fully implemented until the late 1970s. Up to that point, TWA relied more on "linear scheduling"—the theory that if you provide the most frequent and convenient schedules between any two points, you wind up with the bulk of the business. The hub concept proved otherwise, and TWA found this out in Chicago where it pitted linear scheduling against United's hub and was clobbered. United was feeding traffic into Chicago from all over its huge system; TWA was largely originating flights out of there and it was no contest.

United's Chicago–Los Angeles flights, for example, were filled not only with originating passengers, but connecting traffic UAL had carried to the hub from scores of smaller cities. Against this kind of competition, TWA finally reduced its Chicago service from more than a hundred daily flights to fewer than forty.

"We discussed the hub concept," Tillinghast says, "but not with the clarity which has emerged in recent years. I think it's unfortunate it wasn't given the emphasis it should have been given."

TWA's reduced concentration on the Chicago market was especially disappointing to one of the most colorful characters who ever worked for any airline. That he happened to work for TWA brought the company a publicity bonanza that began in 1968 and is still producing dividends.

In the mid-1960s, a certain author dropped into Gordon Gilmore's office in New York with a request.

"I'm writing an airline novel," he told Gilmore, "and I need a special character. A tough, trouble-shooting airline mechanic that everybody turns to in a crisis, even other airlines. I've been told TWA has such a person."

"We have only one guy who fits that description," Gilmore said. "He's in Chicago and his name's Roy Davis."

Roy Davis was a chunky man with the physique of a fireplug, a perpetual cigar in his mouth and the reputation of being able to tackle any assignment tossed at him. He started with TWA in 1942 at La Guardia as an apprentice mechanic. He had been an auto mechanic in Pittsburgh and ran his own garage, but his real love was flying—he had a private pilot's license and applied to TWA for pilot training.

Unfortunately, his ratings were limited to single-engine aircraft and TWA wanted only applicants with twin-engine time. So Davis began his airline career putting de-icer boots and changing brakes on DC-3s, cleaning out the hangar "and all the dirty jobs," he reminisces. "If you got to change spark plugs, you were pretty hot stuff."

His supervisors couldn't help noticing him—he never goofed off, came to work on time and never complained about any task. He wound up working for ICD in Washington and one day was asked if he'd be willing to go overseas as a mechanic for a couple of weeks.

"With all the guys around here, how'd you happen to pick me?" he asked.

"We know who works around here," the supervisor replied.

The "couple of weeks" lasted through the entire war and beyond. He returned to the U.S. in 1946, passed some tests and returned to Paris as general foreman. One night a Connie landed in a heavy fog, went off the runway and became hopelessly mired in red clay mud. They were trying futilely to dig it loose when Davis, chomping on his cigar, finally said, "The hell with it—I'm gonna fly the damned thing out."

Larry Trimble was TWA's vice-president of the European division at the time and came out to the airport with his young son to see what was going on. They climbed aboard the Connie and the son noticed Davis in the cockpit.

"What are you going to do, Mr. Davis?"

"Fly it out," Roy growled.

"If you bust up this airplane, my daddy'll have to fire you."

"Shut up, go in the back and sit down!" Davis ordered.

He lowered the flaps to get as much lift as possible, gunned the engines until they howled in protest, and finally broke loose. The word got back to Kansas City that TWA had a troubleshooter deluxe, and in 1951 Ray Dunn summoned Davis back to the U.S. He worked first at Idlewild and then in Philadelphia as general foreman. The latter base was dispatching 50 percent of its flights late and Davis got the on-time departures up to 90 percent. He was transferred briefly to Pittsburgh and then to Chicago where he spent the next twenty-three years. In the Windy City's O'Hare Airport, he continued his informal career of rescuing mired aircraft—he took a couple of 880s out of the snow and drove a 707 out of a snowbank. It was this last incident that the novelist heard about while researching his projected book and sent him to Gilmore for the identity of the mechanic.

Thus did author Arthur Hailey meet the real-life counterpart of his famous fictional character in *Airport,* TWA's "Joe Patroni." Hailey interviewed Davis several times in Chicago, drawing on Roy's own experiences and personality to create Patroni. Davis, who admired Hailey tremendously, noticed that he never took notes while they talked.

"You know, if you're writing a book I'd think you'd be writing down what I'm telling you," he observed.

Hailey smiled and took out a tape recorder. "This is what we talked about yesterday," he said. "I dictated our conversation when I got back to the hotel." He turned on the recorder and Davis couldn't believe what he was hearing.

"It was verbatim what I had told him," he marvels. "What a brilliant memory and what a terrific guy."

Davis could say the same thing about George Kennedy, the actor who portrayed Joe Patroni in the movie. They met in Minneapolis, where most of the picture was to be filmed, and formed an instant and lasting friendship. Physically they were miles apart—Kennedy is a big man of impressive stature while Roy has trouble looking over an automobile steering wheel. But they were not that dissimilar in personality; both burly, strong, articulate and blunt. Kennedy, one of those rare actors who thinks putting on airs is like spitting on the flag, endeared himself to Davis the minute they met.

"Glad to know you, Mr. Kennedy," Davis said politely, and a bit warily.

"My name's George," Kennedy corrected. "Now, I heard about your taking that 707 out of the snow and I can do the scene better if you talk to me about it."

From then on, Davis became Kennedy's teacher and personal technical adviser. They would talk for hours, not only about Kennedy's role, but airlines and aviation in general. The actor listened, fascinated, to Roy's stories about his early TWA days at La Guardia making $110 a month, staying in a cheap room on Astoria Boulevard, living mostly on White Castle hamburgers and going to church every Sunday hoping someone would ask him home to dinner.

"I'd go sightseeing in Times Square for entertainment," he'd tell Kennedy, "usually with about ten cents in my pocket and I'd have to resist buying a hot dog because if I ate, I'd have to walk home. I never hired anyone at TWA without telling 'em, the one thing I never want you to do is go hungry—if you don't have enough eating money before your next paycheck, come to me."

On Kennedy's part, he regards his friendship with Davis as something to treasure.

Airport's producer, Ross Hunter, had set up the Minneapolis luncheon to let some of the fictitious characters meet their real-life counterparts. Actress Jean Seberg was there—she was playing Tanya Livingston, the airport manager's girl friend and an airline passenger service representative. Hailey loosely based her character on Ginny Jones Henline, a TWA PSR in Chicago, who had been brought to Minneapolis with Davis. Recalls Kennedy:

> The luncheon lasted about three and a half hours, and I picked Roy's brains the whole time. What it was like to fly. All about his job. He's not really a shy man, but I pretty well had to drag it out of him. I asked him a lot of questions about flying. I confessed to him that ever since I was a little boy I had wanted to learn how to fly, but that now I was too old. He said horseshit or words to that effect—that he had once soloed a guy who was seventy-one. 'If you want to fly, fly,' he told me. So later I did—I took lessons and got my license.
>
> After the picture was finished, I'd see Roy now and then. He'd find out I was looking for him. He'd be working on some plane and he'd leave it to come up and bullshit with me for a half hour. I'd be in a city five thousand miles from Chicago and I'd ask some airline guy 'Do you know Roy Davis?' and he'd say 'Sure.' I'd mention that I'd like to get a message to him that I was coming through Chicago in a couple days and would like to see him. And damned if that message didn't reach him. I had trouble realizing this at first—that the airline community is peculiar that way. No matter who you fly for or work for, there's a brotherhood, a comradeship unlike any other industry's. Let something go out of whack and you don't have a replacement part, you borrow the part from another airline. I know Roy did it, all the time. At first it was as difficult for me to comprehend as someone from Ford fixing a General Motors car, but I found out the airlines don't work that way.
>
> When we filmed the scene where Patroni gets the 707 out of the snow and mud, a captain was standing right by George Seaton [the director] to make sure everything I did was technically accurate. I remember asking the captain if reverse thrust was one continuous motion or did I flip the throttles piecemeal? If he saw me doing something wrong, he'd tell me 'It might be better if you did so and so.'
>
> *Airport* was my first glimpse of airline life and the airline breed. Since then, it has grown to the point where I'll be on TWA or some other

airline and the crews will kid me and ask if I'll fix something if it goes wrong or will I take over the controls in an emergency. It's a lovely, warm kind of joke and I love it. But I'll never forget that the real hero of *Airport* was Roy, not me.

Universal, which made the movie, asked TWA to aid with the entire filming, but Gilmore backed away from total involvement largely because of the frightening explosive decompression scene when a bomb goes off in a rear lavatory. No other carrier provided full-scale help and Roy's contribution was directed entirely toward working with Kennedy—and supplying him with the cigars Patroni smoked. Kennedy doesn't smoke and had to learn how.

The world premiere was held in San Francisco and Davis was invited, along with his wife Jeannie. Sitting in front of them in the theater was Captain Bill Dixon, TWA's general manager of flying at the San Francisco base. Along came the scene where Patroni chases the regular crew of the mired 707 out of the cockpit and says, "You may be able to fly this thing at thirty thousand feet, but you ain't any good on the ground." Davis saw the back of Dixon's neck turn red and he snuck down in his seat. Dixon turned around. "Sit tall in your seat, Roy," he growled.

While Gilmore balked at all-out TWA participation, he couldn't have milked much more favorable publicity out of *Airport* than he did. Kennedy wore TWA coveralls with the logo prominently displayed, and some airline observers noted with great satisfaction that while TWA reaped most of the mention, the movie itself was a two-hour commercial for the Boeing 707. *Airport* went on to spawn three successful sequels, with Kennedy playing Joe Patroni in every one. He did the original film for $20,000, but Dean Martin, Burt Lancaster and director Seaton had 10 percent of the picture.

"At one point," Kennedy says, "Burt went to Dean and told him he had been offered four million for his percentage. Martin said, 'Don't be foolish—it's like a slot machine; *Airport* will be running as long as there are movies.' But Burt did sell and Dean's still collecting."

When Roy Davis retired in 1982, just a few months shy of forty years' service, Kennedy showed up at his retirement party—an intimate little affair attended by 700 friends and admirers. That was the official count, anyway. Kennedy swears there were nearly 2,000 present, at least half of them outside the banquet hall trying to listen to the festivities. Kennedy's gift to him was a sweatshirt carrying the words, I'M THE REAL JOE PATRONI. Arthur Hailey sent a tape praising Roy as more of a hero than the fictitious character and Kennedy added the final accolade.

"Actors get to portray heroes," he said, "but seldom a hero who's still alive."

When Roy retired, he had accumulated thirty-eight weeks of unused vacation time. "The trouble was, there never seemed to be a good time to take a vacation. I couldn't go in winter because it might snow and in the summer we had a hundred and twelve flights a day."

But when schedule cuts hit Chicago, Roy decided it was time to leave. Someone asked him why he didn't at least wait for the forty-year mark. His answer was pure Roy Davis. "Because with the schedule reductions I could see guys faced with furloughs, like one supervisor with two kids in college.

It was time to move over for the younger men who aren't protected by seniority."

The strength of the 707, so dramatically portrayed in *Airport,* was no more fiction than Hailey's inspired use of Davis for his Patroni character.

On December 4, 1965, a TWA 707 collided with an Eastern Constellation at 11,000 feet over the small town of Carmel, New York. The impact tore off more than thirty feet of the jet's left wing, leaving less than two-thirds of the wing intact. The Connie was in even worse shape: Its entire control system had been severed—rudder and elevator boost package, control cables for elevators and ailerons, and even the trim tab cables.

The Eastern pilot performed a miraculous job of flying by manipulating his throttles, and pancaked onto the side of a small hill. The only fatalities were a passenger who failed to get out after the plane began burning, and the captain who went back into the aircraft in a vain attempt to save him.

Aboard the 707, commanded by Capt. Charles Carroll, control problems were compounded by fire ignited when the left outboard engine was severed. Fortunately, the flames didn't spread and were soon extinguished by the windstream, but Carroll had his hands full trying to keep his plane in the air long enough to reach Kennedy. For nineteen tortuous minutes, he stayed airborne and staggered into JFK with no wheel brakes left. He landed using just his thrust reversers. The only injury was suffered by a hostess who got a bloody nose when the collision impact knocked her off her feet.

This was the second time a 707 had been landed safely with one-third of a wing gone. Only six months before the Carmel collision, the engine on a Pan Am Boeing exploded and took off nearly thirty feet of the wing. So it was more in awe than humor that some wag sent a tongue-in-cheek message over TWA's teletype system after Carroll's landing, amending the airline's "no go" list—those items that *must* be in perfect condition before an aircraft is allowed to move one inch from the gate. The order, transmitted to all TWA stations, read:

AMENDMENT TO INOPERATIVE EQUIPMENT LIST— EFFECTIVE IMMEDIATELY—ALL BOEING 707S MAY BE DIS- PATCHED WITH RIGHT OR LEFT WING MISSING.

The pilots loved the airplane, although it was an inherently unforgiving beast. "After the Connies," Bob Buck says, "the jets were like dying and going to heaven."

"God, they had power," Hal Blackburn adds. "You could go almost as fast on two engines as on all four. Lose one and you'd hardly notice the difference. In a Connie, when you feathered a prop, you'd have a force of about a ton and a half dead weight on that wing."

Dick Pearson, now vice-president of maintenance and engineering, re- members one incident when a 707 engine tossed a turbine blade and "froze"—so violently that the engine twisted in its mountings and ended up *facing the fuselage* without coming off. "It was one hell of a demonstration of how Boeing builds airplanes. The pylon that holds the engine on the 707's wing is attached at five points. Three would normally be sufficient, but Boeing wanted that little extra strength. We had to take a 707 apart once and it was like dismantling a steel bridge. When we bought the 747, I went up to Seattle to see the 747's structural tests. They bent the wings thirty feet above their normal plane and you could see the fuselage skin wrinkle. But when the wings came back to level, not a rivet had popped and the wrinkles had totally disappeared."

Despite the inevitable occasional friction between an airline and an aircraft manufacturer, TWA and Boeing have always felt mutual admiration. This was evidenced perfectly during the aftermath of the August 29, 1969, hijacking of a TWA flight between Rome and Athens. The hijackers, two Palestinian terrorists, forced Capt. Dean Carter to land at Damascus, Syria, and after everyone was off the plane they blew off the nose with a bomb. Syrian authorities arranged for passengers and crew to be flown out, except for two Israeli citizens who were on the plane, and Carter refused to leave as long as they were in custody.

Bill Meador, advised in Kansas City that the airplane could be salvaged, contacted Boeing after ascertaining the extent of damage to the nose. Boeing diverted a nearly completed 707 nose section from its assembly line and stuffed in the wiring, plumbing and instrumentation that fitted TWA's specifications. Wiring and plumbing components were left extra long so they could be pruned later to the required lengths. The nose, mounted in a special jig, was loaded on a "Pregnant Guppy"—an old Stratocruiser modified to carry oversized cargo and looking for all the world like a huge whale with wings. Meanwhile, Meador sent John Geyser of his engineering staff and seven other technicians to Damascus.

It took the Guppy almost nine days to reach Syria. It first ran into headwind delays over the North Atlantic and the weary crew finally decided to take a more southerly route, via Santa Maria in the Azores. TWA had arranged for fast clearances at the various refueling stops over the original route but wasn't advised that the route had been changed until Meador got a cable from Madrid—"There's a strange airplane here claiming to be working for TWA and they want full service for which we have no authorization."

"Give them anything they need and get them on their way fast," Meador cabled back. Meador continues his own account of the Guppy's odyssey.

I heaved a sigh of relief, figuring it was downhill the rest of the way to Damascus. Next thing we knew, we got a wire from Palermo, Sicily—one engine had blown a jug and their repair kit didn't have the right spare parts. They had tried to contact a Pratt and Whitney representative, but that was a little hard to do on a Saturday afternoon in Palermo. We started telephoning around and finally found that spare parts were available at Israeli Aircraft Industries in Tel Aviv. The fellow who located the parts wired Rome that they would be on an El Al flight into Rome and should be flown over to Sicily as soon as possible.

Now we had another problem. We had to let our people in Damascus know what was happening, but we didn't dare mention that Israel and El Al were involved. So the wire we sent to Geyser said the Guppy's parts were on TWA 840 from New York to Rome. John knew instantly that the wire was a cover-up for the benefit of the Syrians.

By now, Boeing had sent fifty-eight technicians to Damascus who were waiting around for the Guppy to arrive. They weren't sitting on their duffs, though. The minute they got to Damascus they started preparing the fuselage for mating to the new section. There was a production break near the forward passenger entry door where the new nose would fit. They cleaned up all the debris and torn metal from that area and jacked up the fuselage, then cut away the old cockpit section at the production break. When the nose finally arrived, they just wheeled it up on a dolly and started welding. It took almost four weeks to connect all the instruments, wiring and hyrdaulic plumbing.

Geyser didn't have very good communications with us in Kansas City out of Damascus, so Dick Wilson, who was our vice-president in Paris at the time, flew to Syria several times to maintain liaison between John and TWA. He'd fly to Damascus, confer with Geyser and the Boeing people, and then go back to Paris where he'd call us and relay messages.

The Syrians, despite all the diplomatic ramifications, treated us royally. They went out of their way to be kind and gave us all sorts of help. There was only one unpleasant incident involving a Boeing mechanic who started taking pictures of the airport, including a shot of a gun emplacement a hundred yards from our plane. Boeing had briefed its people thoroughly about not taking photographs but this one guy didn't get the message and Geyser nearly had a coronary when it happened. The authorities confiscated the film and gave the mechanic twenty-four hours to leave the country.

TWA sent a flight test crew to Damascus headed by Capt. Lofton Crow, but it was decided to make only one flight out of there—to Rome, where TWA had excellent maintenance facilities and personnel who could check over the repaired 707. It left Damascus carrying Carter and the two Jewish passengers, flew to Rome for a thorough inspection, and then returned to Kansas City where it was examined again before returning to service.

For psychological reasons, TWA changed the aircraft's serial number so no crew member would know he was flying in the patched 707 "with the nose job." Then Meador very quietly had the number changed a second time just in case anyone had caught onto the first switch. One day he encountered a captain who teased him about all the secrecy.

"You thought you were pretty smart, changing that number," he said. "I found out what the new tail number was just by checking the FAA records in Oklahoma City."

"That so?" Meador said. "Have you ever seen it or flown it?"

"No, I've been watching for it, but I haven't seen it yet."

Meador just smiled. "I didn't have the heart to tell him," he chuckles, "that he had just walked off that same airplane."

There were other TWA 707s that underwent "surgery," although not as drastic and not under such dramatic circumstances.

A travel agency arranged some round-the-world charters with 707s reconfigured to all-first class—fewer than sixty seats in a cabin that normally held more than 120. Each trip took twenty-one days with twenty-three stops so the passengers needed such airborne roominess. But this special luxury was nothing compared to a 707 that was supposed to start its airline life as a prosaic, very spartan cargo plane.

The story began in the summer of 1965 with a TWA captain named George Duvall and a book commemorating the 500th anniversary of the Gutenberg Bible. It had been published by a friend of Duvall's who asked the pilot if there was any chance of giving the first copy to Pope Paul VI. Duvall contacted Charlie Billerman, then director of sales for Europe and the Far East and stationed in Rome.

"Sure," Billerman said. "Fly it over here and I'll arrange a presentation to the Pope."

A few weeks after the book was delivered, Billerman received a call from the Vatican's security chief, who happened to be a good friend of his. His Holiness, said the security chief, was thinking of making a trip to New York to address the United Nations. "Would TWA be interested in flying him?" he asked. Billerman managed to say yes without jumping over his desk.

They met to discuss plans and protocol. "You must do it exactly as I'm about to outline it," the Vatican official emphasized. "First, Mr. Tillinghast should write a letter to Cardinal Spellman in New York expressing TWA's great interest in flying His Holiness. Spellman will endorse the idea and send the letter to the apostolic delegate in Washington who will put it in a diplomatic pouch to be sent to the Vatican."

Billerman wrote down all the instructions and mailed them to his counterpart in New York. Days went by and still no invitation from Tillinghast. The security chief kept reminding Charlie that time was getting short and other arrangements would have to be made if TWA didn't want the honor of flying the Pope. Charlie called New York and asked his colleague why the delay?

"I can't keep them waiting much longer," he warned.

"Well, Charlie, we're handling it a little differently. We're going to sort of informally approach Spellman and—"

"Goddammit!" Billerman yelled. "You do it exactly the way I outlined in my letter or we'll blow the whole deal."

"I'm a friend of Spellman and I know what I'm doing," the New York sales officer insisted.

"You know what you're doing? Look, *I* know what I'm doing. I've got a stairway right up to heaven." He hung up and then placed a call to a TWA vice-president who lowered the boom on Billerman's counterpart. The official and formal invitation from Tillinghast reached the Vatican through the suggested channels, but Billerman was confronted with another problem, relayed by the security chief.

"Charlie, as you know, we're the guests of the Italian government in this city so we're going to have to let Alitalia in on this. We'll let TWA choose whether to fly His Holiness from Rome to New York or from New York back to Rome."

Billerman hesitated and then said, "We'll fly him back."

The security chief was surprised. "That's a twist," he remarked. "Are you sure?"

"That's the way I want it."

"Then that's the way it'll be."

To this day, Billerman does not know why he picked the return trip and there were those in TWA who thought he had pulled the publicity boner of the century. As it turned out, the Pontiff's televised arrival on Alitalia showed very little of the Italian airline's DC-8; in ten minutes he was off the plane and into the motor caravan heading for downtown New York. When he left Kennedy, however, TWA's 707 was on television for more than an hour.

The Boeing was something special. Somebody, Billerman does not remember who, mentioned that TWA was taking delivery of a brand-new 707 cargo plane and suggested it could be converted into a passenger plane. What the Kansas City shops came up with was a three-compartment airplane—two large rooms for Pope Paul VI and the rear of the jet for the accompanying press party. Also installed was a specially constructed altar in the forward section, to which was added an ancient cross borrowed from a Southwestern mission. The crucifix was installed on the bulkhead behind the Pope's desk, over the objections of one TWA official who argued that "all those crosses are Spanish or French." Fortunately he was overruled and the security chief told Billerman, "It was a beautiful touch."

The captain was George Duvall, henceforth known to his fellow airmen as "Pontius Pilot." Billerman still has a photostat of the Pope's ticket with the price the Vatican was charged: $890.60 for first class, one-way.

Some years later, Pope John Paul II flew to the U.S. on Alitalia, but used a TWA 727 for touring the nation and flew back to Rome on a TWA 747 whose upper lounge—the "Crow's Nest" as the crews call it—was transformed into working and sleeping quarters for the Pontiff. It was an honor that came naturally to an airline that always has taken its global responsibilities and global reputation seriously. Over the years, TWA's overseas personnel acquired the status of unofficial ambassadors—Charlie Billerman's friendship with a Vatican official was typical, not unusual. But the best example of an enlightened relationship between an airline and a foreign country took place in proud Saudi Arabia.

20

Over There

TWA's technical mission to Saudi Arabia dates back to World War II when Franklin Roosevelt presented King Ibn-Saud a DC-3 as a gift.

From that single plane sprang Saudi Arabian Airlines, which TWA helped build into one of the world's best international carriers. A TWA captain, Joe Grant, flew the DC-3 over there and for the next thirty years Saudi Arabia became a place to live and work for hundreds of TWA people—at one time TWA had more than three hundred maintenance personnel alone assigned to the Saudi Arabian mission, plus two hundred more in sales, pilot training, in-flight service, reservations and passenger handling.

Anyone who served over there remembers it with affection and pride. Typical is Don Heep, now retired, who went to Saudi Arabia in 1974 with his wife Betty, as general manager of marketing operations. When they got there, the original DC-3—*Alpha Alpha X-Ray*—was still carrying passengers (eventually it was put into a Jidda museum). The Americans lived in villas, completely furnished by Saudi Arabian Airlines. The first arrivals were scattered throughout the city, but the government later built a compound called "Saudi City." Heep had been station manager in Los Angeles, but not even long exposure to the denizens of Hollywood could prepare him for the Saudi Arabian experience.

The TWA wives had to adjust to the rather lowly status of women in an Arab country. Moslem law forbade women to drive and this applied to the American wives, who had to rely on native drivers for shopping trips. They also were required to wear dresses that went south to the ankles and north to the neck—no shorts or slacks. One wife went to a store in slacks and the proprietor refused to wait on her. Some British women tried wearing miniskirts but stopped after the religious police rapped them on their legs and sent them home.

Most of the wives played bridge during the day. For those who golfed, there were courses, but with no greens. They had houseboys for servants, but these were erratic. "They'd disappear, go home to their village, get their wives pregnant and come back to us when the baby was born," Betty Heep recalls.

Grocery shopping was an adventure. Any product containing pork was absolutely forbidden and so was anything containing alcohol, even vanilla. TWAers were technically not allowed to drink in their own homes, but the Saudis never enforced this regulation. The Americans even learned to make a version of bathtub gin—actually an Arabian brandy that used sugar as its base, plus a little yeast. Slim Morgan, who went to Saudi as a maintenance advisor in 1967, comments:

The Saudis knew we were making it because we'd go to the market and buy two hundred pounds of sugar. But so long as you didn't get greedy and start selling the stuff to cab drivers, they didn't object. It was the same with pork. You not only couldn't buy it in any store, but you weren't supposed to bring any into the country—or *Playboy* magazines or Frank Sinatra and Barbra Streisand records—they were on a sort of blacklist because they were considered pro-Israel. We'd come through Customs and they all knew us. They'd open our luggage and we'd say, 'No pork, no *Playboy,* no records,' and they'd laugh. We couldn't resist bringing in hams and we'd tell the inspectors with a straight face, 'That's reindeer.'

We'd go back to the states on annual leave and bring back frozen turkeys stuffed with pork sausages. Our wives would even wrap sliced bacon in Saran Wrap and hide it in their bras to smuggle it through customs—we called it 'breast of bacon.' Their airline would not serve alcohol on any flight, not even on the Jidda–New York nonstop. Americans would bring their own bottles on board and they'd look the other way, provided that you stayed sober and didn't get obnoxious. They didn't need liquor service to compete. If you were doing business over there, you rode their airline.

Morgan went over for a two-year stint and stayed ten years. The perks were plentiful. Not only were the homes furnished free, but there were no utility bills and gas was only fifteen cents a gallon. The automobiles came free, too. Morgan was given a Chevrolet station wagon when he arrived and drove it for three years until a Saudi official suggested he needed a new car.

"Fine with me," Slim agreed. "I'd be happy with another Chevy or a Plymouth."

The official called him the next day. "Slim, I'm terribly sorry, but we're having a little trouble locating a Chevy or Plymouth. Would you be satisfied with a Mercedes?"

When Morgan got to Saudi Arabia, the airline had a half-dozen Convair 340s, three DC-9s, a pair of Boeing 720Bs and eight 707s. When he left, in 1977, it was operating the same 707s plus a dozen Lockheed 1011s and nineteen Boeing 737s, and had several 747s on order. "The Saudis made great strides in technology, including maintenance, although it was a problem at first. We couldn't find any Saudis who wanted to work with their hands; they all were trying to get into white collar jobs. I really enjoyed it. It was like starting out all over again, with a hell of a lot of spirit among the people and doing things that would have been heresy in the States because you didn't have to wade through red tape."

In its early years, Saudi Arabian Airlines or SAUDIA was pretty much of a carrier run for the royal family, any member of which could bump a regular passenger off a flight. TWA pilots flew most of the trips thirty years ago and had to get used to some strange sights. A Saudi thought nothing of bringing aboard all his worldly possessions, including livestock. A goat or sheep in the cabin was routine. Some passengers would cook their own meals on flights before TWA introduced modern in-flight service.

The main goal was to train native Saudis to eventually take over the airline in every phase of operations. Vern Laursen and Russ Derickson, two TWA captains who trained SAUDIA pilots, say their flight crews are virtually all Saudi Arabian nationals by now. TWA has eight pilots over there serving as line check and training captains. Insists Derickson:

"I could take four or five of those Saudis and compare them with any American pilot flying in the states. They're good. They're well disciplined and dedicated. Any day they're not flying you can find 'em at the airport, sitting around and talking about their jobs. They have all procedures memorized and they deliver whatever the manuals call for—if a Saudi is supposed to pull some switch at three thousand feet, believe me it's pulled at exactly three thousand feet."

Jidda today has what is advertised as the largest airport in the world, with three terminals. One is for the exclusive use of the royal family, a second is for regular passengers and the third is used by pilgrims bound for Mecca. TWA at this writing has only about twenty-five people still there, including the supervisory pilots, and soon the Saudi Arabian adventure will be history. But the mission will never end in the hearts of its participants, Saudis as well as Americans. If TWAers grew to respect and even love the country and its people, the affection was reciprocated. Many Americans were asked to extend their tours of duty at the Saudis' own request. Don Heep was one and Morgan was told, just before he left, "Slim, if you stay you'll have twenty years of work."

It has been said, with some degree of truth, that TWA is two separate airlines—international and domestic. Certainly, the international division is a world of its own, populated by its own special breed to whom distance is measured by time, not miles. This was true even in the days of the pioneering Connies and is even more apt today. The jets have, indeed, compressed the world. TWA has one hostess who lives in Singapore and commutes to Los Angeles for her assigned flights. A number of flight personnel reside in Europe but fly out of New York.

The international crews have their own stories, and it is not surprising that many center around the legendary figure of purser Buddy Ledger of whom it was once said, "Buddy works a trip like the social director of a Catskill Mountain resort." Because most of the international crews are senior, they tend to be a bit uninhibited and informal, Ledger being a prime example.

Buddy was working a London trip and was told that a woman passenger had been insulting the hostesses. "Flying whores" was one of her more polite descriptions. The woman was traveling with her very embarrassed son who confided to Buddy that his mother already had been thrown off an American flight. Ledger nodded understandingly and approached the obnoxious passenger. First, he went into the possibility that even the magnificent 747 on which she was riding could encounter some dire emergency, in which case people would have only ninety seconds to evacuate the plane and that the flight attendants were trained to guide the evacuation.

"Sometimes," Buddy continued, "we have only fifty seconds or even less and in that case, we have to play a little came called 'pick and choose.'"

"What do you mean, pick and choose?" she asked.

"Madam, it's like being on a sinking ship when they have to pick and choose who gets into the lifeboats first, such as women and children. Same thing as on this airplane. If we get into a serious situation, we have to pick and choose who gets off first. And do you know who does the picking and choosing? Those hostesses you've been calling whores."

The woman looked a little sick. "Are you serious?"

"That's right, madam. You'll be the last. They'll pick and choose everybody before they get to you. And furthermore, if they can't decide it'll come down to me. And I assure you, madam, if that happens you are not going to be picked!"

She never said another word the rest of the flight.

Ledger firmly believes that every flight, particularly the long overseas trips (he flies the polar route between Los Angeles and London), is a cross-section of humanity that requires psychology to handle. "Some people are in mourning, some traveling on business, some are on vacation. The last thing they expect is to spend eleven hours enjoying themselves. I try to get 'em to relax, that's the important thing."

His methods are not exactly conventional. He will be on a 747 leaving London and announce seriously, "We have one flight going to New York, another flight going to Chicago, and if you're heading for either place you're going the long way around because our destination is Los Angeles." Explains Buddy:

"That little sentence puts people at ease. They smile a little and start to relax. I'll go up to a little girl and ask her if she wants some coffee. She'll shake her head and I'll say, 'No? Then how about a little whiskey?' Everybody around her will start to laugh. And *relax*."

Ledger even makes cracks about his cabin crew's longevity. "Your cabin crew today," he told one group of passengers, "is so senior you might as well be flying with the 1910 Olympic team." He wasn't really kidding. TWA once took a picture of a Ledger 747 crew whose seniority added up to some three hundred years. Yet Buddy, like many of his fellow pursers and flight service managers, is a proud man who deeply resents passengers making cracks about older hostesses.

"People will come on my airplane and say, 'Look at that hostess—she's older than my mother.' I wish I could ask a passenger if he'd rather have a pretty face or a professional. I might kid about seniority, but I try to get across the idea that people are going to have a pleasant flight because they have professionals on the plane. I've seen veteran hostesses who check the food before they serve it and throw it away if it doesn't look right. And when you get into an emergency, you want a flight attendant with experience, who knows her job, who won't panic. I've been through twenty-six emergencies in my career and I have yet to have one of these veterans fail me."

Bill Borden, TWA's vice-president of In-Flight, agrees. "One thing about a senior crew is that they've lost their youth, but not their enthusiasm. They've never lost the art of conversation. They may not be young anymore, but we get very few complaints simply because they know how to talk to people. The new breed, unfortunately, includes those who serve the drinks and the food and then go hide. Not the old-timers—they still get a kick out of their job."

TWA's pursers conduct pre-flight briefings of the cabin attendants.

Ledger always asks one last question: "What's the most important thing to do in an emergency?" Those who have flown with him and know him well will roar back an identical response: "GET OFF YOUR ASS!"

Ledger stories are told often when two or more TWA people get together. Like the time he kept eighty passengers from getting off a delayed Trans World flight to board a competitor with available seats to the same destination. Buddy, seeing some passengers start to gather up their belongings, improvised hastily. "Ladies and gentlemen," he announced, "I've just been informed by British Customs that no one will be allowed to leave this aircraft."

Perhaps the most renowned Ledger yarn does not involve a TWA flight. He was invited to lecture at a school for delinquent kids. Buddy's message was that if they followed the straight and narrow like he did, they could wind up with a great airline like TWA, etcetera, etcetera.

"Today I have two cars, a condo in Hawaii, a lovely home here in Phoenix, a mountain cabin near Flagstaff, and I owe it all to TWA," he declared.

One smart youngster raised his hand. "Mr. Ledger, how could you get all that on a purser's salary?"

"Well," Ledger said. "I met my wife on a TWA flight and she's rich!"

Ledger wasn't assigned to cither papal flight, but one of his frequent passengers was Cardinal Spellman. He had him on one trip and heard the pilots bragging that Spellman had given them religious medals. Ledger is nothing if not forward. He went back in the cabin and accosted the cardinal. "Your Eminence, you've given those medals to a bunch of heathens—I'm the only Catholic in this crew."

Spellman said, "Buddy, go back to where you hung my coat and you'll find a medal in the pocket."

Ledger located the coat and pulled out a box which he opened. There was a medal, in solid gold. When the cardinal deplaned, Ledger stopped him to show him the medal. "It's beautiful, Your Eminence," he enthused. "Better than what those heathens in the cockpit got!"

Spellman looked at the medal and grinned. "It should be, Buddy—that's the one the Pope gave *me*. You got the wrong box."

All the international crews, cockpit and cabin alike, have become very cosmopolitan, knowing the better restaurants in any country TWA serves. But this culinary culture was acquired gradually. In the earlier days of international flights, many of the pilots were naive and inexperienced in the ways of foreign travel. Ledger took three pilots to a fancy restaurant in Paris and the airmen, unwilling to admit to a mere purser that they couldn't read the menu, began ordering blind. Relates Buddy:

"One got an all-vegetable plate and the other two wound up with lobster thermidors. That wouldn't have been so bad except that one of the latter asked the waiter for catsup. The maitre d' saw him pour the catsup over the lobster and summoned the chef, who not only started screaming, but threw all four of us out of the restaurant."

Ledger could be incorrigible, even with VIP passengers. He had actor Yul Brynner on a polar flight and Brynner, normally a pleasant person, was in a foul mood. They had just reached cruising altitude when a hostess told Buddy, "Mr. Brynner wants to see you."

Ledger went to the star and asked, "What can I do for you, sir?"

"I don't want any of your girls asking for my autograph," Brynner said grouchily. "I just don't care to be bothered."

"Certainly," Ledger said. "What's your name?"

"Huh?"

"Just give me your name and I'll tell the hostesses not to bother you."

"Yul Brynner," the actor muttered.

Ledger couldn't resist it. "How do you spell it?" he asked sweetly.

Ledger once had a flight to London that lost an engine right after takeoff and had to go back to New York. The passengers were put on another plane that also had engine trouble and returned. They finally got to London some twelve hours late. The first passenger off the plane stopped long enough to slap Buddy's face; she had missed a connection. The second one was late for an appointment and snarled, "You oughta be shot." The third kissed him. "I'm just glad to be alive," she murmured.

"Every flight's like a miniature play and we're on the stage," Ledger philosophizes. "The only difference is that we don't get much applause. The plots are different, too—no two flights are exactly alike. You work a cabin one day and another cabin the next and the second one's a different stage."

Ellie Shaub, a TWA hostess since 1958, says a veteran flight attendant can sense a certain mood on every international flight. "It's set within the first thirty minutes and what causes it I don't know. Sometimes you can feel it before the flight leaves. It's almost a mass psychology. A few people begin to interact among themselves and eventually the mood goes all through the airplane. I've always wondered who or what really starts it. Do we as flight attendants set the mood or does it originate with one or two passengers?"

George Ann Bell, a hostess since 1955, agrees with Ellie that there is an unexplainable mood that permeates a flight but thinks "It comes from the passengers and what they've gone through before they board the airplane."

The veterans are well aware of a phenomenon in their profession—what some refer to as "hostess menopause." It is best described as a period when the job unexpectedly and suddenly becomes boring and palls on even the most dedicated flight attendant; sometimes there is even an element of fear or apprehension.

"In my case," Ellie Shaub says, "there was a decided letdown after three years. It passed, but twenty years later it hit me again. Now I'm in love with the job once more." Doris Owen, who has thirty-four years seniority, concedes, "You go in cycles, but usually you snap back."

Celebrities are frequent on TWA's polar flights out of Los Angeles and all three of these professionals still wonder about a tendency on the part of male passengers to imitate a male star. Ellie had Burt Reynolds on a flight and when he ordered a plain soda, virtually every other man in first class ordered the same thing. George Ann, like all hostesses, has her favorite VIPS (Dannie Kaye and Don Rickles are among them) but at the other end of the scale is a certain well-known comedienne. "She won't talk directly to any flight attendant; she talks to them through somebody else, like 'Tell that girl to bring me another drink.'" And no hostess is ever surprised at what can happen on an airplane, from throwing blankets over passengers with overactive libidos (which happens occasionally on long flights when the flow of liquor is only a few gallons less than the fuel in the wing tanks) to terrifying moments of hysteria.

George Ann encountered the latter on a trip from Rome to Cairo. Just before leaving Rome, an Egyptian woman in first class was watching her perform the lifejacket demonstration and suddenly began screaming. She took off a shoe and threw it at George Ann, yelling so loudly that the captain took a 45-minute delay while they tried to calm her down.

On board was another Egyptian who offered to talk to the hysterical woman. He conversed with her a few minutes and then approached the hostess. "You aren't going to believe this," he told George Ann, "but she has been in New York visiting her son and new daughter-in-law. The yellow lifejacket you were demonstrating reminded her of the yellow dress her daughter-in-law was wearing—and she hates the daughter-in-law."

Ellie worked a flight on which a single Saudi Arabian family occupied the entire first class section of a 747—twenty-one seats. They paid TWA $42,000 for their tickets and Ellie heard later their hotel bill in London ran $25,000 a day. But the airline and its crew valued such passengers no more than they did those who traveled on TWA's military contract flights during the Viet Nam war. These were bid mostly by senior hostesses like Ida Staggers—and she bid them even though she sometimes wondered why.

"We were so loving to those kids," she remembers, "and I guess it was right that we were, if only to make their lives a little bit happier, because they didn't know what they were going into. We were their mothers for just a little while, maybe even their grandmothers. One thing I refused to do was give them my address. It would have torn me up to hear from them. One sweet, wonderful kid conned me into it and I got two heart-rending letters from him after he had gone into combat. I never did it again."

Ida Staggers retired in 1972 at the age of sixty in accordance with a union contract that made it mandatory. She didn't want to—she would have preferred flying for another ten years. She never married. People would ask her why and she'd reply, "Heck, I did get married—to TWA." When she left the airline, she had flown more than a thousand individual trips, an estimated 10 million miles over a 36-year period, and no one who ever flew with her, from captain to the most junior hostess, didn't love her. She was Bob Buck's special favorite. He loved to tell of a layover in Paris when Ida came down to breakfast looking as if she hadn't slept a wink. Buck commented that she must have had a bad night.

"I did," she sighed. "There was some Englishman with a girl in the room next to mine. All night long he kept shouting, 'Good girl—good girl!'"

Ida flew the Viet Nam trips during the last four and a half years of her career. Hostess Martie Escarzega encountered her on one of her last flights—typically, Ida had bid a ten-day trip over Christmas and New Year's. Martie was waiting for Ida's 707 to come into Okinawa for a crew change.

I'll never forget her as she stepped off that plane, fresh and smiling, wearing her white gloves, which was a regulation ninety-nine percent of us ignored, especially in a place like Okinawa. She was sporting a little candy cane in a perky ponytail as she called out, "Now don't you girls take down my decorations."

We climbed aboard, tired, sleepy and feeling sorry for ourselves—ten thousand miles away from home at Christmastime. But once inside, the sadness left my heart. I had tears in my eyes but from shame, not sorrow. Ida had brought Christmas to that drab, blue-gray, six-abreast one-hundred-and-sixty-five-seat 707 interior. There were wreaths on the cockpit and lavatory doors, candy canes above every seat, and on the forward bulkhead a big sign reading "Merry Xmas From Your TWA Crew." It was signed by everyone working Ida's flight and I found out later she had paid for all of the decorations and candy herself.

Ida Staggers, TWA hostess.
She wore her wings in two places: on her uniform and in her heart.

TWAers who served overseas could write their own book—one filled with nostalgia, it should be added, because today the airline relies primarily on foreign nationals to operate its international stations. Stew Long, who supervised the overseas bases for years, says, "If we have thirty-five Americans working in Europe and elsewhere, it's a lot."

TWA's manager in Spain for years was Frank Howell, who went to Madrid after his Philippines assignment and wound up wielding more influence with the Spanish government than the U.S. ambassador. Spain's national airline, Iberia, was one of the foreign carriers TWA helped to mature from a shoestring operation into a jet age competitor, although in Iberia's case the aid was unofficial. An Iberia official once asked Frank why he was so cooperative; Howell even helped Iberia set up its own air travel credit system.

"If I can help you develop a national airline," Howell said, "both of us can develop the air travel market for Spain." Iberia used TWA manuals for awhile and even had a TWA color scheme briefly on its planes. When TWA first went into Spain, the Madrid airport had a single 5,000-foot runway and a shack for a terminal. Baggage was stored in a TWA airport office. Howell noticed that the handful of European airlines serving Spain would go to the Spanish Civil Aviation Authority individually. He talked them into forming The Airline Association—Frank was its first president—and this unified group worked with the Spanish government to modernize the Madrid airport.

Howell also was the first president of the American Club of Spain, an organization of U.S. businessmen working there. It started with thirteen members, all U.S. citizens, but in 1960 Howell convinced the organization it should take in Spaniards; it now has 1,500 members.

Air travel development in Spain was difficult at first. Spaniards generally are not wealthy and also needed permits to travel outside the country, but as American investments began to grow in Spain, traffic increased correspondingly. TWA started with three DC-4 flights a week, replaced these with Connies and finally was operating daily service.

The most fascinating and unusual source of business was flying Basque sheepherders to the United States to become ranchers and improve wool production. The project was the brainchild of John Bidegaray, an official of the U.S. Wool Growers Association who worked with Howell on the project. The Spanish government insisted that the U.S. make certain concessions before the Basques were allowed to leave. The whole emigration plan was about to fall apart when Howell remembered that one of his numerous friends in Spain was Camille Cianfarra, the Madrid correspondent for *The New York Times* who later was to die on the *Andrea Doria*. Howell told the reporter his problem.

"I know how you can do it," Cianfarra said. "You write me up an article on all the trouble you're having. I'll polish it up and hold it until you tell me to release it."

Howell waited until he realized it was impossible to get the government to move, and called the reporter. "Let it go," he said.

The headline in the *Times* a day or so later read: SPAIN REFUSES TO COOPERATE WITH U.S. WOOL NEEDS. Howell got a call from a government minister to come down and get the desired papers. There was a copy of the *Times* on his desk when Howell walked in.

"You didn't have to do that," the official said sadly.

Some 25,000 Basques wound up in America and almost all of them prospered. Sen. Paul Laxalt of Nevada and President Reagan's good friend is the son of a Basque sheepherder, one of the first TWA flew over.

"They never caused any trouble," Howell says. "They were law-abiding, hard-working, and if you gave 'em a hundred sheep to start out with they'd have more than a thousand before you'd know it. A Basque doesn't like fine print. You shake his hand, live up to your part of the bargain and you've got a friend for life."

While the program was highly successful, it had its rocky moments. Four Basques arrived in Boston on TWA and were supposed to fly westward on another carrier. None could speak anything but Basque and all four assumed Boston was their final destination, so they got off the plane and disappeared. For three days, TWA officials in Boston searched for them in vain. On the fourth day, a policeman spotted the Basques sitting in a park and brought them into a precinct station.

Spanish and French interpreters were summoned, but they couldn't get through—Basque is a language of its own. Finally, a policeman found on one of them a piece of paper with John Bidegaray's name and phone number. A desk sergeant called Bidegaray, who spoke Basque fluently and talked to one of the wandering sheepherders. When everything was satisfactorily explained, the desk sergeant asked Bidegaray, "What did he say to you?"

Bidegaray laughed. "He said, 'We're in America, but where the hell are the sheep?'"

Howell expected to stay in Spain for two years. He was there twenty and stayed another seven after he retired, working on a big golf course project. During those two decades, he helped establish schools for travel agents in the larger cities and he brought the ones in smaller towns together for the first time. These agents refused to talk to each other, figuring it was like collaborating with the enemy. Frank would hold dinners for them without telling them who would be there, and arranged free trips on TWA to the U.S. for educational purposes. He was always preaching tourism and when he left, he had received three decorations from the Spanish government for his promotional efforts. He not only knew General Franco well, but set up his first press conference with American newsmen. He got Tillinghast and Breech audiences with the Spanish dictator and it was no coincidence that when Howell retired, Tillinghast flew to Madrid for the retirement dinner. He gave Howell a gold putter as a farewell gift.

There were many TWAers like Frank Howell in Spain and Joe Brummit in Ethiopia, who served the airline overseas through the years—perhaps not with their influence, but certainly with their philosophy: that in a foreign country, an American is the foreigner, and must understand and willingly tolerate local traditions, customs and methods. Patience was more of a necessity than a virtue with TWA people working on foreign soil. No one knew that better than Stew Long, who points out that compared to most European countries, U.S. labor unions are pro-management and blissfully peaceful. Says Long:

Everywhere we operate internationally, there are unions or labor syndicates to deal with. At one time, I had three hostess domiciles reporting to me—Hong Kong, Rome and Paris. The Rome and Paris girls had two separate unions and the Hong Kong hostesses had none. There was no way to keep them separated. We had to mix 'em up, so the Hong Kong girls started flying with the Rome girls and so forth. Before that, cultural differences had to be considered. For example, I'd assign five rooms to five Hong Kong girls on a layover in Bombay and they'd use only one room. I found out it was because they believed the hotel was haunted and they refused to sleep alone. When I started mixing up the three bases, they began comparing salaries and fringe benefits and all I got was chaos. It became so bad with the three domiciles playing one off against the other that I closed all three and put American girls back on. You can't operate under three different sets of rules.

Under most European union or syndicate rules, it's almost impossible to fire anybody. If TWA employees in the U.S. go on strike and shut down the airline, under foreign labor laws we'd still have to keep all international employees on the payroll at their current salaries. Furloughing doesn't work because in most foreign countries, a furloughed employee gets one month's pay for every year of service. In Portugal during the winter we have only two flights a week, but we still have to keep one hundred and twenty-three people at the airport. You can't get rid of 'em unless you're willing to get out of the country entirely. It cost TWA two million dollars to close the Rome hostess domicile because we had to pay all the girls off. That two million was a settlement figure and it would have been more if I hadn't been able to convince an Italian judge that none of the girls really worked in Italy and only a few were Italian.

We have no grievance procedures for international employees. They don't need 'em—they have enough protection without adding what we give American employees. There's no such thing as a merit increase, either. Why have a merit increase when international salaries are pegged to the cost of living? That's why El Al almost collapsed. There's no way that airline could exist with a thirty-eight percent increase in salaries every year.

I guess in the old days it was more exciting and more fun. Now all we do is close stations. I've closed more than anyone in TWA—Casablanca, Nice, Zurich, Vienna, East Africa. . . . In the early days we went everywhere just to see what would happen and then we'd find the market was too thin.

Long, now stationed in New York, spent thirty years in Europe. Most of the time he was an executive so he was luckier than Bob Berle—who was overseas for thirty-five years and in that time had twenty-six bosses. There was a common denominator in all officers and employees alike, however, and that was respect for the foreign competition. Long rates Swissair as the best run and Lufthansa next, but he admires them all. TWA, in fact, enjoys better relations with foreign airlines than some of them have among themselves.

A few years ago, Iberia and Portugal's TAP were feuding and TWA, serving both countries, was right in the middle. One day TWA would be told it couldn't carry any local passengers between Spain and Portugal and the next day it could. General Franco finally got fed up and, perhaps with Howell's urging, sent the head of Iberia to negotiate with his counterpart at TAP.

"I don't care what the settlement is, but you settle and stop this argument," he reportedly ordered.

The Iberia and TAP respective chairmen met and put all five major issues on the table. For three days they argued until Iberia's chairman threw up his hands.

"All right," he surrendered, "I agree with your position on all five issues."

The TAP executive stared at him. "I won't accept," he declared.

When TWA seniors hold reunions, stories about foreign assignments abound. Long once hired an expensive British photographer to take color pictures for a TWA calendar. His first mission was to photograph a Constellation over the Acropolis in Athens. He spent three weeks trying to line up a perfect shot and each day something would go wrong. The Connie would be too low or too high. The sun wouldn't be right. Too many clouds. Not enough clouds. Finally, all conditions were perfect—the aircraft flew over at precisely the desired angle and altitude in a bright blue sky dotted with fleecy clouds. The photographer took the shot, packed up and went home. That was fortunate because if he had stayed close to Stew Long, he would have been murdered. He had forgotten to take the cap off the lens.

Of course, hiring any outsider to perform a task could be risky. TWA signed an author to write a book on the food and liquor of the nations it served. The writer arrived in Athens where TWA's manager, Jack Davenport, met him and took him to a distillery owned by a wealthy Greek family exceptionally proud of its brandy. The author tasted the brandy and delivered his verdict.

"I've drunk a lot of brandy in my time," he told his expectantly smiling Greek host, "but this is the lousiest I've ever tasted."

Davenport got him out of there before the distillery owner could assault him; the book was never written.

One of the most memorable yarns is told by Fred Spuhler, who once accompanied columnist Art Buchwald to Paris on a TWA flight. They were booked at the same hotel but when they checked in Buchwald was told he had no reservation. The desk clerk, unaware that he was annoying a journalistic atomic bomb, was surly and unimpressed with Art's threat: "If I don't get a room within an hour, you're gonna see the damndest column you ever read."

The clerk expressed total indifference. Spuhler offered Art his own room but Buchwald declined and finally got a room elsewhere. Fred eagerly awaited the promised column and was not disappointed. Art told about having to sleep on the street outside the offending hotel and added the coup de grâce.

"If you want to keep warm," he wrote, "they'll cover you with unhonored reservations slips."

End of the Beginning

When Charles Tillinghast assumed command of troubled Trans World, he gave people equal priority with planes.

"The most important thing was management stability," he explains. "To have a climate in which every officer and employee could plan and do their jobs in a normal manner."

The stability he provided included himself. Tillinghast directed the airline's fortunes for nearly sixteen years—first as president, then chief executive officer and board chairman. Those sixteen years included setbacks as well as triumphs—strikes, the agony of fatal crashes, bloodletting deficits and mistakes in route expansion. But TWA was not alone in experiencing trouble; it is part of the environment in an industry so marginal and vulnerable in earning capacity that the altitude at which a captain decides to fly can make the difference between a profitable trip and a money-losing one.

What was important was that TWA was finally standing on its own feet, master of its own destiny and far more secure than it had been in two decades of uncertainty and rule-by-whim under Howard Hughes. If it could be criticized for some wrong decisions, at least they were decisions made by the airline itself. Tillinghast's greatest gift to TWA was its independence from the brilliant but tragically insecure and remote Hughes.

TWA, of course, changed for more reasons than its divorce from Hughes. Along with the entire industry, it had to adjust to conditions it had never before faced. The enormous cost of fleet modernization and expansion was just one factor; the $22 million price of TWA's first Boeing 747 was more than double the market value of all U.S. airlines combined in 1938—the year Hughes first bought into TWA.

The jets, with their incredible productivity born of speed and capacity, turned air transportation into mass transportation. In 1960, when the jet age was less than two years old, only 10 percent of the U.S. adult population (eighteen and over) had ever flown in a scheduled airliner. By 1983, that figure was over 70 percent, with women accounting for more than half of the pleasure/personal trips and one out of every five business flights. Where once it had cost an intrepid passenger $300 for the privilege of flying TAT coast-to-coast in thirty-six hours, the same trip could be made in a jet in six hours at half the cost. Only five and a half decades after Lindbergh flew to Paris, TWA and its competitors were carrying a million passengers a month across the Atlantic at a cost considerably less than tourist fares on a 1927 ocean liner.

Achievement of progress was expensive. A single engine on a 747, priced at more than $1.1 million, cost more than one of TWA's original Connies; it was, however, ten times more reliable, just as the jet planes themselves were far safer and swifter. Between 1918 and 1953, commercial airplanes had struggled from a top speed of 90 mph to 350, the latter achieved by the DC-7. But the jets jumped from that 350 mph maximum to 590, an increase of 240 mph. In brief, the jets achieved a speed advantage over the fastest piston airliner that was almost as great as the accumulated speed increases of the previous thirty-five years.

Furthermore, the turbine engine was far cheaper to maintain. The Wright engines on TWA's Constellation fleet had a TBO (Time Between Overhaul) of less than 800 hours. The airline had a TBO of 1,000 hours on its initial jet engines, but by 1962 this had jumped to 4,000 hours. Even this proved too conservative; TWA had some of its first turbine power plants going 21,000 hours before needing to be pulled for overhaul. Eventually, the FAA eliminated all TBO schedules and merely required that a few critical components be replaced or inspected at specific intervals. Inasmuch as it cost TWA $90,000 to overhaul one jet engine (almost as much as an entire DC-3), the savings were considerable. On the pistons, TWA had been changing 24,000 spark plugs every month.

Under Bill Meador, TWA expanded its inspection methods to include x-raying of key structural parts to determine any sign of wear or fatigue. Also adopted was the use of ultrasonic waves that revealed cracks invisible to the human eye. It paid off in safety. When an early model 707 operated by a foreign carrier lost its tail in severe turbulence, Meador followed the course of the investigation closely. He ordered all of TWA's 707s inspected by the ultrasonic method. On one or two of the oldest planes the technicians found minute fatigue cracks in the fittings that held the vertical tail fin to the fuselage. Mechanics reamed out the holes and replaced the fittings on the affected aircraft. Preventive maintenance, like preventive medicine, had always been a TWA creed and it was to be emphasized even more strongly with the jets. The airline had to prove to the FAA that it could determine precisely the structural life of any component and keep the airplane flying indefinitely, as long as those components were monitored regularly.

This was in direct contrast to the British who, at one point, set an arbitrary limit of 60,000 hours as the life expectancy of any 707, based on the crash of a chartered older model Boeing that suffered structural failure. This high-time 707 had passed the 60,000-hour air frame mark, which scared the British but didn't impress Meador and his engineers one bit. TWA at the time had one 707 that had logged nearly 63,000 hours airframe time and had passed the x-ray and ultrasonic tests easily. When Britain announced it would not permit any 707 (or DC-8) to fly into or out of England after the 60,000-hour mark, Meador and several other U.S. airline maintenance experts went to London and convinced the British government their limit was impractical and unnecessary, given American inspection procedures. "The British," Meador says wryly, "forget everything until an aircraft hits sixty-thousand."

Of less consequence than fatigue cracks, but still intriguing, was a minor mystery that developed while TWA's first jets were going through overhauls. When the cabin carpets were removed for cleaning, mechanics found puzzling tiny dents in the metal floor. They finally figured out the source:

women's high-heel shoes, which concentrated a lot of weight on two points only a half-inch square. Whole sections of flooring had to be replaced.

Guiding TWA through the first ten years of the jet age and beyond was the imperturbable figure of Tillinghast. For the first time in more than twenty years, the proverbial buck had stopped at the desk of Trans World Airlines' president. After Floyd Hall departed, Tillinghast's right-hand man was Ray Dunn, who assumed Hall's title of senior vice-president and system general manager. Although Floyd was sorely missed, Tillinghast could not have found a more able and loyal replacement than this self-educated, self-effacing little man with the bald head and ingratiating smile. If there had been a popular election to name Hall's successor, Dunn would have won hands-down.

They formed an interesting and thoroughly competent team, Tillinghast and Dunn, differing though they did in personality. Their common denominator was inner toughness and resilience. Tillinghast demonstrated it in long-range policy matters, from financing to route planning; Dunn in handling the day-to-day problems of a global airline whose wings in 1963 embraced thirty-nine U.S. cities and twelve cities in ten foreign countries. Dunn lived on a diet of almost daily but temporary crisis, but Tillinghast lived with the constant knowledge that a wrong decision could affect the airline's future for years to come. He did not and could not decide alone—he had a capable board headed by Breech and a capable executive staff—but in the end most of the responsibility would be his.

His regime spanned a decade and a half, a period in which some of commercial aviation's most momentous events occurred: the final end of the piston era and the complete switchover to jets; the introduction of giant jumbo jets; the birth of supersonic transports; the worst airline strike in history; the end of the line for such industry giants as Rickenbacker, C.R. Smith, Juan Trippe and Pat Patterson, all of them stepping aside for younger men; and the end of the line for some of TWA's own greats—Dunn, Cocke, Breech and Rummel.

It took TWA six years to phase out its piston fleet. First to go were the Martins; the last 404 bowed out April 29, 1961, operating as Flight 411 from Baltimore to St. Louis via Washington, Columbus, Dayton and Indianapolis. Next to retire was the original Constellation, Model 049. The last of the one-time queens was withdrawn from service January 1, 1962, and three months later, all twenty-five of the 049s still on the roster were sold to an aircraft leasing firm for a total of $700,000, far less than what one cost new.

On April 6, 1967, the age of the pistons ended for TWA when the last Connie in passenger service landed in St. Louis as the final stop in a trip from New York. Aboard Flight 249 were Ray Dunn and Carl Haddon, who had been Lockheed's project manager on the initial Constellation program. Dunn handed out scale-model propellers as souvenirs for every passenger on the plane, but demonstrated no visible signs of sentimental nostalgia himself. That wasn't surprising—he still remembered all the maintenance headaches of the Constellation years and the teething troubles of the magnificent, but temperamental 1649, last of the Connie line and the plane of which Floyd Hall once remarked: "We lose money every time we start its engines."

As the pistons left, the jet fleet multiplied. Ten years from the date of TWA's first jet service—with that lone 707—the airline was operating 226 pure jetliners: 121 various models of the 707, 59 727s, 25 Convair 880s, 19 twin-engine Douglas DC-9s and two giant Boeing 747s. On order were 45 additional jets: 2 707s, 13 more 747s, another 8 727s and 22 Lockheed 1011s, a wide-body tri-jet that promised to be the most sophisticated airliner ever built because it incorporated much of the technology that had gone into the design of Lockheed's proposed supersonic transport.

Commercial supersonic flights, once considered in the realm of science fiction, appeared to be on the verge of reality even as the jet age reached its tenth anniversary. Russia flew an SST prototype late in 1968 and the joint British/French SST, the Concorde, made its maiden flight early in 1969. Boeing had defeated Lockheed in a government-sponsored competition for the best American supersonic design and Tillinghast had no intention of seeing TWA left behind at the SST gate. In the fall of 1963, TWA took options on four Concordes and increased the tentative order to six a few months later. Even as it signed for the first four, it also deposited a $600,000 check with the FAA to reserve delivery positions on six Boeing SSTs.

The Concorde options, however, were purely defensive. Juan Trippe—as usual, infatuated with every new technological advance—had ordered the Concorde and Tillinghast had no alternative but to follow suit. If the British/French SST was to prove successful, it promised to revolutionize air travel. Tillinghast could have nightmares envisioning Pan Am operating a three and a half hour supersonic service across the Atlantic while TWA's conventional jets were taking six to seven hours. Nor was it entirely Pan Am-generated duress; the Concorde's manufacturers were claiming that without the SST, TWA would lose $100 million worth of first class traffic annually to airlines operating the 1,500-mph jet.

Rummel agreed with Tillinghast that he had no choice, but expressed doubts about the Concorde's viability. Rummel kept telling the French and British they had to build a better airplane—the original design was far too small. To placate American technical critics like Rummel, they did move the pressure bulkhead back to provide a few more seats. "It didn't help much," Rummel says, "because there really wasn't any way to make it bigger without a bigger engine, for one thing—and that they didn't have. I made a lot of trips to London and Toulouse with slide presentations proving we could never operate the plane economically, but in the end we had to put in a defensive order."

But TWA did get into the conditional contract a provision that the Concorde's price wouldn't exceed $20 million; if it went over that amount, TWA could cancel the agreement and get back its downpayment with 5 percent interest. At the time the contract was drawn up, the manufacturers were quoting $7.5 million per aircraft. By 1973, when TWA announced it would not exercise its options, the price per airplane was up to $65 million.

"We asked for our money back plus interest and we got it with no problem," Rummel says. "They were real gentlemen."

Defensive aircraft orders were part of the jet age's growing pains. With air traffic increasing at an annual rate of 15 percent throughout the 1960s, no airline could afford to be caught short in equipment capacity. There was little concern when TWA ordered the mighty 747 in 1966. Once again, Pan

Am had forced the issue by contracting for twenty-five of the huge planes but with North Atlantic traffic growing even faster than domestic, TWA's twelve jumbos seemed like a prudent and conservative investment. But Tillinghast says what really hurt TWA and many other major airlines was United's 1965 decision to order some hundred new jets—747s, DC-10s, more 727s and twin-engine 737s.

"In the early 1960s and particularly from 1963 on," he recalls, "it was my view and that of our board and top management that if TWA merely ran the show right, got its house in order and acquired a decent fleet, it could make a lot of money. This was true up until 1965, but somewhere along the line, in 1965, a bad shadow came on the horizon. This was the single order by United for about a hundred airplanes. Now we had to consider what this would mean in terms of competitive capacity. And we had to be worried. By 1967 the problem of over-capacity began to be very real. We were ordering a fleet of 747s and L-1011s and I started to feel great concern as to how well we could make out if other people began to develop over-capacity. My fears were realized. As a result of over-capacity and a recession, we bottomed out in 1970 and '71."

Over-capacity and recession weren't the only problems to hit TWA in this period. On July 8, 1966, the International Association of Machinists (IAM) struck TWA and four other airlines—United, Eastern, Northwest and National—throwing the nation's air transportation system into chaos. The crippling walkout, which lasted forty-three days, might have been averted except for some airline strategy that backfired. Tillinghast and Art Lewis, Floyd Hall's top aide at Eastern, urged that the five airlines holding contract talks with IAM negotiate jointly. If no agreement were reached, they argued, the shutdown of five major carriers would result in a national emergency requiring White House intervention.

What they didn't anticipate was the IAM's decision to make the airline dispute a test case in an effort to break President Lyndon Johnson's wage-price guidelines. LBJ had put a 3.2 percent ceiling on any wage increases. Instead of applying pressure for settlement, Johnson applied pressure in the other direction—he urged the airlines to hold out and they were forced to accede. They were a regulated industry and if the President of the United States told them not to settle for anything above 3.2 percent, they had to go along. The IAM was perfectly willing to hold joint negotiations; the union, too, knew that if negotiations collapsed, a national issue would be created, namely the validity of Johnson's arbitrary ceiling on wage boosts.

The union refused to break, and the strike was a disaster. Unaffected airlines were sagging under the load of extra traffic. American, for example, with both TWA and United struck, was operating its transcontinental flights at a 100 percent load factor and averaging thirty standbys for every flight. Under this pressure, the airlines had to settle and the final agreement called for wage increases of slightly under 5 percent, which was what the carriers would have accepted in the first place if it hadn't been for those White House guidelines.

The only good thing to come out of the long and costly strike was one of the classic airline stories. American's harried reservations agents were swamped with heart-rending pleas for space on sold-out transcontinental flights, mostly from people who swore they were "personal friends of C.R.

Smith." One agent had twenty-eight such calls in one day and the twenty-ninth added the inevitable line, "By the way, I'm a good friend of C.R.'s." The agent was fed up.

"And I suppose you also know Marion Sadler [American's president]?" the agent suggested sarcastically.

"Know her?" was the reply. "Hell, I've been dating her for three years."

The effects of the strike on TWA, however, were not very humorous. The airline turned in a 1966 profit of $29.7 million, but this was $20 million less than the 1965 net and Tillinghast was vastly disappointed. Given the money-coining efficiency of the enlarged jet fleet, 1966 should have been a record year. Even so, the directors still were able to authorize the first cash dividend to stockholders in thirty years, and only the third dividend ever paid (a 25-cent dividend was voted in 1936 and a 10 percent stock dividend in 1953).

In the back of Tillinghast's mind was a plan to somehow offset the cyclical nature of the airline industry, its vulnerability to recession and labor unrest. His idea was not new; it was simply diversification, which few airlines at that point had ever tried. TWA had stuck its toe hopefully and on a relatively small scale into the waters of diversification in 1964, when it contracted with the National Aeronautics and Space Administration to provide base support services at the Kennedy Space Center in Florida. Three years later, Tillinghast dove into the water. He merged TWA with the Hilton International hotel chain, the hotels becoming a wholly owned subsidiary of the airline.

Tillinghast had put TWA's diversification possibilities into the hands of Tom Huntington, vice-president of a new department Tillinghast had established under the title of "special services."

"Tom was a controversial fellow," Tillinghast allows. "Like many people, he had his good points and his bad points. I told him to begin diversification studies. It had seemed to me, rightly or wrongly, that the airline business had certain ingrown economic problems and that the strongest airline would be the one with the strongest capital structure and the strongest cash flow. So, one of the first things Tom looked at was the hotel business. He developed several plans, but it was clear to us that it would require a lot of capital. The possibility of a Hilton acquisition came up while we were discussing these plans.

"I have no recollection as to when the talks first began, except it was about the time Hughes sold his TWA stock. It was Barron Hilton, Conrad's son, who approached us. Barron was anxious to get into the airline business and become controlling stockholder in TWA. It didn't work out that way—we bought Hilton International, not the other way around."

The purchase price was roughly $17 million, a figure that represented TWA's initial equity in Hilton International. The chain owned or operated forty-two hotels in twenty-eight countries; TWA acquired outright ownership of three hotels, 50 percent of a fourth, and took over the operation of the remaining thirty-eight under lease or management contracts. Under terms of the purchase agreement, Hilton International put two men on the TWA board; initially they were Lester Crown and Conrad Hilton, Jr.

Tillinghast passed the word throughout the airline's executive ranks: "You guys know how to run an airline and they know how to run a hotel, so stay the hell away from the hotels." That policy still is in effect, for the man in charge of the hotel chain, Curt Strand, is regarded as one of the best in the industry and is now on the TWC board. And Tillinghast himself regards the acquisition as one of the best moves TWA ever made.

"It seemed to be so much more financially advantageous to buy a situation that already was a going concern than to start our own. That judgment has been vindicated a thousand times. The hotels have been a gold mine. In terms of what we paid for them, we got the purchase price back every year."

Not all of TWA's officers took kindly to Tillinghast's keep-your-mitts-off-Hilton edict. Senior vice-president of finance Jim Kerley, Floyd Hall's old adversary, frankly thought the airline should have a say on how its own hotel chain was run—an opinion that brought him into direct conflict with Tillinghast, who remarks:

"It seemed obvious that the smart thing for us to do was to let them run their own show as well as they had been running it under Curt Strand, and indeed this turned out to be a great formula. Now Jim Kerley was a very able financial man, but a very aggressive type who thought Hilton needed help in steering their boat. He wanted me to force him on the hotel chain and I absolutely refused—which hindsight tells us was a very sound judgment."

There were a few other diversification proposals that didn't pan out. One involved acquisition of Sun Line, a cruise ship operator. "It got away because the CAB took so damned long to approve it," Tillinghast grumbles. "Another one that never got started was a cargo handling and warehouse operation. It didn't fly because it was proposed at a time when we were buying 747s and 1011s, which involved heavy capital demands."

Eventually, however, TWA did spread its diversification efforts into other fields, under the direction of L. Edwin (Ed) Smart who carved his own niche in TWA's history. He was a protege of Tillinghast, who hired him fresh out of Harvard Law School and took him into his law firm. Smart went over to Bendix after Tillinghast left and stayed there until Tillinghast brought him into TWA in 1966 as senior vice-president of external affairs. Actually, Smart took over from Huntington in charge of diversification in time to help conduct the Hilton negotiations.

A stocky, pleasant-faced man, Smart masterminded what is generally regarded as the industry's finest diversification program. He brought under the Trans World banner the Hilton chain; the Canteen Corporation, a vending and food service business; Spartan Food Services, which operates restaurants in the Southeast; and finally the Century 21 Real Estate Corporation, one of North America's largest franchisers of independently owned brokerage firms.

Spartan and Century were added after Smart restructured the airline, setting up a holding company—Trans World Corporation—under which TWA, Hilton International and Canteen were the initial subsidiaries; Smart became board chairman of the parent corporation. The decision to diversify may well have been the most crucial move Tillinghast made in his entire TWA career, for it provided the airline with a buffer against the roller-coaster fluctuations of the industry—even when the airline lost money, the other subsidiaries usually did well enough to cushion the effects and turn profits over to Trans World Corporation.

Acquisition of Hilton International meshed nicely with the renewal of merger talks with Pan Am early in 1971. Trippe's airline then owned its own hotel chain, Inter-Continental, and not a few were intrigued with the idea of combining not only two great air carriers but the hotel properties as well. There was more behind the latest merger proposal, however, then the attractiveness of marrying airlines *and* hotels. Both TWA and Pan Am had been hit hard by the 1970–71 recession, and the worsening of the overcapacity problem brought on by the 747. The two carriers were competing against twenty foreign airlines over the North Atlantic alone, plus U.S. supplemental airlines, which in the summer of 1969 had carried more passengers across the Atlantic than Pan Am.

The renewed merger talks were initiated by Najeeb E. Halaby, former FAA chief, who had been named Pan Am's new president, with Tillinghast and Ed Smart representing TWA. No real agreement was reached except in principle, and it was never decided which would be the surviving carrier. An educated guess would have been TWA, because Pan Am was in even worse shape than Trans World; the positions of 1962, when TWA had its hat in hand, had been reversed. The merger talks went on all summer but by fall collapsed, not because of failure to reach an agreement but because the Nixon administration let it be known that the government would never sanction the marriage.

TWA and Pan Am were to try once more three years later, but these negotiations wound up in an exchange of routes. TWA gave up its hard-won Pacific routes—Taiwan, Guam and Honolulu—thus ceasing the money-losing around-the-world service it had inaugurated in 1968. It also agreed to abandon service at Frankfurt, Hong Kong, Bombay and Bangkok. Pan Am agreed to pull out of Paris, Barcelona, Nice, Vienna and Casablanca, in addition to dropping its London service out of Chicago, Los Angeles and Philadelphia.

The CAB authorized the route swap for a two-year period. When the agreement expired, TWA restored service only to Frankfurt, never reclaimed its uneconomic Pacific authorization and was glad to leave such low traffic points as Nice and Casablanca. It did buy the Barcelona route from Pan Am, because it fit well with its Madrid service, but ultimately TWA tossed in the towel at the African points of Kenya, Tanzania and Uganda—this service, started in 1967, proved unfeasible because of excessive crew costs and lack of traffic.

Even though the airline was contracting, struggling with heavy equipment commitments (such as the twenty-two L-1011 Tristars ordered in 1968 at a cost of $14 million per plane) and the general vicissitudes of jet age transitions, morale in the company stayed high. Not even the technical complexities of the turbine revolution could shrink the priceless asset of humor that could exist at any strata of airline life.

One such example involved a young TWA mechanic working the radio while a grizzled lead mechanic was taxiing a 707 from the hangar to a JFK gate. Ground Control, which can make a tobacco auctioneer sound slow-spoken, began giving the youngster his taxi instructions with the speed of a beserk machine gun.

"You're cleared from hangar via taxiway November two proceed to inner maintain inner to Mike at Mike turn to outer and continue on outer to George at George turn to inner and . . ."

The junior mechanic was panic-stricken—he had been told that all clearances had to be read back and he couldn't have absorbed this one with a tape recorder. Bravely, he began.

"Ah, Ground Control . . . uh, TWA cleared to . . . the . . . the . . . month of November . . . uh . . . turn to George inner and . . . uh . . . aw, shit!"

The lead mechanic came to his rescue. "Screw 'em," he advised cheerfully. "Just say 'Roger.'"

Stories like that warmed the ailing, gallant heart of Ray Dunn, who had been a mechanic himself and loved the breed for what it was—wonderfully resourceful, fiercely independent and occasionally militant, with a touch of cynicism failing to hide their basic sentimentality. Typical was the job TWA's maintenance and engineering magicians did in restoring the battered hulk of a 45-year-old Northrop Alpha mail plane to its original condition—a job done so perfectly that the aircraft wound up prominently displayed in the new National Air and Space Museum, complete with TWA's markings. The restoration, done solely by volunteers at the Kansas City maintenance base, took eight months and was completed shortly before the museum opened in 1976.

Unhappily, Dunn hadn't been around to oversee the work. His failing health forced his retirement in 1969; his doctrine of technical excellence that had marked TWA even in its darkest days had become a legacy. Ernie Breech had once promised Dunn, "When I leave, Tillinghast will become chairman and you'll move up to president." But Breech, whose own health was poor, decided to bow out at the same time as Dunn. Breech was named TWA's first honorary chairman and received a greater accolade December 3, 1969, when the airline opened a new hostess training center in Kansas City—the Ernest R. Breech Academy. The durable Oz Cocke retired in 1969, too, followed by Bob Rummel shortly thereafter.

Tillinghast had always given Dunn a lot of independence. Only finance and public relations were outside his jurisdiction. He was mostly a crack operations man, but when Hall left he also took over Marketing. It was at his urging that TWA dropped its then-advertising agency and took on Wells, Rich and Green. The other agency, Dunn complained, was "dead in the water." It was a sagacious decision even though the old agency had come up with one of the most famous gimmicks in advertising history—the "Up, Up and Away" song that can still raise goose-bumps on the skins of veteran employees.

Dunn had hiring and firing power, too. His most surprising victim was Tom McFadden, vice-president of marketing, who then joined Floyd Hall at Eastern. That Dunn axed him came as no surprise to Hall, however; Floyd once said, "Tom's trouble is that he thinks Marketing should run the whole damn airline." And when Ray decided to leave for health reasons, he was able to help pick his own successor.

There had been some talk of Jim Kerley replacing Dunn, but Tillinghast decided against this. Dunn's nominee was Forwood "Bud" Wiser, former president of Northeast and regarded throughout the industry as an excep-

tionally capable executive. Dunn had known him for some time and respected him. Wiser joined TWA first as executive vice-president and moved
into the presidency when Tillinghast became board chairman and chief executive officer.

Wiser started on a happy note—the introduction of the magnificent 747s,
an airplane loved by passengers and pilots alike. Before the jumbo went into
service, TWA's directors held a board meeting on one with Ed Frankum
happily flying the huge plane—Frankum always insisted it was impossible to
make a bad landing in a 747. It was Bob Buck's favorite, too. "Just a big
707 with a lot of improvements," says Buck, who was flying 747s when he
retired a few years ago.

Wiser served as president for five years. They were eventful, but eventful
is not synonymous with pleasant. There were highs, such as a TWA 707
becoming the first U.S. commercial transport to land in mainland China in
twenty-three years (the charter flight carried technicians and equipment for
coverage of Nixon's visit to China) and introduction of the L-1011, probably
the easiest airliner to fly ever built. But there were lows, like the 1973 strike
of flight attendants that lasted forty-five days—the longest walkout in the
airline's history.

The strike was a tragedy, reflecting a gradual deterioration in company-
attendant relations even though TWA had been one of the first carriers to
let married women fly (thereby ending the old quit-if-you-marry policy).
This was in 1957 and Bill Borden, then writing training manuals, decided it
was safe to marry a hostess. The flight attendant who became Joan Borden
was a hostess instructor. Recounts Borden:

"At night I'd come home and she'd tell me she didn't like what I had
written and I'd tell her I didn't like what she was teaching, so we decided it
was best for our marriage that she go back to flying the line. We arranged to
meet one weekend in Washington where Joan had a layover. I went to her
hotel to check in and the desk clerk wouldn't let me stay in her room. He
refused even when I showed him our marriage license."

Buddy Ledger got involved in flight attendant contract negotiations when
the hostesses wanted their own retirement plan. This was in the early 1970s
when TWA still required resignation at age thirty-two; the retirement proposal would let attendants work until they were sixty and retire on a pen-
sion. Things were at an impasse when Tillinghast called in the negotiating
teams and gave them an impassioned fight talk about their solemn, sacred
duty to TWA. After he left, Ledger rose and delivered the following speech
which fell a few miles short of matching the Gettysburg address but made
his point.

"Gentlemen, I'd like to tell you a story. The Salvation Army was trying to
reform a lady of ill repute. They convinced her to walk the straight and
narrow and they sent her out to the Bowery with a drum. When a crowd
gathered around, she began talking.

"'I was nothing but an alcoholic. BOOM-BOOM! I took drugs. BOOM-
BOOM! I slept with sailors and soldiers. BOOM-BOOM! I slept with any
man who'd pay me. BOOM-BOOM! And, ladies and gentlemen, I want you
to know I'm sick of all this goddamned BOOM-BOOM!'

"Gentlemen, all I've heard from you tonight is BOOM-BOOM!"

The room broke up. The hostesses got their retirement plan.

It wasn't easy, however, for TWA to grant employees group benefits no matter how deserved they were. Just before Wiser resigned in 1975, the airline was in such financial distress that it met several payrolls only by selling six 747s to the government of Iran, and six months later had to sell Iran another three.

Wiser left under unhappy circumstances. Unknown to anyone, including Tillinghast, he had developed a nervous disorder and was not well. "Up until 1974 or '75," Tillinghast recalls soberly, "Bud seemed to be doing a great job. Then something seemed to happen to him and I didn't find out until years later the nature of his disability."

Tillinghast was planning to relinquish his title as chief executive officer at the time but he called Wiser in—it was June of 1975—and informed him he would not succeed Tillinghast as CEO. Wiser took the news calmly, but when Tillinghast came in the following Monday morning, Wiser had cleaned out his desk and left. The shocked Tillinghast, with no immediate replacement in sight, went back to running the airline for another six months.

Actually, he already had his eye on one man. The airline had recruited him from Eastern in 1968, a young accountant with a flair for finance. He joined TWA as assistant treasurer and two years later was named vice-president and controller. In 1974, he became senior vice-president of finance and when Wiser left, Tillinghast began asking questions around the company.

"I talked to various people at TWA about him," Tillinghast says. "His name came up as someone who had earned the greatest respect as a manager. Another thing in his favor was that, frankly, we had an employee problem at the time—there wasn't much respect for management's problems. He seemed to me to be the kind of fellow who'd impress people on the line. He had the reputation of being a square-shooter, an honest, conscientious leader. There was only one other candidate and that was Dan Reid—he had done a great job for us in San Francisco, he had been vice-president of the New York region, and Bud Wiser had selected him to be executive vice-president—actually Bud's successor if Wiser had moved into my job as was originally planned. Dan had many qualifications and some shortcomings. These things are never black and white; they're always complex."

On January 6, 1976, Carl Edwin Meyer, Jr., became the first president of TWA to be picked from within the company since Jack Frye.

He was tall, balding and deceptively soft-spoken; a lot of people thought he was too easy-going until he cut two vice-presidents from his own staff to show that draconian economy measures started at the top. By the same token, however, few if anyone at TWA knew that, for him, dismissing a fellow executive was an agonizing, emotional experience. A sensitive, caring man, he had paid his dues to leadership.

At first it was hard for Meyer to appear and speak in public—he even nervously rehearsed speeches in front of his wife. Gradually he gained confidence and began to enjoy himself before audiences—he even became skilled at impromptu humor. He was at one Seniors' meeting when the club treasurer was asked to deliver his financial report just before Meyer was introduced.

"Well," announced the treasurer, "we took in a little, we spent a little and we got a little left."

There was loud laughter and when Meyer rose, he glanced in the direction of the treasurer. "I'd like to ask you to come out of retirement and handle TWA's finances," Meyer suggested amid more laughter.

He was far better prepared for his job than any predecessor since Frye, simply because he was no neophyte when it came to TWA's problems. As a top echelon officer, he knew the airline's basic weaknesses: lack of efficient short-haul equipment and a route structure that was theoretically sound but full of holes in a practical sense. Industry pundits loved to point to TWA's routes as ideal—a domestic network that fed an international network. But it really wasn't that ideal largely because the domestic operations suffered from built-in deficiencies, and not enough of the right airplanes was just one of them. Except for National Airlines, TWA's domestic system was the most embattled in the industry—it had virtually no monopoly markets. By comparison, United and Eastern were carrying 90 percent of the traffic on 25 to 30 percent of their routes and American wasn't far behind.

Meyer realized all this. He had many long talks with Tillinghast before he was named president, although he didn't realize he was being seriously considered until two months before the choice was made. "Charlie played his cards pretty close to the vest," Meyer says, chuckling.

Meyer had a little breathing room during his first year, when cost reductions plus 1975's booming international traffic turned the airline around financially. But he knew that given TWA's inherent domestic vulnerability, there had been no permanent cure. So with the directness that typified his management style, he went to the mat with the man who for several years had directed TWA's scheduling policies—vice-president Mel Brenner.

Brenner had come to TWA from American, where he had earned a reputation as one of the industry's most brilliant masters of the art of scheduling—juggling equipment, markets and routes into an efficient system. But both Tillinghast and Meyer had become concerned that Brenner's *modus operandi,* while it undoubtedly had worked for American, was not working for TWA with its smaller fleet and dearth of major market dominance. It was Brenner who had insisted on butting heads against United and American in Chicago, where the former had twenty-one gates, the latter fifteen and TWA only eleven. Sums up Meyer:

"Mel's theory was that you really had to meet 'em head-on in high density places like Chicago, which required more and more airplanes and bigger and bigger losses. He was intelligent and articulate and a lot of what he said was right, but not for TWA."

The resolution was simple but far-reaching. Meyer established a new long-range schedule planning department with eight scheduling experts under the direction of Neil Effman, a strong believer in the hub concept. Significantly, Effman's group was independent of Brenner, who naturally resented it even though Meyer explained, "At that time, I didn't want to put day-by-day scheduling and long-range planning under the same guy." Brenner resigned shortly after the Effman task force began studying the system's restructuring.

What eventually came from the Effman team was a two-fold plan: to make St. Louis the hub around which most of the domestic system revolved, and to develop JFK as a second major hub, one that linked the domestic system with the international routes. (The latter would not be fully realized until several years later, when National merged with Pan Am and sold Trans World its JFK terminal directly adjacent to TWA's international terminal.) The creation of both hubs actually was made possible in 1978 by the most controversial piece of legislation in aviation history: the Airline Deregulation Act.

TWA fought deregulation as it was first proposed, along with most of the airlines—only United and Frontier supported it originally. But once Meyer was assured that the law would not discriminate against established carriers, he adopted the philosophy of "if you can't beat 'em, join 'em." He felt TWA was being structured to ride with the turbulence of decontrol—only two months before President Carter signed the Deregulation Act, the holding company of Trans World Corporation had been established.

The story of what has happened to the industry under deregulation is too familiar to bear repeating in detail. Almost overnight markets were invaded by new carriers with vastly lower operating costs that enabled them to undercut established airlines. The whole uninhibited atmosphere of deregulation touched off a disastrous fare war; by 1983, nearly 80 percent of airline passengers were traveling on discounted fares, many so low that an airline like TWA could lose money on some trips even with a full airplane. One example was TWA's Oklahoma City–Los Angeles route; Southwest Airlines moved into the market with low fares that TWA had to match. And by matching them, TWA wound up losing $1 million a year in this one market even though its load factors averaged a healthy 70 percent.

Meyer believes the flexibility of deregulation has partially offset the senseless self-destruction of the fare wars. "We could not have gone through the massive restructuring of our routes, which was absolutely essential to our survival, without that flexibility," he insists. "We couldn't have added more spokes to the JFK hub and expanded the St. Louis hub. For this company, deregulation turned out to be very much a blessing."

Under deregulation, Meyer made TWA a tougher and leaner carrier. It had nearly 36,000 employees before deregulation, but as of mid-1983 had less than 30,000. Its fleet was pruned to around 160 jets—admittedly marginal, for as Meyer himself conceded, "We're skating right on the thin edge of having enough equipment." More significant than sheer size, however, was the fleet's increased efficiency. Those 160 planes included ten new Boeing 767s and fifteen leased McDonnell Douglas Super 80s. The former replaced the 707 and substitutes in some seasonal markets for the slightly larger L-1011. The 142-passenger Super 80, originally intended as a replacement for the older 727s, actually can take over for the 707 on some routes. (The lease deal enabled TWA to retire the last of its once mighty 707 fleet in October of 1983.)

But the new planes and hubs notwithstanding, TWA still struggles under high operating costs. Early in 1983, Meyer was faced with a threatened mechanics' strike that probably would have wrecked the company; he settled for wage increases the airline couldn't afford, but he left no doubt that TWA's people must help him increase productivity and efficiency as the only way to reduce costs.

Yet like all the presidents who preceded him, Meyer knew he had to rely on the basic loyalty of each employee—the men and women who have gone through so much for so long. They have yet to let the airline down. In the spring of 1983, a group of investors called Odyssey Partners instigated an attempt to break up TWC, the holding company, with the argument that the stock of each subsidiary company should be worth more than that of the whole corporation. If the move had succeeded, TWA would have been cast adrift on its own, stripped of Trans World Corporation's solid protection, so badly needed in the uncertain, unpredictable atmosphere of deregulation.

The Odyssey proposal was soundly defeated, and among those who voted against this effort to demolish Ed Smart's carefully erected and mutually dependent corporate structure was a solid phalanx of TWA's stock-holding employees. Once again, they proved that the airline's sinews, blood and bones really lie in the 29,000 men and women who form its present work force, and the thousands who served before them. They have written the real history of Trans World Airlines and have also forged its future. They have taken TWA through one adversity and crisis after another, and always with pride, style and an unconquerable spirit.

When Gordon "Parky" Parkinson retired in 1968 after serving TWA for forty years, he had planned to take his wife to California for Christmas at their children's. They had passes, of course, but Parky had laid aside about $200 for expenses. Shortly before Thanksgiving, when his retirement had been announced, he came home and confessed, "Honey, I just spent our Christmas money."

"On what?" she demanded.

"I guess you'd better come with me and I'll show you."

He drove her to the old Kansas City Municipal Airport and stopped in front of a newly erected billboard. There, in large red letters, was Gordon Parkinson's farewell message.

"THANK YOU FOR FLYING TWA."

Epilogue

In 1975, about a year before Howard Hughes died, he asked Jack Real to collect some data on what airlines might be for sale.

Real came back a few days later with a suggestion that Hughes might consider National Airlines. It was in the throes of a strike and Real had picked up reports that Bud Maytag, National's president, was shopping around for a merger with Delta or Northwest.

"The stock's selling for around nine dollars," Real told Hughes. "I think you could make a tender offer of about twelve."

"I'll think about it, Jack."

A few days later, Real again brought up the possibility of buying National.

"Well, maybe," Hughes hedged. "I'll think about it some more."

Real knew him only too well. "Howard, I don't think your heart's really interested in National. You want another airline."

Hughes nodded.

Real said, "Can I guess?"

"Sure."

Real wrote a name down on a piece of paper and handed it to Hughes. "This one?"

Hughes nodded again.

"Howard, you don't want it. It would be a disaster."

"I don't care," Hughes muttered.

Nothing more was said on the subject. Hughes' health began to deteriorate; he died February 12, 1976, in a Learjet streaking from Mexico to Houston in a vain effort to get him to a modern American hospital.

February. The same month that had played such a coincidental role in the career of Jack Frye.

The name of the airline Jack Real wrote on that piece of paper was not really a name but a set of initials.

TWA.

"And I'd Like to Thank . . ."

Literary acknowledgments admittedly smack of those never-ending expressions of gratitude from Oscar winners who thank everyone from grandmothers to grips. They also can be padded like a dishonest expense account, because every author likes to create the impression that he or she has spent more time and effort on research than scientists trying to find a cure for the common cold.

In self-defense, however, I must point out that writing the history of a great airline is no solo flight. A great many people aided me in a great many ways. They turned over treasured and valuable files, correspondence, documents, books and pictures. They submitted to interviews ranging from five minutes to five hours. They searched in their hearts as well as their minds to give me not merely facts but feelings about the airline they served and loved.

The story of TWA is my fifth airline history. I know from experience that inevitably I have missed some facts because I have missed some people. "Why didn't you interview so-and-so?" is a common cry in the aftermath of publication. To those I did miss I can only express sincere regrets and assure them their omission was inadvertent. There comes a time when research must end and writing must begin. The research on this book consumed more than half the time allotted to the project.

I owe not just thanks but a deep debt of gratitude to the following:

Jerry Cosley, TWA vice-president of public affairs, for supporting the project from the beginning and insisting that I "tell it like it is, warts and all."

John Corris of TWA's public affairs, for the many hours he spent arranging interviews, conducting many of them with me or by himself and supplying me with voluminous background material.

Gordon "Parky" Parkinson for providing an incredible amount of original source material and guidance on interview subjects.

Former TWA presidents Carter Burgess, Charles Thomas and Charles Tillinghast for the courtesy of their time, the honesty of their answers, and the privilege of meeting them; the same sentiments to TWA president C.E. "Ed" Meyer and Board Chairman L. Edwin "Ed" Smart.

David Tinnin for his superb study of the TWA-Hughes litigation, *Just About Everybody VS. Howard Hughes*, a work so detailed, accurate and highly recommended by several TWA officials that it became my single most valuable reference aid. (I've never met Mr. Tinnin but I relish one story the airline tells about him: he once was arrested in Russia and was released when he flashed his TWA Ambassadors Club membership card—the only identification he happened to have on him at the time.)

Jack Real, president of Hughes Helicopters, for sharing with me an insight into Howard Hughes that could come only from a man who had been Hughes' friend and

326

confidant. Of all the people I talked to about Howard Hughes, he showed the deepest, fairest understanding of this often misunderstood and maligned man. I asked Real why he didn't write his own book about HRH. He told me had been asked to several times but always refused. "I wouldn't want to tell the story unless I told it all. And to tell it all, I'd have to hurt people. Life's too short to hurt people even though I know they were guilty. Howard was a very decent man, generous to a fault. There were many, many kind acts I could tell you about, but I won't because each time he'd say, 'Now, Jack, I don't want anyone to know about this.' We all hear the bad things about him, the selfish things. The idiosyncrasies—the long hair, the dirty gray beard, the long fingernails routine of his last years. I overlooked them. Hell, everyone's got a lot of warts at that stage of their lives. I looked at the whole man and that's what I'll remember: his understanding, kindness and intelligence."

To the people whose names are listed alphabetically below, my heartfelt appreciation for the information they provided in the form of personal interviews and other forms of aid:

Cliff Abbott	Ray Dunn	Ed Jandacek
Lucille Adams	Rod Edwards	Bob Johnson
Susan Ahl	Sharon Eldred	Al Jordan
George Andre	Ken Ensslin	Arlene Kellogg
Joe Bartles	Sal Fallucco	Dan Kemnitz
Dick Beck	Hubert Farrell	Dick Kenny
George Ann Bell	Bill Fields	Tommy Kerg
Joe Bell	Lee Flanagin	Hal Kurtz
Bob Berle	Ken Fletcher	Vern Laursen
Ed Betts	Ed Frankum	Buddy Ledger
Frederick G. Betts	Irv Gartrell	Newt Lieurance
Charlie Billerman	Esther Giles	Stewart Long
Russ Black	C.V. Glines	Mick Martinez
Hal Blackburn	Bill Green	Dick Maurer
Bill Borden	James Greenwood	Alice Mayher
Joan Borden	Johnny Guy	Bob McCormick
John Brock	Floyd Hall	Frank McGough
Joe Brummit	Elma Harrigan	Bob McKay
Bob Buck	Jim Harrigan	Red McKenney
Jean Buck	Betty Hawes	Bill Meador
Bob Bunch	Steve Hawes	Walt Menke
Frank Busch	Thelma Jean Hayes	Bill Mitchell
Bill Bushey	Don Heep	John Mitchell
Otis Bryan	Betty Heep	Bob Montgomery
Al Clay	Ginny Henline	Fran Moran
Fleta Cocke	Hap Henline	Slim Morgan
Jerry Condon	Jack Hereford	Harold Neumann
John Cooper	Peggy Hereford	Kay Nolan
Roy Davis	Ted Hereford	Steve Oliver
Nan Dayhoff	Larry Hilliard	Doris Owen
Russ Derickson	Ulrich Hoffmann	Niki Pappas
Jimmy de Revere	Frank Howell	Wayne Parrish
Bill Dixon	Harry Jacobsen	Fred Pastorius

Dick Pearson
Jean Phillips
Stan Phillips
George Prill
Jon Proctor
Roger Don Rae
Daisy Richter
Dave Richwine
J.D. Rideout
Russ Robbins
Robby Robinson
Frank Ruocco

Tom Sawyer
Fran Schulte
Ellie Shaub
Ray Silvius
Carlyle Smith
Emil Smyer
George Spater
R. Dixon Speas
Fred Spuhler
Bill Sonneman
Ida Staggers
Ruby Stever

Paul Strohm
Anne Saunders
Tom Taylor
Lem Tew
Julia Thomas
Helyn Thomsen
Bill Townsend
Dave Venz
Ed Wells
Gordon Williams
Brien Wygle
Jerry Zerbone

Bibliography

Adventures of a Yellowbird, Robert W. Mudge, Branden Press, ©1969

The Airline Builders, Oliver E. Allen, Time-Life Books, 1981.

Airlines of the U.S. Since 1914, R.E.G. Davies, Putnam, 1972.

An American Saga—Juan Trippe and His Pan Am Empire, Robert Daley, Random House, 1980.

Billion Dollar Battle, Harold Mansfield, McKay,, 1965.

Birth of an Industry, editors of Official Airline Guide, Reuben H. Donnelly, 1969.

Bonfires to Beacons, Nick A. Komons, U.S. Government Printing Office, 1978.

The Chosen Instrument, Marylin Bender and Selig Altschul, Simon & Schuster, 1982.

The Civil Aeronautics Board, Robert Burkhardt, Green Hills Publishing Co., 1974.

Conquest of the Skies, Carl Solberg, Little, Brown, 1979.

Crosswinds, Najeeb E. Halaby, Doubleday, 1978.

Delta, the History of an Airline, W. David Lewis and Wesley P. Newton, University of Georgia Press, 1979.

Ernest Gann's Flying Circus, Ernest Gann, Macmillan, 1974.

Ernie Breech, J. Mel Hickerson, Meredith Press, 1968.

Flying the Line, George E. Hopkins, Air Line Pilots Association, 1982.

Fly Sheba, Lem Tew, privately printed, 1977.

The Flying White House, J.F. terHorst and Ralph Albertazzi, Coward McCann Geoghegan, 1979.

The Ford Story, William Larkins, Robert R. Longo Co., 1957.

From Skygirl to Flight Attendant, Georgia Panter Nielsen, Cornell University, 1982.

Gable and Lombard, Warren G. Harris, Simon & Schuster, 1974.

Howard, by Noah Dietrich and Bob Thomas, Fawcett, 1972.

Howard Hughes, by John Keats, Random House, 1966.

Howard Hughes, the Hidden Years, by James Phelan, Random House, 1976.

Inside Africa, John Gunther, Harper Brothers, 1953.

Just About Everybody vs. Howard Hughes, David B. Tinnin, Doubleday, 1973.

King Cohn, Bob Thomas, Putnam, 1967.

Legacy of Leadership, TWA, privately printed, 1971.

L-1011—The Lockheed Story, J. Douglas Ingalls, Aero, 1973.

My Story, Ingrid Bergman, Delacorte, 1980.

Of Magic Sails, Barbara Bean, Graphic Alliance, 1975.

The Plane That Changed the World, Ingalls, Aero, 1966.

Rockne, Jerry Brondfield, Random House, 1976.

Shelton's Barefoot Airlines, Philip Schleit, Fishergate, 1982.

The Sporty Game, John Newhouse, Knopf, 1982.

Stunt Flying in the Movies, James and Maxine Greenwood, Tab Books, 1982.

The Water Jump, David Beatty, Harper & Row, 1976.

Index

McNary, Sen. Charles, 15
Meador, Bill, 149, 150, 177, 178, 193,
    284, 295, 296, 312
Menke, Ruth, 153
Menke, Walt, 99, 100, 153, 154, 157,
    182, 204, 211
meteorologists, 42, 54, 56
    see also weather
Metropolitan Life Insurance Company,
    268, 273, 274
Metzner, Charles M., 272, 274, 275,
    276, 277, 279
Meyer, Carl Edwin, Jr., 321–323
Meyer, Johnny, 151, 155, 168, 170, 221
Mitchell, John, 195
Mitchell, William "Billy," 40
Moffitt, Capt. Ted, 221
Montgomery, John, 53
Moran, Fran, 216, 245
Morgan, Slim, 112, 300
Muir, Malcolm, 178, 179
Mutchler, Cliff, 97, 98, 102
Myers, Maj. Henry "Hank," 109, 110

National Airlines, 264, 325
National Air Transport (NAT), 3, 4, 13
New York Central Railroad, 9, 21
Nichols, Jack, 114
Nilsen, Capt. Art, 129
Noonan, Bill, 165
North American Aviation, 3, 13, 15,
    34, 36, 39, 41, 61
Northeast Airlines, 248, 271, 272, 275,
    276, 277, 278
Northrop, Jack, 27, 33, 35
Northrop Alphas, 27, 319
Nyrop, Don, 283

Official Aviation Guide, 21
Olds, Irving S., 249, 253
Owen, Doris, 304

Palmer, Don, 87, 88
Pan-American Airways, 62, 73, 81, 83,
    86, 87, 89, 92, 122, 123, 127, 130,
    170, 171, 179, 201, 245, 271
    TWA–Pan-Am merger proposal,
    167–169, 263–265, 271, 288, 318
Parkinson, Gordon "Parky," 30, 54,
    56, 105, 144, 154, 173, 209, 324
Parrish, Wayne, 285, 286

Patterson, Pat, 48, 73, 117, 123, 226,
    246, 283
Paul VI, Pope, 297, 298
Pearson, Dick, 294
Pennsylvania Railroad, 4, 8, 12
    Airway Limited, 9
Peters, Jean, 221, 222, 242
Peters, Mrs. Bessie, 103
Phillippine Air Lines (PAL), 125–128
Phillips, Dan, 120, 121
Phillips, Jean, 117, 138, 139, 141, 143,
    144, 145, 146
Phillips, Stan, 145, 146
Pierson, Warren Lee, 142, 148, 149,
    172, 204, 225, 233
pilots, 6, 23, 43, 49, 50, 51
    salaries, 7, 29, 137, 138
    stories about, 1950s, 194–200
Pittsburgh Aviation Industries Corpor-
    ation (PAIC), 17, 18, 22
Plinton, Jim, 227, 228
Plumridge, Capt. Reg, 213
Post Office Department, 14, 39, 40, 46,
    67, 176
Power, Tyrone, 84, 160, 161
Pratt, John Lee, 22, 23
Pratt & Whitney, 13, 237, 267
    Hornet engines, 33, 36, 44
    JT8D engine, 259
Preeg, Capt. Felix, 70
Prescott, Bob, 69, 248
Pretsch, Ernie, 198
"Price is Right, The," 265
priority system, 102

Quesada, Elwood R. (Pete), 281
"Quickie Vacation," 176, 177

Rankin, James Lee, 272, 273, 274, 275
Rappatoni, Capt. Jim, 221
Raymond, Art, 33, 34, 35, 57
Real, Jack, 85, 91, 174, 200, 202, 220,
    236, 246, 250, 325
Reed, Francis, 256
Reid, Dan, 321
Rice, Ella, 230
Rice, George, 10
Richter, Daisy, 75, 142, 143
Richter, Paul, 18, 20–23, 27, 34, 44,
    48, 55, 68, 72–76, 86–88, 95, 102,
    116, 118, 132, 133